FIFTEEN HURRICANES THAT CHANGED THE CAROLINAS

FIFTEEN HURRICANES THAT CHANGED THE CAROLINAS

POWERFUL STORMS,
CLIMATE CHANGE, AND
WHAT WE DO NEXT

Jay Barnes

THE UNIVERSITY OF NORTH CAROLINA PRESS
CHAPEL HILL

Set in Garamond by Copperline Book Services, Inc.
Manufactured in the United States of America

The University of North Carolina Press has been a member
of the Green Press Initiative since 2003.

Cover photo by Art Newton. Courtesy of the *State Port Pilot*.

Library of Congress Cataloging-in-Publication Data
Names: Barnes, Jay, author.
Title: Fifteen hurricanes that changed the Carolinas :
powerful storms, climate change, and what we do next / Jay Barnes.
Description: Chapel Hill : The University of North
Carolina Press, 2022. | Includes index.
Identifiers: LCCN 2021049432 | ISBN 9781469666303 (paper ; alk. paper) |
ISBN 9781469667461 (ebook)
Subjects: LCSH: Hurricanes—North Carolina—History. | Hurricanes—
South Carolina—History. | Climatic changes—North Carolina. |
Climatic changes—South Carolina.
Classification: LCC QC945 .B349 2022 | DDC 975—dc23/eng/20211201
LC record available at https://lccn.loc.gov/2021049432

This book is dedicated to
the responders, the men and women who often
risk their own lives to save others during the
worst of our hurricane disasters

And to my wife, my love, Robin

CONTENTS

FIFTEEN
HURRICANES
THAT
CHANGED
THE
CAROLINAS

INTRODUCTION

My interest in hurricanes began with Hazel. It swept through the Carolinas a few years before I was born, but its lingering impact on my family and neighbors in Southport, North Carolina, cast a deep impression. My dad used to talk about how tides had lifted large menhaden boats into the pine forest near the plant where he worked. Stories of the devastation at Long Beach, where hundreds of mostly empty cottages were carried away, were a big part of my hometown lore. Clippings from the *State Port Pilot* and my parents' hand-drawn track maps sat in a large folder marked "hurricanes" under my mother's desk, another source of wonder. Black-and-white photos of the shrimp fleet tangled in power lines and scattered among downtown backyards were particularly dramatic. The storm was a benchmark in time. For years, people described things as either "before Hazel" or "after Hazel." Among the locals, recollections of its visit seemed to hang in the air, ready to emerge any time conversation turned to wind, tide, or storm.

Years later, my fascination with Hazel and an interest in local history became something more. In June 1995, the University of North Carolina Press published my first book, *North Carolina's Hurricane History*—the first comprehensive history of hurricanes in the Tar Heel State. Covering great storms dating back to the first European explorers, it chronicled a history that continued to unfold with each new hurricane season. Hurricanes Bertha and Fran roared ashore the following year, in 1996, causing billions of dollars in destruction and compelling an updated, second edition. And the storms kept coming. A third edition followed Hurricane Floyd in 1999, and then in 2013 the fourth edition of *North Carolina's Hurricane History* was released, with new chapters covering another decade of Tar Heel storms. There's a never-ending theme here—it seems there's always another memorable hurricane around the corner.

I'm not a meteorologist, but I've always been interested in tropical cyclone dynamics and forecasting, and the basic principles and individual weather records are a critically important part of the summaries I write. Knowing the highest tides, the fiercest winds, and the heaviest rainfall is key to understanding each storm's fury. And there's always more to learn from the science of these storms, especially as we face a future with warming oceans and rising sea levels.

➤ The awesome fury of Hurricane Hazel is evident in this photo by Hugh Morton, taken near the peak of the storm at Carolina Beach. Morton and several other reporters witnessed the destruction, including *Charlotte News* staffer Julian Scheer, seen here struggling against the rising tide. This photo won Morton first place in spot news in the 1955 Southern Photographer of the Year competition. (Photo from Ed Rankin and Hugh Morton, *Making a Difference in North Carolina* [Raleigh, N.C.: Lightworks, 1988]. Courtesy of Hugh Morton.)

➤ On October 15, 2007, on the fifty-third anniversary of Hurricane Hazel, Jerry Helms (*left*) and the author (*right*) joined local residents on Oak Island to unveil a historical marker commemorating the storm. (Photo by Jim Harper. Courtesy of the *State Port Pilot*.)

But admittedly, I'm most interested in the stories—and the powerful impact hurricanes have on our communities and people. From daring rooftop rescues to tragic human losses and economic ruins, these storms deliver more than their share of drama. The outpouring of compassion that typically follows these disasters in some ways helps offset the storms' emotional toll. Truckloads of donations, organized teams of volunteers, and widespread examples of neighbor helping neighbor give hope through each hurricane recovery. There's also meaningful context to be gathered for each storm: the extent of forewarning (if any), the anxious preparations and evacuations, the frequent loss of ships at sea, the methods and outcomes of recovery efforts, the scope of physical changes to the landscape, and the social and economic fallout all combine to tell the story of each hurricane disaster.

Those who cannot remember the past are condemned to repeat it.
—George Santayana, *The Life of Reason*, 1905

For many Carolinians, recent hurricanes have left bad memories of flooded homes and exhausting recoveries. Others may have suffered less but witnessed unprecedented flooding in their communities. Our personal adventures with hurricanes have always offered valuable lessons. With each storm we learn a lot from the challenges we face, from the first forecasts and warnings to the final home repairs. More broadly, there may be a silver lining for communities that struggle through multiple floods and storm recoveries: they're generally better prepared the next time they face a major disaster. Experience is indeed a great teacher, especially when it comes to hurricanes.

Beyond what we might learn firsthand, broadening our understanding of storm history teaches us a few things too. A review of the great hurricanes of the past can offer lessons to help gain perspective on our persistent vulnerabilities. That's the working premise of this book and of the others I've put together over the years, including *North Carolina's Hurricane History*, *Florida's Hurricane History*, and *Faces from the Flood: Hurricane Floyd Remembered*.

Fifteen Hurricanes That Changed the Carolinas takes this central idea, with a scope that includes both North and South Carolina, and looks to the future: *These are the great storms of the past three centuries. What have we learned and what might we expect in the years to come?* The fifteen chosen here, from the Great Carolina Hurricane of 1752 to 2018's Hurricane Florence, each stand as epic encounters for their time. They are among the deadliest, most severe, and most memorable hurricane disasters Carolinians have faced. Each left its own mark, and collectively they've affected the entirety of the two states—from the Lowcountry and the Blue Ridge Mountains to the Outer Banks and most everywhere in between.

These fifteen storms tested the resolve of those they affected and challenged the government's ability to respond, within the context of the Carolinas' emergence as colonies and then as states. Their stories are unique. No two hurricanes are really the same, though some may share traits or have similar impacts. Sometimes, though, their visits have been as different as night and day. And over time they've had a mounting impact as the Carolinas have steadily grown in population.

Each storm profile ends with a few takeaways—simplified lessons from the past that might be applied to today's thinking about hurricane risk. Some are obvious but fundamentally important, while others represent lessons learned. Mostly, these takeaways are just as relevant now as they were when the storms made landfall, even for those hurricanes that swept ashore centuries ago. There's a lot to be learned from hindsight.

————————————

I've got news for Mr. Santayana: we're doomed to repeat the past no matter what. That's what it is to be alive.—Kurt Vonnegut, *Bluebeard*, 1987

Any conversation today about our hurricane future is necessarily linked to climate and emerging climate science. Oceans are warming. Sea levels are rising. Almost every week, new scientific studies and climate-focused editorials make the news, better defining the global changes underway and projecting the future consequences of anthropogenic (caused by humans) warming. Much of the news seems dire, but it's good to gain some perspective on these threats. In chapter 16, "Future Storms," climate scientists, government leaders, emergency management officials, meteorologists, economists, and others talk hurricanes and weigh in on what to expect in the Carolinas. There's a lot to sort out here, especially when comparisons are drawn through the long-view lens of history.

This final chapter poses other important questions: What have we learned from the past to help us better cope with future hurricane disasters? How are communities across the Carolinas becoming more resilient to lessen the impact of some future Hugo or Florence? What about the costs? What measures are currently being deployed, and what more needs to be done?

The questions aren't new, but in the context of recent disasters such as Matthew, Florence, and others, they present new and real challenges for community

Wreck of the *Priscilla* in August 1899. (Photo courtesy of the Outer Banks History Center, Manteo, North Carolina.)

leaders and policy makers. Discussions around risk, resiliency, cost, and growth are especially difficult in the aftermath of a disaster, when building back quickly is often the priority. But there's growing interest in getting it right, through smart planning and measures that will lessen the impact of the next great hurricane disaster. If anything, this book offers one compelling conclusion: more devastating hurricanes will strike the Carolinas, and their physical, social, and economic impacts will be significant, just as they've always been.

CHAPTER ONE

THE GREAT
CAROLINA HURRICANE
OF 1752

The city of Charles Town, founded in 1670, was the first English settlement in what we know today as South Carolina. It was founded by William Sayle, who sailed from Barbados with three shiploads of English emigrants to establish a new royal colony. Sayle and his party surveyed the nearby coast, navigated up the Ashley River and established a settlement on Albemarle Point, a landmass that has since disappeared. Others soon joined the colony, including Sir John Yeamans who arrived the next year with about 200 African slaves. Sometime after Sayle's death in 1671, the colonists decided to relocate the town to a point of land between the Ashley and Cooper Rivers, where Charles Town was re-founded in 1680.

The new location provided better access to navigable waters, but the boggy peninsula was crisscrossed with creeks, marshes, and ponds. On a normal day drainage was an issue, and the settlement's modest homes and other structures were tested by heavy rains, high tides, and hurricanes. Sanitation was poor, leaving townspeople vulnerable to disease. Over the years, creeks and wetlands were filled to make room for more homes, shops, and storehouses, and the city grew in size. Often, it was the flotsam and debris left after storms that helped fill the low spots and build up the town.

Over time, the citizens of Charles Town endured despite the many challenges they faced from sickness, starvation, hostile invasions, destructive fires, and bad weather. Always fearing the introduction of disease, they erected a pesthouse on Sullivan's Island, a required quarantine station for newly arriving passengers from incoming ships. Surveyors plotted nearby lands where crops were grown, and the sea offered a bounty of fish and shellfish, providing sustenance to the town's citizens. By the turn of the eighteenth century, Charles Town was prospering but facing big challenges too. As the English capital of the Carolina colony, it was frequently raided by Spanish and French forces and

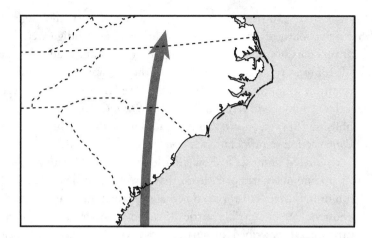

Charles Town Harbor in the mid-eighteenth century. (Engraving courtesy of the Library of Congress, Washington, D.C.)

occasionally by bands of hostile Native Americans. Pirates sometimes invaded to pillage and plunder, including Edward Teach himself, who held the city hostage in the spring of 1718. But due to its perilous location at the edge of the sea, Charles Town faced perhaps its greatest test when tropical storms and hurricanes wrecked homes, sank vessels, and ruined crops. Through planters' journals, shipping records, and personal letters from the period, historians have chronicled a string of hurricanes that battered the city, including those that caused "extensive mischief" in 1700, 1713, 1724, and 1728.

By 1750 Charles Town was a thriving commercial port, the largest and wealthiest city south of Philadelphia. Cotton, rice, and indigo were loaded out aboard merchant schooners, while imports from Europe and the Caribbean made for brisk trade along the wharves. The city was growing, attracting wealthy planters who converted nearby coastal wetlands for rice cultivation, tended by large numbers of African slaves. The *South Carolina Gazette*, which began publishing in 1732, offered a running account of the city's growth, detailing the construction of new churches, hotels, and public buildings. The publication also offered glimpses of how Charles Town coped with raging hurricanes, including one particular storm that historians still consider to be a turning point in the city's history and perhaps its worst hurricane on record.

"The most violent and terrible hurricane that ever was felt in this province" was how the *Gazette* described the hurricane of 1752. Historians have labeled it the Great Carolina Hurricane of 1752, and most have endorsed the notion that it was likely Charleston's greatest storm to date. It arrived in mid-September, after a scorching summer when temperatures in the Lowcountry topped 100 degrees for extended periods. It was followed by a second powerful hurricane just two weeks later, marking one of a handful of occasions when Charleston was battered by two hurricanes in the same year.

There's a lot that isn't known about these hurricanes, as weather records from this era are limited. But historians have pieced together enough information to surmise that the mid-September storm was likely a Category 3 or 4, with landfall just below Charles Town on Edisto Island. It struck near the time of high tide, adding height to the storm's surge. College of Charleston historian Laylon Jordan concluded in *A History of Storms on the South Carolina Coast*, "If storm surge and lunar high tide coincided, the cataclysmic effect was compounded, as with the great hurricane of 1752, which propelled a seventeen-foot tidal wave directly over Charleston, already a flourishing seaport of five thousand inhabitants."

In early July of that year, 200 German immigrants sailed from the Port of Rotterdam to England, where they loaded water and provisions for a sixty-day transatlantic journey aboard the *Upton*. Their destination: Charles Town, South Carolina, and the promise of free land grants offered by the provincial governor. The passengers—mostly families with children, none of whom had ever sailed at sea before—packed the vessel's tight quarters. After completing the difficult journey, they arrived in Charles Town Harbor and anchored in the Ashley River on the afternoon of September 14. That evening, few aboard were able to sleep due to great anticipation for the new lives that awaited them—and the raucous weather that had begun to rock the *Upton*.

The hurricane rolled in that evening. Afterward, the *South Carolina Gazette* summarized the storm's arrival:

On the 14th in the evening, it began to blow very hard, the wind being at N.E. and the sky looked wild and threatening: It continued blowing from the same point, with little variation, 'till about 4 o'clock in the morning of the 15th, and at which time it became more violent, and rained, increasing very fast 'till about 9, when the flood came in like a bore, filling the harbour in a few minutes: Before 11 o'clock, all the vessels in the harbour were on shore, except the *Hornet* man of war, which rode it out by cutting away her main-mast; all the wharfs and bridges were ruined, and every house, store, &c. upon them, beaten down, and carried away (with all the goods, &c. therein) as were also many houses in the town; and abundance of roofs, chimneys, &c. almost all the tile or slated houses were uncovered; and great quantities of merchandize, &c. in the stores on the Bay-street, damaged by their doors being burst open: The town was likewise overflowed, the tide or sea having rose upwards of Ten foot above the high-water mark at spring-tides, and nothing was now to be seen but ruins of houses, canows [canoes], wrecks of pettiauguas and boats, masts, yards, incredible quantities of all sorts of timber, barrels, staves, shingles, household and other goods, floating and driving, with great violence, thro' the streets, and round about the town. The inhabitants, finding themselves in the midst of a tempestuous sea, the wind still continuing, the tide (according to its common course) being expected to flow 'till after one o'clock, and many of the people being already up to their necks in water in their houses, began now to think of nothing but certain death.

The *Upton's* passengers and crew were helpless against the hurricane, the ship tossing back and forth with every wave while dragging anchor through the night. The roar of the wind and rain undoubtedly drowned out the anguished cries of the families below deck. Their harrowing experience continued into the morning. Winds and tides carried the ship over the marshes of Wappoo Creek on James Island, and along the way twenty passengers were seriously injured and later died. After the storm, workers had to dig a channel some 100 yards long and thirty-five feet wide in order to drag the ship out of the marsh. The surviving immigrant families later settled in Dutch Fork, where even today stories of the wreck of the *Upton* are part of their early family history.

The *Upton* was one of many ships scattered by the storm. The *Lucy*, also sailing from England, dragged anchors to a high marsh some seven miles up the Cooper River. The midmorning storm surge tossed sloops and schooners over the seawall and into homes along the bayfront. The *Gazette* reported that "Capt. Walker's pilot-boat, [was driven] against the governor's house [the Pinckney mansion of East Bay Street]; and his sloop the *Endeavor*, bound for Jamaica, after beating down his Excellency's coach-house, stables, &c. was dashed to pieces against Mr. Raper's house [near Market Street]." The *Endeavor*'s mast broke through the home's balcony door. Another vessel, also dragging anchor, was carried from White Point through Vanderhorst Creek. Along the way it bashed the southwest corner of the new Baptist church and grounded on the west side of Meeting Street. The fourteen-gun sloop of war HMS *Hornet*, with its main mast cut and its seven weighty anchors, drifted across the harbor but was the only ship left afloat after the storm. In all, about twenty merchant ships—many loaded with cotton—were wrecked, along with an unknown number of lighter vessels.

The tides were equally destructive to homes, shops, and other structures across Charles Town. Horses, hogs, and chickens drowned in the streets. Startled residents retreated to second-story rooms and rooftops to escape the flood. With the added effects of the storm's fierce winds, even the city's grand homes were no match for this hurricane. Nearly all buildings with tile and slate roofs were stripped bare. Chimneys fell, walls collapsed, and several people were killed in the melee. In *Lowcountry Hurricanes*, author Walter Fraser described the tragic outcome for one family trapped in their Church Street home: "The Bedon family waited too long to leave, and the rushing, swirling torrents of water sucked under and drowned Mrs. Bedon, her three children, two white servants and five black slaves." Across the city, 500 buildings were destroyed.

In its account of the tidal surge, the *South Carolina Gazette* wrote of residents "up to their necks in water in their houses," who began to think of "certain death." In his 1809 historical summary, Charleston historian David Ramsay described the surprising turn of events for residents as the flood reached its peak: "They retired at eleven to the upper stories of their houses and, contemplated a speedy termination of their lives. At this critical time providence mercifully interposed and surprised them with a sudden and unexpected deliverance. Soon after eleven the wind shifted, in consequence of which the waters fell five feet in the space of ten minutes." By three o'clock that afternoon, the wind had died completely and the storm was gone. Royal governor James Glen ordered the militia in to guard the town and prevent looting, promising to prosecute anyone "taking advantage of the calamity."

In *Ships in the Streets: The Charlestown Hurricanes of September 1752*, Amy Glen described the impact of flooding on the city's land records:

The Statehouse, now known as the courthouse at Broad and Meeting Streets, was built in what was thought to be a flood-proof location. Colonists hoping to have their land resurveyed or newcomers to the colony inquiring about the land they purchased prior to arriving in the colony witnessed chaos at the Surveyor General's office and were at risk of being unable to determine which plot of land belonged to them. Floods from the hurricanes had burst through the office doors of the office, with "the original Warrants of Survey, all the Duplicates of Plats of this Province, the Books of Record thereof, the Reports on His Majesty's Quit Rents & ca. were . . . floating about in four and a half Feet Salt Water."

As the storm's massive surge washed over Sullivan's Island, all buildings were swept away, including the pesthouse sheltering fifteen people—ten of whom drowned. The remaining occupants were carried six miles away to Hobcaw Point (west Mount Pleasant) and only survived by grasping rafters as the structure broke apart. An unknown number of slaves drowned on Sullivan's when their shanties were carried away. In the city, Saint Michael's Church had been under construction, and it suffered badly when surging waters rushed up Meeting Street and met floodwaters racing down Broad Street. Waters swirled "at least waist high" through the church. Stories emerged of city laborers grasping broken fences and debris and riding the tide into thickets and cornfields. Others saved themselves by floating out upper windows and clinging onto trees. Across the county every plantation for forty miles lost its outhouse; many suffered losses of cattle, crops, and stately trees. So many trees were downed, covering roads, that travel through the region was difficult for months.

Of all the destruction in the city, perhaps the most troubling to the colonial government was the damage caused to fortifications. Defensive works were hit hard by the storm tide. Along with waterfront piers and wharves, several bastions, or artillery structures, were undermined and washed out, some with their cannon still attached. Granville's Bastion was heavily damaged, and "the platform with the guns upon it floated partly over a wall." At Fort Johnson on James Island, where three people drowned, the barracks were destroyed and guns dismounted, their wooden carriages swept away with the tide. Similar destruction affected the "curtain wall," a four-to-five-foot-thick fortification on the city's land side. Rebuilding these defenses was a priority for the royal governor and was probably completed more quickly than expected after the chance arrival of a thousand Acadian refugees who were an important source of labor in the months following the hurricane.

Colonial authorities saw the reconstruction of Charles Town as an opportunity to improve the urban landscape. The city's seawall had crumbled during the storm, leading to the construction of the original Battery. More low areas were filled, adding elevation to some sections. Wealthy Charlestonians began constructing homes of masonry instead of wood, a trend begun years before after a devastating fire in 1740. Governor Glen even stated that with the storm, "Numbers more must have perished had not our Houses been very Substantial." Many of the new homes were also built on "high basements," elevated half stories that provided some protection from flooding. Fears of another hurricane led residents to consider other protective measures, such as extra-heavy doors and window shutters. Many, though, believed those measures of little consequence, as the storms were a "Mark of [God's] Displeasure against your Transgressions." It took a few years, but Charles Town bounced back. As historian Laylon Jordan wrote, "On receipts of rice and indigo they built better than before."

All indications are that the Great Carolina Hurricane of 1752 was an extremely powerful cyclone but relatively small in diameter, as coastal damage reports south and north of the Charles Town region were not significant. The storm's northwest track likely continued after landfall, such that sparsely populated interior portions of the Carolinas would have received the worst of the storm as it tracked inland. Dr. Cary Mock, geography professor and climatologist at the University of South Carolina in Columbia, found one remarkable record that could shed light on the 1752 hurricane's inland course. Though Columbia didn't exist at the time, at Granby (Cayce) in late September, the Congaree River reportedly rose twenty-eight feet in two hours, rising to the highest mark known for that location in the eighteenth century.

Few records exist of the September 1752 hurricane before it arrived in Charles Town; it was first observed passing along Florida's east coast. There was, however, at least one known perilous offshore encounter. In *Lowcountry Hurricanes*, Fraser described how the English slave ship *Africa* was overtaken by the hurricane's mountainous seas off the coast of Savannah. Bound for Charles Town, its hold packed with anguished slaves, the ship tossed about in the storm throughout the day on September 13: "One large swell rides atop others, creating enormous waves. And it was this type of sea that Captain Dorrington attempted to navigate to save his ship, crew, and cargo of slaves. All aboard must have thought the ship was going down at any moment. Huge waves battered a side of the *Africa* and threatened to capsize it. As the ship wallowed dead in the water, waves swept its deck of small boats and washed 'four white seamen' and a 'Negro' overboard to their deaths; amazingly the *Africa* remained afloat."

The hapless ship was driven ashore into the breakers near the north Edisto River, where all aboard were later rescued by the *Cunliffe*.

No one knows the total number of lives lost from this hurricane, though estimates range from 95 to more than 200. It's likely, though, that those estimates undercount the actual toll, as no official reporting system was in place for such records at that time. The financial losses were significant for the South Carolina region too, especially for the lucrative rice crop that helped fuel Charles Town's prosperity. What little rice survived the storm was worthless, "a great deal pounding away to powder." Rice production in South Carolina following the hurricane dropped to 37,000 barrels from over 82,000 the year before.

GOOD TO KNOW

- Hurricanes (in the Atlantic and eastern Pacific Oceans), typhoons (western Pacific) and cyclones (Indian) are the same type of storm—they're all tropical cyclones. They're fed by heat that builds in the atmosphere and ocean each year, and in the Northern Hemisphere they spin counterclockwise. They become named tropical storms when maximum sustained winds reach 39 mph, then hurricanes when winds reach 74 mph.
- The Atlantic hurricane season runs from June 1 through November 30, though tropical cyclones often occur before or after the official season. Activity peaks in mid-September. In 2021, the National Hurricane Center (NHC) began issuing tropical weather outlooks on May 15 and may lengthen the season in the future.
- The average Atlantic hurricane is about 300 miles across, though they can be smaller or much larger. The center of circulation, or eye, is an area of calm winds typically fifteen to forty miles across. The storm's highest winds and tides are usually found adjacent to the eye, in the *eyewall*.
- According to the National Oceanic and Atmospheric Administration, fourteen tropical storms form in the average Atlantic season, seven of which become hurricanes, based on the most recent thirty-year record. The averages over the last 100 years are closer to twelve

Hurricane warning flags flew over downtown Southport on numerous occasions during the 1950s. Hurricane Hazel's winds shredded them in October 1954. (Photo by Art Newton. Courtesy of Punk Spencer.)

and six. The 2020 season was especially active, producing a record thirty storms, surpassing the twenty-eight named in 2005.

- North Carolina ranks fourth in the United States for the number of hurricane landfalls since 1851; South Carolina ranks fifth. Not surprisingly, Florida ranks number one.

- Anemometers measure wind speeds as maximum sustained winds (average speed over one minute) and gusts (momentary peak recordings). Unofficial wind reports are typically those recorded by private instruments whose accuracy cannot be verified.

- Hurricane intensity is measured in barometric pressure—the lower the pressure, the stronger the storm. For many years barometric pressure was measured in inches of mercury; standard measurements are now made in millibars.

- The naming of tropical storms and hurricanes officially began in 1953 when the U.S. Weather Bureau began using women's names for each storm. Since 1979, men's and women's names have been alternated. If all names on the yearly list are used, as happens in especially active seasons, forecasters now turn to a supplemental list of names (use of the Greek alphabet ended with the 2020 season). The names of particularly destructive hurricanes are retired and replaced with new names selected by the World Meteorological Organization.
- The Saffir-Simpson scale (Categories 1–5) measures hurricane intensity by wind speed; a *major hurricane* is classified as 3 or higher. No Category 5 hurricanes are known to have struck the Carolinas since 1851. Early meteorologists and historians assigned the term "Great" to describe powerful hurricanes, especially those producing significant destruction.
- *Cape Verde hurricanes* are storms that originate near the Cape Verde islands off the African coast. They typically form during the middle portions of the hurricane season, and after crossing the Atlantic they are often more intense than early- and late-season storms that originate in the Caribbean, western Atlantic, or Gulf of Mexico. Florence, Floyd, Fran, Hugo, and the Sea Islands Hurricane are all examples of Cape Verde storms.
- A *storm surge* is a wind-driven, abnormal rise in sea level that accompanies a hurricane as it strikes the coast. The *storm tide* is the observed water level—a combination of the storm surge and normal lunar tide. *King tide* is a nonscientific term often used to describe exceptionally high lunar tides—usually occurring with a new or full moon and when the moon is near its *perigee* (when it passes closest to Earth). Tide records may use different *datums*, or reference points, especially in older records. Many early flood measurements refer to *mean sea level*, the average height of the sea for all stages of the tide. Others may be shown relative to *mean lower low water*, the average of the lower low-water heights of each tidal day observed; *mean higher high water*, the average of the higher high-water heights

of each tidal day observed; and more recently, *ground level*, the height measured above dry land.

- Published dollar-damage figures are estimates in the year they occurred, without adjustment for inflation. Reported figures for any given hurricane may vary widely—even among government agencies. For many years, the NHC calculated total damages by doubling insured losses. In 2011, that methodology was updated to consider other factors for greater accuracy. In 2017, the NHC partnered with the National Center for Environmental Information to again modify its official reports to represent financial losses more accurately. Figures listed in this book have been provided by the NHC, other government agencies, and insurance industry sources.

- Reported death statistics also vary by source. For most historic hurricanes, the totals are estimates. Early records are likely underreported and often include deaths at sea. More accurate fatality reporting began in the early twentieth century. For many years the NHC reported direct deaths (fatalities caused by floods, storm surge, wind, etc.) as well as indirect deaths (auto accidents, electrocution, carbon monoxide poisoning, etc.). Changes in counting methodology proposed by the Centers for Disease Control and Prevention in 2017 were largely adopted by the states, eliminating the direct-indirect distinction and more broadly including deaths by other causes.

Two weeks after the storm, Charles Town's residents were still sorting through wreckage, removing dislocated vessels, repairing homes, and struggling to put their lives back together. The cleanup task was daunting, but progress was being made. Churches were scrubbed of mud and debris and readied for funerals. The rebuild was just getting underway, when once again the skies darkened and winds lifted with the approach of another hurricane.

Fortunately, the second storm was not a direct strike on the city. The *South Carolina Gazette* reported that on September 30, the wind and rain began around 4:00 P.M. but cleared out soon after seven that evening. It was a short-lived storm with violent winds and heavy rains that mostly affected goods and furnishings and "the tops of houses" left exposed by the previous hurricane. Thankfully, too, its short visit in Charles Town did not bring destructive tides, though when it arrived, near the time of low tide, water levels were near those of normal high spring tides. Thirteen offshore vessels were caught in the hurricane; several were beaten and wrecked on the coast. The storm was considerably more severe in Winyaw (Georgetown), where the flooding was much greater and the destruction far worse than from the first hurricane. Landfall was closer to Cape Fear, placing Charles Town on the western edge of the storm as it passed. Still, heavy crop damages were reported in the region and, when combined with losses from the first hurricane, led to a twelve-month government ban on exports of corn, peas, and rice so that residents would have enough food to survive.

Though South Carolina was really only grazed by this second hurricane, the impact in North Carolina was enormous, from Smithville (Southport) through Johnston in Onslow County, where the town was destroyed and the courthouse was swept away by extreme tides. In his seminal volume *Early American Hurricanes, 1492–1870*, historian David Ludlum lamented the lack of contemporary news reports of the storm's impact from "what appears to have been one of the most violent hurricanes ever to strike the Cape Fear country and the Outer Banks of North Carolina."

Charleston has had a long and troubled history with hurricanes, and the Great Carolina Hurricane of 1752 stands out among others for its violence and impact on the city. Ludlum noted the severity of the storm and the value of comparison among early hurricanes: "Little doubt existed among the early writers on the subject that the hurricane of 1752 was the most severe in the Charleston area in colonial times. Ramsay (1809) declared: 'This was the greatest and most destructive hurricane that has ever taken place in Carolina.' Dr. Prioleau, who made a study for the Medical Society about 1805, thought 'the hurricane in the year 1752 far, very far exceeded, both in violence and devastation, the one in 1804.'" Ludlum, whose comprehensive history was published in 1963, also concluded, "In modern times at Charleston only the hurricane of 1893 could be placed in the same class with that of 1752."

TAKEAWAYS

- *Early hurricanes were not well understood.* Early colonists were largely unprepared for destructive hurricanes; many were European immigrants who were unfamiliar with hurricanes' extreme winds and tides. Colonial ports such as Charles Town were dependent on trade by sea, and tropical cyclones were a dangerous threat to their homes, their fleets, and their livelihoods. Not only was there no early warning system whatsoever, but most early residents in the Carolinas didn't understand the movements of hurricanes, their rotational winds, their seasonality, or their true destructive potential. Victims viewed the storms as simply "God's wrath."

- *Each storm is unique.* We know the 1752 hurricane that devastated Charles Town was relatively small in diameter, packed a powerful punch, and moved through quickly. Others, such as Hurricane Florence, are large, slow-moving rain makers. Each hurricane arrives with its own combination of factors that determine the kind of impacts it will have. Some are tightly wound windstorms that bring major damage, while weaker hurricanes have far less destructive winds. Some are known for their copious rains, while others are relatively "dry." They may be large in diameter, or they can be relatively small; size is not correlated with strength. Typically, they move along at a forward speed of about 8–15 mph, but some spin forward much more quickly, especially at more northerly latitudes. Some maintain a straightforward and predictable track, while others might wobble, stall, back up, or change direction. In the Carolinas, even a storm's angle of approach matters, often determining whether it skirts along the coast or tracks deep inland. These factors vary with each hurricane, helping determine the kinds of impacts to be expected.

- *Architectural adaptation has long been a successful strategy.* As the residents of Charles Town learned, properties at low elevation risk flooding from the sea, and structures built with simple wood frames can be vulnerable to high winds. After the 1752 storm, when repairing their homes or building new ones, residents built higher and stronger. Masonry replaced wood, windows featured protective shutters, and "half basements" put living quarters higher above the ground and above potential floods. For any home, the placement, materials, and construction methods—even the shape of the roof—can be the difference between heavy or modest damages during a severe hurricane. Over time, not only have building materials and methods improved, but construction codes have helped better protect structures from high winds and high water. Older homes can sometimes be retrofitted with roof truss tie-downs and other features to make them more resistant to hurricane winds. But experts agree: don't expect to build a hurricane-proof house.

- *Elevation is key.* Whether from persistent rains or ocean surge, rising water is a powerful and destructive force when a hurricane rolls through. For inland homes near rivers and beach houses by the sea, a structure's floor elevation helps determine its vulnerability to flooding. The higher the better. Today, most new homes in the Carolinas built in vulnerable coastal areas are raised on pilings to meet elevation requirements put in place in the 1970s and '80s. Sometimes, existing flood-prone homes can be elevated but at significant cost. And flood insurance rates will vary depending on elevation. When buying a home or property anywhere flooding is possible, think beyond "location, location, location" and consider "elevation, elevation, elevation."

CHAPTER TWO

THE GREAT ANTIGUA-CHARLESTON HURRICANE OF 1804

In July 1804, the war of words between two of America's more prominent early statesmen came to a head. For months, letters exchanged between Alexander Hamilton and Vice President Aaron Burr had escalated in tone and rhetoric. Hamilton, a leading Federalist, detested Burr, and years of public insults and political maneuvering fed a great animosity between the two men. Hamilton had helped prevent Burr's election to the presidency in 1796. Thomas Jefferson won the presidential race in 1800 over John Adams but only after narrowly defeating his own running mate, Burr, after a tie in the electoral college sent the final vote to the U.S. House of Representatives. As Burr became vice president, tensions between Hamilton and Burr escalated.

Lin-Manuel Miranda's Pulitzer- and Tony-winning play *Hamilton* offers a modern take on the intrigue: At 5:00 A.M. on July 11, 1804, both men set out from separate docks on the New York City waterfront and were each rowed across the Hudson River for a secret rendezvous. They weren't meeting to work out their differences but instead to engage in a duel in Weehawken, New Jersey. Duels were illegal but at the time were still believed by some to be an honorable means for resolving conflicts—and at least in New Jersey they seldom resulted in formal charges. On a secluded ledge twenty feet above the river, they stepped off ten paces and fired their flintlock pistols. A lead slug tore through Hamilton's abdomen; he died forty-one hours later in New York. Incidentally, Hamilton's nineteen-year-old son Philip had died just three years earlier in a similar duel, using the same guns on the same stretch of New Jersey riverfront—precipitated by a strident defense of his father's political views.

Because Alexander Hamilton had been such a prominent figure, the vice president was now a fugitive and was charged with murder in New York and New Jersey. He first fled to Washington, where he thought he might evade capture. Newspapers aligned with public sentiment, expressing outrage at the murder and casting Burr as a ruthless threat to the republic. Later that summer, partly to

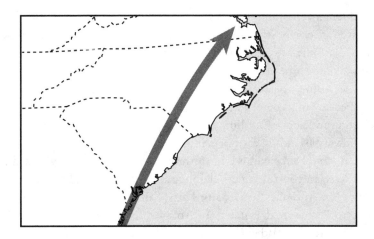

Slaves working in Lowcountry rice fields. (Engraving from *Frank Leslie's Illustrated Newspaper*. Courtesy of the Library of Congress, Washington, D.C.)

avoid public scrutiny, Burr traveled to the Georgia coast to stay with his friend, South Carolina native Maj. Pierce Butler, on his Saint Simons Island plantation. To avoid detection during his travels, Burr is thought to have used the alias Roswell King. During his stay on Saint Simons, he also spent time with John Couper's family at nearby Cannon's Point plantation, where he enjoyed hunting, fishing, French wines, and the pleasant company of a young mademoiselle visiting from France. On September 7, 1804, it was there on Couper's plantation property that Burr was caught up in one of the most ferocious and deadly U.S. hurricanes of the nineteenth century.

Weather historians later labeled it the Great Antigua-Charleston Hurricane of 1804 because of its devastating effects in the northern Caribbean and along the Georgia and South Carolina coasts. The storm tracked through the northern Windward Islands in early September and went on to sweep the Leewards with great fury. Fierce winds and storm-driven waves sank or wrecked hundreds of vessels across the region, claiming an unknown number of lives. Ports in Dominica, Antigua, Nevis, Saint Kitts, Saint Barthélemy, Saint Thomas, and Puerto Rico were devastated. In Antigua, few meteorological details are known, but letters and other records suggest the hurricane was among the worst in the island's history. High winds blew down buildings, and more than fifty vessels were sunk in and around English Harbour. In Saint Kitts, the storm washed homes from their foundations and wrecked every ship at anchor—close to 100 vessels. The impact was similar in other ports along the storm's path. Other great hurricanes of this era had left their mark on the region, especially those of 1772 and 1780. Though they may have claimed more lives, the 1804 hurricane was likely comparable in intensity.

The storm tracked through the Bahamas and continued northwest, approaching the northern Florida coast on September 6. Though it remained just offshore, high tides and strong northeast winds buffeted Saint Augustine, sinking nine of ten ships at harbor but causing relatively little damage otherwise. As it tracked closer to land, it made a gently sweeping curve to the north and northeast, obliquely striking land along the Georgia coast and passing inland over coastal South Carolina. Based on reports of wind direction, we know the eye likely passed over Saint Simons Island, just east of Savannah, and west of Charleston—exposing most of the South Carolina coast to the hurricane's stronger, eastern side. The storm center continued to track northeast, eventually passing through inland portions of eastern North Carolina and extreme eastern Virginia. Not a lot is known of its journey from North Carolina northward, though a severe gale was reported in New England on September 11 and 12 that sank vessels in Boston Harbor and toppled a church steeple in Salem. Historians have mixed views on whether those events might have been associated with this hurricane.

Three elements make the 1804 hurricane an ideal candidate for this book: its size, believed to have been "larger than Hugo," with powerful winds reaching far beyond the central core; its intensity, with at least strong Category 3, if not Category 4, strength at the time of landfall; and its track, imperiling the entire coastal region from northern Florida to southeastern Virginia. In fact, it would be hard to select a hurricane path that could do more harm to the Sea Islands, Savannah, Beaufort, Charleston, and Georgetown than that of the 1804 storm. Reports of heavy damage and casualties began in northern Florida and stretched northward. On the Georgia coast, extreme tides and winds were "the worst in memory," as evidenced by the letter Vice President Burr wrote to his daughter Theodosia during his stay on Saint Simons Island: "The water that fell from heaven was as salty as salt water at sea. . . . The house in which we were shook and rocked so much that Mr. C. began to express his apprehensions for our safety. Before three, part of the piazza was carried away; two or three of the windows burst in. The house was inundated with water, and presently one of the chimneys fell."

Burr, who was visiting John Couper's plantation, realized as the storm grew worse that he was stranded in the home and unable to return to Hampton plantation across the marsh. After watching countless large trees fall around the property and seeing floodwaters fill the first floor, Burr, Couper, family members, and several slaves all made a treacherous retreat to a nearby storehouse some fifty yards from the home. There they waited, listening to the storm's roar until evening, when suddenly the winds abated. Burr insisted that he return to Hampton, enlisting two young slaves to row him across a fully flooded Jones Creek. The three set out for the short journey, unaware that the lull was only the eye of the storm. Howling winds soon returned, now blowing violently southwest, testing the small skiff and the fortitude of its passengers. Burr was ultimately delivered to Major Butler's home, and the slaves managed to return safely.

On nearby Little Saint Simons Island, Butler grew Sea Island cotton and owned over 100 slaves, managed by a "headman," a slave named Morris. As the storm worsened throughout the afternoon on September 7, the frightened slaves scrambled to the flatboat that had transported them to the island, anxious to return to their cabins at Butler's Point. Morris, knowing the boat would be no match for the storm's winds and waves, cracked his bullwhip to get their attention, then ordered them to instead retreat to a large log house built on the island that would serve as better refuge. They followed him there and packed themselves inside. Though floodwaters surrounded them, all survived. Afterward, Butler was so impressed with Morris's lifesaving efforts that he offered him his freedom and awarded him an engraved silver tankard that read, "For his faithful, judicious, and spirited conduct in the hurricane on the 8th of September, 1804, whereby the lives of more than one hundred persons were, by divine permission, saved." Morris accepted the silver cup from his master but declined the offer of freedom, as it did not include freedom for his wife and children.

On many plantations across the Georgia and South Carolina Lowcountry, the outcome was far more dire. In *Lowcountry Hurricanes*, Walter Fraser described some of the tragic events, mostly for slaves working rice and cotton. Plantation owners' homes were typically constructed on high ground, often with the best available materials—tabby concrete and heart pine. Slave quarters were far less substantial: modest cabins or shanties built near the working fields, on lower ground. On many islands, the shanties were the first buildings destroyed. Just like on Saint Simons, the coastal islands were covered by the storm's ocean surge. Hundreds of slaves were drowned. Major Butler lost nineteen. On Broughton Island, a rice plantation owned by prominent Charlestonian William Brailsford, more than seventy slaves—men, women, and children—drowned when their flatboat capsized as they tried to escape the flooded fields. Most of their bodies were swept out to sea and never recovered.

Along the middle portions of the Georgia coast, other plantations, small farms, and villages near the water were inundated by tides "seven feet above normal high water." But the storm arrived at the time of low tide and during a spring tide cycle—which produces a lower-than-normal low tide. Therefore, some weather historians have speculated that the hurricane's surge could have approached sixteen feet.

Dozens of ships offshore were crippled, wrecked, or lost, with only a few able to limp into port after the storm. *Gunboat #1* was said to have been swept seven miles over marshes to Whitemarsh Island, where it finally came to rest in a cornfield. Most small boats were sunk or wrecked, and high winds tore away roofs, blew down houses, and leveled even substantial trees. Among the losses were an unknown number of horses, cattle, and hogs.

On Cockspur Island, at the mouth of the Savannah River, the hurricane peaked at midday on September 8. The island was home to Fort Greene, a strategic fortification completed just a few years earlier in 1794. On the morning the storm arrived, the commanding officer and several soldiers were in Savannah procuring fresh water for the fort, leaving a small contingent behind. Twenty-one people, including several soldiers, wives, children, and slaves occupied the fort and its garrison. By 10:00 A.M., waves were lashing at the battery walls, and shortly after noon, the storm tide reached its peak. Waves "swept the island from end to end." Terrified by the roar of the wind and alarmed by the tide's rapid rise, the group scrambled to the second floor of the blockhouse and then eventually onto its roof. During this time, Fraser noted that "powerful waves moved a forty-eight-hundred-pound cannon more than thirty feet." Around 1:00 P.M., the blockhouse collapsed into the flood, causing the roof to break away with twenty-one escapees holding on for their lives.

Their screams muted by the roar of the storm's ferocious winds, the desperate group was separated when waves broke the roof into pieces. Many were carried out to sea, while others were pulled under the dark waters, never to be seen again. Seven survived by clinging to their roof section while it was swept onto Wilmington Island; one other survivor was able to climb into a treetop. Only thirteen lived to describe these events; most of the women and children perished.

Wilmington Island was similarly covered by the ocean surge. One island plantation home collapsed on the afternoon of the eighth, killing the owner's wife and infant daughter. On nearby Hutchinson Island, tides seven to ten feet higher than normal covered rice fields and swept away countless plantation buildings and dwellings. The greatest loss, again, was that of nearly 100 slaves.

Storm tides pushed up the Savannah River, delivering a destructive surge to the piers, wharves, and ships in harbor at Savannah. Most vessels either capsized or were swept onto the city's wharves. All along the bluff, dozens of large brigs, sloops, and smaller craft were smashed and beaten by waves, where they mixed with a floating soup of broken lumber and stores of cotton, tobacco, and other goods. The waterfront was in "total ruin." In *Early American Hurricanes, 1492–1870*, David Ludlum quoted one survivor who wrote that "there is not a house in the lower part of the town but what has suffered very materially from the high tide which rose to the astonishing height of from twenty to thirty feet above the highest spring tides." Though the hurricane's surge was no doubt extreme, flooding of that degree appears unlikely—the U.S. Weather Bureau later accounted the flood in Savannah as ten feet above mean sea level.

Intense northeast winds battered the city from late morning until well after they reached their peak about 5:00 P.M. The *Georgia Republican* reported that in Savannah the storm raged for seventeen hours, "and sand picked up by the gale was blown into the upper stories of houses as high as 30 feet above ground level." In typical fashion, these winds tore away roofs, razed buildings, toppled countless trees, and caused mayhem across the city. The Presbyterian Meeting House lost its steeple, and the Christ Episcopal Church was heavily damaged. Perhaps the most devastating result in Savannah was the collapse of dozens of massive brick chimneys, which destroyed fine homes but also crushed their inhabitants to death.

Up the coast in South Carolina, the hurricane was equally vicious and the destruction immense. Plantations along the May River were devastated, with entire homes and slave quarters carried away with the tide. Five slaves were known to have drowned on Daufuskie Island, but throughout the region it's likely that many deaths went unreported. In Beaufort, the newly constructed causeway—which had taken the Port Republic Bridge Company seven years to complete—was washed away by the storm tide "in a few minutes." Ludlum wrote that "all dwellings on Bay Point were swept away as the eye of the savage hurricane roared in from the Atlantic. Cotton fields around Beaufort were overflown to a depth of 4 to 5 feet by the immense water surge." Other reports suggested that flooding in Beaufort was nine feet higher than ever known at that location.

The eye of the hurricane was observed at Saint Simons Island but tracked just east of Savannah. It was likely quite small in diameter, moving inland somewhere near Beaufort, which was consistent with the severity of the storm in that region. Across a broad expanse of Lowcountry, small creeks became raging rivers, washing away numerous bridges and isolating communities. The few roads that were not covered by floodwaters were impassable because of fallen trees, hindering recovery efforts.

Fifty miles northeast in Charleston, the hurricane also raged during the morning of the eighth. Winds blew northeast through the night, then turned east during the morning and southeast by afternoon—all while maintaining hurricane force. Like in Savannah and Beaufort, the harbor in Charleston was a "horrendous scene," though peak high water didn't arrive until just after noon. Fortifications and breastworks were overwashed and destroyed on James Island and at Fort Pinckney. Sailing ships of all sizes were sunk or tossed over the city's wharves; many were left wedged in streets and warehouses along the waterfront. Among those wrecked were the *Lydia*, which crashed into a brick weighhouse at Blake's Wharf, and the *Mary*, one of several vessels swept into Governor's Bridge, causing tremendous damage. The Charleston *Times* reported that the slave ship *Christopher* sank at Geyer's Wharf, "the negroes taken out with much difficulty." The *Times* was able to publish the day after the storm, but because the ships at harbor were ruined, it took weeks before news of the hurricane could be delivered to northern cities like Baltimore, New York, and Boston.

The *Charleston Courier* on September 10 also left some clues as to the severity of the surge: "A storm which it is said has not been equaled within the memory of any citizen of Charleston, commenced Friday evening last, accompanied with very high wind from the North-East, and continued without any considerable abatement, till one o'clock [Sunday] morning. . . . In this part of the city, we state from actual observation, that the tide rose three feet higher than it has ever been known since the hurricane of 1752; and several feet higher than the usual spring tides—the whole of Water-street was covered, and in Meeting-street it was nearly two feet in depth."

In addition to the destructive tides, high winds were also a menace throughout the city. Powerful gusts, likely near Category 3 strength, peeled away roofs and toppled chimneys, claiming several lives. Slate tiles were a hazard as they blew down into the streets. Fallen trees covered some sections; in other areas trees were stripped of their leaves. Weeks after the hurricane had passed, fruit trees near the coast reportedly "bloomed and bore fruit for a second time."

At nearby Sullivan's Island, nearly twenty houses were destroyed when they were washed from their foundations by ocean waves. Fraser noted that "the sea covered almost the entire island, from Fort Moultrie to the Cove." Many of the island homes were occupied, and daring rescues saved numerous lives. One child drowned, the island's only reported fatality.

Before this storm, the September hurricane of 1752 was considered Charleston's worst hurricane disaster. Since that time, the city had experienced a lot of change. South Carolina became the eighth state in 1776, and in 1783 Charleston was renamed from the old Charles Town. Bustling exports had helped fund investments in updated fortifications and infrastructure, including new roads, bridges, docks, and seawalls. All had been progressive moves to secure the city's place among the finest in the United States. Charleston's strategic location, impressive churches, fine homes, and busy hotels had attracted additional planters, barons, and wealthy shipping interests. Newer homes had been built of stronger materials and at higher elevations than those of the early eighteenth century.

Through the 1790s, construction had been underway on a stronger, higher seawall along East Bay Street to help protect the city from storms—in the area known today as the High Battery. A hurricane in 1797 undermined and damaged the unfinished project, and another in 1800 caused significant damage to the recent repairs. The costs escalated, but work continued right up through the arrival of the 1804 hurricane, which again broke apart and heavily damaged the palmetto-log-and-stone project. The *Charleston Courier* reported, "New East Bay Street, which, since the gale of October 1800, has been repaired at great expense, is again destroyed; the sea made clear breaches through it, and rushing into Water-street, and the adjacent parts, compelled the inhabitants to quit their houses, in the lower stories of some which the water was 14 inches deep."

The Battery project had become a symbol for Charleston's hurricane woes but also its best example of reconstruction and renewal. Following the 1804 hurricane, it was rebuilt again, this time with granite block, stronger and higher than before. This project was finally completed in 1818 and provided the city with an elegant promenade offering broad views of the surrounding river. In 1854, exactly fifty years after the 1804 storm, another hurricane undermined and partially damaged the seawall again in the White Point Garden section, after which the decision was made to raise the height another two feet. More storm surge damage occurred during the 1893 hurricane, which led to the placement of concrete reinforcements under the walkway. Other construction to extend the Battery occurred during the West End Improvement phase, completed in 1909 and 1911, with a second phase of boulevard extension improvements in 1917 and 1919. A walk along the Battery today steps over the ongoing history of Charleston's efforts to hold back hurricane floods.

As the immense hurricane tracked to the northeast, Georgetown and surrounding areas were also lashed by high winds and flooding, the worst of which arrived around 8:00 P.M. on the eighth. Winds there shifted to south-southeast when the storm center passed west of the city around midnight. Rains and tides overfilled nearby creeks, submerging Georgetown's wharves and bayfront. Fraser described how winds and surging waters destroyed several large homes at North Inlet, including one occupied by a family of fourteen who escaped and retreated to a modest hill, where rising floodwaters surrounded them. Blasted by fierce winds and trapped on a patch of earth only ten feet square, they thought they were doomed. As the winds shifted and the tides relented, they were able to wade through chest-deep water to reach higher land. There they waited through the night, as the storm's slow forward pace kept hurricane conditions in the area well into Sunday, September 10.

Off Cape Romain, several vessels battled the angry seas, many loaded with cotton, corn, and rice. The schooner *Ino* was demasted and the brig *Consolation* was capsized, but both were driven onto the beach with their surviving crews. Among the vessels lost was the schooner *Favourite*, which went down after its cargo of corn shifted in the hold. Four passengers and five crew members all perished; one passenger saved himself by grasping a floating chicken coop. Tossed by massive ocean waves for more than twenty-four hours, he was miraculously spotted and rescued by the crew of the *Venus*.

Not a lot is known of the hurricane's passage into eastern North Carolina. In his 1809 *History of South Carolina*, David Ramsay relayed that the storm was not felt north of Wilmington. But Ludlum concluded this to be in error, with evidence that in North Carolina "trees were blown down as far as 100 miles from the sea coast." There were also reports of more offshore wrecks, including the *Wilmington Packet* driven onto the beach at Cape Fear on the eighth. Although there's no doubt the hurricane lost steam as its core passed overland, its strength at landfall, slow pace, and large overall size likely meant that it was

THE OTHERS

The Carolinas have a rich hurricane history that spans some 400-plus years. The hurricanes selected for this book were chosen because of their meteorological prowess, overall impact, and unique relevance to our understanding of hurricane risk. They include many of the deadliest, costliest, and most intense tropical cyclones of record in the Carolinas. Hurricanes have, of course, rolled through the region for centuries, with many early storms remembered most for their devastating impact on offshore shipping and the resulting casualties at sea. In choosing these fifteen, there was some bias toward the selection of impactful, more recent hurricanes, for which the damage reports, weather records, and personal accounts are more complete.

Flooding was chest deep in downtown New Bern during Hurricane Ione in September 1955. (Photo courtesy of Milt Langston.)

Thanks to the careful work of weather historians, we know there are plenty of other memorable hurricanes that might have been contenders for this group of fifteen. From early unnamed storms that sank ships and wrecked settlements to any one of several recent billion-dollar flooding disasters, there's a long list of possibilities. Here are a few.

Two powerful hurricanes rolled through the Carolinas within two weeks in September 1752. The first was the Great Carolina Hurricane that ravaged Charleston and surrounding areas—selected as the first of the fifteen profiled here. The second made landfall just above Cape Fear on September 30 and swept northward, where it "washed away" the town of Johnston, the Onslow County seat. When tides and winds destroyed the county courthouse, all records and deeds were lost. Portions of the courthouse were said to have washed "across the New River, there two miles wide." Virtually every building in town was wrecked and eight residents were killed. So great was the loss at Johnston (in present-day Camp Lejeune) that the town was abandoned, and a new county seat was established at Wantland's Ferry (known today as Jacksonville).

The Great Chesapeake Bay Hurricane of 1769 was among the most destructive colonial storms of the eighteenth century. Before it swept Williamsburg, Virginia, and areas north, it pummeled the North Carolina coast with high winds and tides. Landfall was near Smithville (present-day Southport), where the courthouse was destroyed by strong gusts and falling trees. In New Bern, tides rose twelve feet above normal, flooding homes and businesses. Among them was the office and printshop of the *North Carolina Gazette*—the colony's first newspaper. The publication's metal type was later found buried in mud and was dug up and put back in service. As the storm tracked northward, witnesses described relentless winds that lasted thirteen hours. Based on pressure measurements taken in Virginia and in Harvard, Massachusetts, the storm likely raced northward at a forward speed of more than 40 mph.

The South Carolina coast was devastated by a cluster of hurricanes in the early nineteenth century, with the Great Antigua-Charleston Hurricane of 1804 the most powerful and deadly of the group. Following this disaster, the coastal region between Beaufort and Georgetown was swept by seven more hurricanes in less than twenty years, the worst of which was a deadly September 1822 storm described as "small but powerful." It struck just below Georgetown on September 27 with a massive surge that covered nearby islands and flooded coastal plantations, drowning hundreds. Most of the fatalities were slaves whose meager shanties were no match for the storm's fury. Following this hurricane, plantation owners began erecting brick "storm towers" across the Santee delta region, round masonry structures with conical roofs, thirty feet in diameter, twenty feet high, and with elevated floors. Upon the approach of a hurricane tide, slaves were taken to these towers, where they would huddle inside to wait out the storm. Today, the towers are mostly gone—only the ruins of a few remain.

In *Graveyard of the Atlantic*, author David Stick chronicled many of the notable shipwrecks off the North Carolina coast from the 1500s through the mid-twentieth century. Thousands of vessels of all varieties and an unknown number of passengers and crew were lost through this period, many thrown down by the heavy seas of tropical storms and hurricanes. Among the most calamitous events was that of a mid-nineteenth-century hurricane that ravaged the coast. Stick concluded, "No authentic information has come to light which would give the names of the many vessels totally lost or the number of persons drowned; it is sufficient to say that the hurricane of July 12, 1842, was one of the worst in the history of coastal Carolina." In this storm, two unknown ships capsized at Diamond Shoals, fourteen were swept ashore near Portsmouth, North Carolina, another fourteen were run aground on the sound side of Ocracoke, and six more were blown out to sea from Ocracoke Inlet and presumed lost.

Among the doomed vessels was the schooner *Lexington* and its crew of four. As the storm tossed the ship off Cape Hatteras, the hold filled with seawater, forcing Capt. William Morgan and his crew to abandon ship. Stick wrote of a note in a bottle, found in Shelby Bay, Bermuda, on October 27 of that year, which read: "I write this and enclose it in a bottle, so that if we should not be saved and the bottle be found, it may be known what became of the vessel and us. At 1 P.M. got into the boat with provisions and water sufficient for six days, having beforehand offered up our prayers to God to protect and save us. Signed Wm. H. Morgan, Captain; John Rider, Mate."

Just four years later, in 1846, an intense and slow-moving hurricane approached the North Carolina coast on September 6. A remarkable surge of water, driven by continuous northeast winds, pushed far into the Pamlico and Albemarle Sounds, flooding rivers and creeks for miles inland. Then as the hurricane passed and its winds rotated to the southwest, this massive expanse of water rushed back toward the sea, overwashing the Outer Banks from west to east. On the night of September 7, a new inlet was created by these events (Hatteras Inlet), separating Ocracoke from Hatteras and making Ocracoke an island. The next day, a second inlet was formed just south of Roanoke Island. It soon became navigable and was named Oregon Inlet for the first large vessel to pass through it, the *Oregon*.

The National Oceanic and Atmospheric Administration Hurricane Research Division's analysis of past tropical cyclones dates to 1851, and from the division's work we know that the Great Carolina Hurricane of 1854 was a major hurricane, Category 3, when it made landfall near Saint Catherines Island, Georgia, on September 8. A reconstruction of available weather data suggests a pressure of 950 millibars (mb) at landfall, with winds of 115 mph. High pressure to the north likely slowed the storm's progress as it carved a path through South Carolina. Its track and severity were similar to that of the Great Antigua-Charleston Hurricane of 1804, following exactly fifty years to the day.

The large, slow-moving storm devastated shipping interests from Florida to New England. Just between Savannah and Georgetown several dozen ships were sunk, scuttled, or run aground. In Charleston, tides poured over wharves and seawalls, flooding homes, shops, and warehouses. The Charleston Hotel, the city's largest and most elegant guest quarters, was blasted by high winds. Its four chimneys collapsed as the roof peeled away, allowing heavy rains to drench the structure's interior plaster walls and fine furnishings. In Georgetown, similar destruction was reported to vessels, docks, homes, and businesses. The *Pee Dee Times* later reported that the storm in Georgetown was the "longest continuous blow in the memory of any inhabitant." Following the storm, Charleston's granite-lined Battery was rebuilt two feet higher to better withstand future hurricanes.

In the absence of any forewarning, merchant ships and passenger liners of this era sometimes sailed into the path of approaching hurricanes with disastrous results. During the September hurricane of 1857 (Category 2 in North Carolina), the 280-foot side-wheel steamer *Central America* foundered in heavy seas and sank some 160 miles off the South Carolina coast. Carrying 578 passengers and crew and some 30,000 pounds of gold prospected during the California gold rush, there was no hope the ship could be saved once its boilers flooded. After a grueling night of battering waves, over 150 women and children were moved into lifeboats the following morning and miraculously saved by nearby vessels. But rolling seas ended the rescue mission later that day, and 425 passengers and crew were lost as the ship went down. In addition to the horrific casualties, the losses in gold were so great they contributed to the Panic of 1857, a nationwide financial downturn that forced a run on U.S. banks. Even today, the sinking of the *Central America* is considered among the greatest maritime disasters in U.S. history. Much of the lost gold and other artifacts was recovered after the shipwreck was discovered in 1988, with the recovery team later embroiled in legal tangles over proceeds from the expedition.

There are other deadly, destructive nineteenth-century storms that could have been considered for this list of fifteen. According to the National Oceanic and Atmospheric Administration's *Deadliest Atlantic Tropical Cyclones, 1492–1996*, which includes accounts of fatalities at sea, the ferocious Norfolk–Long Island Hurricane of September 1821 killed more than 200 as it raced from Ocracoke northward, though most of those deaths likely occurred in the Caribbean, Virginia, New Jersey, and New York. The following year, the aforementioned September 1822 storm claimed 300 lives in coastal South Carolina and offshore waters. An August hurricane in 1881 (Category 2 in Georgia) caused more than 700 deaths in Georgia, South Carolina, and adjacent waters, and a September hurricane in 1883 (Category 2 in North Carolina) was responsible for 106 deaths, fifty-three of which were in the lower Cape

Fear region of North Carolina. And the October 1898 hurricane, the strongest ever known to strike the Georgia coast (Category 4), was responsible for 179 deaths from Georgia to North Carolina. It delivered a record sixteen-foot storm tide at Brunswick, Georgia. This storm's greatest impact was along the coast from Fernandina, Florida, to Savannah and inland toward Augusta, sparing the South Carolina Lowcountry from the most extreme winds and tides. A reconstruction of available data determined the storm reached a low pressure of 938 mb at landfall, a similar intensity to that of Hurricane Hazel in 1954 and Hugo in 1989.

Other, more recent storms have left their mark on the Carolinas. Among them are destructive hurricanes in August 1911 (Category 2 that struck below Charleston) and August 1940 (Category 2 that made landfall near Beaufort, South Carolina, claiming fifty lives and delivering widespread flooding to western North Carolina). Heavy rains from the latter storm caused more than 600 landslides in Watauga County alone, burying homes beneath mud, rocks, and trees and killing twelve people.

The Great Atlantic Hurricane of 1944 was large, powerful, and deadly. Though it never made landfall in North Carolina, it brushed the Outer Banks as it tracked northward, knocking down power lines and leveling small homes near Manteo. In the beach town of Avon, soundside flooding washed 96 of the town's 115 structures off their foundations. On Ocracoke, the tide rose two to four feet inside many homes. Fish were reportedly trapped under furniture as the waters receded. At Cape Hatteras, the weather station recorded a barometric pressure of 947 mb, the lowest of record at that location. But the storm's greatest impact was at sea. While passing some 400 miles off the Florida coast as a Category 4, the storm sank the U.S. Navy destroyer USS *Warrington*, claiming 248 lives. Off the North Carolina coast, U.S. Coast Guard cutters *Jackson* and *Bedloe* capsized and sank in heavy seas while guarding a Liberty ship that had been torpedoed near Cape Hatteras. German U-boats were active at that time in attacking Allied vessels that moved along the Outer Banks. In all, the 1944 storm claimed 390 lives.

In 1955, less than a year after Hurricane Hazel's wrath, two hurricanes and one tropical storm all made landfall on the North Carolina coast within six weeks. Connie (Category 2), Diane (tropical storm), and Ione (Category 2) each made their own news headlines through late summer. In the Tar Heel State, the combined damages from the three storms exceeded those of Hazel the year before. Ione set several rainfall records and flooded large portions of the coastal plain. A weather station in Maysville recorded nearly fifty inches of rain over a forty-two-day period. It was during this time that eastern North Carolina was dubbed Hurricane Alley by news outlets across the United States.

Two twenty-first-century hurricanes made the list of fifteen, though a few others might have been considered—all of which struck the North Carolina coast. Hurricanes Isabel in September 2003 (Category 2), Irene in August 2011 (Category 1), and Dorian in September 2019 (Category 2) each pounded the Outer Banks and might have been contenders given the extent of the coastal flooding and property damage they left behind. The once-mighty Isabel (Category 5 near the Bahamas) turned northward and weakened before slipping up Core Banks, over Pamlico Sound, and eventually into eastern Virginia as a tropical storm. It sliced open a new inlet near Hatteras and flooded hundreds of homes from Carteret County northward. Like so many other Carolina hurricanes, Isabel's toll extended through the mid-Atlantic region. It caused fifty-one total deaths in eight states and brought losses that surpassed $3 billion—though most of those losses were tallied in Virginia and Maryland.

Irene, in late August 2011, was another strong hurricane that weakened considerably before approaching the Pamlico and Albemarle Sounds region. Though "only" a Category 1 at landfall, Irene caused record flooding in numerous northeast North Carolina communities. After the storm, media attention was focused on the dramatic washout of N.C. 12 at Rodanthe and the resulting isolation of Hatteras Island residents. But historic flooding and broadscale misery befell thousands of residents on the other side of the Pamlico, Croatan, and Albemarle Sounds. Nearly 30 percent of homes in Pamlico County were flooded. Irene claimed forty-one lives in the United States, including four in North Carolina. It was credited with more than $1 billion in damages

Aidan and Keagan Charron navigate the flooded
sidewalks near Sir Walter Raleigh Street in downtown
Manteo during Hurricane Irene's record flooding
in August 2011. (Photo courtesy of Paul Charron.)

in the state, though its path through the mid-Atlantic and northeastern
states racked up much greater losses—at $13.5 billion, it ranks among
the twenty most costly hurricanes in U.S. history (through 2021).

One of the most powerful Atlantic hurricanes in history swept toward the Carolinas in 2019. Category 5 Hurricane Dorian blasted the
Bahamas with 185 mph winds, matching the Labor Day Hurricane of
1935 as the strongest landfalling hurricane ever observed in the Atlantic
Basin. It devastated the islands and became the costliest storm in Bahamian history. Then, in a familiar pattern, it weakened, curved northwest, followed the Gulf Stream just off the Florida coast, and eventually
swept over Cape Hatteras as a Category 2 before tracking through the
Northeast and into Canada. Along the way, storm tides flooded portions of Charleston while two tornadoes touched down in South Carolina. Another twenty-five twisters were reported in North Carolina.
Flooding on Ocracoke Island was the most extreme in a generation,

with several residents chased into their attics as floodwaters peaked. The surge arrived quickly; witnesses said waters rose five feet within ten minutes. Thankfully, no drownings were reported on Ocracoke, though the storm was credited with three fatalities in North Carolina.

Notably absent from this book is the devastating flood of October 2015 that resulted from record rainfall over eastern South Carolina—a flood that easily ranks among the state's greatest natural disasters. It wasn't a hurricane, though Hurricane Joaquin's presence in the open Atlantic at the time played a role. The combination of a surface low-pressure system along a stalled frontal boundary over the southeast U.S. coast, an upper-level low over the Midwest, and an extended plume of moisture from Joaquin conspired to drop more than twenty inches of rain in South Carolina's central and coastal counties over five days. Widespread major flooding resulted across the Pee Dee, Santee, and Ashley-Cooper-Edisto River basins, with more than a dozen reporting sites surpassing the state's 107-year-old five-day rainfall record. Significant urban flooding affected the Columbia metro area. More than 1,500 water rescues ensued; tragically, nineteen fatalities were recorded, most flood related. South Carolina emergency management officials reported losses of close to $1.5 billion.

a formidable inland storm. Assuming the diminished hurricane continued to track north or northeast, it undoubtedly caused problems across the eastern half of the Tar Heel State, long after its initial landfall.

After the September 1804 hurricane passed and the cleanup began, the storm's heartbreaking toll became clear: this was the deadliest and most destructive hurricane ever experienced in the Lowcountry since the region was first settled. Charleston newspapers and historians of the time quickly began to make comparisons with the 1752 hurricane and with another vicious storm in 1783. They generally considered the 1752 hurricane to have been the most intense, but the 1804 hurricane was much longer in duration and caused far more destruction over a broader area. Property damages in Savannah alone were more than $500,000; in Charleston the toll exceeded $1 million. In and around the cities, disease outbreaks struck once drinking wells became contaminated by flooded privies.

On the many plantations that dotted the Georgia and South Carolina coasts, planters were devastated by the loss of crops, livestock, buildings, and boats—and slaves. The destruction of food crops such as corn, potatoes, rice, and vegetables was so great that starvation was a widespread problem through the following winter. Sadly, it was the loss of so many slaves that spelled ruin for some. Rebuilding dikes and reordering rice fields was an expensive and labor-intensive undertaking; some fields lay fallow for years. Ultimately, large tracts were sold at deeply discounted prices. Recovery was slowed too by the disruption of all land travel due to the large number of washed-out bridges and impassable roads. It took many years, but eventually the entire region was rebuilt and became prosperous again, just as it had in the aftermath of past hurricane disasters.

No economic losses, however, could compare with the devastating loss of life attributed to the hurricane. Five hundred deaths were estimated in Georgia and South Carolina—mostly drownings on coastal plantations. This figure likely doesn't include some wind-related deaths in Savannah, Beaufort, and Charleston or the many fatalities that occurred at sea. The storm's shocking toll far exceeded that of other historic hurricanes in the region before that time. Nine out of ten deaths were African slaves, drowned by sweeping tides or crushed by collapsing homes. Some died crossing rivers, and others were lost when their ships went down at sea. After the storm, windrows of bodies lined beaches and marsh flats near the hardest-hit areas. Plantation owners, many of whom owned dozens of slaves, were ill-prepared for a hurricane flood of this magnitude. A few had judiciously moved their slaves as the storm began, carrying them with their families to safer areas on high ground. A handful had even rescued their slaves from the floods, saving their lives. But in far too many cases, slaves were left in vulnerable, low-lying shanties or out on coastal fields where there was no refuge from the onslaught of wind and water. Few planters had adequate plans; many simply failed to act.

The Great Antigua-Charleston Hurricane of 1804 remains one of the most violent and tragic hurricane disasters in the history of the Lowcountry. Though North Carolina was spared the worst, South Carolina's entire coastal region was visited by the core of the storm, with dire consequences. It's hard to imagine a more threatening combination of track and intensity for a hurricane in coastal South Carolina than that of this storm. Destruction in the Caribbean was heavy, but the loss of life in the Lowcountry was devastating. Combined with the losses in northern Florida and Georgia, the 1804 hurricane exacted a high toll that wouldn't be surpassed by another U.S. hurricane for nearly eighty years.

TAKEAWAYS

- *Lowcountry plantations were hurricane death traps for countless African slaves.* The vigorous economic growth that was a boon to cities such as Savannah, Charleston, and Georgetown through the eighteenth and early nineteenth centuries was fueled by the region's highly success-ful agricultural endeavors. Sea Island cotton, rice, indigo, and food crops produced healthy profits for wealthy planters who managed large coastal tracts. The planters' success was entirely dependent upon multitudes of African slaves, kept in place partly by the remoteness of the islands where they lived. But plantation owners and slave masters were ill-prepared for the threat of approaching hurricanes. The vulnerability of slave quar-ters was rarely considered, and relocation or other measures to protect the slaves' safety was too often an afterthought. Some wise planters did construct safe houses on high ground, but as documented during the 1804 hurricane and many others of the period, hundreds, perhaps even thou-sands, of slaves were drowned by the swift arrival of hurricane tides.

- *The course a hurricane follows as it passes overland determines the extent of its destructive impact.* Every hurricane will leave its mark. Some may skirt along the coast; others strike the shore and travel deep inland. In the Carolinas, a powerful landfalling hurricane tracking longshore and just inland may be the most potent of tracks. The 1804 hurricane was an example, carving a decidedly treacherous path from Georgia to North Carolina. After making landfall on the Georgia coast, it swept northeast-ward, its center passing through Beaufort, just west of Charleston, just west of Georgetown, and presumably west of Wilmington and across the coastal plains of North Carolina. This track placed the entire South Carolina coast and large portions of North Carolina's coast on the more dangerous eastern side of circulation. Every barrier beach, coastal bay, and river for some 350 miles was subject to the worst of the hurricane's extreme storm tides and maximum winds. For a large hurricane such as the one in 1804, its close proximity to the Atlantic may have helped sustain its energy. And for any modern hurricane following such a track, the population centers along the coast—from Savannah, Hilton Head, and Charleston to Myrtle Beach and Wilmington—would all get hit by the core of the storm.

CHAPTER 3

THE BEAUFORT HURRICANE
OF 1879

In the late nineteenth century, seaside resorts in coastal North Carolina were frequented by vacationers from across the state, just as they are today. One of the most popular resort destinations was the prestigious Atlantic Hotel in Beaufort. Built in 1859 by Capt. Josiah Pender, the hotel was constructed on pilings over the water at the foot of Pollock Street and at the time was described by the *Goldsboro Messenger* as "the largest coastal resort hotel in North Carolina." During the Civil War, the resort was transformed into a hospital but was then completely refurbished in 1866, and by 1870 the Atlantic Hotel was again hosting vacationers. The three-story structure featured broad verandas on each level and was wrapped with windows to catch the prevailing summer breeze off the water. Its charm and location attracted business leaders and families who traveled by train from Raleigh, Charlotte, Asheville, and Richmond, Virginia. It was popular with "high quality guests" and featured sailing lessons, a billiards room, the best cigars and liquors, croquet on the nearby lawn, and nightly string-band dances. The resort did not endure for long, however, as it became the scene of a tragic episode in North Carolina's hurricane history.

On August 17, 1879, preparations were underway for a special convention in Beaufort. The *Raleigh Observer* announced on August 16, "Major Perry of the Atlantic Hotel, Beaufort, will give a Grand Dress Ball in honor of the North Carolina Press Association on Thursday night, August 21.... Major Perry will spare no pains in making it one of the handsomest of the season." The hotel was already brimming with guests, including Governor Thomas Jarvis, his wife, and numerous prominent friends from around the state. The Gatlings of Raleigh, the Stronachs of Wilson, and the Hugheses of New Bern joined the governor and his family. They had all arrived in Beaufort with no knowledge of the hurricane that would soon sweep through the region. In her book *The Atlantic Hotel*, Virginia Doughton wrote that "local boatmen recognized the ominous signs on August 15, like the Man O'War bird, and began moving their boats up the creek." On the morning of Sunday the seventeenth, a duty officer from nearby Fort Macon came to Beaufort to warn Major Perry that a

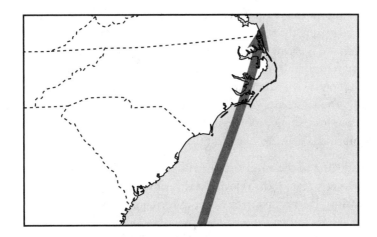

Some of the highest winds ever measured on the Carolina coast were recorded at the Cape Lookout lighthouse in August 1879. (Photo courtesy of the Outer Banks History Center, Manteo, North Carolina.)

dangerous gale was expected in the area. Doughton wrote that "Perry became adamant and shouted that the U.S. government wouldn't tell him how to run the Atlantic Hotel." He later told guests "there was nothing to worry about," and they retired with no knowledge of the powerful hurricane that was soon to strike.

Hurricanes of this era almost always arrived with little warning. In the early 1870s, recognizing the need to relay timely storm information along the Atlantic coast, the U.S. Army Signal Service built a telegraph line connecting coastal observation stations from New England to Florida. On March 8, 1876, a signal service station at Cape Lookout was dedicated, operating from the second floor of the lighthouse keeper's house—just eight miles from the Beaufort waterfront. It was from this location that the officer on duty watched his instruments on the morning of the 1879 hurricane. He reported:

The howling of the wind and the rushing of the water past the station woke us at 5 A.M., 18th. Velocity at this time being 80 mph. and rapidly increasing. The rain pouring down in torrents, the sea rushing past the house at a fearful rate and rising rapidly. It soon undermined the Signal Service Stable, The Light House Establishment Store House and a cookhouse, which were blown down and carried away by the rushing tide. The Signal Service mule which became loose when the stable washed away tried to come to the dwelling house but could not face the raging storm; she turned and rushed into the foaming billows. The fence around the lighthouse next went carrying the keeper's fuel along with it. The whaling schooner *Seychell* of Provincetown, Mass., 50 tons, Capt. Cook, fishing in these waters, was at anchor in the Hook, parted her chains. . . . At the time the vessel crossed Wreck Point she was drawing 12 feet of water, thus showing the tide to have been fuller than ever known at this place.

Amazingly, the signal officers at Cape Lookout were able to survive the storm and witnessed some of the highest winds ever reported on the North Carolina coast. The station's anemometer cups were blown away at 6:35 A.M., at which time the register showed a velocity of 138 mph. The tides continued rising and the winds steadily climbed until 7:35 A.M., when a wind-speed estimate was made of 168 mph. Though extreme winds (gusts) at this level might have been possible, and seem to suggest Category 4 strength, barometric pressure readings from surrounding locations give evidence the storm was more likely a Category 3—as officially recognized by the National Oceanic and Atmospheric Administration's reanalysis team. Wind readings from surrounding locations can't corroborate either, as anemometers were also reportedly destroyed at nearby Fort Macon and in the North Carolina towns of Portsmouth, Hatteras, and Kitty Hawk and in Cape Henry, Virginia.

By 1:00 A.M. on August 18, heavy rains and gusting winds were sweeping over the North Carolina coastline. By 3:00 A.M., many Beaufort residents were pacing in their homes as the winds increased dramatically and the storm's surge began flooding Front Street. The 140 guests at the Atlantic Hotel were stirred by the storm in the early-morning hours. One guest reported, "About 4 o'clock A.M. the tide had risen very much, and the wind was so strong that it was impossible to stand. But those who had witnessed repeated storms at Beaufort told us there was nothing to fear. At about 5 o'clock, the water had risen to the floor of the hotel, and it was thought best to remove the children and ladies. This determination was taken so late that many of them had hardly time to dress, and a few were not dressed."

The *Charlotte Observer*'s report of the guests' escape at 5:00 A.M. was compelling:

> The hotel began to rock. A Raleigh lady grasped her husband's arm and led the way out into the storm. The fury of the gale was indescribable; to the ladies the water was more than waist deep. . . . Children had to be carried through the waves, and it was all that men could do to stand up under the furious lashings of the storm. Two boys . . . having been forgotten during the excitement, threw themselves from a second-story window, fell in the water and were washed ashore. Two other children were washed far from the beach and were picked up in an exhausted condition.

Many of the hotel guests escaped with few clothes or belongings and were forced to swim or wade through the chest-deep waters that had engulfed Front Street. The surging tide washed boats and debris as far into town as Broad Street. Most of the hotel refugees were taken in by the good people of Beaufort, where they were sheltered in hallways and kitchens.

As the hurricane's surge continued to rise, the Atlantic Hotel and other waterfront dwellings crumbled. Shops and ship's stores along Front Street were "washed off the blocks" and collapsed into the tide—at least one of them with the shop owner's wife and children still inside. In the chaos that followed, the Beaufort waterfront was the scene of heroic rescues and great tragedies. The entire Stronach family was saved from the collapsing hotel by an African American man, Palmer Davis. Davis carried the Stronach children in his arms through neck-deep water and falling debris. He also rescued the teenage daughter of Seaton Gales of Raleigh. Davis was later recognized by Governor Jarvis as the hero of the hour, although there were others who risked their lives in the dreadful storm.

The Hester brothers from Morehead City were also credited with saving lives as they helped several guests to safety. Henry Congleton, a local boat hand, drowned in the tide as he attempted to rescue desperate vacationers from the top floor of the hotel. Two young men from New Bern, Owen Guion and

Justice Disosway, were among those trapped on the hotel's third floor. They apparently made a last-minute escape when they jumped into the rising water, clinging to their mattresses with money in their mouths.

In addition to Congleton, two other men drowned in the collapse of the Atlantic Hotel: John Dunn of New Bern, a guest at the time, and John D. Hughes, a local young man who was one of the first to offer assistance to frightened vacationers. After rescuing several guests from the second and third floors, Hughes returned to the hotel during the peak of the storm. Thinking he saw a young woman in a window, he approached the structure just as battering waves and wind caused the hotel to collapse. His death was in vain, however, as he had apparently mistaken the window's billowing curtains for a woman's nightgown.

Among those who escaped the hotel with no time to spare were Governor Jarvis and his wife. It's been told that the governor, like many other survivors, lost all of his personal belongings and was forced to flee in his pajamas with his shoes in his hand. In the chaos of the escape, his shoes were lost, but he managed to lead his family to the safety of a cottage several blocks away.

After the storm passed and the tide receded, the Beaufort waterfront was piled high with the wreckage of the night. Trunks of damaged goods littered Front Street, along with drifts of lumber and broken skiffs. Crowds of dazed people, many of them barefooted, sifted through the rubble in search of lost belongings. Thousands of dollars' worth of jewelry was reportedly lost in the destruction of the hotel. Governor Jarvis called out fifty men from the garrison at Fort Macon to guard the debris strewn about the waterfront.

The citizens of Beaufort took in more than 150 refugees and offered them clothes, shoes, and whatever food was available. Governor Jarvis, in need of proper clothing, was given an ill-fitting sailor suit that had last been worn in the War of 1812. No shoes could be found that would fit his large feet, so he wore a pair of oversized boots. Mrs. Jarvis borrowed a calico housecoat and was thankful to be dressed for the trip back to Raleigh.

On the morning of August 19, the refugees were transported by boat to Morehead City, where they boarded a train to take them home. At New Bern, a large crowd had gathered at the station to express sympathy to Major and Mrs. Hughes for the tragic loss of their son. At 8:30 P.M., the train arrived at the station in Goldsboro, where forty editors of the North Carolina Press Association were waiting to meet the survivors. Members of the association had canceled their trip to the coast upon news of the hurricane and instead met at Goldsboro's Gregory Hotel. The newsmen would later report on the weariness of the group and the tragedies of the storm.

When the remaining survivors arrived in Raleigh, Governor Jarvis encouraged them to gather at the Yarborough House Hotel for refreshments. There the storm-battered group made a toast to their survival, and the reception lasted into the night. One newsman reported that the governor looked "as weather-beaten as he used to after one of Lee's campaigns." That evening, discussions about rebuilding the Atlantic Hotel began. Apparently the idea was modified, as the New Atlantic Hotel was not built in Beaufort but in Morehead City, where it became a vacation landmark for many years.

The devastating effects of the Beaufort Hurricane of 1879 were felt far beyond the Beaufort waterfront. The storm apparently made landfall just above Topsail Island, swept Carteret County, and crossed the Pamlico Sound, returning to the Atlantic near Norfolk, Virginia. From there, it continued to the northeast and brought record tides to Atlantic City and Boston. In Portsmouth, Virginia, over 150 buildings were damaged, many unroofed by strong gusts. At Johnsontown, on Virginia's eastern shore, *Monthly Weather Review* noted that "thirty panes of glass were blown from the observer's house outward against the wind's direction." Dozens of ships were wrecked from Smithville (Southport) to Cape Cod. The *Review*'s report concluded that "the amount of damage done by this storm cannot be enumerated within the limits of this Review. . . . The damage to maritime property must have been enormous, reports already at hand show that over one hundred large vessels were either shipwrecked or suffered serious injury, while the number of yachts and smaller vessels which were destroyed or seriously damaged must certainly exceed two hundred." The U.S. Life Saving Service, with operable stations spread along coastal beaches from Massachusetts to the Outer Banks, was called to action during the storm. These stations were credited with rescuing the shipwrecked crews of the *Water Lily* near Hatteras Inlet, the *Ida B. Silsbee* in Pamlico Sound, and the schooners *Flora Curtis* and *Emma D. Blew* on the New Jersey shore.

In *Hurricanes and the Middle Atlantic States*, author Rick Schwartz described one of the more chilling scenes after the storm: "In all his years of sailing the Chesapeake Bay, Captain Noah Foster had never seen anything like it. Off Gwynn's Island, Va., on the lower bay, he encountered a schooner, the *J. C. Henry*, sailing erratically. A dead woman was lashed to the rigging of the deserted ship. Who was she? What happened?" The mystery was solved with the rescue of two brothers who were carried overboard but later found clinging to wreckage. Along with their parents, the Donnellys, they had sailed into the storm from Philadelphia. Mrs. Donnelly could not swim. In an effort to save her, she had been tied to the ship—a common practice during vicious storms. Sadly, Mr. Donnelly was then swept overboard; his wife soon perished in the relentless waves.

Perhaps the storm's most visible effects were evident in eastern Carteret County. In addition to the destruction in Beaufort, the losses in Morehead City were heavy and included 1,000 feet of railroad track, the Morehead Market House, several windmills, a Methodist church, the city wharves, and dozens of shops and homes. Virtually every structure for thirty miles lost its chimney in the ferocious gusts. Thomas Webb, a night watchman at the railway depot, nearly drowned when the rapidly rising water separated him from the mainland. He saved himself by tying his body to a drifting platform with his pants. When he was later found, exhausted, he had lost most of his clothes in the raging wind and water.

The hurricane's storm surge opened at least two inlets on Bogue Banks, just west of Fort Macon. Great destruction was reported in the barrier island communities of Diamond City and Portsmouth. Beaufort Inlet was reshaped, as almost 800 yards of sand were washed away on the western end of Shackleford Banks. Twenty-one dwellings were leveled in the town of Smyrna, and other communities suffered extensive destruction, including Cedar Island, Ocracoke, Hatteras, and Kitty Hawk. In all, the storm was responsible for forty-six deaths in North Carolina and Virginia.

Like those of other storms, stories of the 1879 hurricane have been passed down in the families of those who survived it. Newspapers wrote about this storm's severity and destruction, and some labeled it the "worst ever." But labels can be deceiving, as each generation may endure a tragic hurricane and then describe it as incomparable. Other hurricanes striking the North Carolina coast may have had greater winds or higher tides, but to the seaside vacationers at the Atlantic Hotel, this storm was indeed the worst.

TAKEAWAYS

- *Structures on or near the water are always most vulnerable.* The Atlantic Hotel was a formidable structure, but it was built over the water and was exposed to the worst of the 1879 hurricane's winds, tides, and waves. It didn't survive. Homes and businesses built close to the ocean, sounds, rivers, and bays will always require special considerations to survive hurricanes. Elevation is the most critical factor; older structures were sometimes built at ground level, but newer ones must meet minimum elevation standards. The types of building materials and methods used are important too. Modern building codes and construction techniques help reduce risk for both flooding and wind damages, though special requirements in coastal zones add costs. When considering buying or building near water, ask a lot of questions of your realtor, builder, and local permitting agency.

- *It seems obvious: heed official warnings.* How fortunate we are today to have state-of-the-art forecasts well in advance of any approaching hurricane. Based on those forecasts, local officials make sometimes tough decisions about evacuating their communities to reduce the risk of injury or death. But not everyone follows those directives. Like Major Perry, the proprietor of the Atlantic Hotel, some choose to ignore official warnings—often from their own sense that "it probably won't be that bad." There's clearly risk in doing so. Residents who live in vulnerable areas should have plans in place before evacuation orders are issued, knowing when to leave, where to go, the safest routes to get there, and what to take with them.

- *The Carolinas' barrier beaches and inlets are always on the move.* Strong currents and shifting sands constantly reshape our fragile barrier islands. Routine winds and tides continuously move sand about, but hurricanes and nor'easters can quickly carve away large portions of beach, knock down dunes, and open or close inlets. In the 1879 hurricane, ocean overwash temporarily opened two new inlets near Atlantic Beach, North Carolina, and shifted Beaufort Inlet eastward by some 800 yards. Other historic storms have similarly altered the Carolina coast, opening new inlets and rearranging navigation routes, requiring mapmakers to redraw their charts. Coastal geologists are quick to point out that storm overwash, which can lead to inlet creation, is a natural and necessary component of a healthy barrier island system.

CHAPTER FOUR

THE GREAT
SEA ISLANDS HURRICANE
OF 1893

In April 1861, the South Carolina militia launched a bombardment on U.S. troops at Fort Sumter in Charleston Harbor, thus beginning the grueling Civil War that divided the United States into north and south. It wasn't long before other violence broke out in places such as Baltimore and Richmond. In Washington, D.C., Clara Barton, a thirty-nine-year-old clerk in the U.S. Patent Office, heard about a group of wounded soldiers arriving in the city and wanted to help. She gathered clothing and medical supplies and tended to their injuries—thus beginning a long and storied career of public service and aid to the suffering.

Barton quickly mastered the collection and transport of supplies and implored government officials to allow her to take her relief efforts onto the battlefield. She was convincing. As the war raged on, she was often embedded with Union forces, resupplying field hospitals and serving the troops in battles at Fairfax Station, Chantilly, Harpers Ferry, Antietam, Fredericksburg, Cold Harbor, and others. The scope of her humanitarian efforts was impressive: throughout the war, not only did she provide comfort to the sick and injured, but she also recruited supporting volunteers, acquired donations, and read and wrote letters for the soldiers. Even after the war, she was instrumental in helping soldiers and their families by establishing networks to identify the missing, injured, and dead. For all these reasons she became known as the Angel of the Battlefield.

While visiting Europe after the war, Barton took interest in the work of the Red Cross in Switzerland and the efforts of Henry Dunant and others to establish international humanitarian treaties in Geneva. After a few years of relief work in France, she returned to the United States to lobby for U.S. approval of the Geneva Conventions. In 1881, Barton founded the American Red Cross and quickly went to work with a public appeal to aid victims of

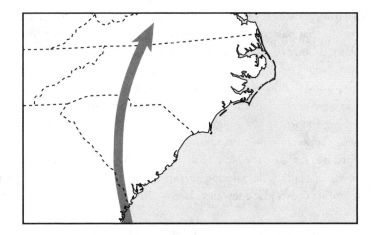

Damaged homes along the beach on Tybee Island, Georgia, after the 1893 Sea Islands Hurricane. (Photo from the Elizabeth B. Pittman collection on the Nicholas, Baker, and Mongin families. Courtesy of the Georgia Historical Society, Savannah.)

forest fires in Michigan. In 1884, she traveled to Pennsylvania with her team of volunteers to the scene of the Johnstown Flood, where more than 2,000 had died. Wherever there was death and suffering, Barton rushed in with food, medicine, and clothing, sometimes saving lives and always bringing comfort to those in distress.

In the summer of 1893, forecasters at the Washington offices of the U.S. Weather Bureau were hopping. The Atlantic hurricane season was well underway, and a flurry of storms kept them busy. On August 23, with limited incoming information, they were attempting to keep up with four hurricanes, including one that passed off the Virginia coast, brushed the Jersey Shore, and struck western Long Island, New York, on the twenty-fourth. It brought heavy damages to New York City, where more than 100 large trees were toppled in Central Park and floodwaters filled much of lower Manhattan. "The Midnight Storm," as newspapers labeled it, was most known for the destruction of resorts on Hog Island. In Washington, Red Cross president Clara Barton was monitoring the storm reports, readying her volunteers for their next potential relief effort. But it wasn't the New York storm that would generate the greatest need—it was instead the devastating hurricane that rolled over the Georgia and South Carolina coasts just a few days later—the tragic Sea Islands Hurricane of 1893.

Like so many other great Atlantic hurricanes, the storm was born near the Cape Verde islands, where it passed on August 16 on a westward track. It became a hurricane on the nineteenth and passed northeast of the Leeward Islands as a Category 3 storm on the twenty-second. It was steadily growing in size as it tracked through the Bahamas on a course that appeared headed straight for the Florida coast.

At the Weather Bureau, forecasters were anxious about the storm, all while still buzzing about the New York hurricane—both posed serious threats, and both were among the first hurricanes for which advance warnings were widely distributed by telegraph. The New York hurricane landed on the twenty-fourth, and the Weather Bureau's warning notices had been a new and welcome advancement, especially for harbors and shipping interests in the Northeast. It wasn't perfect, but some warning was better than none. The big improvement was largely thanks to the placement of underwater cables in the Bahamas and portions of the Caribbean through the early 1890s, such that reliable reports of changing weather could help forecasters keep up with approaching hurricanes.

While the New York hurricane raged to the north, government forecasters prepared to issue their next hurricane warning to the south. On August 25, telegraphic bulletins were distributed from Florida to New York, warning of a large storm some 500 miles east of Florida. In harbors and government installations up and down the coast, red storm pennants were flown to warn of possible hurricane conditions. As the massive storm approached land on the twenty-sixth, it was influenced by a western ridge that caused it to veer northward and track just offshore, parallel to Florida's east coast. Residents on Georgia's Sea Islands were already reporting increasing winds and large rolling waves on the beach. The Weather Bureau issued another bulletin that night: "The hurricane center will likely strike the coast of the south Atlantic states on Sunday, pass inward, and break up into general rains on Monday." Early on the twenty-seventh the storm passed by Saint Augustine, and that morning's Weather Bureau bulletin was quite specific. It stated that the hurricane "will move northwest, striking the coast of Georgia Sunday evening or night." Never before had there been this kind of specific advance warning for a hurricane landfall in the United States. Some coastal interests heeded the warnings and quickly prepared as best they could. A very few left low-lying areas. But unfortunately for thousands of poor and isolated residents of the Sea Islands of Georgia and South Carolina, the warning messages were never received.

The weather along the coast deteriorated rapidly throughout the afternoon on the twenty-seventh as the storm drew closer. Because of its large size, outer bands of wind and rain arrived well before the worst of the storm. As predicted, the hurricane made landfall just below Savannah as a Category 3, with sustained winds of 115 mph and a central pressure of 954 millibars (mb). The eye passed directly over the Savannah Weather Bureau office, where a barometric low of 958 mb was observed. From there the storm center moved inland, passing west of Beaufort and across the South Carolina Midlands. By the time it reached Columbia, the hurricane had diminished to Category 1 strength. It continued weakening as it tracked through Charlotte, eventually curving to the northeast as it passed over central Virginia and through the Northeast.

The Sea Islands Hurricane of 1893 is mostly known for the horrendous toll left by its deadly storm tide, which claimed more than 2,000 lives along the coastal islands of Georgia and South Carolina—making it the deadliest hurricane in U.S. history at that time. The storm arrived on a full moon, increasing the height of the lunar high tide, which unfortunately fell around the time of landfall at 9:00 P.M. on the twenty-seventh. The massive storm delivered an equally impressive surge, estimated at sixteen feet on some of the hardest-hit islands. The U.S. Army Corps of Engineers reported flooding of up to 19.5 feet above mean sea level at Savannah Beach, though there has been speculation that this measurement included wave action. Some computer models have suggested a few areas could have experienced considerably greater flooding levels.

In his 2006 report *Storm Tides in Twelve Tropical Cyclones*, former National Hurricane Center forecaster Brian Jarvinen noted five locations where high-water marks were recorded in the 1893 storm, relative to mean sea level: Fort Pulaski, 15.0 feet; Isle of Hope, 12.5 feet; Bluffton, 13.5 feet; Beaufort, 12.6 feet; and Charleston, 10.1 feet. With landfall near Savannah, the storm's worst flooding was on its northern side, with the greatest inundations occurring along the southern South Carolina coast. Though the storm's damages were widely distributed, nothing compared to the complete destruction of homes and the horrific loss of life among the poor African American communities in the coastal region known as the Sea Islands.

More than eighty islands dot the coast from the Savannah River to George-town, some facing the Atlantic, others sandwiched between rivers and bays. Most consist of low-lying terrain, often wrapped in marsh with few spots higher than ten feet above sea level. Near Beaufort, many were former plan-tation properties, and the African Americans that called them home in 1893 were themselves former slaves and slave descendants (after the Civil War, Sea Island slaves were among the first to be freed). These were Gullah families, and their island communities consisted of modest log cabins built on small farm tracts. Many owned their own land; some were renters or tenant farmers. Oth-ers were laborers who worked in the region's burgeoning phosphate-mining industry. As the great storm approached, all were vulnerable and uninformed, with virtually no chance of surviving the hurricane's deadly tide. The storm's nighttime arrival added to the terror; it's hard to imagine the hysteria that must have overcome these communities once the floodwaters surged near midnight.

As the storm tide washed over the islands, it carried everything with it, sweeping away homes, trees, livestock, and people. In the darkness, some residents managed to scramble onto floating debris or climb large oak trees to escape the floods, only to be blasted by extreme winds. In many areas, few survived the surge. Near Beaufort, twenty-one bridges were washed away and all major ferries were destroyed. Wells were contaminated, crops were ruined, and docks, boats, and railways were washed out. The phosphate operation on the Coosaw River, where 3,000 had been employed, was demolished with the wreck of hundreds of dredges, flat barges, and tugboats—all of which were either sunk or scattered into the forests along a twelve-mile stretch. The storm marked the end of the industry in the area. In Beaufort, high waters flooded shops and homes, but apparently only three fatalities were reported. Bluffton was spared significant damage, thanks to its higher elevation.

The hurricane's impact reached far beyond the hardest-hit islands near Beau-fort. As far south as Saint Augustine, Florida, and as far north as Cape Look-out, North Carolina, this storm sank ships, knocked down homes, and flooded communities. At Fort Pulaski, near the mouth of the Savannah River, the lighthouse keeper, several soldiers, and their families took refuge in a stairwell at the fort when their homes were swept away by tides. Nearly every building on Tybee Island was damaged, and much of the seventeen miles of railroad that connected the island with Savannah was ruined. The storm surprised many who became trapped there; among those lost was one African American family who had made their home inside an abandoned boxcar on the north end. The boxcar was swept away when ocean waters covered the island. Several families that had come to Tybee for rest were forced from their homes as the tides rolled in, moving from house to house in chest-deep waters seeking higher ground. Many homes washed off their foundations; other structures fared well, including the newly built Hotel Tybee and the Cottage Club. The Norwegian bark *Harold*, anchored at the island's pesthouse for quarantine, was pounded by high waves while its crew rode out the storm lashed to the riggings. The ship was driven ashore near the Tybee Island lighthouse, and all but one of the crew survived.

In Savannah, nearly thirty vessels were wrecked or sunk at anchor. Wharves were upended or scuttled; streets were a tangled web of downed trees and twisted telegraph and streetcar wires. "Colorful explosions" of sparks were seen where wires crossed. At the Central Railroad, 50,000 barrels of pitch rosin washed into the streets and spread across twenty acres. High winds knocked down "many fine trees" and several industrial smokestacks and toppled the steeple of the First African Baptist Church. Collapsed chimneys and blown-out windows allowed hurricane rains to pour into homes and shops, including that of the *Morning News*, where water poured into the printing room and temporarily stopped production. After midnight, electric power was out and knee-deep floodwaters surrounded the presses, but gaslights were brought in so that the staff could continue printing the morning edition. The paper reported that fifteen bodies had been found in the city but that "more casualties were expected."

Offshore, the hurricane's massive swells and fierce winds played havoc with passing ships. In *Lowcountry Hurricanes*, Walter Fraser chronicled many of the vessels lost in the storm. Among them was the British brig *Astoria*, loaded with Georgia pine and rendered helpless when winds ripped away its sails off Hunting Island. The crew of twenty climbed the rigging to ride out the storm, where they remained for twelve hours while their ship sank below them. They were finally rescued by the passing steamer *D. H. Miller*. A similar fate fell upon the British ship *Nettie Murphy* off the Georgia coast. With the ship being battered by mountainous seas and taking on water, the captain and crew of eighteen ascended their riggings and were later rescued by the Norwegian brig *Medea*. The *Freeda A. Wyley*, another transport loaded with timber, was overcome by the storm off Savannah and began to sink near the beach. After enduring the hurricane throughout the night from atop the remaining riggings, the captain and crew of eight returned to deck the following morning where they began offloading lumber in an effort to right the hull. They built a fire in the ship's sand box, ate lunch, and hoped for rescue. The following day, on September 29, they were finally saved by the schooner *Annie Kranz*. In their haste to leave, they left the cook fire burning, which ultimately set the vessel ablaze. The burned hulk of the ship later washed ashore near what is today Fortieth Street in Myrtle Beach. Other losses included the steamboat *Abbeville*, which broke in two on top of Smarts Wharf in Savannah; the schooner *Beatrice McLean*, washed into the woods on Saint Catherines Island; and the schooner *Anna S. Conants*, heavily damaged and abandoned off the coast.

Others simply vanished at sea, their cargos lost and crews never heard from again. In David Stick's *Graveyard of the Atlantic*, he referenced many of the ships caught up in the storm. In a region spanning from Brunswick, Georgia, to Cape Hatteras, he noted the losses of the transport schooners *Mary J. Cook, L. A. Burnham, A. R. Weeks, George W. Fenimore, Oliver H. Booth, Gertie M. Rickerson, John S. Case,* and *Lizzie May*. "None of these eight ships was ever seen again; no trace of them or crews ever found. They just disappeared, swallowed up in the center of the hurricane, battered to pieces, turned over, sunk in the middle of nowhere. Fifty-five crewmen, one passenger, and 2,808 tons of shipping lost, before the hurricane even reached the coast."

On the North Carolina coast near Cape Fear, there were, however, some remarkable rescues attributed to one man, Dunbar Davis, keeper of the Oak Island Lifesaving Station. Davis scanned the horizon for ships in distress as the weather grew worse on the afternoon of August 27. His crew of seven was on leave; the station was not fully manned between April and September. Over the span of the next seventy-two hours, Davis worked tirelessly, with the help of several local volunteers, to pull ashore more than two dozen crew members from five troubled vessels. He built a large driftwood fire on the beach, which served as a signal for the desperate sailors, and surprisingly most of the rescues occurred in that vicinity. By the afternoon of August 30, Davis had not slept, and Stick noted, "The record to that time contained three vessels: schooner *Three Sisters*, grounded, captain and mate washed overboard, crew of five saved; brig *Wustrow*, beaten to pieces in the breakers, crew of nine safely ashore and cared for by near-by farmers; schooner *Kate E. Gifford*, grounded and breaking up, crew of seven rescued in breeches buoy."

And it wasn't over for Davis. As he was about to head back to his station for some much-needed rest, a yawl containing seven men was spotted in the Oak Island surf—despondent crew from the three-masted schooner *Jennie E. Thomas* that was foundering some thirty miles offshore. With them was a captain and two crew that had been previously rescued from the *Enchantress*, another disabled schooner. Davis helped the "bruised and nearly-naked" men onto the beach. They then joined the others at his station, where they were given food, water, and fresh clothes. Davis became a local hero; his lifesaving efforts were later immortalized in story and song. The Oak Island Lifesaving Station is now a private residence on Caswell Beach.

One of the more harrowing offshore experiences was that of the passengers and crew aboard the *City of Savannah*, a luxury steamship that had sailed from Boston with twenty passengers, a crew of forty-seven, and a cargo of pork, furniture, and boots. When it didn't make its scheduled Sunday evening arrival in Savannah, local officials and family members were fearful. They knew the ship had likely sailed into the teeth of the hurricane.

Capt. George Savage put his passengers at ease as they passed Cape Hatteras and waves began to build. The ship had already endured violent seas off the New Jersey coast, likely remnants of the New York hurricane just days before. They sailed past two empty lifeboats, an ominous sign. As they rounded the coast near Charleston early Sunday, the twenty-seventh, the skies ahead were dark, and the ocean swells were growing. With heavy rain and winds buffeting the ship, the captain joined the passengers in the dining salon for their evening meal at 5:00 P.M. Suddenly, the ship jerked violently and the captain was thrown from his chair, causing him to jump up and return to his crew— leaving the passengers to finish their meal with no knowledge of the calamity awaiting them.

Soon after, giant waves broke over the bow, knocking the pilothouse from the main deck. Another huge wave broke away the ship's smokestack; a blast of steam shot into the sky. With only sail power, the captain struggled to steer between the waves and was finally forced to order the sails lowered. Fire broke out in the engine room, and the ship went adrift. By 8:00 P.M. it reached the shoals off Hunting Island. Windows and skylights were broken, and two feet of water filled the main salon. Through the night, passengers and crew endured the worst of the hurricane. Captain Savage was now dragging anchors to slow the ship before it crashed into the shoals; it finally struck bottom sometime before dawn fifteen miles off Fripp Island. Listing on its starboard side, waves continued to bash and tear away at the hull of the ship.

The weary passengers, seasick and exhausted, crawled across the wreckage from their staterooms to find life preservers. There was no fresh water to drink, and little food remained. By midday the storm had moved on, and through the afternoon of the twenty-eighth they could only wait and hope for rescue. At nightfall, the ship's crew ascended the rigging to sleep; some of the passengers followed. The next morning, the captain made the decision to send the women and children off in the ship's two remaining lifeboats. They put off, each with four strong men aboard, and successfully made their way to Saint

The Carolina Yacht Club in Charleston following the 1893 Sea Islands Hurricane. (Photo courtesy of the South Caroliniana Library, University of South Carolina, Columbia.)

Helena Island, where they were later rescued. Late that afternoon, as his ship continued to deteriorate in the waves, Captain Savage finally spotted the *City of Birmingham* in the distance and signaled for help. The *Birmingham*, sailing from New York, had already rescued seven shipwrecked sailors off Cape Fear before it found the *Savannah*. Lifeboats were launched to pick up the remaining, exhausted crew. Word spread of the successful rescues, and that night more than 1,000 people gathered along Savannah's Central Railroad Wharf to cheer the *Birmingham*'s arrival. Today, the site of the *City of Savannah*'s demise is a popular fishing spot, simply known as "the wreck."

Up the coast in Charleston, the hurricane also ravaged through the night of the twenty-seventh, though the storm center passed inland, well west of the city. Charleston still received the fury of the hurricane's eastern side, which pushed high tides and large waves over the city's seawalls, heavily damaging docks and wharves and stranding dozens of vessels. The flooding was detailed in records from the Preservation Society of Charleston:

> The Western Union office failed about 3 o'clock Sunday afternoon. The last telegraph out of Charleston read: "The gale is severe. Reported that Sullivan's Island has been swept over by a tidal wave and completely submerged." . . . All of the city south of Calhoun Street lay under a sheet of

water, which stood three to five feet deep below Tradd Street.... The eye passed late in the day, and the water rose another five feet. At 8 o'clock the west section of the city was six to ten feet under water; at 11:00 P.M. the tide was six to eight feet high over the East Battery.

After the storm, only a single pier on the Cooper River remained in place: the stone structure at the customhouse. Twelve of the East Shore Terminal Company's fourteen piers were swept away. The High Battery was heavily damaged, and some of the large stone pavers were lifted into the street. The bathing house at White Point Garden "vanished." The newly built Ashley River drawbridge was heavily damaged and left dangling over its battered support pilings. The attendant reported that three schooners, a barge, and the pile driver *Maud S.* had all rammed the bridge. Friberg's Shipyard at the foot of Council Street was swept away, and vessels that had been hauled out for repairs were upended. The *News and Courier* reported that "Council Street looked like a lumber mart."

Newspapers reported four fatalities in Charleston and three on Sullivan's Island. Charleston Harbor and its waterfront were heavily damaged by the tides, and high winds blasted homes and commercial structures. Winds in the city were clocked at 96 mph, with gusts to 120 mph. Damage to buildings, windows, and trees was thought to have been less severe than that of the hurricane of 1885, though there still were torn roofs, downed telegraph wires, and plenty of other evidence of the storm. The *News and Courier* attributed the reduced wind damage to "extensive and solid repairs of all classes of buildings, and especially of roofs," that had occurred following the 1885 hurricane and the 1886 earthquake.

Though not widely reported at the time, the hurricane's massive size was a major factor in the broad distribution of damages all along its path. As it tracked inland, six to twelve inches of rain overfilled rivers across South Carolina and into North Carolina. High winds damaged crops and forests over a wide swath, particularly through the South Carolina Midlands. Reports from the village of Summerville described impassable streets, filled with large fallen oaks. Heavy damages were reported as far inland as Orangeburg and moderate damages as far west as Spartanburg. In Kernersville, North Carolina, tornadic winds tore through town as reported by the Winston-Salem *Union-Republican*: "A terrific cyclone struck here at five o'clock this morning.... A hundred houses wrecked and a woman killed. Many were injured. Factories, stores and residences were unroofed and some were blown away." On the twenty-eighth, maximum winds of 72 mph were reported in Southport and in Wilmington, even as the storm center tracked well inland west of Charlotte. Newspapers reported that "the sea washed across Wrightsville Beach Island."

In his 2006 report, Jarvinen noted how this storm compared with one modern-day successor: "This hurricane seems to be one of the largest on the Atlantic coast when measured by the radius of the 1000 millibar contour. It caused extensive wind damage to every county in South Carolina, parts of eastern Georgia and the southern part of North Carolina. It was much larger than Hurricane Hugo in 1989 although not as intense at landfall. It was possibly as intense before it made landfall. . . . The impact of this large hurricane to South Carolina and North Carolina was much greater than that caused by Hurricane Hugo in 1989."

Though the hurricane indeed affected a broad region, no location experienced devastation that could compare with the horrific inundation of the Sea Islands near Beaufort. Joel Chandler Harris wrote of his visit to Saint Helena Island for an 1894 edition of *Scribner's Magazine*:

> A house was here, or a cabin. Near by a shoal of dead bodies had been seen drifting along, or were washed ashore. . . . All around, and for miles and miles, farther than the eye can reach, as far as a shore bird can fly, the results of the storm lay scattered. Here a house has staggered upon its end, there a boat has been flung into the arms of a live oak. . . . This woman, standing apart, as lonely as the never-ending marshes, had lost three children. She had five. In the fury and the confusion of the storm, she had managed to get them all in a tree. The foundations of this place of refuge were sapped, and the tree gave way before the gale, plunging the woman and her children into the whirling flood. Three were swept from under her hands out into the marsh, into the estuary, and so into the sea. They were never seen any more. . . . But what this woman said did not run in the direction of grief. "I glad to God I got two lil' one lef."

Among the hardest hit were Lady's Island and Saint Helena Island. At the time, Saint Helena had a population of 6,000, and along with other nearby islands the population of the area was close to 35,000. These islands were home to the largest concentrations of independent Black landowners in the state. The actual number of fatalities will never be known, as many bodies were never recovered. Estimates ranged from 2,000 to 3,500. But thousands did survive, managing to somehow float to high ground or escape into treetops. In *The Storm Swept Coast of South Carolina*, R. C. Mather told the story of a Seabrook man who carried his sick wife in his arms to a neighbor's house, leaving his sleeping children in his cabin. As the storm tide rushed in, the cabin was swept

Debris filled the streets of Beaufort, South Carolina, after the 1893 Sea Islands Hurricane. (Photo courtesy of the Beaufort County Library, Beaufort, South Carolina.)

into the darkness, and he was unable to return for them. "When with morning light the tide had receded, he went home and found his cabin washed up on higher ground, and his children still sleeping in their little loft."

Those remaining alive were destitute, losing not only family and neighbors but all of what few possessions they owned. Food crops were ruined; wells filled with salt water. The carcasses of cows, horses, goats, chickens, and dogs floated in the knee-deep floodwaters that lingered on the islands for days following the storm. Some 30,000 surviving Gullah had no shelter, food, or fresh water to drink. The risk of disease was great; no one knows how many additional lives were lost in the days and weeks that followed. Harris's article in *Scribner's Magazine* added, "The truth would not be missed very far if the number were placed at three thousand. Not all of those were lost in the storm. Two thousand persons, the great majority of them Negroes, were drowned or killed on the night of the storm. The others died from exposure, from a lack of food, or from the malarial fever that was epidemic on the islands during the hot September days that succeeded the disturbance."

Telegraph lines were down throughout the region, and it wasn't until August 30 that word of the disaster in the islands first reached Charleston. The following day, Governor Ben "Pitchfork" Tillman returned to Columbia from a visit to the Chicago World's Fair and received a shocking telegram that "not less than 600 people" had drowned near Beaufort. Former congressman Robert Smalls, a Beaufort resident, issued a national appeal for help: "We earnestly ask for aid in feeding and clothing the hungry and naked." Charleston mayor John Ficken called a town meeting on September 2 and a relief committee was formed, with $1,500 pledged to help feed those in need in Beaufort. A railway car was then dispatched with 2,500 loaves of bread, twenty-five pounds of corned beef, 100 boxes of soda crackers, fifty barrels of grits, and five barrels of molasses. It was desperately needed but wholly inadequate.

In *The Great Sea Island Storm of 1893*, Bill and Fran Marscher described the painfully slow and inadequate response to the disaster at hand: "Although the governor expressed compassion and pleaded for donations from the public, he grossly underestimated what it would take to relieve the suffering and put the stricken people on the road to recovery." Racial and political bias played a role in the response. Tillman, a Democrat who had helped quell Black suffrage in his state, did little to recognize the overwhelming needs of the storm victims, almost all of whom were Black Republicans (he went on to lead disenfranchisement efforts in South Carolina the following year). "The people have the fish of the sea there to prevent them from starving," he told reporters, while making no overtures for funding from state coffers. There was no state-sponsored relief effort, no high-level tour of the scene, and no willingness to understand the scope of the unfolding human catastrophe at the coast.

Weeks passed, and finally it became apparent that local donations would never meet the need. Tillman called on Clara Barton to step in, and on September 18 the governor met with Barton at the Charleston Hotel, where he formally asked her to bring her American Red Cross organization to South Carolina to aid the survivors. By early November Barton and her volunteers had established a warehouse and office in Beaufort to oversee the recovery. In part, their efforts were hampered by the arrival of a second Category 3 hurricane that made landfall near Georgetown on October 13.

Fortunately, Barton was somewhat familiar with the Sea Islands and its people, as she had spent several months on Union-occupied Hilton Head Island during the Civil War. But she was appalled by the governor's lack of financial support and, later, that of the U.S. Congress. The South Carolina legislature had adjourned "without making the slightest provision for the sufferers," and Congress denied Barton's specific request for funding. The only federal assistance she received were garden seeds, several tents, and two deep-draft boats. She launched an appeal through numerous northern newspapers for donations of food, blankets, building materials, and cash. She established sewing circles to produce warm clothes for the approaching winter. Barton, who was

Workers at Red Cross headquarters in Beaufort, South Carolina, prepare rose potatoes for planting in February 1894. Draining flooded fields and planting food crops was a priority for Clara Barton and her Red Cross volunteers in the aftermath of the 1893 hurricane. (Photo from the Clara Barton Collection. Courtesy of the Library of Congress, Washington, D.C.)

seventy-two at the time, had taken on the largest such endeavor of her career. She went to work in Beaufort with just a handful of volunteers and $30,000 in donations, facing a daunting task—feeding and clothing 30,000 homeless victims. Each family of seven was rationed "a peck of grits and a pound of pork, per week."

Then the problem grew bigger. After touring the islands, Barton knew the task was far beyond feeding and clothing—with homes and crops washed away, reconstruction and replanting were essential. The islands still held seawater, so massive ditch-digging projects were begun to prepare fields for crops. The Red Cross strategy was clear, too: the storm victims would help themselves by rebuilding their own communities. But Barton was nearly overwhelmed as the number of storm victims grew, and ultimately up to 70,000 requested assistance. Racial tensions flared, too, when white citizens complained they weren't receiving the same level of help, as a great many across the state had suffered losses in the storm.

Through the next year, the Red Cross succeeded thanks to generous donations from the north, meaningful local support, and the tireless work of Barton, her team, and the Gullah people. Shipments of medicines, tools, seeds, and

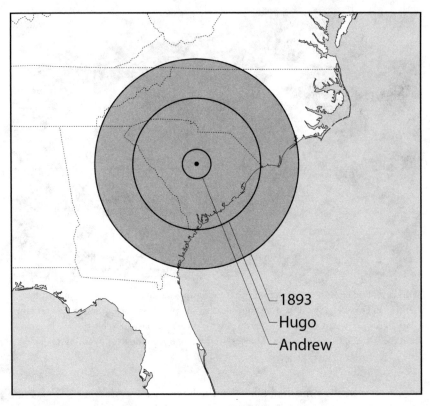

1893
Hugo
Andrew

The 1893 Sea Islands Hurricane was an exceptionally large storm. Tropical-storm-force winds extended more than 225 miles from the storm center, and every county in South Carolina experienced damage. The storm was considerably larger than Hurricanes Hugo and Andrew, shown here for comparison. (Map from Brian Jarvinen, *Storm Tides in Twelve Tropical Cyclones (Including Four Intense New England Hurricanes)* [Washington, D.C.:National Oceanic and Atmospheric Administration/Tropical Prediction Center/National Hurricane Center, 2006].)

building materials arrived in Beaufort and were distributed to the islands by oxcart and small boat. The massive relief effort concluded in June 1894, with the island communities showing major improvement. Barton wrote in her autobiography, "The submerged lands were drained, 300 miles of ditches made, a million feet of lumber purchased, and homes built, fields and gardens planted with the best seed in the United States, and the work all done by the people themselves."

The year 1893 was extraordinary for tropical cyclones in the United States. The Sea Islands Hurricane was the deadliest in U.S. history until that time and was followed just weeks later by a second tragic hurricane in Louisiana that claimed another 2,000 lives. In South Carolina, the Sea Islands storm caused an estimated $10 million in damages but was also blamed for more lasting economic harm—the demise of the state's phosphate industry and the eventual end of rice cultivation. Though most of the attention was focused on the devastated islands, significant property, timber, and crop damages stretched across the state and into North Carolina, with many of these losses never tallied. A few wealthy Charlestonians who suffered damages to their homes and businesses recouped some of their losses through successful hurricane insurance claims, a strategy that was growing in popularity at the time.

Farther up the South Carolina coast, a hurricane landfall near Georgetown in mid-October slowed recovery efforts near Beaufort but also created its own chaos. The Category 3 storm packing 120 mph winds tracked inland through Raleigh, leveling forests and delivering severe flooding all along its path. Winds gusted to 115 mph in Southport, and flooding in Wilmington was thought to be "sixteen inches higher than ever known before." More than a dozen fatalities were reported at Winyah Bay, and twenty-two more died in North Carolina. Across the Carolinas, the two storms combined to leave unprecedented upstate destruction, wrecking the economies of both states at a particularly bad time— the midst of a nationwide economic depression.

After the second hurricane passed the city, the Charleston *News and Courier* offered a theory to explain these menacing storms: "If there is, any connection between 'sun spots' and cyclones, as some scientists affirm, the sun must have some large spots on it just now."

TAKEAWAYS

- *Hurricane warnings have little value if people never receive them.* Today, we take for granted the excellent work done by National Hurricane Center forecasters and the timely warnings they distribute through news media, social media, and countless other sources. Hurricane news coverage can be almost overwhelming and sometimes even criticized for being unnecessarily hyped. But how lucky we are to know about approaching storms far in advance. The 1893 hurricane season was a turning point in the evolution of our nation's early warning system, though the inability to communicate storm information to Sea Islands residents still led to one of the greatest hurricane tragedies in U.S. history.

- *Recovery from hurricane disasters requires leadership on the state and national levels.* This seems obvious today, as recovery efforts following modern U.S. hurricanes typically involve presidents, governors, Congress, state legislatures, FEMA, national nonprofits, and a multitude of local government agencies. But that hasn't always been the case. Unfortunately, a combination of factors led politicians to turn away from the needs of the desperate victims of the 1893 hurricane. Recovery from disasters of its scale is beyond the means of local governments and citizens. Through the twentieth century, state and federal agencies began taking on larger roles in providing coordination and financial support for hurricane recoveries.

- *Nonprofit relief organizations and faith-based groups have become important players in hurricane disaster recoveries.* Clara Barton knew her American Red Cross was the only hope for victims of the Sea Islands Hurricane. With this storm, the Red Cross affirmed its value as a volunteer organization and has been on the ground through most every U.S. hurricane since. The needs following any of today's hurricane disasters are so great that they're beyond what any one organization can offer. Emergency planners and government officials now use a team approach, with strategies to incorporate networks of volunteers and their organizations in key roles throughout the recovery process. Voluntary groups such as the Red Cross and faith-based organizations such as the Salvation Army and Samaritan's Purse work alongside other nonprofits including out-of-state church missions, civic clubs, and many others to play an important role in providing food, water, clothing, home repairs, and other aid to storm victims.

- *Thankfully, mass casualties from hurricanes have (mostly) declined over the years.* The shocking number of deaths that resulted from the Sea Islands Hurricane came during a period when other storms caused similar mass casualties. Following a second hurricane in 1893 that killed 2,000 in Louisiana, the nation's deadliest hurricane struck Galveston, Texas, in 1900, claiming more than 10,000 lives. Through the mid-twentieth century, advances in forecasting and communication helped reduce the casualty rate in the United States, a welcome trend as communities became better prepared and coastal evacuations became routine. But hurricanes like 2005's Katrina, with more than 1,800 deaths, remind us that big storms striking heavily populated areas can still bring devastating loss of life. In the Carolinas, the death toll from great storms such as Hazel, Hugo, Floyd, and Florence haven't reached those levels, but each fatality is one too many.

- *Big hurricane disasters sometimes bring long-term economic consequences.* Hurricanes often deliver painful economic losses to the communities they strike. Even with state and federal aid, today's multibillion-dollar disasters can devastate the finances of homeowners, businesses, and local governments. In addition to property losses, economic activity suffers, especially in the near term. Coastal tourism takes a hit, flooded factories sometimes close, and agricultural losses can wipe out a year's worth of profits. Historically, disasters such as the Sea Islands Hurricane have had an even more lasting effect. South Carolina's prosperous phosphate industry was virtually wiped out by the 1893 storm, and the extensive damage done to rice fields contributed to the demise of rice cultivation through the region—a lucrative industry there for more than 200 years.

CHAPTER FIVE

THE GREAT SAN CIRIACO HURRICANE
OF 1899

On any given summer day, a small navy of pleasure boaters can be found anchored along the sheltered beaches behind "Shack," the nine-mile-long barrier island that forms the southwestern leg of the Cape Lookout National Seashore near Beaufort, North Carolina. Rimmed by vast tidal flats and sandy beaches, Shackleford Banks features miles of windswept dunes and myrtle thickets. Its only full-time residents are the wild horses that have roamed its dunes for centuries. The island's natural beauty reveals no trace of the once thriving community built among the dune forests that vanished at the end of the nineteenth century.

No one is exactly sure when the first settlers moved onto Shackleford, but a fiercely independent clan of fishers and whalers prospered there for more than a century. The "Ca'e Bankers" built simple homes, and by the mid-1800s as many as 800 lived in or near the main village—dubbed Diamond City for the distinctive black-and-white pattern painted on the nearby Cape Lookout lighthouse. They made their living fishing, clamming, and harvesting right whales that migrated near shore. But a string of raucous hurricanes in the 1890s forced them to abandon their community and flee the island, and the disastrous San Ciriaco Hurricane of August 1899 was the final straw.

This hurricane was one of the most powerful cyclones known to move through the western Atlantic in the nineteenth century. It crossed the Lesser Antilles with winds of 150 mph, making landfall in Guadeloupe on August 7. A barometer reading of 930 millibars (mb) was recorded in Montserrat, placing this hurricane in elite company among the strongest of storms. It made landfall again in Puerto Rico as a Category 4 on August 8, the date of the Catholic festival for Saint Cyriacus—hence the storm's name in Spanish, San Ciriaco. Winds blasted the southeast coast at 140 mph as the storm swept the length of the island in only six hours. The results were devastating. Thousands of homes were blown down by fierce winds or washed away by raging rivers and mudslides. Floods filled the city of Ponce, where more than 500 died. In all,

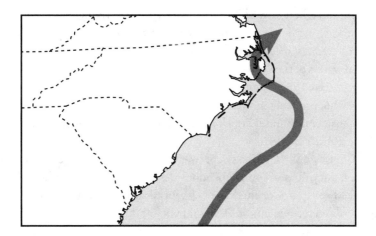

Surfman Rasmus Midgett of the Gull Shoal Lifesaving Station sits atop the wreckage of the barkentine *Priscilla* in August 1899. (Photo courtesy of the Outer Banks History Center, Manteo, North Carolina.)

more than 3,300 lives were lost, making this hurricane the deadliest in Puerto Rican history.

The following morning, the hurricane swept over the northern portions of the Dominican Republic as a Category 3 with 120 mph winds; it would sustain that intensity for nine more days. It tracked through the Bahamas, where at least another 300 more lives were lost on land and at sea. Its northwestward movement brought it toward Florida's eastern beaches, though on August 13 the gently curving storm moved well offshore past Fort Lauderdale. U.S. Weather Bureau forecasters speculated that it could strike Charleston. As it followed the warm waters of the Gulf Stream, it paralleled the coast on a northeast track that might have carried it east of Cape Hatteras and out of harm's way. But on August 16, probably influenced by a high-pressure ridge, its forward speed slowed considerably and its track shifted northwest, steering it toward North Carolina's Outer Banks.

On August 17, San Ciriaco swept over Core Banks, Ocracoke, and Hatteras with great fury. Reports of tremendous destruction from Morehead City to Nags Head were later printed in newspapers across the country. In Carteret County, island settlements at Diamond City and Portsmouth were especially hard hit. The hardy families who lived there were accustomed to foul weather and remote lifestyles, but numerous hurricanes and nor'easters near the end of the century had tested the endurance of the Ca'e Bankers. These storms left drifts of barren sand that replaced the rich soils of their gardens, and saltwater overwash killed trees and contaminated drinking wells. These communities had already begun to see a decline in population before 1899, largely due to the unwelcome effects of hurricanes.

For the residents of Diamond City and Shackleford Banks, the San Ciriaco Hurricane was the final blow. Few if any of their homes escaped the rushing storm tide that swept over the banks. First, the waters rose from the sound side, as northeast winds pounded the islands during the hurricane's approach. Then, as the storm passed, the winds shifted hard to the southwest, surging the ocean's tide over the dunes until the waters met. Cows, pigs, and chickens drowned, fishing equipment was destroyed, and many homes were ruined. The aftermath was a truly ghastly scene, as battered caskets and bones lay scattered, unearthed by the hurricane's menacing storm surge.

Following the San Ciriaco storm, the people of Diamond City and Shackleford Banks gathered their remaining belongings and searched for new places to live. Many moved to the mainland, settling in Marshallberg, Broad Creek, and the "Promised Land" section of Morehead City. Others moved down to the island of Bogue Banks and became squatters among the dunes of Salter Path. But most chose to relocate within sight of their former community, three miles across the sound on Harkers Island. Some even salvaged their island homes, floating them across the water on barges and repositioning them on new foundations. Today, visitors to Shackleford Banks will find no structures or remaining visible evidence of Diamond City.

One of the great tragedies of the August 1899 hurricane fell upon several families from Down East Carteret County. August was mullet-fishing time, when a large group of men would gather their nets, tents, and provisions for a two-week expedition to Swan Island. Their means of transportation was a small dead-rise skiff, twenty-one feet long and about five feet wide. Each shallow skiff could carry two men and their equipment, and each craft featured a small sail on a removable mast. These shallow-draft boats provided effective transport on the protected waters of Core Sound.

This particular August, a group of twenty fishermen had already established their camp on the remote island when the first signs of the San Ciriaco Hurricane were recognized. At first, the brisk winds and gathering clouds appeared to be just a good "mullet blow," which would get the fish moving. But on the morning of August 17, the tide was unusually high, and heavy rains began to sweep through the sound. Alarmed by the rising water, the fishermen considered leaving but chose to stay on the island for fear of the ever-increasing winds. They were later forced to pack all of their nets and supplies aboard their skiffs, as the tides washed completely over the island. They moored their skiffs as close together as they could and crouched under their canvas sails for protection from the driving rain. This proved useless, however, as they soon had to bail the water that rapidly filled their boats.

The fishermen worked frantically to keep their skiffs afloat while 100 mph winds churned the waters and tested their anchor lines. For several hours, the courageous men rode out the storm in the dark, until finally, in the early hours of August 18, the winds subsided. The tide was now unusually low, as the hurricane's winds had pushed a surge of water westward up the Neuse River. Battered but still together, the fishermen debated making a run for the mainland, as they could now put up sail. They knew this journey of less than ten miles would test their skills. Not all agreed to the plan, but after a few had left, the others soon followed. This proved to be a great mistake. The lull that gave them the opportunity to leave was nothing more than the passing of the hurricane's eye over Swan Island. Within minutes, the storm's winds were again full force, this time gusting from the southwest. The small skiffs were now out on West Bay, and most were capsized by the wind and waves when a ten-foot surge of water washed back from the Neuse River.

Only six of the twenty men survived. Among those who were rescued were Allen and Almon Hamilton, who saved themselves by quickly taking down their mast and sail, throwing their nets overboard, and lying low in their skiff as it was tossed about. Fourteen others were not as fortunate. Of those who drowned, ten were from Sea Level: Joseph and John Lewis, Henry and James Willis, Bart Salter, John Styron, William Salter, John and Joseph Salter, and

Micajah Rose. Four brothers from the community of Stacy were lost: John, Kilby, Elijah, and Wallace Smith.

Ocracoke Island was also hard hit by San Ciriaco. The August 21 edition of the *Washington Gazette* reported, "The whole island of Ocracoke is a complete wreck as a result of the fierce storm which swept the entire coast of North Carolina, leaving ruin and disaster in its path. . . . Thirty-three homes were destroyed and two churches were wrecked. Practically every house on the island was damaged to some extent. . . . The barometer went down to 28.3 [958 mb], which is the lowest ever known there and the storm was the most severe ever known to the oldest inhabitants." The article also reported that waves twenty to thirty feet high pounded the beach and that the hurricane's storm tide covered the island with four to five feet of water. Hundreds of Banker ponies, sheep, and cows drowned. The dazed survivors of Ocracoke endured "much suffering" after the storm from a lack of food and water.

The residents of Ocracoke and other Outer Banks communities were wise to the effects of rising hurricane tides. Many had installed "trapdoors" in the floors of their homes to allow rising water to enter, thus preventing the structure from floating off its foundation and drifting away. Some simply bored holes in the floorboards to relieve the water's pressure. Big Ike O'Neal described his adventure in the 1899 storm to Associated Press columnist Hal Boyle: "The tides were rising fast and my ole dad, fearful that our house would wash from its foundations, said 'Here son, take this axe and scuttle the floor.' I began chopping away and finally knocked a hole in the floor. Like a big fountain the water gushed in and hit the ceiling and on top of the gusher was a mallard duck that had gotten under our house as the tides pushed upwards."

Hatteras Island was devastated by the hurricane. The Weather Bureau station in Hatteras Village was hard hit, as the entire southern end of the Outer Banks fell within the powerful right-front quadrant of the storm. Winds at the station were clocked at sustained speeds of over 100 mph, and gusts were measured at between 120 and 140 mph. Ultimately, the station's anemometer was blown away, and no record was made of the storm's highest winds. A barometric pressure reading was reported as "near twenty-six inches" (880 mb), though that improbable reference is not supported by other readings in the area—the National Oceanic and Atmospheric Administration reanalysis team has concluded San Ciriaco was a Category 3 at landfall in North Carolina. Still, it's understood that this hurricane ranks as one of the most powerful ever seen on the Outer Banks.

One of the most detailed accounts of the storm was a report filed with the Weather Bureau office in Washington, D.C., by S. L. Doshoz, the Weather

Bureau observer at Cape Hatteras. The following excerpt from his report describes the extent of the storm surge and the struggle for survival endured by the residents of Hatteras Island:

August 21, 1899

This hurricane was, without any question, the most severe of any storm that has ever passed over this section within the memory of any person now living, and there are people here who can remember back for a period of over 75 years. I have made careful inquiry among the old inhabitants here, and they all agree, with one accord, that no storm like this has ever visited the island. Certain it is that no such storm has ever been recorded within the history of the Weather Bureau at this place. The scene here on the 17th was wild and terrifying in the extreme. By 8 A.M. on that date the entire island was covered with water blown in from the sound, and by 11 A.M. all the land was covered to a depth of from 3 to 10 feet. This tide swept over the island at a fearful rate carrying everything movable before it. There were not more than four houses on the island in which the tide did not rise to a depth of from one to four feet, and a least half of the people had to abandon their homes and property to the mercy of the wind and tide and seek the safety of their own lives with those who were fortunate enough to live on higher land.

Language is inadequate to express the conditions which prevailed all day on the 17th. The howling wind, the rushing and roaring tide and the awful sea which swept over the beach and thundered like a thousand pieces of artillery made a picture which was at once appalling and terrible and the like of which Dante's Inferno could scarcely equal. The frightened people were grouped sometimes 40 or 50 in one house, and at times one house would have to be abandoned and they would all have to wade almost beyond their depth in order to reach another. All day this gale, tide and sea continued with a fury and persistent energy that knew no abatement, and the strain on the minds of every one was something so frightful and dejecting that it cannot be expressed. In many houses families were huddled together in the upper portion of the building with the water several feet deep in the lower portion, not knowing what minute the house would either be blown down or swept away by the tide. And even those whose houses were above the water could not tell what minute the tide would rise so high that all dwellings would be swept away.

At about 8 P.M. on the 17th when the wind lulled and shifted to the east and the tide began to run off with great swiftness, causing a fall of several feet in less than a half hour, a prayer of thankfulness went up from every soul on the island, and strong men, who had held up a brave heart against the terrible strain of the past 12 hours, broke down and wept like children upon their minds being relieved of the excessive tension to which it had been subjected all through the day. Cattle, sheep, hogs and chickens were drowned by hundreds before the very eyes of the owners, who were powerless to render any assistance on account of the rushing tide. The fright of these poor animals was terrible to see, and their cries of terror when being surrounded by the water were pitiful in the extreme.

Doshoz also reported on his own personal ordeal and struggle through the hurricane flood:

I live about a mile from the office building and when I went home at 8 A.M., I had to wade in water which was about waist deep. I waited until about 10:30 A.M., thinking the storm would lull, but it did not do so, and at that time I started for the office to change the wind sheet. I got about one-third of the distance and found the water about breast high, when I had to stop in a neighbor's house and rest, the strain of pushing through the water and storm having nearly exhausted my strength. I rested there until about noon when I started again and after going a short distance further I found the water up to my shoulders and still I was not half way to the office. I had to give it up again and take refuge in another neighbor's house where I had to remain until about 8 P.M. when the tide fell so that I could reach the office. I regret that I was unable to change the wind sheet so that a record of the wind could be made from the time the clock stopped running until the [anemometer] cups were blown away, but I did all that I could under the circumstances.

The San Ciriaco Hurricane also affected the northern Outer Banks with high winds and storm flooding. At Nags Head, rising waters from the Atlantic met the wind-driven waters of Albemarle Sound, flooding the entire area, even in places where the island was a mile wide. Overwash from the storm covered many portions of the Outer Banks, destroying dozens of homes and cottages. Some of the residents of Nags Head refused to leave their homes as the storm approached, as they were confident the flood would soon subside. But the water kept coming, and at last, some families had to be moved to safety by patrolmen from the lifesaving station.

Nineteenth-century hurricanes were often compared by the number of ships they caused to be wrecked or lost at sea. Powerful storms frequently battered the North Carolina coast and earned the region the nickname Graveyard of the Atlantic. So many vessels and sailors were lost through the years that young captains were often given special awards for their first safe passage by the treacherous shoals off Hatteras. In his book *Graveyard of the Atlantic*, David Stick lists seven vessels that were wrecked between Cape Fear and Virginia during the San Ciriaco Hurricane: the *Aaron Reppard, Florence Randall, Lydia Willis, Fred Walton, Robert W. Dasey, Priscilla,* and *Minnie Bergen*. Also, the Diamond Shoals lightship was driven ashore after its mooring lines were broken by the storm's mountainous seas. Six other ships were reported lost at sea without a trace: the *John C. Haynes, M. B. Millen, Albert Schultz, Elwood H. Smith, Henry B. Cleaves,* and *Charles M. Patterson*.

It is known that at least thirty-five sailors from the wrecked vessels were saved as their ships broke apart in the surf. Newspaper accounts concluded that at least thirty lives were lost in these shipwrecks, but the real number of deaths was probably much higher. A newspaper report from Norfolk, Virginia, following the August hurricane described the aftermath: "The stretch of beach between Kinnakeet to Hatteras, a distance of about eighteen miles, bears evidence of the fury of the gale in the shape of spars, masts, and general wreckage of five schooners which were washed ashore and then broken up by the fierce waves, while now and again a body washes ashore to lend added solemnity to the scene."

Of all this hurricane's wrecks and rescues, perhaps the most chilling account was that of the Norwegian bark *Drot*, which encountered the storm in the open Atlantic off the Florida coast. In *The Great Bahamian Hurricanes of 1899 and 1932*, Wayne Neely described the tragic end for the vessel and crew. After a massive wave scuttled the ship and swept the captain and seven crew members overboard, the eight remaining seamen crafted a makeshift raft from loose deck boards and held on for their lives. Pounding waves soon broke the raft into two sections. Two men held one portion of the timber; one eventually released into the sea, the other clung to the raft and was later rescued off Cape Hatteras by the German steamship *Titania*. The other raft, with six crew members aboard, rode the storm's giant swells through day and night. Eventually, it was too much for three of the men, who "lost their minds" and cast themselves overboard. Neely described the gruesome final stages of their journey after days at sea without food or water: "Realizing that they would die of thirst or starvation, the three men agreed to draw lots—the loser would be killed and consumed by the other two. The German lost the wager and was immediately killed by Thomason and Anderson, who quenched their thirst by drinking the blood from his veins." On August 31, two weeks after the sinking of the *Drot*, the two survivors were picked up by the British steamer *Woodruff*. Eventually, they were taken back to Norway and tried for murder.

On the North Carolina coast, one of the most dramatic rescues was that of the barkentine *Priscilla*. This 643-ton American cargo vessel was commanded by Capt. Benjamin E. Springsteen and was bound from its home port of Baltimore to Rio de Janeiro, Brazil. When the *Priscilla* left port on August 12, its captain was unaware of the powerful hurricane that would soon meet his ship head-on.

On the morning of the sixteenth, the wind began to blow, requiring that the ship's light sails be taken in. As the day advanced, the winds continued to increase, and orders were given to take in all but the *Priscilla*'s mainsail. But by late afternoon, the driving wind had blown away or destroyed all of the vessel's riggings, and Captain Springsteen was now adrift under bare poles on a rapid southwest course. Early on the morning of the seventeenth, after a stressful night of rolling seas and hurricane winds, soundings were made to test the water's depth. With each passing hour, the water became more shallow, and the captain knew the storm was driving his ship ashore. Through the torrents of rain and wind, the order was passed to the crew to prepare to save themselves as the *Priscilla* was about to wreck.

After tossing about for the entire day, the ship finally struck bottom at about 9:00 P.M. on the seventeenth. For the next hour, the *Priscilla* was bashed against the shallow shoals as huge breakers crashed over its hull. Within moments, Captain Springsteen's wife, his son, and two crew members were swept overboard and drowned. Shortly afterward, with a loud crash, the ship's hull broke apart, and the remaining horrified sailors held tightly to their wreck. Five more terrorizing hours would pass before the captain and his surviving crew would be carried by massive waves toward the beach.

Even though the hurricane's winds and tide were ferocious, surfman Rasmus Midgett of the Gull Shoal Lifesaving Station set out on his routine beach patrol at 3:00 A.M. on the eighteenth. The ocean was sweeping completely across the narrow island, at times reaching the saddle girths of his horse. But Midgett knew that disaster was at hand by the scattered debris that was washed about by the surf. Barrels, crates, buckets, and timbers provided clear signs that a wrecked ship was nearby. Although the night was dark and the storm was intense, this courageous surfman knew that lives might be in jeopardy.

Finally, after an hour and a half of patrol in extreme conditions, Midgett stopped on the dark beach at the sound of voices—the distressed cries of the shipwrecked men. Realizing that too much time would be lost if he returned to the station for help, he decided to attempt the rescue alone. One by one, he coaxed the *Priscilla*'s crew off the wreck and into the water, where he helped them to shore through the pounding breakers. Seven men were saved in this manner, and they gathered on the beach, exhausted.

Three of the crew remained on the wreck, however, too bruised and battered to move. Midgett swam out to save them and physically carried them to shore, one at a time. He then brought the men to a high dune, where he left them to wait. He offered his coat to Captain Springsteen, who had received a serious wound to the chest. All of the men were bruised and bleeding, and some had had their clothes stripped away by the churning surf.

Midgett quickly returned to his station for help, and several men were dispatched to retrieve the survivors. In all, he had saved ten lives while risking his own in the treacherous surf of the San Ciriaco Hurricane. For his efforts, he was later awarded a Gold Lifesaving Medal by the U.S. secretary of the Treasury.

The San Ciriaco Hurricane tracked thousands of miles over twenty-eight days and became the longest-lived Atlantic tropical cyclone on record. After crossing Hatteras and sweeping up the Pamlico and Albemarle Sounds, it returned to the Atlantic off the Virginia coast as a Category 1 hurricane. From there it moved northeast, paralleling Long Island, New York, on its way out to sea. It became extratropical on August 18 just off the coast of Nova Scotia and continued to move away from land. But more than a week later, on August 26, remnants of the system reemerged as a tropical storm some 700 miles southwest of the Azores. The storm held that status for a week, before passing through the Azores as a Category 1 hurricane on September 3.

Like that of many hurricane disasters of this period, San Ciriaco's death toll is best represented as an estimate. In Puerto Rico and the Bahamas alone, it's believed more than 3,400 perished, and the storm's total probably surpassed 3,850—placing it among the Western Hemisphere's ten deadliest hurricanes. Estimates vary on the number of deaths in North Carolina; some news reports counted sixty, though twenty-four was the most-often-quoted figure. As violent as it was, the hurricane's sharp turn toward the Atlantic following landfall on the Outer Banks likely reduced its impact over inland areas and spared lives and property. But unfortunately for coastal North Carolina residents, it wasn't the last hurricane disaster of the 1899 season.

A second destructive hurricane battered North Carolina later that fall, on Halloween. Residents of the region had come to accept this kind of misfortune; it was the third time in less than twenty years that two hurricanes had hit the Tar Heel State within a single season. One newspaper columnist at the time speculated that these violent storms were "God's punishment for allowing dancing on Sundays in local clubs."

The Halloween storm came ashore well to the south of where the San Ciriaco Hurricane struck in August. Like Hazel in 1954 (though far less powerful), it made landfall in northeastern South Carolina and cut a path through eastern North Carolina into Virginia. Even though the two storms of 1899 crossed different sections of the coast, the second's widespread effects brought great damage to some of the same locations. The October hurricane was most intense in the vicinity of Southport, Wilmington, and Wrightsville Beach, and registered as Category 2 in both North and South Carolina.

After the hurricane rolled through in the early morning hours of the thirty-first, afternoon winds and rains abated and a large crowd boarded the Seacoast train in Wilmington, headed for Wrightsville Beach to survey the damage. When the train turned the corner toward Wrightsville Station, those on board weren't prepared for the vast destruction before them. The massive railroad trestle was warped and twisted; the tracks were in shambles. The depot was piled high with seaweed, and debris filled the streets "as far as the eye could see." More than twenty cottages were either washed into the sound or wrecked by the rolling surf. The public pavilion, Ocean View Hotel, and old Hewlett barroom were among the losses. The Carolina Yacht Club and Atlantic Yacht Club were also severely damaged, both having been washed from their foundations and carried by the tides. The surge on Wrightsville was reported to be eight feet.

Landfall had been near Myrtle Beach, which at the time mostly consisted of undeveloped barrier beaches and coastal marshes. In Southport, the tide rose five feet above normal high water, and many houses along the waterfront were badly damaged. According to the *Wilmington Messenger*, "Large droves of cattle drifted across the river, dead and alive. They were run off by high waters all over Bald Head Island, which never was known to be covered before." The destruction at Carolina Beach equaled that at Wrightsville. The railroad tracks were damaged, numerous cottages were destroyed or "missing," and witnesses said waves rolled through the town. Along the Wilmington waterfront, the Cape Fear River flooded the wharves from one end of the city to the other.

North of the Cape Fear region, the New River Inn and over a dozen cottages were swept away in Onslow County. In Morehead City and Beaufort, the effects of the Halloween hurricane were as unwelcome as those of the San Ciriaco storm. High water again flooded the low-lying reaches of these coastal towns. Newspapers proclaimed the storm brought New Bern "the worst experience in

Wreckage rests on the remains of the railroad tracks at Wrightsville Beach following the October 1899 hurricane. (Photo courtesy of the Lower Cape Fear Historical Society, Wilmington, North Carolina.)

her history." The water was two feet higher than during the August hurricane, and as had happened on the Wilmington waterfront, fires broke out on the docks when barrels of lime were flooded. Few reports were offered from other coastal villages, such as Portsmouth and Ocracoke, but the Halloween hurricane no doubt affected much of the North Carolina coast.

TAKEAWAYS

- *Getting hit by two or more hurricanes in one season is not uncommon.* On the Carolina coast, no one can predict what to expect with each hurricane season. With luck, years may pass between hurricanes. But some years can be very active, with two or more landfalls striking the same area in a single season. Remember Bertha and Fran in 1996? Or Dennis and Floyd in 1999? It turns out that back-to-back hurricanes are not uncommon in the Carolinas, with the 1899 season just another example. Hurricane watchers mostly worry about "the big one," anticipating the next epic storm disaster. But occasionally, some communities will suffer through two, or even three, tropical cyclones within weeks—from which the cumulative toll can far exceed that of a single storm. In 1955, Hurricane Connie, Tropical Storm Diane, and Hurricane Ione all struck the North Carolina coast in August and September. The combined losses in North Carolina from these three exceeded the losses from Category 4 Hazel the year before.

- *Today, we're past the point of retreat from many of our vulnerable barrier beaches—at least in the near term.* The people who settled Diamond City were a hardy bunch, though they were ultimately chased from their village on Shackleford Banks by hurricanes. The storms took a toll, and the people finally decided it wasn't practical to live on the island. From their new homes on the mainland, they were still able to ply the local waters and make a living fishing. Native American tribes who predated European settlers took a similar approach, establishing seasonal fishing camps on the barrier islands but maintaining their settlements just inland. Many of today's coastal island communities look far different than the windswept dunes of Shackleford. Miles and miles of homes, condominium developments, hotels, shopping centers, and restaurants line portions of the Carolina beachfront today, all thriving communities that take advantage of the public's love for sun, surf, and sand. They're home to tens of thousands of year-round residents and welcome millions of seasonal vacationers. In the near term, it's unlikely we'll see retreat from these communities, even as sea levels rise, beaches continue to erode, and storms continue to strike. Most of these cities and towns have developed strategies to cope with their fragile environments, such as restricting the removal of trees, replenishing beach sand lost to erosion, and placing limitations on how and where structures are built. But they'll always be especially vulnerable to destructive hurricanes, and the sand that lies beneath them will always be on the move.
- *For centuries, hurricanes claimed countless lives at sea until forecasting and warning improvements finally curbed the losses.* When Congress authorized the U.S. Army Signal Service in 1870, it was created with shipping interests in mind. Each year, hurricanes were responsible for huge losses—in ships, valuable cargo, and the lives of countless sailors and passengers. In 1890, weather forecasting responsibilities were transferred to the U.S. Weather Bureau, and then in 1898, President William McKinley directed the bureau to expand its early warning system into the West Indies. The telegraph network linked weather observers in places such as Nassau and Key West with Washington, so that information about potential tropical cyclones could be relayed to coastal interests. In cities such as New York, Philadelphia, and Baltimore, ships remained in port when threatening storms were thought to be approaching. But the system wasn't perfect, and through the

late nineteenth century, hurricanes continued to ravage ships of all sizes and types along the Carolina coast. The two hurricanes of 1899 added to the toll. It was just a few years later, with the advent of radio, that ship captains were able to keep up with news of approaching weather. The Wireless Ship Act of 1910 required radios aboard oceangoing merchant vessels and passenger liners. Better forecasting and improved communications led to far fewer lost vessels and sailors.

CHAPTER SIX

THE GREAT ASHEVILLE FLOOD
OF 1916

When we think about devastating hurricanes, we usually consider landfall along the coast as "ground zero," where the forces of wind and water are at their peak. This is typically the case; there are many coastal hurricanes among the fifteen storms in this book. Sometimes, depending upon a storm's size, strength, and track, inland portions of the Carolinas many miles from the ocean can also suffer. Examples fill these pages, including hurricanes menacing Columbia, Charlotte, Raleigh, Rocky Mount, and other cities. Even the mountainous counties in the west have been battered by deadly winds and floods brought on by dissipating hurricanes as they spun inland. There's no better example of this than the events that became known as the Great Asheville Flood of 1916.

Two hurricanes were responsible for this disastrous flood, though they made landfall nine days apart and hundreds of miles away from the Asheville region. The first set the stage; the second would eventually break U.S. weather records. This cycle of events began on July 5, 1916, quite early in the season, when a Category 3 storm struck near Pascagoula, Mississippi, with 120 mph winds. At the time, it was the earliest known major hurricane to make landfall in the United States. The following day the storm center hovered over central Mississippi and Alabama; it lingered for three additional days with steadily decreasing intensity. Heavy downpours destroyed crops throughout the region, including in portions of western Georgia. The dissipating storm finally weakened to a tropical depression on the ninth as it tracked northward through Alabama and into Tennessee, soaking the slopes of the Appalachians with heavy rains. Some areas near Asheville saw ten straight days of wet weather.

Rainfall totals across the mountains were impressive but not disastrous. Between July 8 and 10, observers in Brevard and Hendersonville recorded over five and a half inches of rain, whereas Asheville recorded less than four. As rains from the Gulf coast storm ended, the French Broad River surpassed flood stage at four feet—and kept rising, reaching 8.8 feet on July 11. For the next few days it began receding but remained high, above normal levels.

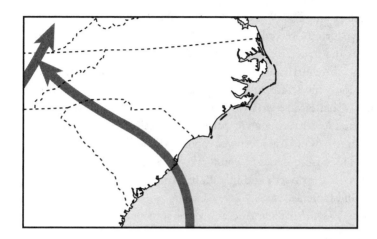

Across western North Carolina, the flood of 1916 was responsible for approximately eighty deaths, though the exact number is unknown. (Photo from *The Floods of July 1916: How the Southern Railway Met an Emergency* [Washington, D.C.: Southern Railway, 1917]. Courtesy of University Archives, University of North Carolina at Asheville.)

More than a week after the first storm's landfall, on July 14, a second hurricane hit the South Carolina coast north of Charleston. Only two days earlier, on the twelfth, ship reports had first identified it as a tropical low south of Charleston. It approached the coast and reached Category 3 intensity on the thirteenth as its eye slipped past Charleston. It struck near Bulls Bay just a few hours later at 4:00 A.M. on the fourteenth, where pressures were estimated at 960 millibars, making this unnamed hurricane a strong Category 2 at landfall.

According to the U.S. Weather Bureau's *Monthly Weather Review*, "This is the first July storm of record that passed northwestward from the region of the Bahamas and struck the south Atlantic coast."

Before this hurricane's winds and rains made their way west, plenty of destruction—moderate to severe—was reported along the South Carolina coast. In Charleston, two lives were lost, as the storm was described as being "of unusual severity, though its path of destructiveness was comparatively narrow." Hundreds of large trees were uprooted and blown down, giving the city a scarred look from which it would take years to recover. But the greater damages were in areas north and inland, in McClellanville, Georgetown, Pawleys Island, and Florence.

Monthly Weather Review described the scene in McClellanville:

> Large tracks of cultivated land in McClellanville section were inundated Friday morning, causing a total loss of crops. Water stood 4 or 5 feet deep in the town and left a heavy deposit of sea sledge covering dead animals and fowls. The tide is said to have been higher than in 1893 or 1911. The crop damage from about 15 to 20 miles northeast of Charleston on to McClellanville and the Santee River is estimated by the competent to judge at from 75 to 90 per cent. Almost all the trees in McClellanville were uprooted. Numerous houses were blown down, but they were of flimsy construction. Loss of live stock was rather heavy from wrecking of barns, and some hogs and other small animals were drowned. Notwithstanding the great material damage there was no loss of human life.

In Georgetown, damages were largely confined to waterfront businesses. On Pawleys Island, evidence of the storm tide was more obvious. The *Georgetown Times* reported, "This storm will go down in history as second only to the storm of '93, when so many memorable tragedies took place.... Along the beach the sand hills are cut as if sliced with a giant knife.... Fishing boats are washed high on the big sandhills and steps carried to the end of the island."

As rough as the initial landfall was at the coast, it was widespread and copious rainfall that makes this storm memorable. Precipitation maps for the period show two distinct regions with the heaviest accumulations. The first was just as the storm passed inland, over a broad area stretching from Kingstree to Florence where up to fifteen inches were recorded. The second pocket of extreme rainfall occurred much later over a section of the Blue Ridge Mountains above Asheville. Both regions suffered heavy damages from flash floods that swept away homes, livestock, crops, dams, bridges, rail tracks, and an unknown number of lives.

Near Lake City, flooding forced families onto their rooftops during the evening hours after the storm passed through. In a July 15 article titled "Florence Bridges Are Washed Away," the Charleston *News and Courier* reported, "Never in the history of this section has there ever fallen such a quantity of rain as fell yesterday and last night. The United States weather bureau at this place gives the official figures for the thirty-six hours as 14.25 inches of rain, an unprecedented record."

As the system tracked northwestward, its heavy rain clouds swirled over upstate South Carolina. On the night of the fourteenth, gusting winds toppled trees around Charlotte leaving piles of debris along city streets. But over the next days, north and west of the city, drenching rains overfilled every creek and river for miles across the foothills and mountains.

In the areas north and east of Asheville the rainfall set records, and when added to earlier rains from the Gulf coast storm, they produced the deadliest flash floods in North Carolina history. Rainfall in Asheville was not excessive, with less than three inches recorded July 14–16. But unprecedented amounts fell in the surrounding area. Ten inches fell in twenty-four hours in Hendersonville, a record that still stands for that location. Remarkably, the greatest deluge was recorded at Altapass, near Grandfather Mountain, where 22.22 inches fell during the twenty-four-hour period ending at 2:00 P.M. on the sixteenth. This downpour established a new twenty-four-hour rainfall record for the entire United States—a record that stood for more than twenty-five years.

By this time, winds from the storm were not a major issue, but the rain brought deadly landslides to the mountain countryside. The destruction was focused around the Swannanoa and French Broad Rivers in Buncombe County, though surrounding communities also experienced destructive slides. Numerous bridges and railroad trestles were washed away as the flooding reached its peak early on Sunday, July 16. The rise and spread of the French Broad was particularly swift. According to records from the Southern Railway Company, "The tremendous rains on the 15th and 16th in the watershed of the river caused it to rise with great rapidity. At 8 A.M., on the 16th, it stood at 13.5 feet, 9.5 feet above flood; by 9 A.M. on the same day, it had risen to 18.6 feet; and at 10 A.M. the bridge on which the gage was located was washed away. The crest of the flood was about 21 feet; the exact figures will be determined later." According to the National Oceanic and Atmospheric Administration's National Center for Environmental Information, the French Broad peaked at 23.1 feet, 19.1 feet above flood stage.

The region surrounding Asheville was particularly busy with railway traffic at this time, and hundreds of rail passengers were marooned between terminals

The French Broad River flows beyond its banks, inundating Asheville during the flood of 1916. (Photo courtesy of North Carolina Collection, Pack Memorial Public Library, Asheville, North Carolina.)

as tracks and trestles were washed out. Five hundred rail passengers from Knoxville, Tennessee, and points west were trapped in Marshall. All bridges there were destroyed, and fifty-three homes were swept down the narrow valley below the town. At least four deaths were reported in Marshall. Though many trestles were destroyed, good communications helped prevent any railway casualties. In the weeks following the flood, Southern Railway launched a massive effort to rebuild the damaged tracks and bridges, establishing work camps for 2,300 laborers. Out-of-work farmers and millworkers from across the region joined the rebuilding effort, receiving room, board, and $1.50 a day for their labor. Much of the work was completed within two months. A white-water-rafting journey today down the French Broad River crosses over "Rebar Rapids," an old bridge foundation where some of the last remaining evidence of the flood's destruction—exposed steel rebar—can be seen.

Along the banks of the Swannanoa and French Broad Rivers, all warehouses and industrial plants were submerged and heavily damaged. One hundred fifty feet of the stone dam at the Weaver power plant were washed away, and electricity was out throughout the region. The flood effectively divided North Carolina, as nine railroad bridges and all highway bridges across the Catawba River were destroyed, as were most across the Yadkin. Mills were destroyed in many

Asheville during the 1916 flood. (Photo courtesy of North Carolina Collection, Pack Memorial Public Library, Asheville, North Carolina.)

locations, including the cotton mill at Monbo. At Mount Holly, the *Charlotte Observer* reported waters crested above forty-five feet, "about twice as high as ever before." The flood swept away the five-story Armon Manufacturing mill and over 1,000 bales of cotton. Estimated property losses in the state totaled $22 million.

The Catawba River flowed far beyond its banks from the North Carolina mountains to the South Carolina Midlands. For hundreds of miles, almost every bridge and railroad trestle on the river was damaged or destroyed. In some areas the surging flood was miles across. Surrounding farms were swamped; rafts of dead livestock were a common sight. Rich topsoil was scoured and washed away, leaving most fields unfarmable. Days later, extreme floods finally reached York County, South Carolina, with great momentum, heavily damaging the Catawba Dam and power plant at Indian Hook so essential to the operation of the region's many textile mills. Farther south on the river, the hydroelectric station at Rocky Creek was also destroyed.

Just months after the flood, reconstruction of damaged towns, bridges, and homes was well underway. Construction also began on massive flood-control projects to help prevent future disasters on the Catawba watershed in North and South Carolina. By 1925, three large dams had been built on the headwaters of the Catawba, creating Lake James. Other massive dam projects created Lake Rhodhiss in Morganton, Charlotte's Mountain Island Lake, and Lake Wylie in York County.

Surging waters from Gashes Creek washed away twelve to sixteen feet of earth over several acres surrounding this well near
U.S. 74 East, the "Asheville–Charlotte Highway," during the
flood of 1916. (Photo courtesy of North Carolina Collection,
Pack Memorial Public Library, Asheville, North Carolina.)

The Great Asheville Flood ranks among the deadliest of all disasters in
North or South Carolina. Estimates vary, but approximately eighty fatalities
are attributed to the flood. Several deaths were reported in Biltmore Village,
the scene of some of the worst residential flooding. According to the *Asheville
Citizen*, "The damage at Biltmore is frightful.... Without warning at 4 o'clock
Sunday morning the Swannanoa river overflowed the village. Men plunged
into the stream carrying their wives and children. Horses turned loose plunged
madly through the flooded streets in the darkness. In an hour the water was
15 feet deep in the streets. Four lives were lost."

One of the tragic events in Asheville took place near Biltmore, where master carpenter James Lipe and his daughter Kathleen were wading through the

incoming flood when the waters became deep and the current swift. They were carried by floodwaters into a tree, where they held on in desperation. Two young nurses and another woman soon joined them, clinging to the tree in neck-deep water. A crowd gathered to aid their rescue, but ultimately all but one were lost to the swirling currents. Kathleen Lipe held on and was rescued some fourteen hours later. Biltmore Village residents who escaped the flood but lost their homes were given food, blankets, and transportation by Edith Vanderbilt, widow of Biltmore Estate's founder, George Vanderbilt.

Another tragedy occurred at Belmont. Nineteen railroad workers were operating a steam-powered crane to remove large trees and other debris stuck against a Southern Railway trestle over the Catawba, when the entire bridge structure suddenly "cracked" and collapsed. The workers plunged into the surging river, grasping for any logs or debris to hold them at the surface. Ten drowned, two went missing, and three were rescued by volunteers who came to the riverbank that evening. Through the night, the crowd on the bank could only hear the cries of the four remaining men, who clung to a poplar tree out in the river some two miles downstream. Former Charlotte police and fire chief W. S. Orr oversaw the rescue and told the *Charlotte Observer*, "I never thought that I would see the time when I would hear a man call upon me in the name of God for help and not give it, if it was in my power. Tonight, it would be suicide, but you can't expect that poor fellow to realize it."

At daylight, a rescue was attempted by two volunteers in a small boat. After reaching the tree and hauling one of the men aboard, the boat capsized, tossing all three into the water. They scrambled in the currents to grab the tree; now there were six men in need of rescue. Hundreds gathered on the banks to witness these events, many on their knees in prayer. Volunteers quickly assembled a raft, but it couldn't navigate the rushing river. Railroad carpenters fashioned a small boat caulked with cotton, but it sank. A motorboat arrived, but the engine sputtered. Then, all eyes were drawn to two men in a flat-bottom boat, who seemed to paddle in from nowhere. Peter Stowe and Alphonse Ross had been recruited in Belmont to save the men, and they did, patiently loading the first three to shore under a chorus of applause. As they returned to pick up the remaining men, their boat capsized, tossing Stowe overboard. He quickly grabbed the boat with one hand and the tree with the other, pulling himself up with the other men. Finally, they were able to right the boat, climb aboard, and paddle back to shore, where they received a hero's welcome. The *Charlotte Observer* reported, "The bloodied and bruised trestle survivors broke down in tears and were reported to ramble incoherently. They had spent 19 hours in the water." The following day's headline was "Praise for Heroic Negroes who Saved

Six White Men's Lives." In 2016, on the 100th anniversary of the flood, a state historical marker was dedicated in Belmont to honor the ten men who died in the Catawba River.

TAKEAWAYS

- *You don't have to live on the coast to get slammed by a hurricane.* Hurricanes that track inland can have devastating effects many miles from the shore. Ask anyone who remembers Hugo in Charlotte or Fran in Raleigh. In the Carolinas, the mountain counties are vulnerable too. Like during the flood of 1916, back-to-back hurricanes—though considerably weakened—visited the region in 2004. In early September the remnants of Hurricane Frances dropped over eighteen inches of rain in Linville Falls in Burke County. Nine days later, Hurricane Ivan brought seventeen inches to Cruso, west of Asheville. Gusty winds blew down billboards and toppled trees, while extensive flooding gripped the region, with twenty U.S. Geological Survey rivergages setting new records. In North Carolina, the winds, floods, and mudslides claimed eleven lives and left damages of more than $200 million.
- *Heavy rains on steep slopes present a unique danger.* Rapid rainfall accumulations from tropical cyclones generate flash floods when creeks and streams are overwhelmed. In mountainous regions, steep hillsides accelerate the rush of water, sometimes with deadly consequences. When the remnants of Hurricanes Frances and Ivan soaked western North Carolina in 2004, tragedy struck in Macon County. On September 16, following Ivan's most intense rains, twenty homes were carried down a mile-long mudslide and debris flow at Peeks Creek—some with residents still inside. Around 10:00 P.M., when the rains were the heaviest, a layer of soil atop Fishhawk Mountain became liquefied and started flowing downhill. Along with the mud came rocks, boulders, and massive trees, sliding off the mountain at 30 mph, crushing homes, killing four, and injuring several more. Among the odd sightings the next morning: wind chimes still hanging from the porches of houses that tumbled hundreds of feet, and a Mercedes-Benz lodged high among the limbs of a tree. Thirty-two other debris flows were recorded in the region during the rain event.
- *Transportation disruptions following hurricanes hinder response and recovery efforts.* When Hurricane Florence soaked the Carolinas in 2018, lingering floods covered roads and highways across the east, effectively isolating many communities for days. Most of the storm's fatalities in the Carolinas

resulted from motorists attempting to drive on flooded roads. Closure of major routes such as Interstates 95 and 40 not only disrupted response and recovery efforts but also required diversion of regular traffic, sending drivers on elaborate detours over state and county roads. Traffic diverted from Interstate 95 jammed local routes and hindered the movement of rescue teams and other officials. Following the Asheville Flood of 1916, it was the railroads that were crippled when tracks and trestles across the west were washed away. Washouts blocked passage for hundreds of travelers, stranding them in several North Carolina towns. The economy of the region was dependent on the railroad system, and the 1916 flood struck a blow to commerce that lasted for years.

CHAPTER SEVEN

THE OUTER BANKS HURRICANE
OF 1933

In the early 1930s, the Great Depression had a firm grip on the nation and had cast its long shadow across the Carolinas. Times were hard from the Appalachians to the coast. In November 1932, Franklin D. Roosevelt was elected president with the promise of a New Deal for economic recovery. By the summer of 1933, there was hope among the people of the nation. But for many coastal North Carolinians, the months of August and September would bring even greater despair than the recent economic turmoil.

The 1933 hurricane season was a record breaker. Twenty tropical storms, including eleven hurricanes, were recorded in the Atlantic and Gulf of Mexico, with five hurricanes making an impact on the United States. It was the busiest season since 1887 and set a record that would stand until 2005, when twenty-eight storms were named (thirty were named in 2020 and twenty-one in 2021). Among the many storms were two hurricanes that raked the North Carolina coast, one in August and another just a few weeks later in mid-September.

The first of the two was a Cape Verde hurricane that sustained Category 4 strength for several days during its course across the Atlantic. After passing south of Bermuda it weakened considerably during its approach to the Outer Banks and made landfall as a Category 1 well north of Cape Hatteras. It crossed Albemarle Sound and by midmorning on August 23, it was on a curving path into Virginia. It passed west of Washington, D.C., and spun northward into central New York before returning to the Atlantic off the Maine coast. It's sometimes called the Chesapeake and Potomac Hurricane because of the extensive damages it brought to this region. A washed-out bridge led to a deadly train derailment near Washington, D.C., with Hampton Roads and Norfolk suffering flooding described at the "highest tides of the 20th century."

At Cape Hatteras, the maximum winds were only 75 mph, though winds north of that location likely reached 90 mph. High tides and severe beach erosion were reported all along the banks. Inland areas suffered extensive crop damage, and damages in northeastern North Carolina were estimated at $250,000.

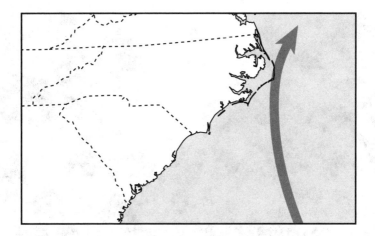

The four-masted schooner *G. A. Kohler* was driven ashore north of the cape, its captain and crew rescued by Coast Guardsmen from Chicamacomico station. But the vessel remained stranded on the beach for the next ten years; its cargo and furnishings were salvaged by locals, including pieces of the wreck used to build the Salvo Assembly of God Church. Eventually the stripped vessel was burned. Occasionally, its remnants are exposed by hurricanes and nor'easters and can be seen on the beach just north of ramp 27 near Avon.

Just weeks after the August storm and following a similar track, another hurricane moved toward the North Carolina coast. By the morning of September 15, it was 250 miles south of Cape Hatteras, and all indications were that it would make landfall late that night or early the next morning. Storm warnings were issued, and the few coastal cities that had hurricane plans put them into effect. The American Red Cross, better organized after its recent experience with tragic hurricanes in Florida, urged the Carolina chapters to prepare for a potential disaster.

When the Category 2 hurricane approached North Carolina it slowed significantly, and a slight turn to the north brought the storm center just offshore near Cape Hatteras. Its slow progression meant that the Hatteras weather station was within the radius of maximum winds for almost eight hours. Though the center of the eye never actually made landfall, intense northeast winds over Pamlico Sound forced tremendous quantities of water to surge to the southwest, flooding the river basins of the Neuse and Pamlico. By this time, it was not only slow moving but a very large storm.

The tremendous storm tide that swept through several Down East communities claimed twenty-one lives and left extensive destruction. Wind-driven

After striking the northern Outer Banks, the August hurricane of 1933 tracked into Virginia and caused the greatest flood in Norfolk history. (Photo courtesy of the City of Norfolk Main Library.)

water remained high on the land until the storm moved up the coast. Then, as if the plug were removed from a bathtub, the water rushed back toward the sea, overwashing Core Banks from west to east and opening Drum Inlet in the process. Winds were estimated at 85 mph at Cape Hatteras just before the anemometer was destroyed. In Beaufort and New Bern, winds gusted to 100 mph. In some areas, wind-related damage was as severe as the flooding. Countless large trees were downed throughout the east, including in the city of New Bern. A *New York Times* reporter wrote, "New Bern has long been known as the 'Athens of North Carolina' because of its many large and beautiful trees. Now hundreds of these trees are either lying in the streets or leaning grotesquely against the battered houses. Many of the splendid trees of East Front, Broad, Pollock, Johnson, and Craven streets were blown down."

The flooding in New Bern was the highest ever known by any resident and was said to have been about two feet greater than in the storm tide of September 1913. The water reached a height of three to four feet in some streets, and rowboats and skiffs were used to evacuate people from buildings that were completely surrounded by water. The tide rose a foot above the tallest piling on the Coast Guard dock, and the dock was wrecked and washed away. The cutter *Pamlico* was unharmed, however, even though it was moored to the dock at the time.

The Neuse River bridge that linked New Bern and Bridgeton on U.S. 17 was washed out at about 1:30 A.M. on September 16. A three-quarter-mile-long section was taken out by the surging waters of the Neuse, and pieces of the bridge were scattered along the shore for miles downriver. Two automobiles were believed to have been stranded on this section, but their occupants were able to escape the bridge before it collapsed. Damage was also reported to the Norfolk Southern railroad trestle and the Trent River bridge. Several boxcars were dumped into the Neuse when the Atlantic Coastline Pier caved in.

One unusual story from the storm of 1933 came from the New Bern area. The roof of Mrs. Sam Smallwood's boathouse was blown off by the fierce winds. It landed, right side up, on a seawall a quarter of a mile downriver, with Mrs. Smallwood's boat, which had been suspended from the rafters, still intact. The boat was retrieved the morning of the storm and was used to take Mrs. Smallwood to higher ground.

The damage in New Bern alone was more than $1 million. Many homes and businesses were severely damaged by both high water and winds. Several lumber factories were destroyed. The rising salt water reached the region's farmlands, and damage was heavy to unharvested corn, cotton, and sweet potatoes. In many locations, tons of tobacco stored in barns were destroyed when they became soaked by heavy rains and rising floodwaters. But by far, the greatest loss and suffering came to those who lived near the water and made their living from the sea. Carteret County was hit hard by the storm, and remote Down East communities were devastated.

The *Beaufort News* described these events in the week following the storm:

> The oldest citizens here in Beaufort have told the News that it was the most devastating storm that they have seen in the past four score years. It was not merely a bad wind that reached gale force for just a few minutes; the disastrous hurricane swept Carteret for more than twelve hours without ceasing for even a few minutes. From early Friday morning rain began falling and this continued unremittingly until about day break Saturday morning.
>
> This terrific tropical hurricane which swept up the Atlantic coast Friday seemed to have hit Carteret near Beaufort Inlet, striking Beaufort and Morehead City first, then continued with its destructive force on to

Merrimon, South River, Lukens, Roe and Lola, with all other communities in eastern Carteret getting their shares of the devastating tempest. . . . Within Carteret County alone there was a property loss of at least a million dollars, eight people were drowned and scores left homeless, hundreds without food and more with barely enough clothing to cover their bodies. Thousands of domestic and wild animals perished in the water and if they are not removed and buried decomposition will result in stench and disease. In the villages where homes and other buildings were wholly or partially demolished, men, women and children by the score stuck nails in their feet and have cuts and bruises and sprains across their bodies. Only a very small percentage have received medical attention and been inoculated with tetanus antitoxin. Sanitary conditions in the stricken area are terrible, and epidemics will in all likelihood ensue if the people do not cooperate whole-heartedly with the sanitary engineers of the State Department of Health.

Capt. Jim Hamilton and his three sons, Nelson, Charlie, and Ralph, all drowned in Long Bay when their twenty-foot skiff capsized in the storm. Like countless other fishermen before them, they had left their home in Sea Level with no knowledge of the impending weather. Their expedition quickly turned tragic as their small boat was no match for the furious seas.

In the Down East community of Merrimon, the tide was estimated at "fifteen or sixteen feet." Only fifteen out of forty houses remained after the tides overwashed the area. The Carraway family endured a horrible ordeal when their house collapsed during the storm. The entire family huddled together as a blast of wind tore down the structure, pinning them in the wreckage amid the rising tides. Mr. Carraway escaped with the help of his son George, but his niece Freda was trapped under the debris. Those who escaped were forced to flee to higher ground when the tides continued to rise, but Freda remained under the house and did not survive.

At nearby Cedar Island, about eight families endured the hurricane, and all their homes were washed off their foundations or severely damaged. Bewildered residents struggled to simply survive in the first days following their ordeal. After the hurricane passed, the local director of the Red Cross, Frank Hyde, launched a relief mission to the Down East villages. No communication with the isolated hurricane victims was possible, so this voyage would provide the first news of the conditions in these areas. Thirty "orders" of food and supplies were prepared for the relief effort, which was assisted by the Coast Guard.

Hyde left Fort Macon for Core Sound early Monday morning, two days after the hurricane's arrival.

The mission reached the community of Lola, on the southern end of Cedar Island, by late morning. James Whitehurst, a reporter for the *Beaufort News*, was traveling with Hyde and filed the following report:

> Upon arriving on shore we were conducted through a throng of half-clothed bewildered people who looked upon us with overjoyed eyes. One young woman with a baby—it appeared to be her first—cried with joy. Every person seemed to have stuck nails in their feet or had cuts and bruises about their bodies. The last food in Lola had been consumed for breakfast, and this had been far from sufficient. . . . The homes had been washed from their foundations, windows had been blown out, roofs and roofing wrenched from the tops of the structures. Wreckage was strewn from one end of the island to the other. Few of the people had shoes on, and virtually every one had on all the clothing they had been able to salvage.

When the Coast Guard boat carrying Hyde moved to the northern end of the island, its passengers found even greater destruction in the village of Roe. Eight or ten homes were described as totally destroyed, and only one was "fit for winter." Most of the homes had floated haphazardly with the tides, and many suffered structural damage. Thick mats of mud, grass, and debris filled several houses and littered the branches of nearby trees.

At South River, similar floods struck late Friday night. The Louis Cannon family narrowly escaped drowning when their home collapsed in the storm. They had gathered in their attic when the waters rushed into the first floor. They eventually escaped by clinging to the rooftop of the demolished house until they became caught in the top of a grove of trees. There they rode out the storm until the waters receded.

The home of William Cannon became a refuge for other South River residents who were forced to flee their homes. The Cannon residence was on higher ground than many other houses, and frightened neighbors and relatives made their way there when the floods moved in. Ultimately, more than fifty people were sheltered in the house. Many stayed through Saturday, until they were able to return to what was left of their homes.

One of the great tragedies of the 1933 storm struck the family of Elijah Dixon, who were staying in a two-story home near Back Creek when the hurricane hit. Dixon, his wife Ellen, and their eight-year-old daughter Hazel, three-year-old son James, and nine-month-old daughter Elva Marie were all plunged into the raging waters when the house collapsed into Back Creek. The family tried desperately to cling to the broken fragments of the rooftop. With his young son around his neck, Dixon jumped into the dark waters to rescue his wife, who was still clinging to baby Elva. In the darkness and confusion, the infant slipped from her arms and drowned. As the weary group again gathered on the roof, they realized that young Hazel was also missing. Reeling from this double tragedy, Dixon still managed to grasp a large branch when the rooftop was swept into a grove of trees. There the battered family remained until later Saturday afternoon, when they were rescued.

Some Down East residents reportedly brought their domestic stock inside their homes as floodwaters approached. Pigs, goats, chickens, and even cows were coaxed up to second-floor rooms to escape the rising tide. Many farm animals were not so fortunate, however. Most of those left to fend for themselves either drowned or were scattered by the storm.

One peculiar story appeared in the *Beaufort News* one week after the storm:

Down at Roe, which is located on the north end of Cedar Island, some men spied a forty-pound shoat [a young hog] lodged in the crotch of a tree Monday morning after the storm about fifteen feet from the ground. This animal had evidently been carried to this place by the high tide and terrific hurricane wind Friday night. In order to prevent the apparently dead pig from decomposing and causing both stench and disease, it was decided that the animal should be removed and buried.

One of the men climbed the tree with a saw and started to remove one of the limbs of the crotch, so that the shoat would fall to the ground. About the second or third stroke of the saw, the pig came to life and let out an unearthly and demon-like squeal that echoed and reached through the woods around Roe. This unexpected resumption of life on the part of the supposedly dead shoat pretty nearly frightened the rescuer to death. After it dawned on the bewildered men that the pig was really alive, they quickly removed him from the tree crotch.

The tragedies of the 1933 hurricane were spread throughout numerous Down East communities. In Oriental, Vandemere, Bayboro, and Arapahoe, local newspapers reported that "hardly a building was left intact." From Ocracoke, there was a report that "four feet of water had covered the island." As the hurricane's storm surge pushed over Ocracoke, residents scrambled for high ground in any way they could. Some had prepared their homes by removing floorboards

HURRICANE LORE

Cable network documentaries have profiled some of America's great hurricanes. Newspaper reporters and local television stations have covered them in detail. But in the Carolinas, when the subject of hurricanes comes around, many residents prefer to tell their own stories. They're quick to describe their experiences and the remarkable events they've witnessed. Some talk of historic storms such as Hazel or Hugo, sharing tales that have been passed through family for generations or told and retold by friends. Others have fresh memories of recent hurricanes. They may include stories of shocking floods, amazing rescues, daring escapes, tragic and heart-wrenching loss, and the sometimes ironic or even humorous events that unfold during these storms. Over time, some stories even mix with legend, solidifying their place among the Carolinas' hurricane lore.

One of the most well-known tales of the Carolina coast is thought to have begun on Pawleys Island during the September hurricane of 1822. It's the story of the death of a young man from Charleston who was traveling by horse to meet his fiancée up the coast. According to legend, he drowned when his horse sank in "quicksand" as he tried to navigate a coastal marsh near Pawleys Island. His ghost later appeared on the beach, warning his grieving fiancée of the hurricane's approach and urging her to leave the island. She and her family fled the terrible storm and when they returned, their home was spared. That's one version of the legend of the "Gray Man" of Pawleys Island, perhaps South Carolina's most famous ghost story.

His shadowy figure is said to appear just before the arrival of hurricanes to serve as a warning to others. Some say he made appearances again in the late 1800s, and news reports suggest sightings occurred before Hurricane Hazel. Two days before Hugo's arrival, Jim and Clara Moore saw the ghostly figure walking the beach but were alarmed when it vanished before them. They told *Unsolved Mysteries* that they evacuated soon afterward and returned later to find their beach home surrounded by debris but mysteriously unharmed. More recently, the blurry image of another Gray Man sighting spread across social media in the days before Hurricane Florence.

Dramatic stories of survival are ready-made for hurricane storytelling. During the Great Asheville Flood of 1916, two young boys apparently climbed a tall tree on the banks of the Catawba River to watch the raging torrent below. As the swollen river surged, the tree unexpectedly collapsed into the river, carrying the boys with it as it raced downstream. Their cries could be heard from the banks as the boys clung desperately to the tree's branches. After several hours, the tree finally got hung up with other debris some four miles downstream. It wasn't until the following day that the two boys were rescued.

When fierce hurricane winds and floods destroy homes and other structures, anyone trapped inside is lucky to live to tell of their experience. When the hurricane of 1752 swept the North Carolina coast, rising water from the storm washed a small boy, about four years old, more than a mile across Onslow County's New River where he was found among storm debris. Barely able to speak after his frightening ordeal, he could say only one word—"Hadnot." The spot where he was found was subsequently named Hadnot Point and is part of present-day Camp Lejeune.

In the same region in September 1815, a powerful hurricane surprised coastal residents and made landfall near Swansboro. According to a report in the *Raleigh Minerva*, the storm caused great damage and loss of life in Onslow County. Mr. Nelson's home on Brown's Banks was swept away by storm surge, taking with it four of his children. Nelson and one of his sons survived by clinging to the wreck of their house as it carried them nearly ten miles to Stones Bay on the New River.

Along the Carolina coast, similar dramatic escapes have been reported from other hurricanes at Edisto Island, Sullivan's Island, Ocean Isle, Oak Island, Topsail Island, Oriental, Ocracoke, and Hatteras Island. Perhaps the best known is that of Connie and Jerry Helms, who floated on a mattress out of a second-story window as Hurricane Hazel surged over Long Beach (now Oak Island), North Carolina, in 1954. Pummeled by heavy rain and waves, they eventually reached the lee side of the island, where Jerry grabbed a tree branch and held on until the tides receded. For the fiftieth anniversary of Hazel, their ordeal was the subject of a 2004 episode of the Weather Channel's *Storm Stories*.

Also profiled on the Weather Channel program was the story told by John and Judy Hardison, who lost their Hatteras home during Hurricane Isabel in 2003. The couple narrowly escaped drowning when Isabel's tides buckled their home and knocked it off its foundation, tossing them into the raging surf. They managed to survive by clinging to a nearby tree, where they held on for over three hours as the storm blasted around them. One year after the storm, the Hardisons' home was nothing but a gravel lot—in preparation for selling their property, all traces of the former house were leveled, including the small tree that saved their lives.

During Hurricane Floyd, fast-rising water in several North Carolina communities crept into homes overnight, shocking residents and waking them from their sleep. Some first learned there was a problem when they awoke to realize their bedding was wet. In some places, the flooding was more than twelve feet deep, forcing residents to scramble to higher floors and attics. In Pinetops, fire chief Steve Buress led a team of first responders who used small boats to rescue dozens trapped in the Dodge City area. In *Faces from the Flood: Hurricane Floyd Remembered*, Buress recalled, "We were checking each house, yelling for them, and you could hear them inside. They would knock on the roofs . . . and hear somebody banging back. . . . We had to take chainsaws in and cut holes in the tops of houses. We had to cut through the shingles on the roof. Then we got them to crawl out the holes and get in the boat. . . . They were literally scared to death, and rightly so."

In nearby Rocky Mount, fire chief Ken Mullen had his hands full when 911 distress calls poured into the station the night Floyd's floodwaters struck the city. His crews responded to dozens of rescue calls, often motoring borrowed boats into neighborhoods swamped by several feet of water. In *Faces from the Flood*, he remembered one surprising sight:

> One story that sticks in my head was this little old lady, about seventy-some years old, that was going to swim out. The guys were

in a boat and saw her coming by. . . . They thought it was a dog. So, they reached down and grabbed her by the hair on her head and started pulling her up. She yelled something like "Let me go boy! I'm gonna swim out of here! Worry about those other people, I'm alright." She would duck under the water, swim about ten yards, come up for air, then she'd duck under again and swim some more. I guess she made it out just fine.

In the 1930s, the Civilian Conservation Corps built miles of large dunes on portions of the Outer Banks. The "sand walls" practically surrounded the town of Avon. When the Great Atlantic Hurricane of 1944 passed offshore, northwest winds pushed water from Pamlico Sound into the village, forming a deep pool. Cars and trucks were completely covered, and houses floated off their foundations, sometimes crashing into one another. One young girl, huddled in desperation with her family in a second-story hallway, became seasick as her home sloshed about in the wind and waves.

Longtime residents have handled flooding in creative ways. Some older structures on Ocracoke were built to cope with rising water. At the first signs of a flooding storm, residents would open their front doors and remove the corks from a series of holes drilled through the floor in the corners of each first-floor room. Allowing water to enter their homes equalized the pressure and kept the structures from floating off their foundations.

Occasionally, memorable hurricane events leave their mark on history. One such storm arrived in October 1837, a long-lived hurricane dubbed Racer's Storm that wandered from the Gulf of Mexico across Florida, into the Atlantic, and toward the Carolinas. On October 9 it swept the Outer Banks, sinking ships from Cape Fear to New England. Its greatest tragedy was the loss of the steamship *Home*. The 220-foot passenger ship, sailing from New York to Charleston, was touted as one of the finest packets ever built—an "elegantly constructed vessel." On the morning of the ninth, it heaved through the storm's heavy seas and began taking on water near Cape Hatteras. Its pumps could not keep up. Capt. Carleton White ordered the crew, and then passengers,

The steamship *Home* founders in a hurricane off the coast of Cape Hatteras in 1837. This region, notorious for its dangerous shoals, was dubbed the Graveyard of the Atlantic by fifteen-year-old Alexander Hamilton after he survived a treacherous voyage there in 1773.

including women and children, to join in the effort to bail water from the hold. Panic ensued as the waves grew increasingly large, intermittently lifting the ship's side paddle wheels out of the water. That afternoon the boilers flooded, and Captain White steered west, desperately hoping to beach the vessel before it went down. At 10:00 P.M. the *Home* finally struck a bar about six miles east of Ocracoke Village.

Two of the ship's three lifeboats were "dashed to pieces" even before they could be put to use. The third was lowered with fifteen passengers aboard but it promptly capsized. Over the next hours, in darkness and boiling seas, a chaotic sequence of passengers and crew abandoned the fractured *Home*, some grasping floating debris, others dropping out of sight. In *Graveyard of the Atlantic*, David Stick wrote of a rather "portly woman" who was tied to a settee (a long upholstered seat) and carried by waves to the shore, where she was pulled from the surf by local residents. There were only two life preservers aboard the ship, both taken by "able-bodied men." In the end, of the ship's 130 passengers and crew, only forty were saved—twenty passengers, nineteen crew, and Captain White.

Afterward, perhaps because of the number of prominent citizens lost to the disaster, Congress launched an investigation into the sinking of the *Home*, with intent to prosecute the surviving captain. It was finally determined to have been an "act of God," but there was one very important outcome from the inquiry that's still in force today: Congress ruled that going forward, every U.S. passenger ship must carry one life preserver for "each soul aboard."

Sometimes, a good story is just a good story. The hurricane of September 1876 made a direct hit on the North Carolina coast above Wilmington and was credited with bringing a minor miracle to Hyde County. It seems that in the town of Swan Quarter, earlier that spring, the local Methodists had decided to build a new church. After finding a choice location in the heart of town, the congregation was displeased to learn that the land's owner, Sam Sadler, wanted nothing to do with the Methodists and had no interest in selling his property to them. Even after church members increased their offer, Sadler refused to sell. Determined to move ahead with the project, the Methodists obtained an alternate piece of property on the edge of town, where that summer they erected a modest frame building. The congregation was satisfied, and their new church was dedicated on a blue-skied Sunday morning in mid-September—the same day a major hurricane was churning past Cuba on its way toward the Carolina coast.

As the hurricane approached and barometers started falling, local fishermen began moving their boats into sheltered creeks and packing away their gear. Once the storm spun over the state, winds drove high waters across Pamlico Sound and piled them on the shores of Hyde County. Swan Quarter was flooded with five feet of water. Homes and businesses were deluged and wrecked, and the town's fishing fleet was severely damaged. But despite all the destruction around them, the residents of Swan Quarter were most surprised by an apparent act of divine intervention.

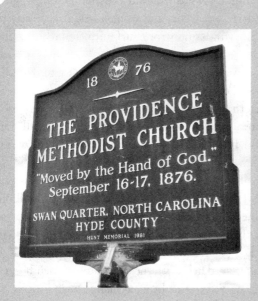

A historical marker in Swan Quarter reminds visitors of the movements of the Providence Methodist Church during the September 1876 hurricane.

During the storm, rising tides lifted the small frame church off its foundation and floated it toward the center of town. After the waters receded, residents were astonished to see that the little church had settled down squarely on Sam Sadler's land, just as the Methodists had originally planned. Sadler was also impressed: according to legend, he later signed a deed and gave his land to the church, and then he joined the congregation. Today, a historical marker stands in front of the Providence Church reminding visitors that it was "Moved by the Hand of God, September 16–17, 1876."

to prevent the tides from washing their houses "off the blocks." Many rode out the hurricane in their attics, and some were forced onto their rooftops.

At the Green Island Hunt Club at the eastern end of Ocracoke, nine people took refuge as the storm approached. The two-story clubhouse was rocked by pounding surf, and by midnight, "the ocean was breaking in the kitchen." As the first floor filled with water, the occupants gathered on the second floor, which also began to flood. Like so many other storm victims throughout the region, the group was forced to crawl through a high window onto the roof, where they rode out the storm. The structure pitched and rolled like a boat, and the constant up-and-down motion washed away the foundation, digging a deep hole in the sand. The frightened men and women held desperately to the rooftop through the gusting winds and strong surf until, at daybreak, the storm passed.

As the tides receded, the survivors climbed down off the clubhouse. To their amazement, the wave action had dug the house so far down that the second-floor windows were level with the ground. The fishermen were also surprised to see their boats cast upon a nearby beach. During the storm, these small craft were blown out into the sound, but when the hurricane passed and the winds shifted, they were blown right back, suffering little damage.

The September hurricane of 1933 left many scars on the North Carolina coast. In all, twenty-one were dead and damage estimates topped $4.5 million. The Red Cross identified a nine-county region with a population of 120,000 as the area of greatest suffering. Their survey indicated that 1,166 buildings had been totally destroyed and 7,244 severely damaged. The Red Cross gave aid to 1,281 families, many of whom received help with the rebuilding of their homes. This effort helped temper the anguish caused by what many Down East locals still revere as one of the "worst ever."

TAKEAWAYS

- *Landfall isn't necessary to produce devastating effects.* By definition, a hurricane makes landfall once the center of the storm reaches land. It's a critical moment that determines a lot about how severe the impact will be for surrounding locations. In the Carolinas, landfalling hurricanes sometimes pass inland, while others bump along the coast, briefly clipping the barrier beaches or crossing North Carolina's Outer Banks. The eye of the September 1933 hurricane came extremely close to landfall at Cape Hatteras but stayed fifteen miles offshore. The area around Buxton was inside the core of hurricane winds, and thus the storm was considered a direct hit but not a landfall. Category 4 Hurricane Helene in 1958 came within ten miles of the North Carolina coast but never made landfall; it still whipped up a 135 mph gust at the Wilmington airport, the highest on record for that location. The center of Hurricane Matthew in 2016 briefly made landfall in South Carolina but slipped past the Brunswick County beaches and never touched land in North Carolina—though it brought $5 billion in damages to the Tar Heel State. Large hurricanes, even those passing by the coast, can have broad reach—putting areas at risk hundreds of miles from the eye.

- *Wind-driven storm tides on sounds and bays are a particular threat in North Carolina.* When a hurricane strikes the coast, winds swirling around the eye create a vertical circulation in the ocean that lifts upward upon land-fall—the phenomenon known as storm surge. During intense hurricanes, this surge can be devastating, overwashing barrier beaches and destroying properties within its reach. In North Carolina, the state's unique geography presents an additional threat. The broad expanses of the Pamlico and Albemarle Sounds separate the Outer Banks from the mainland, and they're subject to great movements of water from continuous hurricane winds. As the September 1933 hurricane slowed and passed along the coast, intense winds swept these waters southwestward with deadly results. Flooding engulfed eastern Carteret County, Oriental, Ocracoke, and other points along the southern reaches of Pamlico Sound. Flooding extended up the Neuse and Pamlico Rivers, effectively blocking their flow and sending high waters into New Bern and other communities. Along the northern banks of the Albemarle Sound, the water was "blown away" to the lowest level ever recorded for that region. Similar wind-driven flooding struck during Florence in 2018, devastating New Bern.

- *Many of the Carolinas' most vulnerable coastal communities are naturally isolated.* Historically, most of the Carolinas' eastern counties have been sparsely populated, apart from coastal cities such as Charleston and Wilmington. Over time, this region grew in population, particularly those communities that attracted summer vacationers, anglers, and retirees. Today, beach towns such as Hilton Head, Folly Beach, Myrtle Beach, Wrightsville Beach, Emerald Isle, and Nags Head bustle with activity, especially during the summer tourist season. But thanks to some unique geography and the broad expanse of surrounding sounds and rivers, other coastal communities remain relatively isolated—and especially vulnerable to hurricanes. In North Carolina, Ocracoke and Hatteras Islands top that list, both prone to big storms and geographically remote in ways that pose special challenges for evacuations, infrastructure maintenance, and access during post-storm recovery. Communities on North Carolina's "Inner Banks" are also relatively remote. Places such as Cedar Island, Sea Level, Oriental, Hobucken, Bath, Belhaven, Swan Quarter, and Engelhard each have long histories with hurricanes and face unique challenges before and after each storm. Many places in South Carolina are similarly remote, especially those small communities scattered along rivers and bays across the Lowcountry.

CHAPTER EIGHT

HURRICANE HAZEL,
OCTOBER 1954

Throughout history, violent tropical cyclones have visited the Carolina coastline with great regularity, though with a randomness that makes it hard to know what to expect in any given year. Sometimes they've struck twice or even three times within a single season. Most often, however, years pass between major storms, allowing coastal residents time to recover and rebuild before the next hurricane. But during the 1950s, a flurry of storm activity exceeded expectations. Two Category 4 storms blasted South Carolina, and seven hurricanes struck North Carolina, with several more passing close by. Their combined effects were devastating. Included in this group was arguably the most infamous of all modern Carolina hurricanes, Hurricane Hazel.

In 1950, before Hazel's arrival, the U.S. Weather Bureau had begun naming hurricanes in the Atlantic, initially with a phonetic sequence common to the military (Able, Baker, Charlie, etc.). But in 1953, forecasters officially began using women's names for tropical storms, a practice begun by a few navy meteorologists in the Pacific during World War II. It didn't take long for the American public to become very familiar with some of these names.

As the 1954 season got underway, Hurricanes Carol and Edna gave coastal North Carolina residents a brief scare and a taste of nasty weather. Carol brought Category 1 winds to the Outer Banks and caused $250,000 in damages but went on to pound Long Island, New York, Connecticut, and Rhode Island as a major hurricane, claiming sixty lives. It caused over $460 million in damages, making it the costliest U.S. hurricane until that time. Hurricane Edna followed less than two weeks later, again tracking past the Carolinas well east of Cape Hatteras, though 70 mph gusts were observed on the Outer Banks. It followed Carol's path into New England, however, slamming some of the same areas devastated by the earlier storm and causing more than twenty fatalities. But the season wasn't over, and the eighth storm of 1954 took dead aim on the Carolinas, eventually becoming among the greatest natural disasters ever to affect either state.

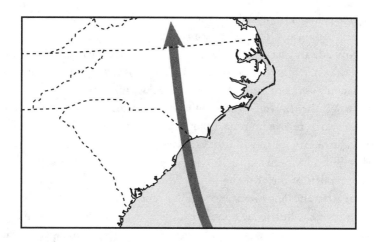

A young woman wades through the streets of Carolina Beach after the passing of Hurricane Hazel. (Photo courtesy of Hugh Morton.)

Hazel began as a trough of low pressure over the warm waters of the tropical western Atlantic. On October 5, 1954, the small storm was identified just east of Grenada and was observed on a west-northwest track that would take it through the Grenadines. Winds were clocked at 95 mph, and the small island of Carriacou was the first to suffer from Hazel's winds and tides.

At the Weather Bureau's Miami office, veteran chief forecaster Grady Norton was working twelve-hour days plotting Hazel's course. Tragically, Norton suffered a stroke on the morning of October 9 and died later the same day. The Weather Bureau scrambled to pick up where Norton had left off, following the daily reports of the growing storm. Although he had been warned by his doctor to avoid the long hours, Norton had ignored his medical condition out of concern for the hurricane's potential for destruction. Following his death, the bureau continued its work without pause. Norton's young assistant relayed timely warnings and later made urgent phone calls to coastal officials as the storm approached the Carolinas.

Hazel continued to draw energy from the warm Caribbean waters and intensified as it curved northward toward Haiti. During the early morning hours of October 12, the well-organized storm slammed into the Haitian coast, raking over both the southern and northern peninsulas. Haiti was devastated. Several small towns were "almost totally demolished," and larger cities such as Jérémie and Port-de-Paix suffered severe wind damage. Torrential rains fell over the island nation, flooding rivers, washing out roads and bridges, and filling homes and businesses with mud. Heavy rains caused a massive landslide that buried the mountain village of Berley, killing almost all of its 260 residents. Extreme winds of 125 mph were reported from several Haitian cities. Tides reached record levels on the southern peninsula, and surge flooding was "the highest in memory." It was estimated that as many as 1,000 Haitians died in the storm.

As Hazel moved through the Windward Passage on the morning of October 13, its strength diminished greatly, the result of a distortion of the hurricane as it passed over the mountainous Haitian terrain. But Hazel rapidly regained intensity and form over the next few hours. After passing the Bahamas it was again a major cyclone. At 11:00 A.M. on the fourteenth, the Weather Bureau hoisted warnings from Charleston to the Virginia capes.

The eye of the hurricane passed about ninety-five miles east of Charleston at 8:00 A.M. on October 15. About this same time, the outer fringes of the storm first touched the U.S. coastline in the vicinity of Folly Beach. Finally, between 9:30 and 10:00 A.M., Hazel's ominous eye swept inland near North Myrtle Beach and just below the North Carolina–South Carolina border. It was there, and in areas just to the north and east, that its most awesome forces were unleashed, although the destruction continued as the hurricane barreled inland.

The National Oceanic and Atmospheric Administration's reanalysis team reviewed the available weather data and concluded that Hazel was indeed a Category 4 when it struck—the northernmost known landfall on the Atlantic coast for any hurricane of that intensity. Capt. Leroy Kinlaw was aboard the fishing boat *Judy Ninda* at Tilghman Point on Little River when Hazel's eye passed overhead about 10:30 A.M. He reported the passage took only thirty minutes and brought on a period of light winds and no rain but no sunshine either. There he observed the lowest barometric pressure reading in the storm, 938 millibars (mb).

The storm surge that Hazel delivered to the beaches in this region was, at the time, the greatest in the Carolinas' recorded history. The tide reached eighteen feet above mean low water at Calabash. Hazel's surge was made worse by a matter of bad timing—it struck at the exact time of the highest lunar tide of the year, during the full moon in October. Local hunters often refer to this as the "marsh hen tide," a time when high waters tend to flush waterfowl out of the protective cover of the marsh grass. Hazel's storm tide was boosted considerably by the unfortunate timing of its approach.

The coastal region where Hazel made landfall was also battered by some of the most destructive winds in Carolina history. Estimates of 150 mph extremes were reported from several locations, including Holden Beach, Calabash, and Little River Inlet. Gusts of 106 and 98 mph were measured in Myrtle Beach and Wilmington, respectively, but winds were estimated at up to 125 mph at Wrightsville Beach and 140 mph on Oak Island. As Hazel swept inland, its winds endured with freakish intensity. Grannis Field in Fayetteville reported gusts of 110 mph, and estimates of 120 mph gusts were made by observers in Goldsboro, Kinston, and Faison. Many anemometers were destroyed along the way. The wind-speed dial at the Raleigh-Durham Airport was watched closely during the storm, and gusts to 90 mph were recorded around 1:30 P.M., though that location was on the weaker, western side of the storm's track. Most incredibly, wind gusts near 100 mph were reported from numerous locations in Virginia, Maryland, Pennsylvania, Delaware, New Jersey, and New York as Hazel tracked through the Northeast on its way to Canada. Many of Hazel's wind-speed records remain unbroken, including a 113 mph gust at Battery Park in New York City, the highest ever reported for that location.

Hazel's violent winds hacked or toppled countless trees across northeastern South Carolina and eastern North Carolina. In the aftermath of the storm, some sections of highway were littered with "hundreds of trees per mile." Some

For those who remember it, Hurricane Hazel remains a benchmark storm for North Carolina. It is the only Category 4 hurricane known to strike the state since record keeping began
in the mid-nineteenth century. The damages at Carolina Beach were extensive, as seen in this
photograph. (Photo courtesy of the Cape Fear Museum of History and Science, Wilmington,
North Carolina.)

were uprooted and tossed about, and others were snapped off ten to twenty feet
above the ground. In Raleigh, it was reported that an average of two or three
trees per block fell. Many landed on cars, homes, and other structures, and
power lines were left tangled and broken. Dozens of other cities and towns,
especially those on the eastern side of the storm track, faced similar losses.

Effects of the hurricane as it moved inland were remarkable. According to a
report from the U.S. Weather Bureau:

Forests of pine and other trees appeared to be scorched by fire. All trees
and plants along the coast appeared to have been burned. Groves of pecan
trees were heavily damaged. Building destruction is said to have been
greater in the interior sections of North Carolina than at inland points
near the coast. From all indications, the hurricane did not decrease in

intensity as it moved into the interior. . . . Inland, out of reach of the rising waters, a tremendous area of North Carolina received heavy damage
from high winds. An estimated one-third of all buildings east of the 80th
parallel received some damage. Roofs and television aerials were the most
widely hit but some radio towers, outdoor theaters, and many signboards
were counted among the losses.

Heavy rains fell from northeastern South Carolina to central North Carolina and Virginia. The areas that recorded the greatest rainfall amounts were
all on the western side of the storm track, and many eastern locations received
as little as one inch. At least ten weather stations in North Carolina established
new twenty-four-hour records for rainfall. These records included more than
six inches in Burlington, High Point, and Lexington and 9.72 inches in Carthage, located in the Sandhills area of the state. A U.S. Geological Survey rain
gage at Robbins, several miles north of Carthage, measured 11.25 inches. Several
locations in northern Virginia recorded more than ten inches, and new rainfall
records were established all along Hazel's northern course.

Although Hazel's greatest destruction occurred in the Carolinas, its inland
track through the mid-Atlantic and northern states was unexpectedly intense.
After passing between Goldsboro and Raleigh at about 1:30 P.M. on October 15,
the storm tracked through Warren County and into Virginia at about 2:30 that
afternoon. At that time, the storm's barometric pressure had only risen to 965
mb, up slightly from its recorded low in Little River earlier that day.

Hazel was a fast-moving storm when it arrived on the coast, with a forward
speed of more than 20 mph. It accelerated rapidly as it passed through Virginia, attaining a forward speed of more than 50 mph. Within four hours, the
hurricane had passed over the state, dumping torrential rains and unleashing
winds gusting to 100 mph. The storm center passed just west of Richmond, yet
winds there were some 30 mph less than in Norfolk, which was on the eastern
edge of the storm.

Damages in Virginia were extensive from both winds and tides. Several
ships in the James River were either sunk or wrecked, including the battleship
Kentucky, which broke its moorings and ran aground some 1,000 feet from its
berth. In all, thirteen Virginians were killed during Hazel, and damages in the
state were conservatively estimated at $15 million.

Power failures were commonplace as the storm churned its way through
Maryland, the District of Columbia, and Pennsylvania. Wind gusts of 98 mph
were reported in Washington, D.C., at 5:07 P.M., and strong winds brought
down trees, power lines, and radio towers throughout the region. Winds in

Baltimore reached 84 mph, and a six-foot tide flooded streets and basements near Baltimore harbor. Wilmington, Delaware, reported gusts to 98 mph, and Philadelphia recorded gusts to 94 mph. Property damages mounted as Hazel sped relentlessly to the north.

As heavy rains poured across western Pennsylvania, flash floods swept away cars and homes, and twenty-six lives were lost. The death toll throughout Hazel's northern course was already high, as twenty-two had perished in Virginia, Maryland, Delaware, and the District of Columbia. Then, as the storm raced through western New York State, more tragedies occurred. There, twenty-one deaths were attributed to the hurricane, of which five were caused by falling objects, five by electric shock, four by automobile accidents, three by falls, and four by other causes.

Very few hurricanes in U.S. history have maintained their vigor the way Hazel did as it blasted through the interior sections of the northeastern states. As the storm passed through the western counties of New York, gusting winds near 100 mph continued to uproot trees, peel back roofs, and snarl power lines. Then, at approximately 10:00 P.M., just twelve hours after landfall on the Carolina coast, Hazel joined forces with a weak low-pressure system near Buffalo. Extremely heavy rain fell on numerous communities in western New York, and some city streets were flooded by almost two feet of water. Many highways and bridges were washed out, and the effects of wind and water once again intensified.

As Hazel crossed Lake Ontario, it carried its rampage into Canada. Several locations reported wind gusts near 100 mph. More than seven inches of rain turned the Humber River, which flows along the western edge of Toronto, into a torrent, washing away homes and automobiles. Scores of victims were trapped in the flash flood that swept through the Toronto area. Here, the destruction continued, as eighty-one more lives were lost and property damages were estimated at $100 million. Five firefighters drowned during a failed rescue attempt in the raging flash flood. Perhaps the greatest tragedy occurred on Toronto's Raymore Drive, where an entire neighborhood of homes was swept away by a wall of water from the Humber River. With no warning, thirty-two drowned when floodwaters struck while they slept. To this day, and especially in the Toronto area, Hazel is remembered as the greatest flood disaster in Canadian history.

Hazel was last seen crossing the Arctic Circle on its way to Scandinavia, where it eventually fell apart. This incredible hurricane had not lost its momentum and had not faded as many storms do when they move overland. Instead,

Hazel's destruction was spread over 2,000 miles on its northward trek from the Caribbean through North America.

On the North and South Carolina beaches near landfall, and in inland areas along its path, the destruction left by Hazel was likened to that of the battlefields of Europe after World War II. Evidence of the storm's violent winds stretched for miles upstate, leaving residents with the task of cleaning up virtually every city street and country road from Horry County, South Carolina, to the Virginia line and beyond.

When Hazel made landfall near the North Carolina–South Carolina border, its storm surge and intense winds reached their peak. At Myrtle Beach, hurricane-force winds began around 6:00 A.M. and continued to intensify until the eye reached the coast at 9:20 A.M. The South Carolina beaches were battered by northeast winds estimated at 130 mph and waves that crested at thirty feet. Hardest hit were locations near the point of landfall, which included Garden City, Myrtle Beach, North Myrtle Beach, Windy Hill, Cherry Grove, and Ocean Drive. Throughout this stretch of coastline, storm-surge levels ranged between fourteen and seventeen feet above mean low water. Although the destruction in South Carolina was greatest on the northern beaches, homes and piers were damaged as far south as Georgetown.

Hazel's mid-October arrival was in some ways a blessing, in that many cottages and businesses were empty. Most of the Myrtle Beach area's seaside attractions had been shut down for the season, the majority of beach shops and tourist businesses had closed, and most beach cottages were not rented.

Among the hardest-hit communities was Garden City, just south of Myrtle Beach. After the storm, only three homes there remained livable; 272 were heavily damaged or simply "missing"—swept off their foundations by the fourteen-foot surge and carried into the nearby marsh. In Myrtle Beach, Red Cross officials estimated that 80 percent of the front-row structures were destroyed. The fifteen-foot surge undermined many buildings, often reducing three-story structures to two. Among the casualties were the storied Patricia Manor hotel, the Gay Dolphin Park, and the USO Recreation Center on Ocean Boulevard South. Every fishing pier along the strand was either heavily damaged or destroyed, including the Garden City Pier, Surfside Pier, Myrtle Beach State Park Pier, Second Avenue Pier, Ocean Plaza Pier, Windy Hill Pier, Tilghman Pier, and Cherry Grove Pier. Most were rebuilt and ready for fishing the following year.

Cherry Grove saw some of the state's heaviest damage. After the storm, more than thirty homes had to be removed from the town's streets. All homes on

Residents of the Carolina coast faced the recurring ordeal of hurricanes for an extended period during the 1950s. (Photo courtesy of the News and Observer Publishing Company / North Carolina Division of Archives and History, Raleigh.)

Atlantic Beach, South Carolina, nicknamed the Black Pearl, is a unique and historic community just north of Myrtle Beach. Settled in the 1930s by African Americans, the oceanfront town became a popular vacation destination for Black families. As it did other communities in the region, Hazel pounded the oceanfront here too, including the Hotel Gordon, along with its adjacent dining hall. (Photo courtesy of Alice Graham, AfroFest Collection.)

the eastern end, known as East Cherry Grove, went missing when the surge covered the community and carved a new inlet where the causeway had been. It was also the scene of the state's only fatality—Leonard Watts apparently drowned near his cottage.

At Crescent Beach, nineteen homes were washed into the streets and had to be removed; 150 were damaged heavily and demolished. The popular Ocean Strand Hotel was destroyed when the surge washed through the first floor, collapsing the structure onto the beach. The hotel's furniture and bedding washed into the ocean and filled surrounding streets.

The night before the storm arrived, Ocean Drive police chief Merlin Bellamy was off duty, grilling steaks with friends at home when he got a phone call about 10:30 P.M. The call was from a forecaster in Charleston who wanted to know if he was prepared for the approaching hurricane. "I was like everyone else, I knew there was a storm that was supposed to pass offshore, but I had no

During the 1950s, the Grand Strand was home to several popular dance pavilions, including Robert's Pavilion on Ocean Drive. Hazel's pounding surf tore the structure apart. Following the storm, a new Ocean Drive Pavilion was built on the former site of the old Robert's, using many of the original structure's timbers. (Photo from the *State* Newspaper Photograph Archive. Courtesy of the Richland Library, Columbia, South Carolina.)

idea it was going to land in our town," Bellamy remembered. He scrambled to get evacuations underway, working into the night to urge residents to leave their homes for a nearby shelter. Many had no transportation, so he loaded them in his squad car and moved them to safety. Into the night he made multiple trips, each time wondering if he'd make it back over the bridge to the island. Though Ocean Drive was near the point of landfall, no casualties were reported in the town thanks to Bellamy's efforts.

Across the border in North Carolina, the south-facing beaches of Brunswick County caught the brunt of Hazel's fury. Sunset Beach, Ocean Isle, Holden Beach, and Long Beach (known today as Oak Island) were hardest hit; virtually every home or structure was washed away or severely damaged. In most cases, oceanfront cottages were first battered by waves and 140 mph winds, then swept off their foundations and tossed several hundred yards into marsh thickets. Fortunately, as was the case in Myrtle Beach, most of the homes were empty. Those few unlucky souls who were caught in Hazel's rapidly rising storm tide either rode out the upheaval of their homes or perished in the ordeal.

Though Hazel's winds were extreme, Myrtle Beach's first- and second-row cottages suffered most from the hurricane's massive storm tide and pounding waves. (Photo from the *State* Newspaper Photograph Archive. Courtesy of the Richland Library, Columbia, South Carolina.)

After surveying the Brunswick beaches in the aftermath of Hazel, the U.S. Weather Bureau office in Raleigh issued the following report:

All traces of civilization on that portion of the immediate waterfront between the state line and Cape Fear were practically annihilated. Grass-covered dunes some 10 to 20 feet high along and behind which beach homes had been built in a continuous line 5 miles long simply disappeared, dunes, houses, and all. The paved roadway along which the houses were built was partially washed away, partially buried beneath several feet of sand. The greater part of the material from which the houses had been built was washed from one to two hundred yards back into the edge of low-lying woods which cover the leeward side of the islands. Some of this material is identifiable as having been parts of houses, but the greater portion of it is ground to unrecognizable splinters and bits of masonry. Of the 357 buildings which existed on Long Beach, 352 were totally destroyed and the other five damaged. Similar conditions prevail on Holden Beach, Ocean Isle, Robinson Beach, and Colonial Beach. In most cases it is impossible to tell where the buildings stood. Where grassy dunes once stood there is now only flat, white, sandy beach.

The *State Port Pilot* reported the story of two survivors who endured the worst of the storm: Connie and Jerry Helms. The young couple had come to Long Beach for their honeymoon and were out roller-skating the night before Hazel struck. The Coast Guard warned other residents of the hurricane's approach, but the newlyweds arrived back at the beach too late to hear the warnings. They went to bed with no knowledge of the ominous storm poised off the coast.

At dawn the next morning, the Helmses awoke to the sound of pounding surf and chairs blowing about their porch. Huge waves began crashing over the dunes as the couple scrambled to leave their cottage. With no time to even pack their clothes, they jumped into their car, but amid the rising water it wouldn't start. They ran to their jeep, but it wouldn't start either. By this time, the surging ocean water was waist deep in the street, and they knew it was becoming deeper and rougher by the minute. They made their way to a nearby two-story house and broke through a door to get inside. As the tides continued to rise, the second floor buckled, and the couple feared they might perish if the house collapsed.

"We started seeing houses exploding then floating away," Jerry Helms recalled. "Sometimes you could see the whole house flying through the air. There was a little cinderblock house next door, and a breaker went over top of the house, and after it went over it was gone. Stoves, refrigerators, and houses were flying through the air. Before we got out of the house we were in, we saw a guy standing in the doorway of another house floating by. He was found the next day buried in the sand."

The couple watched as the entire island went underwater and every house within sight was swept away or pounded to splinters by massive waves. Large timbers, roof sections, and appliances of every kind whisked past the cottage where they had taken refuge. Then, as the water swirled just inches below the second-story windows, the Helmses knew that their shelter was about to give in to the storm. Tying themselves together with a flannel blanket, the newlyweds escaped the collapsing house through a high window. Connie Helms, who could not swim, climbed onto a cotton mattress while her husband jumped into the raging waters.

"We went right out to sea on that mattress," Jerry recalled. "By that time, all the two-story houses were covered by water, and most of the other stuff was already gone. But we never had a chance to think about what was happening or be scared. We were just trying to hold on to that blanket and stay alive."

The currents did not take the couple out to sea but instead carried them toward the leeward side of the island. To stabilize their makeshift life raft, Jerry grabbed a section of a house that drifted by and positioned their mattress on top of it. A short time later, their raft became lodged in some treetops near Davis Creek. There the couple endured the storm for several more hours.

"It got real calm when the eye passed over, and then it started raining real hard. It felt like little bullets," Jerry recalled. "There was a lot of times we thought we were gone. The only thing that saved us was the good Lord and that blanket."

When the winds subsided and the floodwaters receded, the Helmses climbed down from the treetops. They then made their way across Davis Canal, still clutching the blanket that had helped save their lives. The couple later found their way to Southport, where they visited Dosher Memorial Hospital for treatment. Later that night they went back to their home in Whiteville.

The following day, Jerry returned to Long Beach with his father-in-law to search for the remains of the car, the jeep, and the cottage. When they arrived on the beach they were disoriented—homes, streets, telephone poles, and other points of reference were gone. But eventually they found both vehicles buried deep in the sand, and the only remaining fragment of the house was one corner, held in place by a single post. About a mile up the beach, they found their refrigerator, still intact, with its door sealed. "The drinks in the refrigerator were still cold and the only thing broken was a bowl of peas, so we sat down and ate lunch out of it," Jerry said. The honeymoon was over for the Helmses, but their incredible struggle for survival was not soon forgotten. In 2004, at the time of Hazel's fiftieth anniversary, Connie and Jerry retold their story for the Weather Channel's *Storm Stories* series.

Several miles west of Long Beach, the resort of Ocean Isle was the scene of the single greatest tragedy Hazel brought to the Carolinas. The beach was connected to the mainland by a small ferry that was destroyed in the early stages of the storm. The only people on the island were store owner Sherman Register, his wife and two children, and another family from High Point who were there celebrating the purchase of a new beach house. Given no means of escape, the group of eleven gathered in one of the island's higher buildings. As the winds and waves increased, the building began to crumble, forcing the group to swim through the breakers to a nearby truck. They managed to drive the truck onto Halfway Hill, the highest point on the island. With the women and children inside, the men tried in vain to keep the vehicle upright as the tides continued to rise. Tragically, their efforts were no match for Hazel's fury, and the truck was soon washed away. Of the eleven, only two survived. One of the survivors was the Registers' teenage daughter Sonja, who was swept off the truck and into the forest on the other side of the Intracoastal Waterway. According to reports in the Wilmington *Star-News*, "Sonja was unconscious when she was found. . . . She was brown-looking, almost gone." Thirty-three cottages that had stood on Ocean Isle were completely destroyed. Only two houses remained, and they were washed almost one mile across the island into the marsh.

In Southport, Hazel's storm tide forced ocean water through the mouth of the Cape Fear River, flooding the waterfront streets with a surge of eight feet. All twenty of the town's shrimp houses and fuel docks were destroyed. Restaurants along the river and several warehouses were demolished. The storm tide lifted thirty-five-ton shrimp trawlers over their docks and swept them into town, where they crushed cars and homes along the way. Along Bay Street, majestic old oak trees were toppled by winds that gusted to 130 mph. For several blocks near the waterfront, large piles of debris choked the town's streets.

Lewis Hardee owned two trawlers and a shrimp-packing house on the Southport waterfront. As the storm reached its peak, his boats floated over the docks and his shrimp house was destroyed. Like many others in the small town, Hardee made his living on the water. "Back then, nobody had insurance on boats in Southport," Hardee recalled. "Things were a mess. Boats were scattered all in the marsh from the Intracoastal [Waterway] to the Coast Guard Station. We all had a warning, but nobody knew it would be like it was."

Hardee had just rebuilt his shrimp house and dock the summer before Hazel arrived and tore them apart. A fire the previous year had damaged the old structures, and his new pier and house had been built with costly cypress decking. Hazel's powerful winds and waves broke them to pieces and scattered their timbers along the shore. "After the storm, I took a carpenter's crayon and went along the waterfront and put my name on every board," Hardee remembers. "You know they weren't hardly seasoned, they were new lumber, just a year old. All two-inch cypress decking. With that lumber I built another new fish house down at the yacht basin."

After Hazel passed, the fishermen of Southport faced the challenge of removing their large trawlers from high ground, repairing their damaged hulls, and returning them to the water. Fortunately, a contractor at the nearby ammunition facility at Sunny Point offered some help. A crew from Diamond

A local woman climbs through debris surrounding the remains of Harrelson's Grocery on the riverfront in Southport after Hurricane Hazel. (Photo by Art Newton. Courtesy of Punk Spencer.)

At Southport, Hazel's storm tide lifted thirty-five-ton shrimp trawlers over their docks and into the streets. (Photo by Art Newton. Courtesy of the *State Port Pilot*.)

Construction Company brought in an eighty-five-foot crane that lifted the large boats from the streets and yards of Southport and placed them back in the water. This task took several days, but the residents and fishermen of this storm-ravaged town were grateful for the help.

Farther upriver in Wilmington, flooding in the Cape Fear reached its highest level in recorded history, 8.15 feet above mean lower low water (this record was later eclipsed during Matthew, Florence, and Isaias). Floodwaters damaged numerous warehouses along the waterfront, and dozens of cars were submerged by the rising water. Overall damage to the city was not extensive and was limited mostly to broken storefront windows and uprooted trees. High winds snapped telephone poles in several locations, leaving more than half the area's residents without any means of communication. Wilmington was without electricity for three days. Two thousand residents were sheltered in twenty Red Cross evacuation centers around the city.

The Wilmington Reserve Fleet in the Brunswick River basin suffered about $1 million in damage from the storm. Several of the large ships broke their mooring lines when high winds "snapped cable an inch and five-eighths in diameter like it was ribbon," according to the Wilmington *Star-News*. Three Liberty ships drifted upriver with the winds and threatened to wreck the Brunswick River bridge. At the peak of the storm, a tugboat captain used his vessel to stop the ships just 100 yards from the bridge. His courageous efforts saved the concrete span that provided the only link between Brunswick and New Hanover Counties.

Carolina Beach was hit hard by Hazel, largely because the popular resort found itself in the hurricane's powerful northeast section. Property damage there totaled $17 million, much more than in any other single coastal community. The heaviest damages occurred along the oceanfront, where the storm's tidal surge bashed homes and the downtown amusement area. In all, 362 buildings were completely destroyed and another 288 suffered major damage.

A number of residents stayed on Carolina Beach through the hurricane and witnessed Hazel's wrath on their town. They saw large waves roll through Mack's five-and-ten store and watched as the steel pier collapsed and sank. Dozens of houses floated off their foundations and "crashed together like bumper cars." One man was crouched in his living room when a surging wave heaved an eight-by-eight-inch timber through four walls of his home. After the hurricane passed, the giant piece of lumber had to be cut into four pieces to be removed.

According to a story by Susan Gerdes that appeared in the *Tidewater*, eighty-year-old Alex McEachern refused to leave his Carolina Beach home upon Hazel's approach. To escape the rising waters, he and his dog climbed atop a freezer

The destructive forces of Hurricane Hazel's storm tide are evident in this image of the Breakers Hotel at Wilmington Beach. (Photo courtesy of the North Carolina Division of Archives and History, Raleigh.)

in his pantry to ride out the storm. Miraculously, even though McEachern's house was torn apart by the wind and waves, the pantry was unharmed; in fact, it was the only room left standing. After the storm subsided, the lucky twosome climbed down from their refuge and found their way into town.

During the early part of the storm, emergency workers used the Carolina Beach Town Hall auditorium as disaster headquarters. But as the floodwaters rose, town officials packed up their equipment and important documents and retreated to the China Cafe, which stood on slightly higher ground. Ultimately, fourteen blocks of the town were underwater. One house caught fire during the storm, but firefighters were unable to reach it because of the flood. As officials looked on, the residence burned down to the waterline, which was about four feet above the ground.

Up the coast at Wrightsville Beach, mayor Michael Brown and police chief Everett Williamson scrambled to coordinate last-minute evacuations of the island. Though Wrightsville was flooded, including the police station, no lives were lost on the island. Hazel's storm surge covered Lumina Avenue and put several feet of water inside businesses such as the King Neptune Restaurant and Roberts Grocery. After the storm, the entire front row of beach homes was missing. Estimated at twelve feet above mean low water, the tide swept over the island, destroying eighty-nine buildings and severely damaging another 155. Property damages were estimated at $7 million, including severe destruction to the town's sewage plant.

When Hazel struck the Wilmington area, only twelve state troopers were on duty, but additional support was brought in quickly. By the following day, fifty troopers from as far away as Asheville had come to assist local police with the round-the-clock task of maintaining checkpoints, directing traffic, and assisting those in need. Numerous accounts of heroic rescues were compiled after the storm, including several rescues made on foot in chest-deep water. Many local officers were said to have faithfully maintained their duties while their own homes were damaged in the storm.

Checkpoints were set up in key locations to prevent immediate access to the hard-hit barrier islands. Thousands of eager sightseers traveled to the coast to witness the destruction, but most were turned away. Looting was a severe problem, and on some beaches, the National Guard was brought in to assist the police with protecting property. According to local news reports, some looters launched small boats and even swam across the waterways to evade police and made off with radios, stoves, refrigerators, and cash.

Even along the coastline north of Wrightsville there was considerable destruction. At Topsail Beach, 210 of the 230 houses were destroyed and property damages were estimated at $2.5 million. The Topsail Island drawbridge was "carried away" by Hazel's furious winds and tides, and a Marine Corps amphibious vehicle was the only means of transport to the island for days. Sneads Ferry and Swansboro suffered from extreme high tides, which deposited fishing boats and pleasure craft high and dry in streets and backyards.

In Carteret County, 120 miles north of where Hazel made landfall, residents witnessed the worst hurricane since the storm of 1933. Hundreds of citizens took refuge in the Morehead City Town Hall and the county courthouse in Beaufort. Damage was extensive in several locations near the water, including Atlantic Beach and the causeway that joins Morehead City and Beaufort. Property damages were reported at $2 million, but fortunately there were no reports of deaths or serious injuries. Thirty-five homes were destroyed, and scores more suffered minor damage.

In Atlantic Beach, Hazel's storm surge pounded the boardwalk area to rubble. Twenty-foot waves washed away a section of the Atlantic Beach Hotel. At the other end of the boardwalk, waves washed through the lobby of the Ocean King Hotel, undermining the structure. The Triple S Pier was battered by the surf, and its tackle shop was badly damaged. After the storm, only 200 of the pier's 1,000 feet remained. The old beach highway that connected Salter Path and Emerald Isle was swept away in two places. In these areas, Bogue Sound connected with the ocean but only briefly, until heavy equipment was brought in to fill in the overwash.

In Morehead City, a fish house, dwelling, and skating rink were washed from their foundations. Large glass windows were smashed and trees were toppled by winds that gusted to near 100 mph. At the peak of the storm, surging waters flooded the basement of the Morehead City hospital. For hours, fire trucks pumped the water out so that basement facilities could continue to be used. Nurses in the basement worked with water up to their knees, scrambling to remove patients and save equipment.

Tony Seamon of Morehead City witnessed the effect Hazel had on the county. He and his father ventured downtown during the storm. "Daddy wanted to check on the restaurant," Seamon recalled, referring to the Sanitary Restaurant, which he owned on the Morehead waterfront. "We drove down Twentieth Street and the wind whipped the water across the road. We came to the old wooden picket bridge and it was submerged. The only way we could drive through that water was to open both car doors and let the water come on through."

As they reached downtown Morehead, Seamon's dad asked him to investigate the damage to the restaurant. "He told me, 'You got to get out and look inside,'" Seamon remembered. After one failed attempt to wade through the waist-deep water, he tried again to make it to the restaurant. "The current through the street was like a river. I eventually went under swimming to avoid the wind. When I got to the restaurant, I could look through the door and see all the tables and chairs floating around. Daddy had made the decision to cut holes in the floor to equalize the pressure. At least the whole place didn't float away."

After the hurricane passed, the Sanitary Restaurant was cleaned up and put into service as a feeding center. The Red Cross set up generators to provide power, food was brought in, and coupons were issued for meals. Work crews involved in cleanup efforts were fed around the clock until power was restored to the area and things returned to normal.

Other portions of Carteret County were hit hard by the storm. Several homes along the Morehead-Beaufort Causeway were totally wrecked, and their debris was piled high in the middle of Highway 70. Huge waves rolled across the causeway for hours, washing away homes and depositing small skiffs and one large cruiser in the roadway. Several cars were abandoned by their owners

Front Street in Beaufort, North Carolina, was under several feet of water during Hurricane Hazel, even though the center of the storm passed more than 100 miles west. At its peak, the tide nearly covered the parking meters shown here. (Photo courtesy of the *Carteret County News-Times*.)

on the east side of the Beaufort bridge when the unwary motorists became trapped by the hurricane's surging tide. The cars choked when water completely covered their engines, and the drivers were forced to wade through the tide to safety.

In Beaufort, the downtown businesses along Front Street suffered heavy losses. Every store was flooded with seawater, which covered the entire street to a depth of three feet. Gusting winds caused plate-glass windows in numerous stores to shatter, resulting in even greater damage from wind-driven rain. City Appliance Company, Bell's Drug Store, and Merrill's Men's Store were among the hardest hit. Numerous small boats were washed into the streets, and at least four cabin cruisers sank in Taylor's Creek. The highest water in Beaufort occurred at 11:15 A.M., when the barometer fell to its low point (for Carteret County) of 984 mb. The tides in Morehead reached their peak an hour later, around noon.

Across the county, Hazel battered homes, boats, and utilities. Many roofs that had just been reshingled after Hurricane Edna were stripped again by gusts of 90 to 100 mph. Power lines and poles were tangled, and communications were cut. A section of the North River Bridge was washed away, but thanks to rapid work by state highway crews, the bridge was repaired just five days after the storm.

Although the Pamlico and Albemarle Sound region was far from Hazel's center as the storm tracked through the state, many communities throughout the area suffered serious flooding. The Outer Banks north of Ocracoke were not severely affected, but cities such as Washington and Belhaven saw extensive damage from wind-driven tides. New Bern, Edenton, and Elizabeth City also reported flooding. Across a wide portion of inland North Carolina, far from the effects of the tides, Hazel's powerful winds brought significant destruction to more than two dozen counties.

Although most of Hazel's fatalities in North Carolina occurred along the beaches of Brunswick County, several deaths resulted from the harrowing winds that raced across the state. In Wallace, Hussey's Tobacco Warehouse collapsed, crushing Warsaw resident Bill Taylor underneath the rubble. In Parkton, a one-month-old infant was killed when a large tree fell on her home. The child's mother was seriously injured, as she had been lying next to her daughter in bed when the massive tree came crashing down. Though at least eighteen injured people were taken to the Goldsboro hospital, there was only one fatality in Wayne County. Wesley Wooten, a Pikeville farmer, was killed after a large tree crashed through his home. He was rushed to the hospital during the eye of the storm, and because the power was out, doctors operated on him by flashlight. He died later that night. Other deaths occurred as a result of electrocution, falls, and automobile accidents. Across North Carolina, hospital emergency rooms were filled with victims of the storm. At least 200 injuries were reported, some serious, in the six hours Hazel visited the state.

By most accounts, it was the most destructive hurricane in Tar Heel history. In North Carolina nineteen people were killed; 15,000 homes and structures were destroyed; 39,000 structures were damaged; thirty counties had major damage; and the storm brought an estimated $136 million in property losses. In South Carolina, Hazel left one dead, more than a dozen injured, and $27 million in damages. But when the hurricane's effects in the Carolinas are combined with those of other states, as well as with those of Grenada, Haiti, and Canada, the numbers climb: ninety-five deaths in the United States and as many as 1,200 deaths overall, with an estimated $350 million in property damages.

Winds from Hurricane Hazel likely gusted above 150 mph in Brunswick County and continued at hurricane force as the storm sped inland. Wind damage was heavy in thirty North Carolina counties, and gusts near 100 mph were reported in several states, including Virginia, Delaware, New Jersey, and New York. (Photo courtesy of the News and Observer Publishing Company / North Carolina Division of Archives and History, Raleigh.)

This memorable hurricane became a benchmark in the lives of many Carolinians who endured the storm. From Horry County to Henderson and everywhere in between, any time the topic of hurricanes is raised, stories about Hazel often follow. Hazel ranks as one of the most destructive hurricanes to strike the United States in the twentieth century. Fortunately, in the Carolinas, storms of its magnitude are relatively rare events, and few have matched its fury.

———

We have looked for your house on the beach but never did find it and believe that it may no longer exist. If we have the site located correctly the house must be completely gone.—From an insurance claims adjuster's letter to a homeowner following Hurricane Hazel, in *Hurricanes and the Middle Atlantic States* by Rick Schwartz

Miles from the coast, this eastern North Carolina automobile dealership lost its sign to Hurricane Hazel's winds when the storm swept inland.

For days and weeks after the storm, Carolina Power and Light workers were busy replacing downed power lines and snapped utility poles along Hurricane Hazel's path. (Photo courtesy of the North Carolina Division of Archives and History, Raleigh.)

TAKEAWAYS

- *Lunar tide cycles have a big influence on the severity of hurricane storm tides.* Hurricane Hazel happened to arrive on the South Carolina coast at a particularly bad time. It came ashore on a full moon high tide, just after the moon reached its perigee—the time of the month when the moon passes closest to Earth. This alignment yielded the highest lunar tide of the year—the worst possible time for a hurricane to strike. The moon's gravitational pull likely raised Hazel's tidal surge by almost three feet, boosting its destructive impact. Hurricane Gracie, another Category 4 that struck a bit farther south just a few years later, happened to hit at "dead low tide," lessening its storm tide and reducing resulting damages. Nevertheless, tides at Edisto Beach still measured twelve feet above mean low water. Coastal residents should look for this possible alignment when a hurricane approaches their location.
- *Beware the hurricane's right-front quadrant.* In the Northern Hemisphere, tropical cyclones spin counterclockwise. Hurricanes striking the Carolinas typically approach from the south, southwest, southeast, or east. As a hurricane hits the coast, its strongest winds and highest tides usually sweep onshore near landfall on the northeastern side of circulation, or in the right-front quadrant. Hazel's arrival near the state border meant that points just north and east of landfall—such as Calabash, Ocean Isle, Oak Island, and Carolina and Wrightsville Beaches—would catch the brunt of the storm. All received Hazel's worst tides and winds. Just south of landfall, Garden City still suffered heavy losses, but as the storm raced inland the hardest-hit areas were just east of the track. This was evident by record winds that rocked the eastern seaboard all the way to Canada. For any severe hurricane approaching the Carolina coast, just a thirty-mile shift in the location of landfall, north or south, can make a big difference for nearby coastal communities.
- *A hurricane's forward speed as it strikes land is a key factor in determining its impact.* In addition to monitoring hurricanes' wind speeds (rotational velocities), meteorologists also track their forward speeds (storm center movement from point A to point B). In lower latitudes, Atlantic tropical cyclones typically move along at about 8–15 mph, but as they recurve northward, they often increase speed. Sometimes, other nearby weather systems influence them, causing them to slow or stall. Hurricane Florence was one whose movements slowed just as it made landfall, causing it to drift over the Carolinas at less than 5 mph, resulting in disastrous rainfall

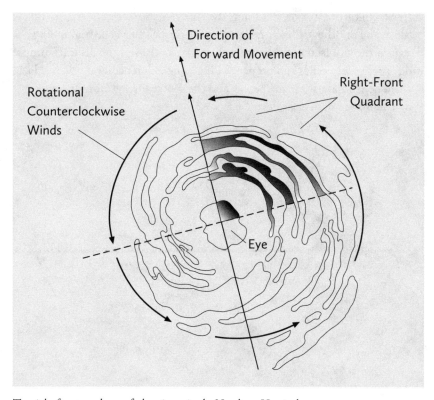

The right-front quadrant of a hurricane in the Northern Hemisphere.

accumulations. Hurricanes moving more rapidly don't linger, generally producing less rainfall and a shorter duration of extreme winds. But faster forward movement has another consequence—accelerated winds on the eastern side of the storm. Hazel was moving quickly when it struck the Carolinas, and ultimately raced through Virginia and Maryland at more than 50 mph. This swift pace amplified winds east of the track, helping Hazel establish new wind-speed records in places such as Norfolk, Philadelphia, and New York City.

• *For longtime residents of coastal Carolina, stories of hurricanes past have become part of family history, retold through generations.* Great hurricanes are tumultuous events that sometimes change the lives of the people who experience them. In the Carolinas, many hold memories of these disasters that are important markers in their lives, sharing them with family and friends any time the topic of hurricanes is discussed. Storytelling is a powerful and important way to help us better understand the threats we face from future storms. For some, they're dramatic stories of rescue and survival. For others, they're tales of the hurricane's fury: the frightening roar of the winds, the insidious reach of the floods, and the disheartening destruction of homes and property. Like Hugo, Florence, and others, Hazel was a benchmark for many people and the source for a great number of personalized hurricane tales.

CHAPTER NINE

HURRICANE GRACIE,
SEPTEMBER 1959

They became infamous. Hurricanes Carol (1954), Hazel (1954), Diane (1955), and Audrey (1957) all became household names in the mid-1950s even as they killed hundreds and racked up millions of dollars in property damage in Louisiana, the Carolinas, and the Northeast. Hurricanes had long plagued the United States' Atlantic and Gulf coasts, but until the early 1950s when forecasters began naming them, many were easily forgotten or confused with other storms. For the news media and the public who followed along, naming the storms gave them each a memory-building reference label that helped mark its place in time. The fifties were also a period when hurricane activity in the Carolinas was peaking. After experiencing relative quiet from the 1920s through the 1940s, North and South Carolina suffered through eleven hurricanes in nine years. Among them was the epic Category 4 Hazel in 1954 and a second Category 4 on the South Carolina coast just five years later in 1959—Hurricane Gracie.

During this period, advances in science and technology were in the news. The space race between the United States and the Soviet Union took off, and around the globe scientists were using new technologies to solve problems. The International Geophysical Year was set for 1958, placing a global focus on earth sciences. NASA was founded the same year, though a U.S. rocket program had been underway since even before the Soviets launched Sputnik in October 1957. But it wouldn't be until the early 1960s that U.S. satellites would send back the first pictures of hurricanes. Tropical cyclone forecasting had shown steady improvement in the 1950s, but the later use of satellites would prove to be the real game changer.

Forecasters could have used that help trying to understand several of 1959's Atlantic hurricanes. Over the Fourth of July holiday, squalls developed surrounding a low-pressure system off the South Carolina coast, and reconnaissance aircraft were dispatched to monitor the "small storm." The system briefly moved south, then turned northeast, and then was blocked by a ridge of high pressure,

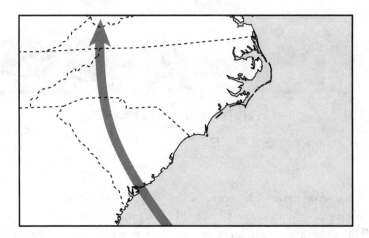

Though Hurricane Gracie made landfall at low tide, floodwaters still filled the streets of Beaufort, South Carolina. (Photo courtesy of the Beaufort County Library, Beaufort, South Carolina.)

sending it west. It became Hurricane Cindy on July 8 and struck near McClel-lanville as a Category 1 the following day. Damages were minimal, though there was one fatality in Georgetown—a motorist killed by a falling tree.

Cindy had toyed with forecasters with its erratic movements. While some hurricanes might move along more linear or gently curving tracks at a predictable pace, others sometimes stop, back up, stall, or turn abruptly, depending upon the steering currents and atmospheric forces surrounding them. The next hurricane along the Carolina coast—Hurricane Gracie—was another fickle storm that challenged forecasters, though it turned out to be far more powerful and destructive than Cindy had been.

The U.S. Weather Bureau regarded Gracie as "troublesome." Forecasters had tracked it as an easterly wave in the Atlantic for days, and as it meandered through the Bahamas between September 22 and 27 it seemed to lose all direction. Gordon Dunn, chief forecaster in Miami, wrote in *Monthly Weather Review*, "At one time or another it moved in about every direction of the compass, [and] proved impossible to forecast in detail." Its intensity fluctuated during this time, until it emerged from the northern Bahamas on the twenty-seventh as a Category 2 storm on a northwestward track. With steering winds now more apparent, the Weather Bureau issued a hurricane watch for the U.S. East Coast from Savannah to Wilmington on the morning of the twenty-eighth, then upgraded its bulletins to hurricane warnings that afternoon. As the storm approached, the warnings were well heeded, and evacuations from South Carolina's vulnerable islands and coastal beaches were described as "almost total."

As they prepared their hurricane warnings, forecasters had a better sense of where the storm was headed, but they faced a new challenge in the final forty-eight hours before landfall. Gracie was getting much stronger. It grew from Category 1 intensity to Category 4 during that time, ultimately packing 140 mph winds as it tracked closer to the South Carolina coast. Dunn concluded, "Its sudden development and intensification is difficult to explain."

Gracie made landfall over Saint Helena Sound around noon on September 29 on a northwest track. An observer on Coffin Point, near Frogmore, reported the eye's passage, which created a dead calm that lasted thirty-five minutes. During that time the sun appeared and was "extremely hot." The storm continued inland west of Columbia and gradually dissipated, as hurricanes usually do overland. It tracked through western North Carolina, over the Blue Ridge Mountains and into West Virginia before recurving across Pennsylvania, New York, and New England as an extratropical storm. As a Category 4 at landfall, Gracie had the potential to be another frightful, epic disaster for South Carolina. But fortunately for the Lowcountry communities standing in its path, several factors combined to somewhat lessen the storm's overall impact.

At the coast, the Weather Bureau's timely warnings were taken seriously. After all, Hurricane Hazel was still a fresh memory for many, while others still remembered the potent August 1940 hurricane that had blasted the coast near Beaufort. On the most vulnerable islands, the call for evacuations was successful. Also, though Gracie had deepened rapidly upon its approach, briefly attaining sustained winds of 140 mph, it experienced some weakening just before landfall.

Though it could have been even stronger, it still struck as a fierce 130 mph hurricane. Reconnaissance aircraft reported a 951-millibar (mb) barometric pressure near the coast. The barometer at the Marine Corps Auxiliary Air Station at Beaufort recorded a low of 950 mb; a five-minute sustained wind was measured at 97 mph and gusts reached 138 mph. In the Weather Bureau's summary report, the storm's remarkable ferocity was noted: "Wind was estimated as high as 152 kt. [175 mph] closer to the exact center of the storm and gusts as high as 130 kt. [150 mph] seem quite credible." These estimated winds were likely considered in the National Oceanic and Atmospheric Administration's reanalysis project's 2016 reclassification for the storm, in which Gracie was upgraded from Category 3 to Category 4. Its 950 mb pressure reading at landfall places it among the fifty most intense hurricanes to strike the United States since 1851.

Because Gracie tracked inland over Saint Helena Sound and passed over a region of relatively low population, its fierce winds reached fewer homes and businesses, another factor that diminished total losses. But the single biggest factor in reducing the storm's overall impact was its arrival at dead low tide. Hurricanes of Gracie's strength might easily deliver storm tides in this region above fifteen feet, but a late-morning low tide significantly reduced the flooding when the storm arrived at noon. Still, an impressive surge hit the coast from Hilton Head to Charleston; tides at Edisto Beach peaked near twelve feet above mean low water. In Charleston, two feet of water filled the lower portions of the city, and the tide reached 8.14 feet above mean low water. The National Weather Service later reported, "The fact that the storm came ashore at low tide limited the impact of the storm surge and could have prevented an epic storm surge disaster along the South Carolina coast."

In Beaufort and surrounding island communities, Gracie produced what was believed to have been the greatest wind destruction in the region's recorded history. The most obvious damage was to trees; tall pines were snapped, and live oaks were split and toppled in every neighborhood. After the storm, mountains of vegetative debris clogged virtually every street and highway for miles along the hurricane's path. Mixed with the fallen trees was an endless tangle of downed power lines, traffic signals, and cracked power poles. Roof damage was severe in Beaufort, and wind-tossed tree branches shattered countless windows in the city. Eight homes were destroyed, and another eighty suffered heavy damages. The *Beaufort Gazette* reported that after the storm, someone

Hurricane Gracie's ferocious winds tore open G. W. Trask's packing shed in Beaufort, South Carolina. (Photo courtesy of the Beaufort County Library, Beaufort, South Carolina.)

in town shared a personal collection of kerosene lanterns, "an extremely handy hobby during this particular kind of emergency." At Parris Island, roofs peeled off storage buildings, and trucks and trailers were overturned. On Saint Helena Island, winds heavily damaged more than thirty homes and tore away the roof of the Ocean Villa Hotel. Thirteen fishing boats sank in Saint Helena Sound; causeways and roads near Beaufort were submerged. Afterward, the loss of electricity and lack of adequate drinking water affected the region for weeks. Farmers in eastern Georgia and South Carolina reported heavy damages too, with high winds shredding vulnerable crops still in the field, especially unpicked cotton. After the storm, travel was extremely difficult. Parts of the Lowcountry resembled a "war zone," prompting Governor Fritz Hollings to call out the National Guard to assist with the cleanup in Beaufort County.

Facing the stronger northeastern side of the eyewall, Edisto Beach was hit with the worst of Gracie—the strongest winds and highest tides. Three-fourths of the 1,200-foot Edisto Pier was washed away. Pounding ocean surf and winds that may have gusted above 150 mph tore into dozens of beachfront homes and undermined others. Sixteen cottages were demolished and another sixty-three were damaged along a two-mile stretch. Many had been newly built or rebuilt in the years since the August 1940 hurricane that had heavily damaged the island and destroyed half its oceanfront structures. Gracie wasn't kind either, bashing cottages and stripping away the sand beach, which was later replenished with dredged sand and shell hash from the backside of the island. Some of these post-Gracie erosion-control efforts remain visible today.

Total damages in South Carolina were estimated at $14 million, with more than half of that amount in Charleston County. As might be expected from a storm with such extreme winds, damages were heavy to trees, power lines, roofs, and windows but also to television antennas, billboards, water towers, and church steeples. In Charleston, fierce gusts shattered storefront windows in the business district and broke open windows at the city council chamber, damaging a priceless eighteenth-century portrait of George Washington painted by John Trumbull. Just inland, in places such as Walterboro, Bamberg, and Orangeburg, residents were chased from their homes by the frightening boom of crashing trees. As the storm tracked west of Columbia, wind and rain left minor damages at the capitol building.

Thanks to the storm's arrival at low tide, flooding was considered "manageable" in Charleston, though according to Weather Bureau reports from that time, the storm still produced the sixth-highest storm tide of record at Charleston Harbor. Rutledge and Ashley Avenues were flooded with overflow from Colonial Lake. Many roads were impassable, and the U.S. Coast Guard buoy tender *Bramble* was used to evacuate a small number of people in the city. On Folly Beach, 125 mph winds and a ten-foot storm tide battered beachfront homes, causing some to collapse. Numerous cottages lost their roofs, as did the Folly Beach Hotel and Pavilion. Two hundred residents who chose to ride out the hurricane were isolated once the only access to the mainland was cut off—they finally received food and water when the Red Cross was able to reach them on the thirtieth.

Rainfall ranged from four to eight inches across southeast South Carolina, with 4.9 inches recorded at the Marine Corps Air Station in Beaufort and 8.3 inches in Walterboro. Pockets of heavy rain extended well into North Carolina and Virginia, with the greatest accumulation measured in Big Meadows, Virginia—13.20 inches. But largely, the rains didn't bring destructive flooding;

Charleston was north of Hurricane Gracie's landfall, but the city still experienced wide-spread flooding from the passing storm. (Photo courtesy of the *State* Newspaper Photograph Archive, Richland Library, Columbia, South Carolina.)

in fact, they were instead a welcome relief for farmers in the drought-stricken upland portions of the Carolinas and Virginia.

Gracie claimed twenty-two lives in the United States, ten of which were in South Carolina and Georgia. There were no storm tide drownings—all the fatalities in South Carolina were the result of fallen trees, electrocutions from downed live wires, and rain-induced automobile accidents. Four were killed in Beaufort, including James Chaplin, who was helping a stranded motorist when he was struck by a "flying timber."

As often happens with tropical cyclones, Gracie spawned numerous tornadoes along its journey inland—one of which became the single deadliest event of the storm. Tornadoes spun out of the hurricane even before it made landfall. "Likely tornado damage" was reported near Walterboro and in Lake City on the morning of the twenty-ninth, and a confirmed twister damaged several homes up the coast in Garden City. As the remnants of Gracie tracked northward past Charlotte and into West Virginia, an outbreak of multiple

U.S. Marines at Parris Island serve hot food to local evacuees following Hurricane Gracie in September 1959. (Photo courtesy of the Beaufort County Library, Beaufort, South Carolina.)

tornadoes ripped across North Carolina, Virginia, and Pennsylvania. Seven touched down in central Virginia on the afternoon of the thirtieth, including several in Albemarle County near the village of Ivy. A "dark funnel" dropped from the sky and tore apart the Mountain Plain Baptist Church at Mechums River sometime after 4:00 P.M. It began by overturning a parked car and was likely one of several that shot across the county, lifting roofs and leveling barns. Within a three-hour span, twelve fatalities were discovered and another dozen residents were injured.

The greatest tragedy occurred in the Morris family's two-story duplex near Ivy. Twelve family members were home preparing dinner when the twister tore the structure apart. Afterward, little remained of the Morris home. Leanna Simms, working at a neighbor's house at the time, witnessed the destruction and crawled across the wreckage to search for survivors. "I could hear children crying," she told the Charlottesville *Daily Progress*. She found one little girl pinned in the debris and pulled her to safety. Rescue personnel arrived on the scene afterward and searched through the night for other victims, ultimately recovering the bodies of ten family members. Miraculously, another of the

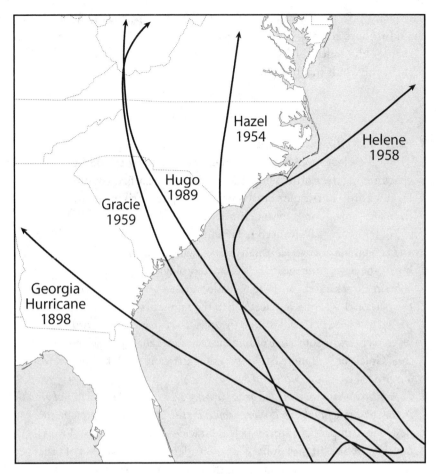

Few Category 4 hurricanes have been known to make landfall north of Florida, at least since record keeping began in the mid-nineteenth century. Hurricanes Hazel and Gracie, however, were only five years apart. Hurricane Helene in 1958 was a near miss, passing just off the North Carolina coast and never striking land. Had it hit the Carolinas, there would have been three Category 4 landfalls in the region within five years.

Morris children was found alive the following morning some distance from the home.

Another touchdown less than an hour later tore through a nearby farm owned by John Clayton. According to Phil James's 2009 account in the *Crozet Gazette*, "The roof was lifted from his main house, which was damaged beyond repair—all while Mrs. Martha Clayton remained at her work desk. . . . Several days later O. B. Enswiler of Lacy Springs, Virginia, personally returned to a thankful Clayton family a water-stained paid-up bank note. He had found it in his yard—fifty miles northwest across the Blue Ridge Mountains—deposited there by the winds that had plucked it from atop Mrs. Clayton's desk."

TAKEAWAYS

- *Hurricanes often spawn tornadoes, sometimes with deadly consequences.* Tropical cyclones are known to spin up tornadic activity, adding to the chaos among the storms' winds, rains, and tides. Tornado outbreaks can form within a hurricane's broad circulation, often striking many miles from the central core and sometimes well in advance of landfall. Prior to the development of advanced radar and public warnings via radio, TV, and cell phone, tornadoes usually struck with no warning. During today's hurricane news coverage, television meteorologists often spend considerable time tracking the shifting tornado watches and warnings issued by the National Weather Service. When the remnants of Hurricane Frances passed just west of the Carolinas in 2004, they spawned a record forty-seven twisters in South Carolina. The tornadoes that spun from Hurricane Gracie proved more lethal than the hurricane itself, killing twelve in Virginia.

- *Population density is a big factor in gauging a hurricane's impact, and growth in the coastal region has put more people at risk.* It's hard to reconcile the destructive impact of a storm such as Gracie—its $14 million in losses in South Carolina (in 1959 dollars) was considerably less than that of other storms of the era and a far cry from the billions in losses major hurricanes often produce today. Though Gracie was a Category 4, its arrival at low tide and its modest rains reduced overall losses due to flooding. But another factor was the number of homes and businesses it affected. Its path from Saint Helena Sound across South Carolina proved devastating for Edisto Beach, Beaufort, and portions of Charleston County, but as it moved inland it passed through a region that was sparsely populated at the time. Hurricanes striking more densely populated areas will always generate more property damage, as seen in the staggering tolls from urban megadisasters such as Hurricanes Katrina, Sandy, and Harvey. In the Carolinas, population growth increases vulnerability over time—especially for hurricanes striking more populous cities such as Hilton Head, Charleston, Myrtle Beach, Wilmington, Jacksonville, or Kill Devil Hills or for those that might reach inland cities such as Columbia, Charlotte, Raleigh, or Durham.

- *Sometimes a hurricane's heavy rains are welcomed.* Tropical cyclones can have natural benefits; most notably their rains help replenish dried soils and recharge underground aquifers. When Gracie rolled through the Palmetto State, rainfall was not extreme by hurricane standards—many areas received from four to eight inches. River flooding was not a major issue, in part because South Carolina was experiencing drought at the time, and river levels were low. Gracie's rains were especially helpful for farmers who count on occasional episodes of tropical moisture to benefit their crops.

CHAPTER TEN

HURRICANE DONNA,
SEPTEMBER 1960

After the string of hurricane strikes through the 1950s, residents along the Carolina coast kept watchful eyes on the storms that brewed during each hurricane season. Storm tracking and forecasting were improving, and hurricane warnings were becoming more focused and reliable, though satellite images of tropical systems were not yet available. After all the repairs and reconstruction, hurricanes were on people's minds. Destructive storms had garnered the full attention of news media outlets, and the advent of television through this period helped many residents stay informed. Late in the summer of 1960, coastal residents watched cautiously as another dangerous cyclone sliced through the Caribbean and headed toward Florida. This new storm left heavy destruction and scores of dead in its wake even before it reached the United States. It then went on to become one of the most potent hurricanes in U.S. history. Its name was Donna.

On August 29, a large squall of heavy rains and high winds wrapped around Dakar, Senegal, on the westernmost tip of the African continent. This was more than the usual summer thunderstorm; it was blamed for the crash of an airliner and the deaths of sixty-three passengers. By September 2, these rains had grown into the origins of what would become Donna, spinning out of the Cape Verde region. It continued building to hurricane strength, and on September 4 it swept over the Leeward Islands packing sustained winds of 125 mph. Its eye passed directly over Barbuda, Saint Barthélemy, Saint Martin, and Anguilla and just south of Anegada. A large percentage of homes on Saint Martin, Barbuda, and Anguilla were destroyed or severely damaged. Many interisland schooners were wrecked, and at least seven fatalities were reported. Heavy rains in Puerto Rico triggered mudslides and extensive flooding. According to U.S. Weather Bureau reports, "At Humacao, where residents had returned to their homes in the river bed or on the flood plain despite issued flood warnings, 90 persons were drowned or unaccounted for. A landslide buried 8 persons near Patillas. Total fatalities were 108, and damage to property and crops nearly $8 million."

Homeowners and merchants along the Carolina coast whose properties faced the ocean suffered the greatest losses from Hurricane Donna in September 1960. (Photo courtesy of the News and Observer Publishing Company / North Carolina Division of Archives and History, Raleigh.)

By the time Donna had bounced along the northern coast of Puerto Rico and passed by Cuba on September 7, it had already claimed more than 120 lives. As the storm approached the southeastern Bahamas, it slowed in forward speed, turned somewhat more to the west, and intensified dramatically. The eye passed over Mayaguana, where hurricane winds were observed for thirteen hours. After winds blew away an anemometer at Fortune Island, observers there estimated the maximum winds at nearly 170 mph. Miraculously, no lives were lost in the Bahamas.

As it turned its sights on southern Florida, this monster hurricane packed winds in excess of 150 mph. On September 7, newspapers labeled it the "Killer Hurricane" and reported that all of South Florida was on alert. At 11:00 A.M. the following day, the dreaded warning flags—red with black squares—were hoisted throughout the Keys. Weather Bureau bulletins placed the hurricane in frightening perspective by stating that it produced the same energy as a hydrogen bomb exploding every eight minutes. Many Keys residents, reminded of the awesome Labor Day storm of a generation before, packed their bags and left for Homestead and Miami.

At 2:30 A.M. on September 10, Donna's twenty-one-mile-wide eye swept over the middle Keys. It had intensified through this time, yielding several extremely low pressure readings. At Conch Key a recording of 933 millibars (mb) was measured, and the official landfall was established at 930 mb, making Donna the sixth-strongest hurricane to make landfall in the United States in the twentieth century. A thirteen-foot storm surge struck the islands. Not surprisingly, the middle and upper Keys were pounded by large waves and the surge, which was highest just north of the center of the storm. At Tavernier the water reportedly rose to within eighteen inches of the record mark established in the Category 5 Labor Day storm of 1935. According to a Weather Bureau summary, "Destruction was almost complete from wind and water over an area 40 miles to the northeast and 20 miles to the southwest of the track."

The impact was devastating. Not only were homes beaten, flooded, or washed away, but the Overseas Highway was washed out in several places. The Tea Table Bridge between Upper and Lower Matecumbe was exposed to the worst of the surge, and boiling seas washed away a 1,000-foot section of the concrete span. The pipeline that supplied fresh water to the Keys was broken in six places, and telephone and electrical cables were also destroyed. Automobiles, yachts, furnishings, and appliances were scattered with the tides and tumbled and tossed into mangrove thickets and streets. A report in the *Florida Keys Keynoter* described the scene at Islamorada: "Nearly every home, resort, and business building fronting the ocean was either gutted or destroyed. Many of the older wooden buildings, some dating back to the '35 hurricane, were floated two and three blocks away. Some ended up on the Overseas Highway, and others traveled even farther toward the Gulf. Even well-constructed concrete block houses could not withstand the force."

Deadly Category 4 winds gusted above 150 mph. At Marathon, gusts snapped large creosoted utility poles in half—poles that had recently been installed and were supposed to withstand winds of 150 mph. At Tavernier, the fastest sustained wind was 120 mph, though that was the maximum reading on the dial. According to Weather Bureau records, "The anemometer needle held solid against the pin for 45 minutes." The highest sustained winds in the Keys were estimated around 140 mph "with possible momentary gusts of 175 to 180 mph." Winds in Everglades City and Naples likely gusted to 150 mph. Homes, office buildings, and stores were unroofed and ripped apart. House trailers appeared to have exploded, and one mobile home park was left devastated, with not one home standing. It was estimated that 75 percent of structures in the Keys were damaged by the storm.

Amazingly, and in stark contrast to the disastrous Labor Day Hurricane of 1935, only four lives were lost in the Keys during Donna. The bodies of two men were found in the waters off Key Largo, and a third victim was a woman who was a Marathon resident. The fourth, who was lost and presumed dead, was a woman who had been swept away in the darkness as she and her husband tried to reach higher ground during the peak of the storm. Along with some friends, the couple had formed a "human chain" and tried to wade through the tide, but the swirling waters carried her away.

As Donna crossed the Keys and moved into the Gulf of Mexico in the early hours of September 10, it alarmed forecasters and South Florida residents when it abruptly took a hard turn to the north. It then slammed into the Florida coast a second time, striking just south of Naples on the Gulf shore with 120 mph winds. In Everglades City, waters retreated well below normal as the storm's eye approached. Then after it passed, the tide swept back with fury, flooding the city's streets to a depth of eight feet. After abandoning their homes, 200 residents escaped to the second floor of the Collier County courthouse, where they watched the tide swirl waist deep in the first-floor lobby. Half the town's structures were destroyed by extreme winds and flooding. Fort Myers Beach suffered heavy losses too, with scenes reminiscent of damage in the Keys— wrecked marinas, tangled utility lines, and unroofed buildings. The famous Naples Fishing Pier, which had withstood many hurricanes since it was built in 1888, was reduced to a ragged row of twisted pilings. Flushed from the surrounding Everglades, alligators, snakes, and rats were a menace in Naples after the storm. Numerous venomous snakebites were reported, mostly from reptiles that had taken up residence in homes, furnishings, and even pickup trucks.

Donna curved inland, crossing Florida on a northeast track, along the way delivering record-breaking destruction. More than 5,000 homes were damaged across the mainland, making Donna *the* memorable hurricane for an entire generation of Floridians. The state's citrus production was heavily damaged;

at least half the grapefruit crop was lost. Winds continued to blast well above 100 mph through most of the storm's path across the state, with isolated gusts reported of 140 mph or more in Hardee and Polk Counties. New record lows for barometric pressure were set in Fort Myers on the Gulf coast (951 mb) and Daytona Beach on the Atlantic coast (973 mb).

In all, thirteen lives were lost in the Sunshine State. But Donna's fury was not over. By the afternoon of September 10, the now–Category 1 hurricane reemerged into the Atlantic near Daytona Beach and then moved off the Georgia coast, where it began rebuilding strength over the warm waters of the Gulf Stream.

The storm passed just off the South Carolina coast and began to rapidly accelerate. As it moved toward land, its forward speed increased to 45 mph, enhancing wind speeds in areas east of its track. Just before midnight on September 11, Donna moved over the North Carolina coastline near Topsail Island as a Category 2 storm with sustained winds of 105 mph. It arrived with an unusually large eye, estimated to be fifty to seventy-five miles in diameter. The hurricane continued on a northeasterly course, passing over Carteret, Pamlico, Hyde, and Tyrrell Counties before crossing over Albemarle Sound and through Elizabeth City. Eventually, it returned to the Atlantic for the second time, near Virginia Beach, on the morning of September 12.

Before its arrival in North Carolina, Donna caused problems in South Carolina too. High tides and gale-force winds buffeted the coast, with considerable damage to boats, docks, and structures near Beaufort. At Ocean Drive Beach winds gusted to near 100 mph and eleven inches of rain were reported. Near Charleston, a tornado damaged or destroyed several homes, causing $500,000 in damages and injuring a dozen residents who were hurt by flying glass. The 1840s-era Bennett Rice Mill was heavily damaged by a twister as well. Tornadoes hit other areas too, including one near Garden City that damaged six buildings. In North Carolina, a tornado destroyed a home in Sampson County with eight residents inside, and all were hospitalized with injuries.

As Donna tracked northward, a large flock of seagulls became trapped in the storm's eye. Military radar confirmed the presence of the birds, which were carried hundreds of miles northward by the storm. This sometimes happens; seabirds were known to be carried far inland with storms such as Fran and Hugo. In Donna, many of the seagull flock finally escaped near Wilmington when the eye distended to more than sixty miles across. But many couldn't endure the winds, and hundreds of dead gulls washed up on the beaches between Carolina Beach and Topsail Island in the days following the hurricane.

Along the North Carolina coast, homes and businesses from Southport to

Nags Head suffered extensive structural damage. Winds gusted in excess of 100 mph, and tides ran four to eight feet above normal. Beach erosion was severe in some locations, and numerous areas of overwash were reported. Fortunately, though, the storm arrived closer to low tide, unlike during Hazel, when astronomical tides were peaking at landfall. Winds were about what would be expected from a Category 2 storm. Wilmington reported a peak gust of 97 mph, but at several locations farther north and along the Outer Banks the peak was higher. New Bern reported a maximum gust of 103 mph; Hatteras recorded 94 mph. Sustained winds in Elizabeth City were clocked at 83 mph, and a 120 mph gust was recorded in Manteo. Especially east of the storm track, these winds toppled trees and utility lines, and they damaged crops as far as fifty miles inland. After the storm, there was a natural tendency for eastern Tar Heel residents to compare Donna's winds with those of Hazel, and from New Bern northward, Donna was the stronger blow.

Wilmington reported a barometric low of 962 mb, making Donna the third-most intense storm ever measured (by pressure) at that location, after Floyd and Fran. At Wrightsville Beach, several homes lost their roofs; some were lifted by winds and tossed down on parked cars. One of North Carolina's first fatalities occurred in Wilmington the night of the storm when Coast Guardsman John Flood was electrocuted while attempting to repair an antenna atop the office of the captain of the port at the customhouse. A gust of wind unexpectedly shifted the antenna into a live power wire as he held it. New Hanover County suffered extensive damage, which some news reports listed as "just as bad as Hazel."

Carteret County found itself on the eastern side of the storm, and the coastal communities of Atlantic Beach, Morehead City, and Beaufort were among the hardest hit. In Atlantic Beach, several buildings were leveled, including the Pavilion and a bakery constructed of concrete blocks. Numerous structures lost their roofs completely, and many decks and porches were ripped away by high winds. Donna's storm tide cut through the protective dune line in several places, overwashing streets and undermining homes. Breakers ripped through the dunes on Knollwood Drive in Pine Knoll Shores, and a second overwash carried away a twenty-five-foot section of Ocean Ridge Road in Atlantic Beach. But perhaps the most impressive overwash occurred just east of the Oceanana Pier, where the Dunes Club was destroyed. The beach club was broken apart by the waves, its wooden dance floor washed onto Fort Macon Road. The roadway was undermined as well, isolating the Coast Guard station and all points east of the overwash. Furniture, dinnerware, and kitchen utensils from the club were later retrieved from nearby dunes.

The eastern overwash from Hurricane Donna at Atlantic Beach, North Carolina, struck
the Dunes Club head on, ripping the structure apart and carrying portions of its floor and
roof across Fort Macon Road. The overwash was later filled in, the roadway restored, and the
Dunes Club rebuilt. (Photo courtesy of the *Carteret County News-Times*.)

On the Morehead City waterfront, restaurants and docks were heavily damaged and tides rose into the streets. Several families had fled their homes for
refuge in the town hall, where children slept on the floor through the night.
At least eight homes lost their chimneys, and "virtually every TV antenna in
Carteret County was bent over or went missing." Some of the heaviest destruction in the Carteret region occurred on the Morehead City–Beaufort Causeway along a low-lying stretch of U.S. 70. This area had been hard hit during
Hazel, and Donna's winds and tides brought even greater destruction. After
the hurricane had passed, reporters flocked to the scene, and one writer for the
Greensboro Daily News described the aftermath:

> Up and down the causeway almost everything is wreckage. Power and
> telephone lines are down across the road, the poles snapped off at their
> bases. The road itself is half-gone in spots, thick chunks of broken asphalt
> jut out of the pits and ravines carved into the sand by the wind-driven
> tides. The Beaufort and Morehead Railroad runs in a single track along
> the north side of the causeway, and it is here that Donna did the railroad
> dirty. The storm cut the sand from under the tracks and left the crossties

hanging—barely in some places—by the rail spikes, and the rails themselves dangling over the water like two long strands of half-cooked spaghetti. A diesel engine leans crazily toward the water—still on the tracks, but with nowhere to go. Behind it, on both sides of what used to be the railroad embankment, stretches a bizarre parade of upturned boats, beds, tables, pillows, smashed planking, pilings, beams and driftwood. A pair of water skis, a child's doll, an outboard motor housing, a sofa that got out of its house without, somehow, making a hole in either wall, windows or door.

At the height of the storm, an ambulance was swept off the causeway by the tide. Driver Bert Brooks and his companion, Cecil Moore, were transporting Annie White to the Morehead City hospital. White was expecting a baby and was being taken there for fear that the hurricane might isolate her from the mainland. The rapidly rising tide caught the ambulance before Brooks and his passengers could make their way across the bridge. They emerged from the vehicle in chest-deep water and managed to retreat to a house on the causeway, where they were able to safely ride out the storm. The ambulance was badly damaged and was partially buried in the sand. Annie White didn't have her baby that night after all but gave birth two weeks later.

The Outer Banks were struck with the full fury of Donna. High winds, gusting to 120 mph in some locations, ripped away roofs and toppled miles of telephone and power lines. The storm's early southeast winds piled a mass of water up the Pamlico, Albemarle, and Currituck Sounds, inundating their banks and tributary rivers. As the hurricane passed, the winds shifted and a raging flood struck the backside of the islands. Dozens of homes on the sound side of Kitty Hawk and Nags Head were severely damaged. Some of the region's famed hunting clubs suffered the most damage in their history. At least three houses were swept into Roanoke Sound near the Little Bridge between Nags Head and Manteo. Violet Kellam, owner of the Oasis Restaurant at the Little Bridge, escaped as her business collapsed around her. She told the *Virginian-Pilot* that "the water rose more than three feet in 15 minutes" and the eye lasted "more than an hour." In some areas, it was reported that "telephone poles popped like firecrackers." Tides filled the streets in downtown Manteo, flooding homes, shops, and other businesses to an extent never seen before. Among the losses was the Waterside Theatre, which housed Manteo's famed *Lost Colony* outdoor drama. Surging tides sometimes retreat as quickly as they advance. After the hurricane passed through Nags Head, "flopping bass and other live fish" were picked up off the streets.

Away from the coast, dozens of towns and cities in the east suffered damages from Hurricane Donna. In New Bern, many large trees were downed, some crashing into homes and businesses. In Washington, Edenton, Swan Quarter, and Elizabeth City, fallen trees and toppled power lines were common, along with washed-out docks and bulkheads. More than seventy miles of power lines were downed north of Swan Quarter, and most communities in the northeastern counties were without electricity. Donna's ferocious winds also reached inland and struck signs, trees, and telephone poles in Kinston, Goldsboro, and Greenville.

Like a few other memorable hurricanes, Donna didn't end its journey by fizzling out after its return to the Atlantic. Instead, it maintained its course toward New England and struck Long Island, New York, as a Category 2 later on September 12. There the storm delivered a ten-foot storm surge and caused extensive damage. Block Island, Rhode Island, recorded sustained winds of 95 mph, with gusts up to 130 mph; a 145 mph gust was recorded at the Blue Hill Observatory in Milton, Massachusetts. Damage was reported all along the northeast coast, from Virginia to Maine. The famed boardwalk in Atlantic City, New Jersey, was bashed by high waves, and winds toppled a radio tower in Massachusetts. Donna eventually weakened when it crossed the Gulf of Saint Lawrence on a northerly track.

Among those caught in the storm in New York was Nobel Prize–winning author John Steinbeck. As Donna raked over his Sag Harbor, Long Island, home, he jumped into the raging waters to secure his boat, only to be blown to shore while grasping a tree branch. He wrote about his adventures in Donna in his 1962 memoir, *Travels with Charley: In Search of America*.

Hurricane Donna caused a record amount of destruction in Florida and brought significant damage to the storm-weary residents of eastern Carolina. By hitting New England with a powerful blow, Donna became a menacing oddity—it was the first storm to strike with hurricane-force winds in Florida, the Carolinas, and New England within the seventy-five-year records of the Weather Bureau. Damage estimates in the United States topped $400 million, with nearly $300 million of that in Florida—although by some reports Donna's total cost was believed to be closer to $1 billion.

According to a memorandum from the National Oceanic and Atmospheric Administration—*The Deadliest, Costliest, and Most Intense Hurricanes of This Century* by Paul Hebert, Jerry Jarrell, and Max Mayfield—Donna's total death toll in the United States was fifty, although a Weather Bureau summary, counting both direct and indirect fatalities, placed the total slightly higher. The geographical distribution of the deaths is a testament to the remarkable endur-

Hurricane Donna's fierce winds and tides destroyed seaside shops at the Circle at Atlantic Beach, North Carolina. Donna was the last in a flurry of hurricanes that battered the Carolinas through the 1950s. (Photo courtesy of the News and Observer Publishing Company / North Carolina Division of Archives and History, Raleigh.)

ance of the storm. In addition to the thirteen deaths in Florida, there were eleven in North Carolina, three in Virginia, two in Maryland, one in Pennsylvania, nine in New Jersey, three in New York, nine in Massachusetts, one in New Hampshire, and one in Vermont. When combined with those of the Caribbean, the toll was 364. In North Carolina, most of the fatalities were along the coast. Three boys drowned when they took refuge in a house that was swept away by the tide. One person was electrocuted, and two died when they were crushed by large trees that crashed into their homes. Two were killed in weather-related traffic accidents; three others suffered heart attacks. Over 100 injuries requiring hospitalization were reported across the state.

Donna's arrival in North Carolina—just a few years after Hazel and the other big storms of the fifties—was difficult for many coastal residents to take. But very few packed up and moved away from their homes near the shore. An editorial that appeared in the *Carteret County News-Times* shortly after the storm summarized the mood of the local people: "Donna left in her wake not only material destruction but crushed spirits. You can fight just so many hurricanes and then the loss of your business, home, plus the drudgery of back-breaking clean-up begins to be a heart-breaking task. Carteret will come back, because there's nothing else to do but that, but the novelty of hurricanes has long worn off."

TAKEAWAYS

- *Long-term cycles influence hurricane activity.* We now look ahead to each Atlantic hurricane season with some idea of how many storms to expect, thanks to seasonal forecasts issued by the National Oceanic and Atmospheric Administration and others, based on careful scientific evaluation of global weather patterns. But for any given location, no one can predict when the next hurricane will strike. For years, hurricane meteorologists have been aware of a long-term cycle in which decades-long periods of increased activity in the Atlantic are followed by periods with fewer storms. During this cycle's warm phase, Atlantic Ocean temperatures rise by about 1 degree Fahrenheit, boosting hurricane development. Each phase may last twenty to forty years. It's believed this warm-cool cycle has been around for at least 1,000 years, affecting not only Atlantic hurricane activity but also snowfall in the Alps, famines in Africa, and droughts in North America. The most recent shift to the warm phase occurred in the mid-1990s, increasing tropical activity since that time. During the last warm period in the 1950s, the Carolinas were hit by eleven hurricanes in nine years (including Donna in 1960), yet during the cool phase that followed, only seven struck over the next three decades. This cycle doesn't preclude disastrous hurricanes during cool periods or quiet years during warm phases. Any year could be the year for the next great storm.
- *Wind damages rise dramatically as wind speeds increase.* Very few people in the Carolinas have experienced the peak winds of a major hurricane (Category 3 or higher), though some might think they have. Just because someone is "in" a strong hurricane such as Hazel, Hugo, or Fran doesn't mean the highest winds have reached their location. Coastal residents who've experienced hurricanes in recent years may have witnessed gusts

approaching 90 mph or more. But for most, our personal experiences with high winds are limited to what we might have seen during severe thunderstorms, possibly reaching 50 or 60 mph. Winds create measurable force against objects such as walls, and it's that force that knocks down trees and damages buildings during a storm. As wind speeds gain velocity, the force exerted doesn't rise in a linear fashion—it increases fourfold for every doubling of the speed. In a strong hurricane, for example, a 120 mph wind will exert four times the force of a 60 mph wind. Thankfully rare in the Carolinas, high-wind hurricanes bring significant danger and are in a separate class than the Category 1 or 2 hurricanes more common to the region.

CHAPTER ELEVEN

HURRICANE HUGO,
SEPTEMBER 1989

Through most of the 1960s and '70s, hurricane activity in the Carolinas was unusually quiet. Few big storms struck through this period—a time of expansive growth along the barrier beaches and across the coastal region. Hurricane Ginger brought Category 2 winds to North Carolina in 1971; Hurricane David did the same in South Carolina eight years later. Then a series of storms in the eighties tested coastal communities' evacuation plans from Charleston to Corolla. Hurricanes Diana (1984), Gloria (1985), and Charley (1986) made their presence known, but it was the last storm of the eighties that turned out to be the "big one" everyone had feared.

Few hurricanes of the modern era have caused greater destruction or loss in the Carolinas than Hurricane Hugo did in September 1989. Hugo was an intense Cape Verde storm that began as a cluster of innocent thunderclouds off the western coast of Africa. On September 10, these thunderstorms became a depression that, while drifting westward, grew into a tropical storm on the eleventh and a hurricane on the thirteenth. It then became a powerhouse. Hugo gradually curved to the west-northwest and slowed its forward speed as it approached the Leeward Islands, packing sustained winds of 160 mph and a central pressure of only 918 millibars (mb). It was the easternmost Category 5 hurricane ever observed in the Atlantic until Hurricane Lorenzo in 2019.

On September 15, three hurricane hunter aircraft deployed to Barbados to intercept the storm and retrieve data about its strength and structure. Two National Oceanic and Atmospheric Administration P-3 Orion research planes were followed by a U.S. Air Force Reserve C-130, each equipped with instruments and dropsondes that would eventually help forecasters model the storm. The first P-3 Orion plane, *Kermit*, flew into the storm at a lower-than-usual altitude, only 1,500 feet, and ended up subject to what old-time hurricane hunters call a "hairy hop." At the time, the plane's radar was not working properly, blinding the crew to the intensity of the storm's core winds. The eye was just twelve miles across. As the plane reached the eyewall, where lateral winds were

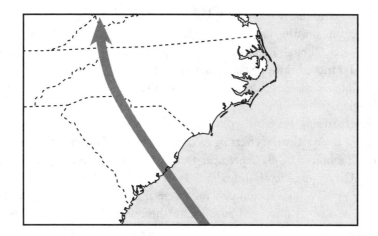

Soldiers from the South Carolina National Guard were on patrol to protect against looting on Folly Beach after Hurricane Hugo. (Photo courtesy of the *State* Newspaper Photograph Archive, Richland Library, Columbia, South Carolina.)

measured at 185 mph, it slammed into an updraft/downdraft that wrenched the aircraft violently, tearing loose instruments, a life raft, and other items that then flew around inside the cabin. About that time, one engine burst into flames. Within seconds, the plane was plunging toward the ocean surface, at risk of going down. But fortunately it emerged into the calm eye as the pilot skillfully pulled the plane out of its dive just 880 feet above the Atlantic. The aircraft and its weary crew then ascended inside the eye and later found a "soft spot" in the eyewall, returning safely to Barbados.

Hugo was impressive as it rolled over Guadeloupe on September 17, Saint Croix on the morning of the eighteenth, and Puerto Rico on the evening of the same day. Though it had attained Category 5 status briefly while over the Atlantic, it moved through these islands ranked as a 4. Throughout the eastern Caribbean, the destruction was massive. Damage estimates for the region exceeded $2.5 billion, and at least forty-one lives were lost.

After battering Puerto Rico with 130 mph winds, Hugo weakened and turned to the northwest, charting a course that would ultimately lead to the South Carolina coast. By September 21, the cyclone was churning the waters of the Atlantic just a few hundred miles east of Florida. At 5:00 A.M. that day, the storm's maximum sustained winds were 110 mph, but by 5:00 P.M. they had elevated to 135 mph. Fed by warm offshore waters, Hugo had increased in intensity again from Category 2 to Category 4 in only twelve hours. This killer storm was gaining strength and presented a serious threat to the U.S. southeast coast.

On September 20, a hurricane watch was issued for the beaches from Saint Augustine to Cape Hatteras. Thousands of Carolina residents prepared for the possibility of evacuation. The next morning, a hurricane warning was issued from Fernandina Beach, Florida, to Cape Lookout, North Carolina. Later that day, the warnings were extended northward to Oregon Inlet. Large-scale evacuations were ordered for beach communities from Georgia to southern North Carolina. South Carolina governor Carroll Campbell ordered mandatory evacuations of the entire coast. All three lanes of Interstate 26 from Charleston were converted to outbound traffic, and eastbound lanes were closed to help accelerate the evacuation. Ultimately, 186,000 residents fled their homes. Inland hotels filled quickly, leaving many evacuees searching for a safe place to stay. There was a true sense of urgency because Hugo was not only strengthening but also accelerating. Instead of swinging northward as some had expected, Hugo slammed into the central South Carolina coast just before midnight on September 21 with a forward speed of 30 mph and maximum sustained winds of 140 mph.

Landfall occurred at Sullivan's Island, several miles north of Charleston. From there, the storm swept inland, maintaining its northwesterly course. As Hugo passed through the central part of the state, it weakened slightly, although winds were still of hurricane force when its eye passed between Columbia and Sumter. By 6:00 A.M. on September 22, Hugo had diminished to tropical-storm strength. At daybreak, it passed into North Carolina just west of Charlotte and carved a path through Hickory and over the Blue Ridge Mountains. The storm continued to accelerate as it passed through the state and was advancing at 40 mph when it moved into extreme western Virginia. From there, the remnants of Hugo continued through West Virginia, eastern Ohio, and western Pennsylvania. The once-powerful cyclone was tracked for two more days as an extratropical storm as it turned across eastern Canada and into the North Atlantic.

Hugo was the most powerful hurricane to strike the United States in twenty years. Reconnaissance aircraft measured a barometric low of 934 mb just before landfall, and an unofficial recording of 933 mb was made at Mount Pleasant. Not since Hurricane Camille struck Mississippi in 1969 as a Category 5 had a storm of such strength made landfall in the United States. Hugo's 140 mph winds blasted portions of the South Carolina coast, the strongest since Gracie in 1959. In downtown Charleston, well south of the highest winds, a 110 mph gust was reported; a navy ship in Charleston Harbor measured gusts to 125 mph. At Folly Beach, also on the weaker, southern side of the storm, a gust of 107 mph was observed. The *Snow Goose*, anchored in the Sampit River five miles west of Georgetown, recorded a sustained wind speed of 120 mph. Inland areas along the storm's track endured hurricane-force winds as well. At Shaw Air Force Base near Cherryvale, the highest gust measured was 110 mph; at nearby Sumter the peak gust was 109 mph. Farther inland, gusts of 70 mph were reported in Columbia. For many inland locations across the state, Hugo set new all-time wind records. Rainfall ranged from five to ten inches, substantial but not enough to cause widespread freshwater flooding—thanks in part to the storm's rapid forward pace.

The storm surge near landfall in South Carolina was extreme, setting a record as the highest ever observed on the U.S. East Coast. A measurement of 20.4 feet was recorded at Awendaw, and the National Weather Service reported 19.8 feet at Cape Romain, Bulls Bay, north of Charleston. Tides were reported of 16 feet at McClellanville, 15 feet at Isle of Palms, 13 feet at Sullivan's Island, 13 feet at Myrtle Beach, 11.9 feet at Folly Beach, and 10.4 feet at downtown Charleston. A fisherman in McClellanville reportedly rode out the storm aboard his shrimp trawler and was said to have "floated over the roofs of two-story houses." Not surprisingly, the impact on waterfront properties was enormous.

The communities nearest landfall suffered the most shocking losses. Monstrous tides swallowed rows of beachfront homes and left marinas with piles of upended pleasure boats. Extreme winds peeled roofs off homes and businesses, flipped and scattered small planes parked at airports, and toppled television broadcast towers. The 150-mile-wide swath of the storm was especially devastating to the forests of the state, as more than 6 billion board feet of timber were

Isle of Palms was one of the hardest-hit beaches during Hurricane Hugo. (Photo courtesy of the *State* Newspaper Photograph Archive, Richland Library, Columbia, South Carolina.)

destroyed. That total was more than three times the loss experienced with the Mount Saint Helens volcanic eruption in 1980. The Francis Marion National Forest just north of Charleston was among the hardest-hit areas. The U.S. Forest Service estimated that Hugo damaged or destroyed 70 percent of the trees in the 250,000-acre forest, or about 1 billion board feet of timber. Many trees were sheared off at a height ten to twenty feet above the ground. Very few of the splintered trees were harvestable, and economic losses of the timber alone were over $1 billion.

Luckily, Charleston just missed the storm's most destructive forces, but damages were still extensive. A ten-foot tide spilled over the historic seawall and flooded the first floor of downtown homes. Later surveys found that 80 percent of the city's roofs were damaged, and over 100 buildings suffered heavy structural damage or were uninhabitable. A large "million-dollar" crane at the Port of Charleston was also destroyed.

At Sullivan's Island, as Hugo's winds and tides reached their peak, the Ben Sawyer Bridge linking the island to the mainland collapsed, tilting the large steel span into the air at a crazy angle. The surge destroyed two, and in some cases three, rows of beach homes that faced the ocean. Losses at Sullivan's Island and Isle of Palms approached $300 million. In Georgetown, historic

McClellanville was hit hard by Hurricane Hugo. A record-setting storm tide swept the town, wrecking homes and heavily damaging the fish houses, docks, and trawlers that were the economic lifeblood of this small fishing community. (Photo courtesy of the *State* Newspaper Photograph Archive, Richland Library, Columbia, South Carolina.)

homes were flooded, and both the Georgetown Landing and Belle Isle marinas were destroyed. Pawleys Island was divided when surging tides carved a new inlet nearly 100 feet across. Fourteen homes were destroyed; three were swept into the tidal creek behind the island. Fishing piers along the strand were no match for Hugo's storm surge either, and most were destroyed or damaged from Folly Beach to Cape Fear. In Myrtle Beach, protective dunes were "gone"; sand and several feet of water covered parts of Ocean Boulevard. Not since Hazel in 1954 had this area suffered such extreme beachfront destruction.

In the small fishing community of McClellanville, where some of the highest tides were reported, a dramatic scene unfolded the night of the storm due to the rush of water through the town. With a population of less than 500, McClellanville prepared as well as any coastal town could when facing a Category 4 hurricane. Many residents made their living on the water, and with word of the severity of the storm, shrimp trawlers were moved to secluded creeks to ride it out. Since many homes were at risk of flooding, several hundred residents were directed to the town's designated shelter at Lincoln High School. There

As the tides receded following Hurricane Hugo, cars parked adjacent to Lincoln High School in McClellanville were found tossed, stacked, and submerged. The school had served as a community shelter, but evacuees were lucky to escape with their lives after the building flooded during the peak of the storm. (Photo courtesy of the *State* Newspaper Photograph Archive, Richland Library, Columbia, South Carolina.)

they gathered in the cafeteria on the afternoon of September 21, unaware of the harrowing experience that would befall them that night.

As Hugo descended on McClellanville, high winds knocked out power early, plunging the evacuees into darkness. Within hours, floodwaters began creeping into the school, at first just ankle deep in classrooms and the cafeteria where the crowd was gathered. But with the doors sealed tight, the water kept rising—knee deep, then waist deep—to the horror of those inside. The fear was overwhelming, as resident Elizabeth Young told the *State*: "The water took over the building. We thought we were going to die. We knew we were trapped and couldn't get out."

In a scramble for their lives, the crowd climbed on top of tables, chairs, and a stage in the cafeteria to raise themselves above the floodwaters. One man in a wheelchair was hoisted onto a table. Young, along with her daughter, prayed while she held her two grandsons, three and four, on top of a refrigerator in the school's home economics classroom. Water inched above her chest. In the darkness, anguished cries from the crowd standing on the cafeteria stage in almost neck-deep water was too much for some. According to the *State*, about fifteen people opted to float near the ceiling in the band room. Among this group was an eighty-two-year-old grandmother who was kept afloat by two family members. Paramedic George Metts described the anguish: "The enormity of our situation was staggering. We were totally trapped. The tidal surge had risen so rapidly that we had no time to call for help. My walkie-talkie had gotten wet earlier and now it had fallen into the inky darkness. We were on our own. The water was still rising and those that could were packed like sardines on that stage."

A few were finally able to climb out a high window onto the building's roof and were nearly blown down by the storm's ferocious winds. About that time, the water stopped rising—and began its retreat. Miraculously, it poured out of the building just in time, and not a single life was lost. In the National Oceanic and Atmospheric Administration's *Natural Disaster Survey Report for Hurricane Hugo*, the authors concluded, "A potentially disastrous error in base elevation was discovered. . . . Later examination revealed that the base elevation of the school was 10 feet, not the 20.53 feet listed on the evacuation plan. This school should not have been used as a shelter for any storm greater than a Category 1 hurricane." Today, Lincoln High School is shuttered—it closed in 2016. On an outside wall of the cafeteria, a plaque just above eye level marks the waterline from Hurricane Hugo.

McClellanville resident Thomas Williams, his wife, and their four children managed their own dramatic escape that night when the surge surrounded their home just down the street from the school. As the storm approached and the winds increased, the family dog barked incessantly at the front door. Williams told South Carolina Sea Grant's *Coastal Heritage* magazine that when he went to the door to look outside, he was shocked at what he discovered. "I'm six-feet-two, and I saw water at eye level—the storm door was holding back the water, keeping it from coming into the house. I shut it quick." At that moment, water exploded through the floor, tossing the refrigerator into the air like "popping a champagne cork." The walls shook and swayed, and the kitchen roof suddenly disappeared, "snatched away—like that," he said. The water was waist high and rising, so he gathered his family in a bedroom, climbed on a dresser, and began pounding the Sheetrock ceiling with his fist to break open a hole. Fracturing his little finger, he kept pounding until an opening was large enough to pass through. He then lifted his family, one by one, into the relative safety of the attic. The house continued to shift and shake. In the darkness, he tethered his family together with a telephone cord: "If we're found tomorrow, at least we won't be scattered all over McClellanville." Williams and his family survived, but their home was destroyed.

As the storm barreled inland, fierce winds gusted above hurricane force and left behind tornado-like damages in every community along the storm's path. The storm center tracked through Manning, Sumter, Camden, and Kershaw on its way toward Charlotte. A school gym near Camden provided shelter for over 100 residents, when high winds threatened the structure. It was evacuated just minutes before the roof collapsed. In Berkeley and Dorchester Counties, hundreds of homes were heavily damaged, leaving 17,000 homeless. In Berkeley County, eight fatalities were recorded. Surveys after the storm found that 70 percent of the trees in this region were knocked down. In the town of Florence, near Interstate 95, high winds peeled away rooftops of several buildings at the Travelers Inn, chasing more than 100 guests from their rooms. Most were evacuees who had fled the coast. Many were dismayed to see that roof debris had crushed their cars in the parking lot.

Across a broad region, including Orangeburg, Clarendon, Sumter, and Florence Counties, hundreds of homes were destroyed or heavily damaged. Many lost roofs; others were bashed by fallen trees. Churches lost their steeples. Agricultural losses were heavy, too, especially for peaches, soybeans, pecans, and cotton. But the one constant, prominent in most every community along Hugo's path, was the unending sight of downed trees—crushing cars, tangling power lines, blocking roads, and presenting monumental challenges for removal crews.

In North Carolina, Hugo had a severe impact too, both on the beaches of Brunswick County and in the cities and towns in the western portions of the state. Damage was reported in twenty-nine counties, most of which were designated as federal disaster areas. As the center of the storm rolled past Charlotte, freakish winds buffeted the region. Sustained winds in Charlotte measured 69 mph; the highest gust recorded was 99 mph at Charlotte Douglas International Airport. Shards of glass rained down from a few of the city's skyscrapers when large windows were blown out. The 400-foot transmission tower at WSOC-TV collapsed onto the station. Pleasure craft on Lake Norman, north of Charlotte, were "piled into a heap like toys." Trees crashed into homes, cars, and power lines, and utility poles snapped. Charlotte lost more than 80,000 trees to the storm, many of which were more than seventy years old. Ninety-eight percent of the city's residents lost power, and for some, repairs were not made for more than two weeks. Power outages caused large amounts of raw sewage to bypass treatment plants and flow into streams throughout Mecklenburg

Hugo was a Category 4 hurricane when it swept ashore, and its extreme winds left a trail of destruction as it carved a path toward Charlotte. (Photo courtesy of the *State* Newspaper Photograph Archive, Richland Library, Columbia, South Carolina.)

Large hardwood trees fell throughout Charlotte when Hugo rolled through, crushing homes and cars. Cleanup of the downed trees took many weeks. (Photo by Jane Faircloth. Courtesy of Transparencies, Inc.)

County. North Carolina's largest metropolitan area was brought to its knees by the storm.

Numerous other cities and towns felt Hugo's wrath as it moved northwest. Gastonia, Monroe, Lincolnton, and Hickory were all hit hard by the storm. Two to four inches of rain fell across the western counties, although Boone received almost seven inches. High winds ripped down power lines throughout the region, and forests in some areas were leveled. In North Carolina, Hugo damaged more than 2.7 million acres of forests in twenty-six counties, with almost complete destruction of 68,000 acres. Timber losses to the state were valued at $250 million. And like in South Carolina, very little timber was salvaged. Forestry agents were overwhelmed by the sheer volume of dead trees. Most of the timber was either splintered by the storm or decayed before loggers could reach it.

In the wake of the hurricane, residents across the Carolinas emerged from their homes in awe of the destruction. So many trees, tree limbs, and utility poles were downed that they completely filled the streets and yards of some neighborhoods. Cleanup efforts began almost immediately but were slowed one week after Hugo when seven more inches of rain fell across several western counties. Chainsaws were essential in clearing streets and lawns, but perhaps the most valued commodity in the aftermath of the storm was one we often take for granted: electricity.

From the South Carolina coast to the hollows of the Blue Ridge Mountains, over 1.5 million people were without electric power the morning after the storm. Utility companies scrambled to put crews to work repairing and replacing downed poles and lines. In some areas, the destruction was so extensive that it was difficult to tell where the lines used to be. Line crews, equipment, and supplies were brought in from around the nation to assist with the effort. Some areas were back in service within days, but others were without power for weeks. Many crews worked sixteen-hour days and spent weeks away from their families to get the job done. Most residents were appreciative of the line crews' heroic efforts, but tempers sometimes flared as some customers remained in the dark while their neighbors' lights were on.

Duke Power was just one utility that reckoned with Hugo's aftermath. In the effort to restore electricity to 700,000 of its customers in North and South Carolina, Duke Power spent $62.5 million in just two weeks. More than 9,000 workers replaced 8,800 poles, 700 miles of cable and wire, 6,300 transformers, and 1,700 electric meters. The overall recovery effort was unprecedented in the utility's history. The importance of restoring electricity after any hurricane was highlighted in a government report following Hugo: "In any large-scale natural disaster, energy is the common denominator. Its loss is capable of causing severe economic dislocation. On the other hand, it is essential to recovery as well. In the case of hurricane Hugo, electric power was the principal infrastructure component that had to be rapidly restored."

Naturalists monitoring wildlife populations in western North Carolina noted that Hugo was responsible for bringing a number of bird species to the area that ordinarily wouldn't be found there. Seabirds sometimes become trapped in the eye of a major hurricane, traveling along with the storm as it moves forward. After Hugo, at least twenty-five species were transported to places such as Shelby and Lake Norman, hundreds of miles inland from their oceanic habitat. Among the birds seen in these areas were black skimmers, least terns, and a white-tailed tropic bird.

The southern beaches of the North Carolina coast also suffered from the effects of Hugo. In Brunswick County, the storm produced an eight-to ten foot storm surge that battered beachfront cottages. Over 120 homes on Holden Beach, Ocean Isle Beach, and Oak Island were either destroyed or condemned because they suffered extensive damage. Severe beach erosion affected these barrier islands, in many cases washing away the protective dunes that lined their shores. Oceanfront fishing piers were bashed and damaged in Brunswick, New Hanover, Pender, and Onslow Counties. But the most significant of the state's coastal destruction occurred in Brunswick County, where damage estimates topped $75 million.

At the time Hugo struck in 1989, it was the most expensive hurricane in U.S. history. Approximately $10 billion in property was destroyed, $7 billion on the U.S. mainland, $2 billion in Puerto Rico, and $1 billion elsewhere. It remains the costliest hurricane in South Carolina's history, with almost $6 billion in losses (in 1989 dollars). A tally of property damages reported by the Red Cross in the state included 3,307 single-family homes destroyed, 18,171 homes with major damage, 56,580 homes with minor damage, and another 12,600 mobile homes heavily damaged or destroyed. In North Carolina, the price tag was around $1 billion, even though the storm made landfall near Charleston, some 200 miles away. As a result, Hugo became North Carolina's most expensive hurricane to that date, though Hurricane Fran, and later Floyd, would shatter Hugo's mark in the 1990s.

As with many hurricanes, reports of the number of deaths associated with Hugo vary among sources. Some reports consider all deaths, while others distinguish between those directly and indirectly caused by the storm. The National Hurricane Center reported forty-nine direct deaths, twenty-six of which occurred in the United States, Puerto Rico, and the U.S. Virgin Islands. This tally includes thirteen fatalities in South Carolina, one in North Carolina, six in Virginia, and one in New York. Other government reports from 1989 count a total of fifty-six or sixty fatalities. Newspapers from the hardest-hit portions of the Carolinas reported numbers that included indirect fatalities, such as heart attacks, automobile accidents, and deaths associated with cleanup in the days following the hurricane. By these counts, the totals were estimated at eighty-two, including thirty-five in South Carolina and seven in North Carolina. Among the fatalities in South Carolina were four from collapsing homes, nine from fire and smoke inhalation, six from drowning, four from electrocution, and two from falling trees.

Dozens of injuries were reported in the days, weeks, and even months after the storm, ranging from severe cuts and broken limbs to electrocutions. Cleanup crews often encountered live power cables, and chainsaw-related injuries were common. But considering the widespread and heavy destruction Hugo brought to the Carolinas, the death toll could have been much higher.

Once the hurricane had moved on, the winds calmed, and the tides receded, everyone in Hugo's path struggled to comprehend the destruction. Whether at the coast, in the South Carolina Midlands, or the western counties of North Carolina, residents in hard-hit communities had to overcome the shock of what had just happened. It was hard to think about what to do next. "No one has ever seen anything like this in our lifetimes," one Sumter resident told the Associated Press. "I know we'll get through somehow, but frankly I don't know where to start."

Emotions ran high. In the days and weeks that followed, news editorials pointed to poor planning on the part of government officials and a pervasive lack of action. FEMA was heavily criticized for moving too slowly and famously called out by South Carolina U.S. senator Fritz Hollings on the floor of the U.S. Senate as "a bunch of bureaucratic jackasses." Local governments, working with state and federal officials, struggled to get recovery efforts underway in some of the hardest-hit areas.

The Hugo recovery, with all its challenges, received national attention as well. Among the analyses was that of the Natural Hazards Research and Applications Information Center at the University of Colorado, which published a detailed review of the recovery effort, highlighting what worked well and what didn't. In summary, it concluded that South Carolina wasn't prepared. Among the findings in the report:

> Problems were found in all four phases of emergency management: preparedness, response, recovery and mitigation. . . . When Hugo hit South Carolina, the warning and evacuation activities worked out well, but,

when the storm was over, no one seemed to know what to do next. Unfortunately, very little recovery planning had been done at any level of government. Given the magnitude of the disaster and the widespread damage, the recovery process had to be improvised. . . . The recovery period revealed significant deficiencies with state and county emergency capabilities and serious problems in two national disaster response organizations, the Red Cross and FEMA. An underlying concern is that most emergency management knowledge comes from direct experience rather than from existing educational and training programs. . . . Disaster management knowledge and techniques are known and used by some but are not being well taught or effectively shared.

The report and its findings echoed the views of many who worked closely through the recovery effort. Fortunately, the report's authors noted that "in general, the representatives from South Carolina's governmental agencies, the Red Cross, and FEMA regional staff supported the report's findings." Though there was considerable rancor surrounding the recovery effort, including what had and hadn't been done, many in the emergency management community now look back on this as a watershed moment in their profession. Soon after Hugo, "emergency management" became the focus of a lot of attention and funding across the nation, as states bolstered their staffing, professional training, disaster exercises, and cross-agency communications to better prepare for future disasters. FEMA implemented changes too, which would soon be tested—just three years after Hugo, Hurricane Andrew slammed South Florida, causing total damages that more than doubled Hugo's toll.

TAKEAWAYS

- *Powerful hurricanes barreling inland are our greatest threat.* In the Carolinas, Category 4 landfalls are rare, and no Category 5 hurricanes have been documented. But when an intense storm such as Hugo does strike, an inland track poses a tremendous threat—especially if the storm strikes a city at the coast and moves through densely populated areas such as Columbia, Charlotte, or the Triangle region of Raleigh, Durham, and Chapel Hill. Coastal cities will always be first to suffer, but the impact of damaging winds and flooding in more populous inland areas escalates the destructive toll and threatens more lives.
- *A rapidly intensifying hurricane that makes an unexpected shift in track prior to landfall is a forecaster's worst nightmare.* Forecasters at the National Hurricane Center have improved their forecast-track performance significantly

over the years. But they'd be quick to say that forecasting changes in intensity still poses a huge challenge. During its final approach to the Florida panhandle in 2018, Hurricane Michael jumped from Category 3 to Category 5 intensity, alarming local officials and wreaking havoc upon landfall. When a hurricane intensifies rapidly just before arrival, it can catch residents—and even emergency management officials—off guard. The same can happen when an approaching hurricane unexpectedly shifts course. That's why, when discussing forecast tracks, you'll hear meteorologists and officials say, "Don't focus on the skinny line, pay attention to the cone of probability." Hugo both intensified and changed course slightly in the hours before sweeping ashore; fortunately, these late-breaking changes were well communicated to coastal residents.

- *The use of satellite imagery was a game changer for hurricane forecasters.* In the early 1960s, the first images of hurricanes from space were beamed down from satellites, heralding a new era in hurricane forecasting. These images allow meteorologists to have a more accurate and complete picture of a storm's size, location, and organizing features and to see how it relates to nearby weather systems. Through the late 1960s and '70s, further improvements yielded more detailed images. By the time Hugo moved through the Atlantic in 1989, satellite images were an important tool in evaluating the hurricane's evolution and movements—something easily taken for granted today.

- *Organized, professional emergency management, staffed with well-trained personnel, is essential for coping with hurricane disasters.* This seems obvious today, but just a few decades ago, there were real gaps in our ability to respond to broadscale disasters such as Hugo. The necessary levels of planning and coordination among federal, state, and local officials were lacking, mostly due to an underestimation of the personnel and resources required to effect response and recovery in a disaster of its scale. At the time, Hugo was the costliest hurricane in U.S. history. Months after the storm, some leaders in the United States saw it as a turning point, after which more emergency management professionals were employed and new funding helped governments better prepare for future storms. Hugo was a bit of wake-up call, and the effort that followed to continuously improve response and recovery is still relevant today.

- *Multibillion-dollar hurricane disasters are here to stay.* Since Hurricane Diane in 1955—a storm some consider to be the first billion-dollar hurricane disaster—we've seen steadily rising costs for U.S. hurricanes. Hugo's $7 billion tally in the Carolinas was shocking in 1989, shattering the U.S.

record for hurricane losses. That sum was eclipsed just three years later by Hurricane Andrew and its whopping $27 billion toll. Since that time, active hurricane seasons and numerous megadisasters have yielded more eye-popping damage figures. In the Carolinas, Florence now tops the list at $24 billion, surpassing Hugo as the costliest hurricane in either state. Costs keep rising, but not because the storms are more severe. The growing damage figures stem largely from three ongoing factors: population growth in U.S. coastal counties, the growth of wealth, and inflation over time. Today, far more people live and work in harm's way than in the 1950s, for example. They live in larger, more expensive homes and own more costly cars, boats, and other possessions. Though mitigation efforts are underway to help reduce future losses, multibillion-dollar hurricanes in the United States have become commonplace, siphoning away ever-growing amounts of federal funding, threatening local economies, and posing increasingly difficult challenges for government decision-makers.

CHAPTER TWELVE

HURRICANE FRAN,
SEPTEMBER 1996

Like several others in this book, the story of Hurricane Fran is really the tale of two hurricanes. Bertha and Fran conspired to make 1996 a record-breaking year in North Carolina's weather history. Fran, a potent September Cape Verde hurricane, was itself an epic disaster, and Bertha's impact on some of the same portions of the coast just eight weeks earlier gave the Tar Heel State a one-two hurricane punch not seen since 1955. As the 1996 season ended, Fran became the state's costliest disaster ever and its deadliest hurricane in eighty years.

Following an overly active 1995 hurricane season that gave the Outer Banks a close call from Hurricane Felix, 1996 quickly established itself as a benchmark year for weather in North Carolina. Not only was the state paralyzed by winter storms that caused twelve fatalities from January through March, but a record fifty-one tornadoes touched down during the year, many associated with powerful thunderstorms in April and June. But by far, the biggest weather stories of 1996 were Hurricanes Bertha and Fran. For the first time in forty-one years, two hurricanes struck the Tar Heel coast during the same season, sending a wake-up call for thousands of North Carolina residents who got a double dose of hurricane trouble.

As families and friends gathered for Fourth of July celebrations along the Carolina beaches, a tropical wave drifted off the African coast and began to churn across the Atlantic. Soon after the last fireworks displays were over, the National Hurricane Center quietly issued its first advisory on the tropical depression that would later become Hurricane Bertha. July hurricanes are not common, though the historical record includes more than twenty-five that have made landfall in the United States since 1851. Bertha reached Category 3 status on July 9, the first Atlantic hurricane to achieve that intensity that early in the season since Hurricane Alma in 1966.

As Bertha tracked toward the Carolinas on July 10, evacuations got underway along the North Carolina coast. By late afternoon on July 11, beach towns such as Wrightsville Beach and Emerald Isle were eerily quiet, except for the

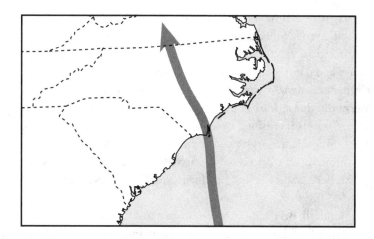

Hurricane Bertha's surging tide undermined the main road through North Topsail Beach. (Photo by Don Bryan. Courtesy of the Jacksonville *Daily News*.)

sound of police cruisers that roamed the near-empty neighborhoods in search of the uninformed. Even before Bertha's arrival, its economic impact was being felt; tourism suffered as vacationers scrambled to leave the coast. But some chose not to leave and continued watching the Category 1 storm.

Then, as has happened many times before, the lumbering hurricane rapidly intensified overnight, due at least in part to its proximity to the Gulf Stream. Bertha's sustained winds intensified by 25 mph in less than twelve hours. By July 12 the storm was a Category 2, and it picked up forward speed just before slamming into the coast between Wrightsville Beach and Topsail Island at about 5:00 P.M. Bertha was the first July hurricane to strike North Carolina since 1908.

After making landfall, Bertha quickly diminished in strength, moved inland across eastern North Carolina and eastern Virginia, and then slid along the northeastern coast to New England. On portions of the North Carolina coast, Bertha provided many residents with their first real taste of hurricane wind and water. Although there was an unconfirmed report of a 144 mph gust at Topsail Beach, most wind readings were well below 100 mph. Frying Pan Light Station, off the coast of Cape Fear, encountered the eyewall and recorded sustained winds of 83 mph and gusts to 108 mph. The highest winds on land were measured at New River near Jacksonville, where sustained winds of 81 mph and a gust of 108 mph were recorded.

Bertha's gusts toppled trees and whipped signs, shingles, and loose objects along much of the central coast. In many communities, the winds were the strongest experienced in decades. Both man-made structures and natural vegetation were put to the test. Particularly hard hit were the communities that felt the storm's eastern eyewall, especially in Onslow, Carteret, Jones, Craven, Pitt, Beaufort, Martin, Bertie, and Hertford Counties. Heavy rains pounded the Carolina coast, too, as Bertha moved inland. Numerous rainfall measurements exceeding eight inches were reported, including a record of more than fourteen inches near Hofmann Forest.

The winds and rains were significant, as were the storm's surging tides, which caused extensive beach erosion and structural damage for miles around the area of landfall. Hardest hit were the beaches and sounds between Cape Fear and Cape Lookout, especially those north of Wrightsville Beach. Fishing piers were damaged from Kure Beach to Carteret County, and miles of oceanfront dunes were stripped of their sand. The highest storm surge, estimated to be between five and eight feet, struck in Pender and Onslow Counties and caused extensive structural damages on Topsail Island and at Swansboro. The surging tide also overfilled sounds, creeks, and inland rivers, destroying hundreds of residential piers and boat docks. Nowhere, however, was the storm's destruction more evident than in the precariously low-lying resort community of North Topsail Beach.

Bertha's thirty-five-mile-wide eye moved inland just below Surf City, focusing the storm's worst effects on the narrow barrier island. North Topsail Beach, viewed by some as having too little elevation for residential development, was hardest hit by the ocean surge. Waves rolled over the area's modest dunes and flooded State Road 1568, washing away tons of sand and causing the road to collapse in at least three sections. As the storm passed, pools of water up to eight feet deep crossed the broken highway, which provided the only access to the northern tip of the island. About fifteen families were stranded in their cottages beyond the scuttled road, and emergency personnel considered sending a Marine Corps helicopter to rescue them.

One couple from Ohio barely escaped a confrontation with the tides. After deciding to ride out the hurricane in their North Topsail home, they apparently changed their minds as the storm reached its peak. They piled into their minivan and attempted the dangerous trek toward higher ground. By that time, however, the water had risen too high, and they were forced to abandon their swamped-out vehicle and wade back to their home through chest-deep water. The following day, rescue crews pulled their minivan out of several feet of water and sand.

As Bertha bore down on Topsail Island, police in Surf City rescued more than fifty people who had belatedly decided not to weather the storm. According to a report in *The Savage Season*, a book published by the Wilmington *Star-News*, police chief David Jones endured another of the storm's close calls. "We went to get a lady that was up at the north end, and we got out of the car trying to get to her house, and the roof picked up off her house and just missed the patrol car and us by about 6 feet," Jones reported. "A whole roof crashed in the road in front of us."

At North Topsail more than 120 homes were destroyed, and hundreds more suffered damage from wind and water. Dozens of washers, dryers, heat pumps, and other appliances were washed into ditches and marshes, forming instant landfills. Scattered among the broken and exposed water mains were cars, buried to their door handles in deep sand. The walls of some homes were peeled open, their contents visible to the outside as if they were oversized dollhouses. These were the scenes that attracted television news crews in the days and weeks following Bertha, as North Topsail was generally considered to have borne the brunt of the storm's fury. In nearby Surf City and Topsail Beach, fishing piers were heavily damaged, and severe erosion swallowed up much of the beach.

Among those who weathered the storm at Topsail Beach was nationally syndicated television talk show host Rolonda Watts. Watts, a North Carolina native, disregarded evacuation orders and stayed put as the storm surge ran underneath her home, which was built on pilings. "I love this stuff. There's nothing greater than being in the mix," she told the Jacksonville *Daily News*. In the hours before Bertha approached the Carolina coast, she wanted to bring satellite trucks down to the area to tape an episode for her *Rolonda* show, but the impending evacuation made that difficult. Fortunately, the television personality and her home were both unharmed by the hurricane.

Elsewhere in Onslow County, gusting winds ripped away the roof of the Dixon Middle School gymnasium, which happened to be serving as an emergency shelter for local evacuees. This caused some tense moments for the frightened refugees, who were quickly moved to the school's cafeteria. In other communities such as Hampstead, Jacksonville, and Richlands, pines cracked and oaks collapsed across countless homes, cars, and roadways. In Swansboro, a storm surge of six to eight feet flooded much of the waterfront area. Upriver, virtually every private dock was lifted, broken, and tossed along the riverbanks in unrecognizable forms. This region saw some of the storm's worst inland flooding.

Farther south, six-foot tides eroded beaches in Cherry Grove, South Carolina, and gale-force winds caused minor damage. In North Carolina, Kure, Carolina, and Wrightsville Beaches suffered as well. Fishing piers were heavily damaged and numerous homes and businesses lost their roofs. At Carolina Beach, parts of Carolina Avenue were under three feet of sand. Among the notable losses was the Ferris wheel at Jubilee Park amusement center. The forty-two-year-old wheel toppled during the storm, crashing into a nearby merry-go-round and landing in a pile of twisted metal. The park's owners, Larry and Ginny Spencer, had no insurance on the wheel but managed to maintain their sense of humor about the loss. Soon after the hurricane had passed, a sign was erected near the park's main gate that read, "Used Ferris Wheel for Sale."

Across the impacted region, most of the damage came with the crack and thunderous collapse of large trees that succumbed to Bertha's winds. In Wilmington, many stately oaks and other hardwoods were lost in the historic downtown district, and around the city, power lines were toppled by falling branches and limbs. One of the notable trees was a large, 200-year-old oak on Fifth Avenue that was split open by Bertha's gusting winds. Residents were surprised to discover that spilling from the belly of the oak were cobblestones and Civil War–era cannonball fragments, likely put inside the tree's hollow as ballast many years before.

Farther north, Bertha's winds and tides caused similar issues. Marinas and docks were battered in New Bern, Oriental, Washington, and Belhaven. Waters from the Pungo River flowed into Belhaven's streets, flooding homes and businesses and leaving behind a mud line on the walls of the old town hall. Damages were also reported in Emerald Isle, Atlantic Beach, and Morehead City, although the destruction lessened east of Beaufort. Ocracoke and Hatteras Islands were spared the worst of the storm, and residents and vacationers there were allowed to return the day after the hurricane.

In Raleigh, well to the west of Bertha's official track, the storm still managed to have an impact. Twelve hours before landfall, the National Weather Service reported that a tornado touched down in southwest Raleigh and crossed into Cary, uprooting trees but causing no serious injuries. Another windstorm whipped across the state fairgrounds, tearing away the roof of the Hunt Horse Complex while a 4-H horse competition was underway. Almost 400 horses and 1,800 spectators were badly frightened, but no one was injured. Both incidents were spawned by the approaching hurricane, along with three other twisters later documented in Maryland.

Even though Bertha, as a Category 2, didn't rank as a "major" hurricane, its overall impact on eastern North Carolina was significant. In all, 750,000 people had evacuated the Carolina coast, and the disruption of the busy summer season created economic losses for many coastal businesses. In North Carolina, more than 400,000 residents were without power; 1,100 homes were destroyed and another 4,000 damaged; seventeen counties were declared disaster areas by President Bill Clinton; and property damages totaled more than $300 million. Bertha claimed twelve lives overall, two of which were in North Carolina—both from automobile accidents related to the storm.

A whole generation of eastern North Carolina residents would remember Bertha as their first meaningful hurricane. It was the first tropical cyclone since Ginger in 1971 to have such a broad and significant impact across the eastern counties. As a rare July storm, it struck in the heart of the tourist season and had a lingering effect on the region's economy. But most incredibly, after such a long period with so few hurricanes, coastal residents soon found themselves battening down for another dangerous storm when Hurricane Fran approached the same portion of the coast just eight weeks later.

In the weeks following Hurricane Bertha, residents along the North Carolina coast did their best to repair their damaged properties and bring their lives back to normal. Downed trees were cut and hauled, signs were replaced, shingles were patched, and docks and boats were repaired. But then, just as the kids went back to school and the Labor Day holiday approached, more talk of hurricanes spread across the airwaves. First it was Edouard, an impressive Category 4 that was deflected by a trough over the Carolina coast in late August, steering the storm offshore midway between Cape Hatteras and Bermuda. Unfortunately, a few days behind Edouard came another storm whose track would not be diverted—Hurricane Fran.

Fran was a classic Cape Verde hurricane that lived and died in the heart of the hurricane season. Its origins were familiar—out of Africa as a tropical wave with a typical westward movement—but its early development may have been thwarted somewhat by the presence of the large and powerful Edouard some 750 miles to the west-northwest. After finally reaching tropical-storm strength and earning its name on August 27, Fran literally traveled in the wake of Edouard, passing northeast of the Lesser Antilles with little impact on the Caribbean. Then deep convection became more concentrated, and Fran's winds reached hurricane strength on August 29. By the following day, however, it was downgraded to a tropical storm, possibly due again to the presence of Edouard. Fran slowed in forward speed, turned toward the northwest, and for the moment seemed too weak and distant to pose a serious threat to the Carolina coast.

As Edouard tracked north on August 31 and became less of an influence, Fran regained hurricane strength and began to accelerate. The subtropical ridge that had once kept Edouard at sea was now itself over the Atlantic and helped steer Fran west-northwest, on a course then roughly parallel to the Bahamas some 100 miles to the east. Over the next three days, the hurricane strengthened consistently, finally reaching Category 3 intensity, with maximum sustained winds of 115 mph, on September 4. At this point, forecasters looked to the next nearby weather system that could influence the hurricane's course— a mid-to-upper-level low-pressure system drifting over Tennessee.

Forecasters and residents along much of the southeast coast were now closely monitoring the hurricane's every move. On September 4, the Hurricane Center issued a hurricane watch from Sebastian Inlet, Florida, to Little River Inlet, South Carolina, based on their impressions of the storm's forward direction. Late that evening, while poised some 250 miles off the Florida coast, Fran reached peak intensity. Its minimum central pressure dropped to 945 millibars (mb), and maximum sustained winds reached 120 mph. By this time, hurricane warnings were in effect for much of South Carolina's coast and all of North Carolina's, including the Albemarle and Pamlico Sounds. Everyone now acknowledged that Fran was a dangerous storm. Thousands turned their attention to the computer-generated landfall probabilities displayed on the nightly news and the internet. No one knew exactly where the storm would strike, but it was frightfully clear that landfall was imminent.

Full-blown evacuations got underway along the beaches of North and South Carolina, based on an expected landfall near Myrtle Beach. Throughout the morning on Thursday, September 5, a stream of cars fled inland, away from the "danger zone" near the coast. As the storm drew closer to the Carolinas, it gradually appeared that landfall would occur a little farther north than fore-casters had earlier predicted—and it did. Fran came ashore near Bald Head Island around 8:30 P.M. Thanks to good early warnings and the storm's lack of rapid acceleration before landfall, most residents who had wanted to leave the beaches had ample time to do so.

At the time Fran made landfall, it was still a minimal Category 3 hurricane, with maximum sustained winds of 115 mph and an estimated minimum pres-sure of 953 mb. The strongest winds were believed to have run in streaks within deep convective areas of the circulation, north and northeast of the center. And Fran was no small storm. Before landfall, reconnaissance reports indicated that hurricane-force winds were measured up to 145 miles away from the eye. Be-fore their televisions were darkened by the loss of power, most residents in the hurricane's path were able to watch the ominous swirl of radar images as Fran advanced over them. By the time it moved inland, the storm appeared to have swallowed up much of North Carolina.

Fran's course overland seemed almost to follow the Cape Fear River, affecting a broad region that extended upstate. Because the hurricane's greatest power was concentrated on its eastern side, the beaches of New Hanover, Pender, Onslow, and Carteret Counties were hammered with the worst winds and tides. To a large degree, this was the same region that had suffered during Bertha just weeks before, but Fran was different. It was a larger, more intense storm, and its impact along most of this stretch of coast was far greater than that of the July hurricane.

Fran's course carried it deep inland, up the Cape Fear, west of Interstate 40, and into the heart of the Triangle region of Raleigh, Durham, and Chapel Hill. Along the way, its howling winds battered every county in its path, fell-ing millions of trees and knocking out power over a major portion of the state. According to National Weather Service reports, the center of the storm tracked through portions of Brunswick, New Hanover, Pender, Sampson, Harnett, Johnston, Wake, Durham, and Person Counties before passing into south cen-tral Virginia. Because of the storm's strength and interior course, damages were heavy all along its path. Destructive winds and flooding rains tore through the region, wreaking havoc reminiscent of Hugo's visit across South Carolina and into western North Carolina in 1989. Gusts above hurricane strength were felt as far inland as Durham, and isolated bursts above 75 mph may even have reached into Virginia.

Officially, Hurricane Fran was downgraded to a tropical storm around 3:00 A.M. on September 6, shortly before its center reached the Raleigh area. It continued to lose energy as it passed into Virginia, where it was downgraded further to become a tropical depression. It still had a significant impact on the Virginia countryside, however, as torrential rains caused flooding in the region near Danville and South Boston. As the storm slowly continued northward over the eastern Great Lakes, it gradually lost its warm central core and was no longer tracked by hurricane watchers. On the evening of September 8, Fran became extratropical while centered over southern Ontario, Canada. With little fanfare, its remnants were later absorbed into a passing frontal system.

From a meteorological perspective, Fran was one of the most intensely studied hurricanes in history. Scientists used a wide range of instruments and techniques to scrutinize the storm on land, at sea, and in the air. These studies yielded loads of data that ultimately helped improve our basic understanding of hurricane behavior. Perhaps one of the most interesting experiments was conducted aboard National Oceanic and Atmospheric Administration hurricane hunter aircraft. Reconnaissance flights had been flown into hurricanes for decades but always while the storms were at sea. Fran marked the first time that researchers had ever flown through a hurricane that was moving overland. "We've never done it before because it was considered too dangerous," said National Oceanic and Atmospheric Administration researcher Mark Powell in an interview with the Raleigh *News and Observer*. "The water is fairly smooth, so the levels of turbulence aren't as intense as they are over land. No one knew what to expect."

The mission flew for three hours after landfall, looping over Raleigh and Durham around 10:30 P.M., then turning around and passing through the advancing eye south of Goldsboro. The aircraft was loaded with various weather instruments, including Doppler radar and special devices to measure the storm's barometric pressure, wind, and rainfall. Powell indicated that the mission was successful in providing "the most detailed picture we've ever had of what happens in a hurricane after landfall." In total, the reconnaissance flights during Fran (all of which were conducted by the U.S. Air Force Reserve) allowed the crew to calculate the coordinates of the storm's center (known as center fixes) seventy-one times in the course of seventeen flight missions.

Other scientific studies were underway as Fran roared ashore. Buoys loaded with weather instruments were deployed off the Carolina coast in advance of the storm. This practice has become somewhat routine in recent years, but Fran apparently was the first storm in which the buoys were in position to report from the eye of a passing hurricane. Also, scientists from the National Severe Storms

Laboratory were in Wilmington when Fran arrived. These scientists normally focus their studies on severe thunderstorms and tornadoes; now, for the first time, they were present to observe the conditions of a landfalling hurricane.

The scientists had plenty to observe. Wind-measuring instruments all over eastern North Carolina were tested by the storm. Unfortunately, a few were destroyed, and some made recordings that were later discounted because the instruments either were mounted at an improper elevation (the World Meteorological Organization standard is ten meters, or thirty-three feet, above the ground) or simply were not reliable. Nevertheless, the National Weather Service was able to confirm wind reports that included gusts of 124 mph at Frying Pan Shoals Light Tower, 122 mph at Figure Eight Island, 105 mph in Southport and New Bern, 100 mph in Greenville, 92 mph at the Duke University Marine Laboratory in Beaufort, 80 mph at Seymour-Johnson Air Force Base in Goldsboro, 79 mph at Raleigh-Durham Airport, and 86 mph in Efland, west of Durham. Wilmington's Doppler weather surveillance radar measured winds aloft in excess of 138 mph as the inner convective bands of the storm approached the Cape Fear area before landfall. After the storm, there were published but unconfirmed reports of gusts of 137 mph at Hewletts Creek in Wilmington and 126 mph at Wrightsville Beach. As is often the case with landfalling hurricanes, reports of sustained hurricane-force winds were difficult to find, although a reading of 90 mph was recorded at Frying Pan Shoals (based on a two-minute averaging period). The lowest barometric pressure observed on land was 953 mb, recorded in Southport at the time of landfall and communicated to the National Hurricane Center by amateur radio volunteers.

According to National Weather Service reports, the heavy storm surge that affected much of North Carolina's southeast coast ranged from eight to twelve feet. Still-water marks measured inside buildings provided these elevations; exterior water levels were generally higher due to wave action. The highest surges were observed at Carolina Beach, Wrightsville Beach, Figure Eight Island, and Topsail Island. Some longtime residents at Wrightsville Beach compared the flood level during Fran with that of Hurricane Hazel in 1954 and found that Fran's was several inches higher. Hazel was a much more intense storm, but it struck some forty miles farther down the coast. Preliminary reports from the Weather Service indicated that Fran's surge was ten feet in Swansboro and New Bern, nine feet in Washington and Belhaven, and seven feet at Atlantic Beach. Still-water surge heights of five feet were measured in Southport and Beaufort, North Carolina. A large portion of the dunes between Figure Eight Island and Emerald Isle had been washed away by Bertha, setting the stage for extensive beach erosion and ocean overwash during Fran. With little dune structure left to protect these areas, the surging tide and breaking waves demolished homes, undermined roads, and covered streets and yards with deep sand and debris.

The destructive floods that hit many portions of the state did not just sweep in with the storm surge but also fell from the skies. Drenching rains bore inland as Fran came ashore, with the heaviest bands of precipitation very closely following the storm track. To make matters worse, some portions of North Carolina received monsoon-like rains even before Fran approached the coast. On September 3, two days before the hurricane's landfall, Carteret and Onslow Counties were inundated with rains measured at up to seven and a half inches in some locations. These rains filled creeks and ditches and saturated soils near the coast. At the opposite end of the state, strong thunderstorms associated with an upper-level low poured incredible rains on several western communities just before the hurricane struck the coast. The area around Bat Cave, Lake Lure, and Chimney Rock received up to eleven inches of rain in just three hours; Sugar Loaf Mountain recorded 12.49 inches. As a result, about seventy homes and businesses were severely damaged or destroyed. And in the central part of the state, the Triangle and northern Piedmont had about four inches of rain in the three days immediately preceding Fran. These rains also saturated the ground and set the stage for the record-breaking floods that followed.

Rainfall totals exceeding six inches were common along the path of the hurricane as it moved overland. Wilmington radar precipitation estimates ranged as high as twelve inches over portions of Brunswick and Pender Counties, and the Newport Doppler system estimated similar amounts over Duplin and Onslow Counties. Cherry Grove Pier in South Carolina reported 8.36 inches, Pope Air Force Base in Fayetteville 6.72 inches, and New River Air Station at Jacksonville 7.05 inches.

As Fran tracked inland, its center of circulation held together longer than expected, partially due to its large size. Fran was as large as Hugo and larger than Andrew, even though it wasn't as powerful as either of those storms. Its central core finally collapsed just southeast of Raleigh, almost directly over the city of Garner. These factors spelled disaster for the Raleigh area. The Raleigh *News and Observer* described the result: "Two large bands of intense winds and rain surrounding the center suddenly rushed together as the storm collapsed inward on itself over Raleigh. That caused the hurricane to drop its heaviest rains on the city." Though reports suggested that up to 9.5 inches fell at some Triangle locations, the Raleigh-Durham Airport officially recorded 8.80 inches, still enough to shatter the old twenty-four-hour record of 6.66 inches set in September 1929. (Hazel brought only 4.93 inches to the Triangle.) Other records marked at the airport included the highest recorded wind gust (79 mph, which

beat the previous record of 64 mph set during a thunderstorm in May 1996)
and the lowest barometric pressure for September (977 mb). A slightly lower
pressure reading of 974 mb had been recorded at the airport during Hazel in
October 1954.

The worst of the rains were yet to come, however. Fran continued to dis-
sipate as it moved into Virginia and dumped its heavy clouds over much of the
state. Some of the most impressive precipitation occurred near Shenandoah
National Park, where rainfall amounts were enhanced by the orographic effects
of the central Appalachian Mountains. The highest recorded amount was 15.61
inches, though numerous stations measured in excess of fourteen inches. Heavy
rains also spilled into portions of West Virginia and Pennsylvania, where flooding was considered the most severe in years.

In addition to monitoring estimated rainfall over the areas affected by Fran,
Doppler radar stations indicated the presence of several tornadoes in North
Carolina and Virginia. According to the National Weather Service, confirma-
tion of such reports was difficult due to the extensive nature of straight-line
wind damage across the region. Some residents near Hampstead reported hearing the distinctive "freight train" sounds of a twister barreling through their
neighborhood, though so many trees were downed throughout the area that
isolating a particular path of destruction was tricky. Weather experts agree,
however, that funnel clouds were very likely present in some of the storm's
stronger convective bands.

Meteorologically, Fran was a major hurricane—a real Category 3 with all the
trimmings. But perhaps even more impressive than the record-breaking wind,
storm surge, and rain were the scope and severity of destruction the storm laid
across the land. Decades had passed since the Tar Heel State had felt this kind
of blow, and its force exposed many vulnerabilities. Not only did the storm
shatter property wherever it went, but it also altered the lives and challenged
the spirits of its victims.

As Fran came ashore near the mouth of the Cape Fear River, residents in
nearby Southport were expecting the worst. Though well informed about the
storm's anticipated intensity, many older inhabitants were ready for comparisons with their lifetime benchmark—Hurricane Hazel—from four decades
earlier. They knew, perhaps better than most, that Fran should be taken very
seriously.

Fortunately, Southport and the Brunswick County beaches were spared
the worst of Fran. Even though the storm's eye passed over Southport, wind
damages there were generally lighter than expected. Slight damages were reported to roofs, signs, and docks, and some of the town's trademark live oaks

were toppled. The nearby Brunswick nuclear power plant, which at the time supplied 20 percent of Carolina Power and Light's electricity, was shut down sixteen hours before the storm arrived, and no damages were reported there. While the inland areas of New Hanover and Pender Counties were buffeted by high winds, an eerie quiet fell over the streets of Southport. The calm lasted so long that some residents ventured into the streets to peer up at the twinkling stars, despite warnings to stay put. After the hurricane had passed, Brunswick County emergency management director Cecil Logan told *USA Today*, "We stayed in the eye for more than two hours, which is unheard of. We stayed in that eye, and the storm tore up everyone else."

At Oak Island, more than 200 homes received some damage, and nineteen were rendered uninhabitable. Many were oceanfront cottages whose septic systems were undermined or damaged by the storm tide. The once-popular Long Beach Pier lost about 100 feet of its length, but other piers on the island were relatively unharmed. At Holden Beach, seven homes reportedly "fell into the ocean," and several feet of dunes were washed away. At Ocean Isle, the septic systems of fourteen homes were damaged, and several cottages were flooded by overwash. Overall, though, these beaches, which had been swept by Hazel's awesome seventeen-foot surge, fared very well in Fran. Because they were on the weaker side of the eye, the storm surge was moderate, measuring only about six feet at Holden Beach. In the weeks following the storm, tourists who were forced to cancel vacations farther north jammed the county's beachfront hotels.

Around Cape Fear, it was a different story. The beaches of New Hanover County caught the brunt of the hurricane and were left with a massive mess. Fort Fisher, Kure Beach, Carolina Beach, Wrightsville Beach, and Figure Eight Island all were exposed to Fran's destructive core. As high winds peeled back roofs and snapped utility poles, the surging Atlantic sucked away dunes and poured into the streets. The tide filled some homes with water and sand and radically displaced others. In Carolina Beach, one house floated off its foundation and came to rest on Canal Drive, some 200 feet inland. The Wilmington *Star-News* reported that the town was under six feet of water at times. Other stories held that cars were floating about during the peak of the storm, bumping into telephone poles and buildings. As the flood worsened, rising water forced the town's police department to move from its headquarters on Canal Drive to the town recreation center. One resident, who believed pounding waves were about to demolish his condominium building, called 911 at the height of the storm to relay information to his next of kin. Some longtime residents emphatically insisted that the damage was "just as bad as Hazel." In all, Carolina

Beach had over 930 damaged homes, forty-one destroyed homes, seventy-five damaged businesses, and over $33 million in private property losses.

At nearby Kure Beach, the scene was similarly depressing. Dozens of ocean-front homes and condos, already compromised by Bertha a few weeks earlier, suffered major structural damage. Several feet of sand were carried inland by the surging waters and deposited in first-floor rooms of vacation resorts. Porches, decks, and awnings disappeared, either swept away by wind and water or buried out of sight. Debris from damaged structures drifted in the flood, covering streets and lawns with a potpourri of lumber, appliances, household furnishings, and broken glass. A portion of Atlantic Avenue washed away, and other streets were barely recognizable. Water and sewer lines were ruptured, sixty-eight businesses were damaged, and more than 260 houses were destroyed. Kure Beach was near ground zero during Fran, and few communities faced more significant destruction.

One well-known facility affected by the storm was the North Carolina Aquarium at Fort Fisher, which suffered only minor structural damage but was forced to rely on its diesel-powered generator to keep air and water flowing to its displays. After a few days, fuel began to run low, and curator Paul Barrington and his staff faced the possibility of having to release or lose their collection of fishes that had taken years to acquire. But fortunately, after reading about the aquarium's dilemma in the Wilmington *Star-News* on September 8, the wife of a Carolina Power and Light worker urged her husband to make the aquarium a priority. By 11:00 A.M., the electricity was back on again, and the fishes were saved.

Up the coast at Wrightsville Beach, a storm surge of close to eleven feet tore down dunes and flooded expensive beach houses. Almost the entire town was underwater at one point. When residents at Harbor Island finally returned to their homes, some found scum lines on their walls four feet above the floor. Up and down the beach, deep sand covered Lumina Avenue, mixed with debris from first-floor cottages and apartments. Beach chairs and washing machines were not the only losses—some people lost personal keepsakes such as wedding albums, home videos, love letters, and music collections. Virtually anything left at ground level was either saturated by rising salt water or washed into the streets. At the Bridge Tender restaurant near the bridge to Wrightsville, witnesses reported that high water "floated bottles off the bar." On the northern end of the beach, a six-foot dune was flattened, edging Mason Inlet even closer to the imperiled $22 million Shell Island Resort. Like the other nearby beaches, Wrightsville suffered heavy damages: more than 560 homes damaged, thirteen houses destroyed, and fifteen businesses damaged.

In Wilmington, it was largely Fran's nasty winds that caused trouble. Bertha had already thinned out the weaker trees, but countless more either snapped above the ground or heaved over, roots and all, during Fran. Power lines and traffic signals were torn and tangled, gas station canopies buckled and fell, and residential roofs were stripped. In some locations, empty tractor trailers were blown on their sides and commercial buildings had their metal roofs peeled away. One of the casualties was the Days Inn, which lost part of its roof during the storm, to the astonishment of guests who had retreated to their rooms on the top floor. Around the city, evidence of Fran's visit was easy to spot on the morning after the storm.

Few landmarks in Wilmington got more attention after the hurricane than the historic First Baptist Church on Market Street, which lost its steeple to one of Fran's early gusts. Sometime after 10:00 P.M. on the night of the storm, Rev. Mike Queen was summoned to his church to inspect the damage. He arrived during the quiet of the hurricane's eye and found that a major portion of the church's 197-foot spire had exploded onto the sidewalk below. The copper-topped steeple, built between 1860 and 1870, was thought to have been used as a lookout post during the Civil War. It had since withstood many hurricanes, including Hazel in 1954 and the 135 mph gusts of Hurricane Helene in 1958. After studying the mountain of bricks beside his church, Queen proclaimed that the spire would be rebuilt. He also described to the Associated Press his perspective on the loss: "God created a world that allows nature to do what it will."

Curator Harry Warren of the Cape Fear Museum summarized the First Baptist Church's calamity thus: "It came down like thunder. Then, it ended up being symbolic of the entire hurricane experience in Wilmington. The next day, every news cameraman in the free world was out there filming in front of it. Satellite trucks were all over the place and these news reporter guys were dressed up like something out of Banana Republic. It was really quite a scene."

Emergency management officials later reported that one-quarter of Wilmington's homes were damaged. According to the Raleigh *News and Observer*, nine businesses sustained major damage, 320 homes were destroyed, 530 homes suffered major damage, and more than 3,000 had minor damages. As in most other communities in the area, power was out across the city. Mayor Don Betts estimated the impact on public buildings to be at least $5 million and described Fran as a "major, major storm."

Across New Hanover County, boat owners had done their best to prepare for the hurricane, some harboring their boats in protected creeks, others trailering them inland. Many, though, underestimated the power unleashed by Fran. Along docks from Snows Cut to Bradley Creek, vessels large and small were tossed, beaten, and sunk. Like toys in a bathtub, many broke free of their moorings and rode the tide to high ground. After the waters receded, Masonboro Road was littered with broken docks and misplaced boats, just as it had been forty-two years earlier after Hazel. One vessel tossed onto high ground was the *Hurricane Rock*, which was selected as the backdrop for Tom Brokaw's post-storm live broadcast of *NBC Nightly News*.

At Bradley Creek, several large boats and the floating dock to which they were tied broke loose during the storm and smashed into the Oleander Drive bridge. Boats at the nearby marina had suffered a similar fate after Bertha. The Scotts Hill Marina was also beaten by Fran's pounding storm surge, sending sections of dock and expensive pleasure craft into the nearby woods. Before Fran hit, a local film studio had scheduled to shoot scenes at the marina for the movie *Buried Alive II*. Afterward, producers agreed to foot half of the bill for the dock repairs so that filming could proceed. According to the Wilmington *Star-News*, losses from damaged and destroyed boats alone totaled $50 million.

Perhaps the most amazing destruction inflicted by Fran fell upon the communities of Topsail Island along the Pender-Onslow coast. Topsail Beach, Surf City, and North Topsail Beach were all slammed hard by Hurricane Bertha in July, only to catch the worst of Fran mere weeks later. Bertha caused extensive property damages, but more important, it washed away the island's protective dunes. Afterward, very little remained to slow the ten-foot storm tide that accompanied Hurricane Fran. Across most of the region, everyone acknowledged that the second storm was more serious. After Fran had passed, Onslow County public works director Dave Clark compared the two hurricanes for the *Star-News*: "We had a little breeze come by here on July 12th. This was a real storm."

The devastation at Topsail was immense. Nearly all of the front-row cottages in Topsail Beach were destroyed, and about half of the second-row homes were either destroyed or heavily damaged. Flights over the island on the morning after the storm were the only means of assessing the scope of the loss. Along one three-mile stretch of N.C. 50 in Surf City, the Raleigh *News and Observer* estimated that about 200 of 500 homes had "obvious roofs and walls missing, foundations crumbled, or windows blown in." In many locations, splintered stubs of pilings and half-exposed septic tanks were the only recognizable features that remained where houses had once stood. More than 300 homes incurred damages that exceeded half their value. Added to the debris on the beach were hundreds of old car tires torn loose from an artificial reef about five miles offshore.

North Topsail was also hit hard again. It was estimated that more than 90 percent of the structures in town were either destroyed or damaged beyond

Following considerable damages from Hurricane Bertha, Hurricane Fran delivered a devastating blow to Topsail Island, breaking apart these beachfront condos. (Photo courtesy of
FEMA.)

repair. Many had never been restored after Bertha, but others had been completely remodeled. Some unfortunate homeowners had literally just finished
repairs during the week of Fran's arrival. After Fran, the town hall and police
station were gone, and roadways and utilities that had been patched together
after Bertha were demolished. The tide that swept over the island was so powerful that it lifted entire cottages and floated them hundreds of yards into the
marsh. Its force was so strong, in fact, that it carved six new inlets across Topsail
Island, slicing up the beach road and isolating entire neighborhoods.

Amazingly, scores of residents remained in their island homes as Fran came
ashore, though not all of them wanted to be there. Several said they simply
waited too late to leave and found themselves trapped once waves pushed over
the beach road. A few stayed because they wanted to "protect their property,"
and others said they stayed for the thrill of it. Some who rode out the storm in
their elevated homes described the ordeal of listening to the thundering surf
break under their feet. They felt their cottages shake and heard the waves wash
through their ground-floor garages.

One of those who hadn't planned to stay but waited too long to leave was
Len Gioglio. Earlier that day, Gioglio sent his family to a nearby shelter while

he remained in his North Topsail Beach cottage to make storm preparations. He knew he had waited too long when he saw deep water covering New Inlet Road, the only escape route off the northern end of the island. His story was told in the *Star-News*:

> As the waters rose Thursday night around his home, Len Gioglio did the only thing he could think of: He tied a rope around himself, lashed it to his battered home, and held his dog in his arms for two terrifying hours as they were slammed by Hurricane Fran.
>
> Each time the 4-foot storm surge slammed them down the rope, Mr. Gioglio, 37, pulled himself and his dog back up the rope, thinking that the next time they might not make it.
>
> "I thought I was going to die," Mr. Gioglio said Sunday, his voice shaky. "You just couldn't imagine how strong the wind was. . . . It rained so hard you couldn't see a few inches in front of you."

Beyond the obvious loss of man-made structures on the island, the natural environment was also tattered after the storm. Heavy beach erosion had moved mountains of sand, wiping out what remained of the dunes and their fragile vegetation. So much construction debris, paper, plastic, glass, appliances, and toxic household products was washed into the marsh or buried in the sand that removal of it all was impossible. Local conservationist Jean Beasley was quoted in the North Carolina Herpetological Society newsletter as saying that Topsail Island was "an ecological disaster, with tons of treated lumber and untreated sewage in the ocean and sound, mosquito trucks spraying every night, and those snakes that had survived the storm being killed by the hundreds as they sought high ground. Every sea turtle nest on the island had been inundated."

Farther up the coast, the town of Swansboro was still picking up the pieces from Bertha when Fran came ashore. Docks that had just been rebuilt were washed away again, and more stately trees were toppled into the streets. Winds and tides battered dozens of homes and shops along the waterfront. Casper's Marina was hit especially hard, and the Snap Dragon restaurant was severely damaged. The Christmas House, a waterfront shop filled with holiday orna-ments, was floated twenty feet off its foundation and flooded with five feet of water. By the time owner Henry Schindelar arrived at the scene the following morning, looters had already made off with gifts and decorations. Schindelar told the *News and Observer*, "It's a mess. I don't know whether to clean it up or just bring in the bulldozer."

In Carteret County, tides along the beaches of Emerald Isle and Pine Knoll Shores caused extensive beach erosion, and sound-side docks were washed away.

At the east end of Emerald Isle, sand and water covered about ten blocks of Ocean Drive, and several homes were torn open by the winds. Some septic tanks were exposed; broken glass and pink insulation spread across the dunes. Initially, Emerald Isle officials thought as many as thirty-six homes might be lost, but eventually all but six were repaired. Winds ripped awnings, porches, and decks and stripped away shingles on countless cottages. East of Beaufort, however, the damage lessened, and most residents felt lucky after viewing the aerial videos of the beaches farther south. But Fran did have a lingering effect on the forests along the coast. Maritime forests, in particular, suffered a severe infestation of southern pine beetles during the summer of 1997 that wiped out thousands of mature loblolly pines. The voracious insects capitalized on the effects of the previous year's storms, first attacking those trees weakened by salt spray and wind damage. The infestation ultimately destroyed most of the large pines, in many cases costing landowners more in tree removal expenses than they had paid for other, more traditional hurricane repairs.

Riverfront communities not in the storm's direct path were nonetheless soaked by flooding tides and heavy rains. Downtown New Bern was submerged by the rising waters of the Neuse, which also undercut the roadway on the U.S. 17 bridge, causing a six-foot section of pavement to collapse. The damaged road forced officials to close the bridge for ten hours. In Belhaven, town manager Tim Johnson reported that 30–40 percent of the houses in town were damaged by floodwaters from the Pungo River, which rose eight and a half feet above normal. In Washington, about three-quarters of the downtown area was underwater at the height of the storm. Residents described the streets as "waist-deep rivers." The combination of floodwaters from the Pamlico River and heavy rains draining from nearby creeks left several blocks of the city underwater more than a day after the hurricane's passing. Even in Elizabeth City, well to the north of the storm's track, Fran's winds pushed water down the Pasquotank River, flooding the town's harbor, wrecking docks and piers, and sinking a forty-two-foot sailboat.

In Jacksonville and surrounding Onslow County, residents endured the eastern edge of Fran's dangerous core, and damages from winds and flooding were widespread. Heavy rains earlier in the week had already filled ditches and creeks, and by the time Fran pushed inland, the New River had spread more than a quarter of a mile beyond its banks. Tall pines snapped at housetop level, crushing scores of cars and homes under fallen timbers. Propane tanks floated into the streets, tractor trailers were bowled over, and telephone poles leaned crazily. Last-minute evacuations were required in some locations. Jacksonville police detective Candido Suarez reportedly commandeered a Jet Ski

Gusting winds from Hurricane Fran toppled trees and damaged homes all along the storm's course from Cape Fear to Raleigh. (Photo courtesy of FEMA.)

and rescued more than twenty people from a flooded street. A city water tanker and surplus military truck carried others to high ground, including dialysis and heart patients.

Much like Hugo in 1989, Hurricane Fran first wrecked communities along the coast, then marched inland with remarkable force. Its center tracked just west of Interstate 40, blasting the mostly rural counties between Wilmington and Raleigh with hurricane-force gusts and hefty rains. Although they never received the media attention accorded to the more populous cities or the hard-hit resort beaches, many small rural towns in Fran's path were badly pounded by the storm. Downed trees, washed-out bridges, and flooded roads isolated numerous communities, slowing rescue efforts and making recovery difficult. Among the eastern highways blocked or closed were portions of N.C. 53, 50, 11, 41, 210, 903, 904, 905, and 411; U.S. 421; and dozens of other state roads. Concerned about the rise of floodwaters, the state highway patrol also closed portions of Interstates 40 and 85 on Friday after the storm.

In Bladen County, downed trees and pouring rains tested the skill of rescue teams called out during the hurricane. An expectant mother put in an

Hurricane Fran left billions of dollars in damages across North Carolina, setting a new standard for hurricane destruction in the state, from beachfront communities to Raleigh and beyond.

emergency call just after midnight, when ambulances had ceased operations due to the storm. But because her baby was breech, emergency workers decided to attempt the transport. Calls to hospitals and military bases for a rescue helicopter were useless because high winds kept the choppers grounded. Risking their own lives, four different crews of emergency personnel headed toward the anxious woman from different directions, each battling the gusting winds and treacherous conditions. Firefighters used chainsaws to cut trees along the way, clearing a path for the ambulances to reach the woman's home. So many trees were downed that it took fifty-three minutes for rescuers from Kelly to travel just ten miles. Eventually, they reached the expectant mother and took her to the county hospital, where the baby was delivered. Mother and child were both reported in good condition.

In rural towns such as Warsaw, Wallace, Burgaw, and Clinton, streets were littered with massive tree branches, loose shingles, and broken glass. Commercial signs were buckled and shattered, and misplaced power lines were draped over storefronts like Silly String. Warped pieces of tin hung from trees across the countryside, having been stripped from the roofs of farmhouses and barns. Some yards were filled with the trunks of massive oaks and huge earthen cavities where the trees had once stood. The Raleigh *News and Observer* reported that "virtually every road in Sampson and Duplin Counties was blocked by fallen trees, utility lines, swollen rivers, or all three." In Kenansville, a strong gust lifted away the copper dome of the Duplin County Courthouse, built around 1911, and dumped it into the street below. The busted shell was later retrieved by a sheriff's deputy.

Fran cut right through the heart of North Carolina's eastern farm belt, and the resulting damages were enormous. In July, Hurricane Bertha had dealt a severe blow to the state's farmers, causing an estimated $189 million in agricultural losses. Fran's impact was much greater and was spread over a broader region. Thousands of acres of crops were blown down or flooded, and heavy losses were reported to livestock and poultry. Especially hard hit were farmers who grew corn, cotton, soybeans, and tobacco. Tobacco farmers lost plants in the fields, but many also lost leaves that had been harvested but not cured. The hurricane knocked out the power to drying equipment in their barns, causing the leaves to sour within days. High winds and flooding were also responsible for the deaths of more than 1 million turkeys and chickens, 16,000 hogs, and more than 400 head of cattle. In some cases, entire flocks of poultry were lost when their buildings were flooded. The North Carolina Department of Agriculture estimated the total loss to farming at $684 million, including more than $185 million in tobacco, $55 million in cotton, and $54 million in corn.

In the hours preceding Fran's landfall in North Carolina, thousands of vacationers and residents along the coast packed their cars and fled inland. Some remained near the coastal area, staying with family or friends, and some sought refuge in public shelters that had been set up in schools and government buildings. Others drove farther inland and rented any available motel room they could find. Even in communities far from the coast, hundreds of families went to local shelters for protection from threatening winds and rising water. The American Red Cross operated 134 shelters in fifty-one counties, housing 9,426 people on the night of the storm. In all, according to National Weather Service reports, almost half a million residents in North and South Carolina evacuated during Fran. But unfortunately, many who left the beaches fled inland to wait out the storm in one place they surely thought would be safe—the Triangle region of Raleigh, Durham, and Chapel Hill.

Fran hit the Triangle hard. Not since Hazel's visit in 1954 had the Raleigh area been subjected to the kind of flooding and wind damage it endured through Fran. Most residents in the region began the evening by watching multicolored radar images spin across their television screens, knowing that the storm's path was undeniable—Fran was headed their way. As the hurricane's collapsing eye approached the region, massive trees tumbled and power lines popped and sizzled. Inside their now-dark homes, almost a million Triangle residents could only sit and listen to the whirling winds outside, waiting fearfully for the next thunderous crash of pine or oak. A few managed to sleep through the ordeal, but most paced through the night with flashlight in hand, hoping for it all to end soon.

Winds in the Raleigh area were nearly hurricane strength, and countless trees gave way to the blow. Pines typically snapped, whereas many large oaks fell over completely, roots and all. Hundreds of homes and businesses were bludgeoned by the falling trees, which sometimes left deep craters rimmed with muddy red clay. Downed trees and branches were everywhere—across highways, through roofs, tangled in power lines, smashed through boats and cars, in swimming pools—and virtually every neighborhood was affected. On the campus of North Carolina State University, more than 250 stately trees were lost. Those who had seen Charlotte after Hugo had instant flashbacks—the images of entire neighborhoods covered with toppled trees were eerily familiar. Raleigh—dubbed the City of Oaks—now seemed to be the city of fallen oaks.

As the decaying hurricane swept over the city, residents huddled in darkened hallways to wait for the worst to pass. Some managed to survive very close calls. Just ten minutes after North Raleigh resident Thao Do left her bedroom for the comfort of her mother's room, a large tree crashed through the roof and landed on her bed. The family told the *News and Observer* that they didn't realize what had happened at first. They heard a loud crashing sound, "like a freight train going through the house." Bruce Do later said, "We didn't realize the damage until we opened up my sister's bedroom and saw the sky."

In Cary, Laura Hamo woke her two young sons, Evan and Eric, and moved them out of their upstairs rooms when the storm grew especially fierce around 1:00 A.M. Just ten minutes later, a sixty-foot oak toppled onto the Hamo house, landing a large branch on Evan's bed. Raleigh resident Patti Clinton escaped a similar disaster when her faithful beagle saved her life by whimpering and waking her just moments before a massive tree smashed the bed where she had been sleeping. Others in Raleigh were not as fortunate. Among the many deaths Fran caused in North Carolina was that of Mary Bland Reaves, who was killed when a single falling tree sliced through her mobile home on Nevada Drive.

Unfortunately, Fran's effects on the Triangle were not limited to punctured roofs, crushed cars, and streets blocked by leafy barricades. A record rainfall on the night of Fran's visit saturated soils already presoaked by earlier rains, and the result was some of the worst flooding in the region's history. Entire blocks of homes were swamped, as were countless businesses and major thoroughfares. In Durham, rising waters flooded city streets and forced hotel residents to flee

Massive trees fell throughout the Triangle area during Hurricane
Fran, including this oak that shattered a bedroom wall on Kens-
more Drive in Raleigh. (Photo by Scott Sharpe. Courtesy of the
Raleigh *News and Observer*.)

in the middle of the night. In Chapel Hill, portions of Estes Drive and Eastgate
Shopping Center were submerged. The Eno River spread beyond its banks and
into downtown Hillsborough, flooding a county building and covering more
of the city's streets than anyone could remember ever being covered.

Wake County endured some of the region's most destructive flooding. Raleigh's Crabtree Creek spread far beyond its banks, inundating the area surrounding Crabtree Valley Mall and much of the heart of the city. The normally
placid creek, a tributary of the Neuse River, rose more than sixteen feet in just

fourteen hours, finally cresting at seven feet above flood stage. The result was a muddy sea that, by 4:25 A.M., filled the lower level of Crabtree Valley Mall with a foot of water and turned the nearby Sheraton Hotel into an island. Merchants in the mall later reported finding water moccasins among their merchandise. As the morning progressed, rescue workers broke through doors at the Sears Pet Center and rescued animals endangered by the rising flood.

Surrounded by six-foot-deep floodwaters that completely buried rows of parked cars, guests at the Sheraton found themselves stranded on the morning of the storm. Included on the guest list were numerous evacuees who had fled the coast in search of safe refuge. One of those was actor James Woods, up from Wilmington, where he had been filming a forthcoming movie. Woods reportedly donned bedroom slippers and a bathrobe the morning after the storm and helped make sandwiches for fellow victims in the hotel lobby. Also among the guests were a heart patient and a diabetic, both in need of medical assistance. They were aided by Ray Williams and Lupton Pittman, two Raleigh men who happened on the scene. After learning of the situation at the Sheraton, Williams and Pittman left, only to return soon after with divers' wet suits, emergency items, and a canoe.

Other parts of the city were also hit hard by flooding, which wrecked houses, stranded motorists, and set the stage for dramatic rescues. On the Saturday following the storm, the *News and Observer* ran a remarkable account of the floods in Raleigh:

> Some of the worst flooding devoured much of the Forest Acres neighborhood near where Crabtree Creek runs under Wake Forest Road.
>
> Jason Ferriss, a house painter who lives in the Forest Acres neighborhood, said he was surprised to find water up to his ankles when he was awakened by his two cats about 4:30 A.M., and got out of bed to find out what was wrong.
>
> "I decided to get my cats to safety on the roof, but by the time I got a ladder up there, the water was up to my waist," Ferriss said.
>
> Ferriss remained on the roof until daylight, and then found an inflatable air mattress in his home, which he began using to swim a few belongings out. He said the water in his house had risen to within a foot of the ceiling by then.
>
> "I lost everything except what I have here," Ferriss said as he loaded three dripping photo albums, a basket of clothes and a rifle into his sister's car.
>
> Several people who live in rentals at the end of Anne Street scrambled to their roofs as water poured into their homes. Two young men from a

Wayne Smith is rescued by Raleigh firemen from the bed of his pickup truck at the intersection of Wilmington and Fayetteville Streets. Smith was trapped for more than an hour in the fast-moving waters that raced through the city after Hurricane Fran. (Photo by Keith Greene. Courtesy of the Raleigh *News and Observer.*)

nearby street who were out checking for damage heard their pleas for help, so they ran home and returned on a power ski.

"They were screaming like the night," said Roger Reece, 25, who along with his friend Tom Quackenbush, 22, got three people to safety on Quackenbush's power ski. The water was about 8 feet deep, the men said. They said they had to walk on top of submerged cars to get to the house.

One man declined to be rescued from his roof, they said, because he wanted to stay there and videotape the scene once the sun rose. "That made me mad as hell," Quackenbush said. "We go to all the trouble to get them life jackets, show up on a Jet Ski, and then he wouldn't come off the roof."

Flooding along Middle Creek in southern Wake County was also severe. A Benson man who was attempting to cross where the creek overran Old Stage Road was swept downstream by the torrent. He eventually climbed into some small bushes, but the currents in the area were so swift that no boat could reach him. Sheriff's deputies later called in a helicopter from Fort Bragg to make the rescue. At the Triple W Airport in southern Wake County, two young

Fuquay-Varina boys were rescued after they were swept 150 feet down a raging creek. A small boat was brought in to reach the boys, who were safely pulled from an isolated bank.

Silver Lake Waterpark, a popular recreational site in Raleigh, burst its dam during the night and emptied its waters across Tryon Road, stranding colorful bumper boats on the lake's muddy bottom. Bass Lake and Lake Raleigh also emptied out when their dams were breached. Yates Millpond near Raleigh was one of the more notable losses, mourned by generations of naturalists who had studied aquatic ecology along its banks. Other lakes, millponds, and farm ponds around the region suffered a similar fate; their waters broke through dams and were pulled by gravity toward swollen creeks that feed major rivers such as the Neuse. According to a North Carolina Division of Emergency Management report, there were three major dam failures and twelve minor failures involving private facilities.

On Falls Lake, the Rolling View Marina was crippled by the storm but not from flooding. Fran's high winds whipped boats from their moorings, sinking about twenty and scattering others across the lake. Falls Lake suffered in other ways, too. A north Durham sewage-treatment plant lost power and flooded during the storm, releasing partly treated sewage into the reservoir that provides Raleigh with drinking water. Numerous other sewage-treatment plants and water plants across the state were also disabled, forcing thousands of residents to heed health warnings in the days following the storm: boil your drinking water!

Across scores of eastern counties, river flooding reached all-time highs during the week following Fran. The U.S. Geological Survey reported that by September 13, water levels on six North Carolina rivers and streams had set new records. The Flat River in Durham County, a tributary of the Eno, reached 17.3 feet; the Eno River at Hillsborough, 21.1 feet; Middle Creek near Clayton, which flows to the Neuse River, 14.3 feet; the Tar River in Granville County, 24.1 feet, and in Franklin County, 25.2 feet; Tick Creek in Chatham County, which flows into the Rocky River, 13.4 feet; and the Haw River in Alamance County, 32.8 feet. Three of these—the Tar River, the Flat River, and Middle Creek—reached the 500-year flood level, according to the U.S. Geological Survey.

Communities downstream from Raleigh along the swollen Neuse River braced themselves for a mighty flood that took days to reach its peak. During the hurricane, floodwaters had already swamped portions of Smithfield, damaging homes and businesses along Market Street. But the worst was yet to come. Falls Lake, north of Raleigh, had risen eleven feet during Fran, reaching a new record high—262.7 feet—just eighteen inches below the rim of the lake's spillway. The U.S. Army Corps of Engineers, which controls the lake's water level, feared that more rains could cause the lake to overflow or, at worst, burst its massive dam. They began a controlled release of water on September 9, dumping as much as 6,400 cubic feet per second into the Neuse by the following day. The result was an extended flood downstream, which took days to manifest in Smithfield, Clayton, portions of Wayne County, and most notably Kinston. The normal rate of release at the Falls Lake dam is 150 cubic feet per second.

After invading the low-lying neighborhoods of Johnston and Wayne Counties during the previous week, the Neuse River finally peaked in Kinston on September 17—more than ten days after Fran had swept through the state. According to the U.S. Geological Survey, the Neuse crested in Kinston at 23.2 feet, more than 9.1 feet above flood stage, largely because of the Falls Lake discharge. The worst flooding occurred in the southeastern portion of the city and in communities along the southern side of the river. More than 200 homes within the city limits were engulfed, and nearby mobile home parks and small houses were also affected. Water was two to three feet deep in the streets of Rivermont, just south of the city. Hundreds were forced to flee as the waters crept into their yards, and many more were rescued by National Guard troops and sheriff's deputies who ran small boats through the streets. Kinston's ailing wastewater-treatment plant was overwhelmed for days, releasing an estimated 4 million gallons of raw sewage into the river every twenty-four hours. Already burdened with similar sewage problems upriver, the Neuse spread an unsavory odor around Kinston that was reportedly noticeable from low-flying airplanes.

Officials in Kinston, like those in other flooded towns, warned residents to avoid contact with polluted waters and to watch out for venomous snakes seeking high ground. Numerous city streets and secondary roads were closed off, and shelters were opened to house victims of the flood. The *News and Observer* described the scene: "On Sunday, life in Kinston took on a surreal quality. Hordes of disaster-watchers with video cameras on their way to flooded neighborhoods drove past a long line of hurricane victims waiting downtown for emergency welfare benefits. Motorists on U.S. 70 saw Jet Skis surfing beside them on the other side of the guardrail."

Flooding along the Northeast Cape Fear River was equally destructive. Dozens of developments in Duplin and Pender Counties suffered through the same kind of soggy invasion that communities along the Neuse endured. Their ordeal was made worse when four additional inches of rain fell on the area in the days following Fran. In Burgaw, scores of homes were flooded immediately after the hurricane, and the waters just kept rising. Homeowners near N.C. 53

used canoes and skiffs to retrieve their belongings. Many homes were hit from two directions: trees that fell during the storm tore holes through roofs, allowing heavy rains to soak furnishings; days later, creeping floodwaters from the river finished the job. In some neighborhoods, the water stood eight feet deep. Countless roads in Pender and Duplin Counties disappeared under the murky flood, and portions of N.C. 53 and N.C. 210 were washed out. Remarkably, dozens of motorists attempted to drive anyway, providing a booming business for Green's Wrecker Service in Maple Hill. According to the Wilmington *Star-News*, owner Leslie Green towed twenty-eight vehicles in just two days, at $150 each. "It's extra if there's a snakebite involved," Green said with a laugh.

Beyond the borders of North Carolina, flash floods also forced evacuations across the Virginia countryside, prompting dozens of dramatic rescues. As Fran plowed through that state's foothills and mountains, it dropped up to fourteen inches of rain on parts of the region. Swiftly rising creeks and rivers forced some families to flee, while others became stranded in mountain hollows and remote areas. Countless residents had to be plucked from their rooftops and their cars by National Guard helicopters, and rescue teams struggled to reach others with boats and military vehicles. The entire city of Elkton was cut off by surrounding floodwaters, and Rockingham and Page Counties in the Shenandoah Valley were also hard hit, requiring dozens of rescues. The Dan River basin, which includes Pittsylvania and Halifax Counties and the city of Danville, crested eleven feet above flood stage—one foot higher than the previous record set during Hurricane Agnes in 1972. Heavy flooding was reported in the South Boston area, and about forty homes were evacuated after water began spilling over a dam on the Moormans River twenty miles northwest of Charlottesville.

Even in eastern Virginia, Fran will be remembered. Wind gusts reached 71 mph in Hampton, and scattered damages were reported. At Virginia Beach, a fifty-by-fifty-foot chunk of the Ramada Plaza oceanfront hotel came tumbling down, exposing insulation and beams between the sixth and ninth floors. Gale-force winds in the Chesapeake Bay pushed waters up the Potomac River, forcing the evacuation of some areas near Washington, D.C. More than three feet of water covered streets in the Old Town district of Alexandria, marking some of that area's worst flooding in many years. Even beyond Virginia, serious floods forced residents out of their homes in West Virginia and Pennsylvania. Like a handful of memorable past hurricanes, Fran left its distinctive mark on the interior portions of several states.

In the hours and days following Fran's trek across North Carolina, Tar Heel residents struggled to recover from the shock of the storm. Most quickly went to work salvaging what they could and beginning the arduous task of cleaning up the mess the hurricane had left behind. Curfews were established in most cities, as officials attempted to maintain order and prevent looting along darkened streets. As with any hurricane, perhaps the most basic necessity sucked away by Fran was available electric power. The Reuters News Service reported that 4.5 million people in the Carolinas and Virginia were without electricity on the day after the storm. Caravans of utility crews poured into the stricken areas almost immediately, some coming from as far away as Florida and Alabama. Carolina Power and Light reported that it recruited about 2,000 additional workers, bringing its total work force to 7,300—about 2,000 more than the army of workers gathered in South Florida after Hurricane Andrew in 1992. Hotels throughout the Triangle were overbooked, and Carolina Power and Light scrambled to find rooms for all of its crews—some were even taken in by grateful residents. The power outage was accompanied by all sorts of side effects. For example, about 295 of Durham's 300 traffic signals were knocked out, causing the city's accident rate to climb 30 percent after the storm and directly contributing to at least one fatality. In some communities, residents were fortunate enough to have their power restored within hours. But for many, the wait for crews to untangle twisted lines and replace damaged poles and transformers stretched for many days. As a result, thousands struggled through the cleanup period without the benefit of lights, hot showers, televisions, electric stoves, and other comforts of modern living.

A few people with portable generators cranked up modest supplies of power. In some cases, those without electricity borrowed from neighbors who had it, running lengths of extension cord from house to house. In areas where the power was out for more than a day or two, stocks of frozen foods quickly began to thaw, so massive backyard barbecues were hastily assembled from Wrightsville Beach to Raleigh and beyond. These impromptu potluck feasts brought neighbors together to talk about the storm and to form alliances of survival skills and kindred spirits.

Immediately following the storm, the four commodities most in demand were ice, chainsaws, generators, and gasoline. Because most gas pumps require electricity to operate, there were only a few locations equipped to serve the needs of countless thirsty cars and trucks. On the morning after Fran passed through, a station on Old Apex Road near Raleigh was one of the few in the Triangle to have working pumps, and motorists waited in line there for up to an hour to fill their cars. The station's manager had sold gas to about 980 people by noon, when the pumps ran out. The traffic was so heavy she couldn't keep up with the sales and resorted to an honor system for patrons buying gas.

In many communities, and especially in the Triangle, hordes of people lined up at building-supply centers like Home Depot and Ace Hardware to buy chainsaws, generators, and plastic tarps. First-time do-it-yourselfers waited for hours to make their purchases. At one Home Depot in Cary, store owners had to hold a lottery and erect bleachers in the parking lot to manage the anxious crowds. At one point, an announcement came over the store's public-address system that another truckload of generators had just arrived, and in less than a minute, a line of 100 potential buyers had formed. The store later reported that it had sold about 400 chainsaws and 400 generators between the morning of September 6 and the following afternoon.

Similar lines snaked around the few open grocery stores, where eager shoppers had come to buy ice and other necessities. The ice was used primarily by those struggling to save hundreds of dollars' worth of steaks, chops, and other items removed from their powerless freezers. Packaged foods also sold quickly—anything that didn't require refrigeration or cooking. Word soon spread regarding which restaurants and fast-food grills were serving hot meals, and thousands of families flocked to the few scattered establishments lucky enough to have power. Of course, relief agencies of all kinds were also hard at work across the state, providing meals, clothing, and shelter to those in need. The Red Cross, the Salvation Army, and numerous church-sponsored groups set up relief stations and shelters to aid untold numbers of victims. Donations were collected to fund the relief effort, including large corporate gifts to the Red Cross.

The difficult physical task of cutting up and removing downed trees kept many families busy to the exclusion of almost all else. Businesses specializing in tree cutting and home repairs were flooded with requests, and most filled their week's schedule within hours that first day. Frustrated homeowners called dozens of companies and could only reach recordings. In desperation, many storm victims whose homes were covered with trees took chainsaws in their hands for the first time, buzzing frantically through the timbers that engulfed their property. For days and even weeks, a whining symphony of saws echoed through virtually every neighborhood in a forty-county stretch along the hurricane's path. And as the trees, branches, and stumps were cut and stacked, mountains of storm debris quickly grew along city streets and country roads. Local officials scrambled to deal with the incredible volume of waste, which required caravans of trucks for hauling and specially designated lots for mulching and burning. Virtually every city and county in the region managed its own "stump dump."

Fran's winds had a devastating effect on Tar Heel forests, much like Hugo had had on South Carolina timber. The North Carolina Division of Forest Resources estimated that the storm damaged 8.2 million acres of woodland.

In some coastal sections, 85 percent of all trees sustained some type of damage, and that figure exceeded 50 percent in the Raleigh-Durham area. Among coastal counties, New Hanover and Pender suffered the greatest destruction; timber losses in Pender County alone exceeded $89 million. In many forested areas, the tremendous amount of dead wood greatly increased the likelihood of fire. Fallen trees blocked fire lanes and breaks, limiting the mobility of U.S. Forest Service personnel and restricting access for firefighters. The economic impact on the state's forests alone was estimated at $1.3 billion.

Down at the coast, the cleanup was particularly grueling, especially along the barrier islands so devastated by the storm surge. At Topsail Island, two FEMA search-and-rescue teams used dogs and sophisticated listening devices to hunt for at least five people who had been reported missing. One team had to be airlifted to the northernmost end of North Topsail Beach because the area was completely inaccessible after the storm. In Wilmington, more heavy rains fell two days after Fran, and authorities warned residents not to drive because logs cut from downed trees were floating about in the streets. A particularly difficult problem to combat was the influx of gawkers who drove around the hard-hit coastal region with video cameras pressed against their windshields, slowing traffic and obstructing the recovery effort. Even the skies were crowded—so crowded, in fact, that authorities were forced to create a no-fly zone over the beaches, where airborne sightseers were making low passes to view the crushed buildings.

Just as they had been after Bertha, hundreds of resort property owners were anxious to return to the affected beaches the day after the storm. This time, however, the destruction was even more severe, and the resolve of town officials was steady. Nevertheless, residents lined up at the bridges, waiting for the first chance to get back on the islands and go to work. Many in the Triangle area were unable to travel to the coast to check on their vacation cottages, so instead they gathered at the state fairgrounds in Raleigh to view a videotape of the destruction. The tape was recorded by the state highway patrol during a helicopter flight down the coast. Trooper Ed Maness, who was behind the camera, told the Raleigh *News and Observer,* "There were times I had to look up from my view finder and out at the coast to see if all that damage was really real."

Soon after Fran barreled through North Carolina, Governor Jim Hunt declared a state of emergency in all 100 counties, the first time such action had ever been taken. He was later described as "shocked" by the extent of the damage. Initially, 1,000 National Guard troops were called to action, and the governor ordered 1,400 of the state's prisoners to help with the cleanup. He also announced that state workers living in the affected counties should stay home for up to a week to help their communities recover. Hunt flew by helicopter from the capital to Wilmington, where he rendezvoused with FEMA director James Lee Witt. Together with other officials, they then flew up the coast and toured the battered shoreline from Brunswick County to Topsail Beach. President Bill Clinton initially declared ten counties federal disaster areas, but as the days went by, that number crept upward—by September 11 there were forty, and ultimately more than fifty counties were so designated. On the fifteenth, Clinton made a brief stop in Raleigh, toured hurricane-damaged neighborhoods by helicopter, and met with Hunt and other officials in a livestock showroom at the state fairgrounds. After pledging to "do whatever we can," he returned to Washington. Ultimately, more than $700 million in federal aid made its way to North Carolina after the storm. In December 1996, the Clinton administration also took the unusual position of agreeing to increase its share of spending for repairs to the state's highways, bridges, and other public works to 90 percent of the eligible costs.

CREATURES IN THE STORM

We know hurricanes are dangerous, disruptive events, bringing risk for loss of life and property. When a severe hurricane or flood strikes, wildlife and domestic animals are in many ways just as vulnerable as people, and stories of their survival have become part of our fascination with these storms.

For centuries, portions of the Tar Heel coast have provided haven for feral horses. These hardy creatures have endured blistering summers and barren winters on the thin strips of barrier beach that line the shore, but the ravages of severe hurricanes have thinned their numbers and caused mass die-offs on several occasions. The San Ciriaco Hurricane of 1899 reportedly drowned hundreds of Banker ponies as well as scores of cows and goats. So many were lost that burning their carcasses became the only effective means of eliminating a potential health hazard on the banks. Fortunately, many survived, and today managed populations of these ponies still roam free on Shackleford Banks, part of the Cape Lookout National Seashore. Similar herds wander the beaches of

An anxious crew of dogs looks for high ground
after being rescued from the sunken neighborhoods
of Princeville after Hurricane Floyd. (Photo by
Dave Saville. Courtesy of FEMA.)

Corolla, Ocracoke Island, the Rachel Carson Reserve near Beaufort,
and remote private islands near Cedar Island. Five wild horses drowned
when they were swept off the Rachel Carson Reserve during Hurricane
Isabel in 2003. These deaths were somewhat unexpected, as the horses
are well adapted to their environment and are known to instinctively
move to high ground during flooding storms.

During Hurricane Dorian in September 2019, extreme tides swept
across Pamlico Sound, flooding Ocracoke and other coastal islands
with some of the highest water in memory. Thankfully, the ponies on
Ocracoke and at Corolla, Shackleford Banks, and the Rachel Carson
Reserve all fared well. Those at Cedar Island were not as fortunate;
only twenty-one of the herd of forty-nine survived the inundation. In
addition to the horses, the island was home to about twenty-five "sea
cows," cattle of unknown origin that have roamed free there for years.
Most drowned during Dorian—only about six survived. Three of the
survivors made the news when they were discovered on the beaches of
Cape Lookout National Seashore about a month after the storm. It was

believed the trio swam or were carried about four to five miles across Core Sound to North Core Banks. The park service returned them to their Cedar Island home, and one was later named Dori, according to the Wild Horses of Cedar Island Facebook page.

During Hurricane Fran, thousands of trees toppled into pastures across North Carolina, some striking and killing horses and livestock. But some trees proved even more lethal in the days following the storm when horses that munched on the wilted leaves of fallen red maple, cherry, or elderberry branches became sick and died. The staff of North Carolina State University's College of Veterinary Science scrambled to save what animals they could and issued warnings to horse owners to remove the downed trees as quickly as possible. Cherry tree leaves contain cyanide, and the leaves of all three species are highly toxic to horses and often lethal.

Waterfowl can be victims of severe hurricanes. Hunters report that ducks seem to disappear after these storms, perhaps seeking cover in areas farther inland. In the book *Reflections of the Outer Banks* by Donald and Carol McAdoo, former Corolla postmaster Johnny Austin described the effects of high winds on some waterfowl: "The ducks and geese used to be so plentiful around here that when a storm came up it wouldn't be unusual to pick up $15 or $20 worth that had killed themselves flying into that top wire of the lighthouse. And you only got five or six dollars a barrel for them, depending on the kind they were, so it took a lot to mount up to $15."

After Hurricane Fran, bird watchers near Raleigh were treated to a rare sight—hundreds of seabirds were spotted around the Triangle. As the storm pushed across the state, it carried with it a collection of birds usually found over the Gulf Stream, including petrels and an Audubon's shearwater. Most of the inland sightings were near Jordan and Falls Lakes. Seabirds usually fly ahead of a hurricane but sometimes travel within the eye as it moves overland. They often drop out over large lakes, then rest before their return to the Atlantic. Wildlife experts reported that the variety and quantity of coastal birds and seabirds found at Jordan Lake on the Saturday after the storm were unprecedented. Similar reports followed Hurricane Florence, when rare sightings of a Trindade petrel, royal and sandwich terns, and a red-necked phalarope were reported at Buckhorn Reservoir near Wilson, North Carolina.

Eastern North Carolina is the northernmost range for American alligators, and gator stories are not uncommon in hurricanes. Flooding simply expands their habitat, and they're often seen moving about in storms. During Hurricane Florence, several incidents made the news, including a big gator on the move at Osprey Cove near Myrtle Beach, recorded in a viral video, and an apparent alligator visit inside the flooded New Bern Riverfront Convention Center on the Neuse River. Storm surge washed through the facility, and afterward workers found large gator tracks on mud-covered carpeting in interior hallways. During Hurricane Dorian, a gator was "arrested" by the Berkeley County, South Carolina, sheriff's office. According to the sheriff's Facebook page, the three-and-a-half-foot reptile broke into a home at Moncks Corner, near Lake Moultrie, northwest of Charleston, and was safely removed by officers. The post stated the department's "zero-tolerance policy for looting" in the storm, "even those looters with a tail . . . and claws."

Hurricane floods often flush out another potential hazard for humans: venomous snakes. Following the Sea Islands Hurricane of 1893, deaths from snakebites were reported in South Carolina. Rattlesnakes and cottonmouth moccasins were the likely culprits. In another late nineteenth-century hurricane, a family was forced to climb up an oak tree to avoid the rapidly rising tide, only to find "the branches filled with copperheads and other serpents." Snakes have sometimes escaped floods by finding refuge in homes and furnishings. After the hurricane of 1876, one Hyde County man found a rattlesnake coiled inside his dresser drawer. The reptile was likely seeking a dry location to ride out the storm.

During Hurricane Bonnie in 1998, the Brunswick Community Hospital in Supply, North Carolina, lost its roof. National Guard troops and health-care workers from New Hanover Regional Medical Center traveled to the damaged hospital through torrential rains at 1:00 A.M. to transfer several patients to safe quarters in Wilmington. Along the way, their convoy of Humvees was nearly swamped by deep standing water that covered the highway. That's where they apparently picked up an unexpected passenger. Robyn Moore, a mental health director from Wilmington, told the Associated Press, "When we hit the puddle, water went over the top of the car, and we heard this huge thump. . . . We see this thing on the windshield, this big grayish-brown thing." When they arrived at their destination, they found a cottonmouth entangled in the Humvee's front grille.

In *Faces from the Flood: Hurricane Floyd Remembered*, volunteer Janice Bailey relayed a story she heard following a rescue near Kinston:

> Well, this man came by the church one day and told us this story we couldn't believe. Out in his trailer park the flooding came up real fast during the storm. I think it was dark. He grabbed a few clothes and things and put his bag on his little porch and went back inside to grab a few more things. While he was in there a snake crawled inside his bag, but he didn't know it. When they came to rescue him with a boat, he got in the boat along with some other people, and they went away. Well, the snake crawled out into the bottom of that boat, and those people screamed and nearly jumped out of that boat. Fortunately, I think it was a game warden driving the boat, so he got it out of there. But can you imagine? I know I'd be over the side pretty quick.

Surging tides sometimes retreat as quickly as they advance. After Hurricane Donna passed through Nags Head, "flopping bass and other live fish" were picked up off the streets. After Hurricane Hazel, a large flounder was found on a sidewalk in Carolina Beach, and blue crabs were seen scurrying on the streets of Morehead City. On more than one occasion, the people of Ocracoke have found fish in their furniture after storm tides washed through their living quarters and deposited marine life. Hurricane Florence submerged portions of Interstate 40 in Pender County, and after the waters receded, the local fire department was brought in to hose away thousands of dead fish deposited there by the floods.

In his book *Ocracokers*, Alton Ballance relays a story told to him by his grandfather. During the San Ciriaco Hurricane of 1899, witnesses reported seeing two porpoises swim through the village of Ocracoke when floodwaters inundated the island. For a short time, they became lodged in the forked branches of an oak tree, but rolling waves helped free the pair. They swam away and were last seen crossing the island and entering Pamlico Sound.

Another marine mammal story was told after Hurricane Isabel in 2003. On the ocean beach near the Cape Hatteras Lighthouse, a group of residents spotted a baby dolphin wash ashore the day after Isabel's passing. The young dolphin was dead, but just up the beach, a larger dolphin, presumably the mother, was seen thrashing in the surf. Residents believed the dolphin was searching for its calf and wouldn't leave the area. A small group gently held the six-foot mammal in knee-deep water, calming it and encouraging it to swim away. Julia Magliano told the Raleigh *News and Observer,* "I told her, 'It's OK. You can leave. The baby's dead.'" The dolphin finally gave a thrust of its tail and headed out to sea.

Carolina Beach resident Granger Soward spotted an unusual visitor at his Canal Drive home during the onslaught of Hurricane Fran. For several hours, Soward and four friends watched the storm surge push into his yard, cover his mailbox, and float cars and debris around his neighborhood. But then, as the storm's eye passed over them, a strange omen appeared at the back door. A large manatee drifted peacefully into the yard and lingered for about an hour before turning back to deeper water.

Along the coast, hurricanes often decimate the nests of loggerhead sea turtles, laid in shallow sands on the upper edges of Carolina beaches. Loggerheads, protected as a federally threatened species, typically lay their nests during the warm summer months, just before the most active portion of the hurricane season. The storms' high waves and heavy erosion are particularly destructive to sea turtle populations, sometimes wiping out hundreds of nests along Carolina beaches.

Wildlife officials note that although some animals may be affected by a severe hurricane, most manage to endure these storms without harm. Experts agree that wildlife can survive a natural disaster such as a hurricane far better than they can survive an oil spill or some other man-made catastrophe. Domesticated animals, however, don't always fare as well.

In the hours and days following Hurricane Floyd, thousands of people across eastern North Carolina fled their homes for local shelters or had to be rescued by boat or helicopter. Often left behind in the lingering floods were their family pets. Dogs, cats, birds, hamsters, and other animals became unwitting victims of the disaster because they could not join their owners in area shelters. Through the brave efforts of numerous search teams, many of the pets were eventually rescued. Farm animals were also among the stranded, and many were brought to safety during some rather unique rescue missions, including several horses and cows that were hoisted to safety by helicopter.

Similar rescues followed Hurricanes Matthew and Florence. Stories emerged of rescue teams finding all sorts of animals in strange and precarious places: dogs, chickens, and even cows were seen waiting patiently on the rooftops of flooded buildings; a 300-pound hog was found resting on a king-size bed inside a flooded home; and a cat was rescued after perching for more than two hours atop a stop sign on a flooded street. Emergency responders navigating neighborhoods by boat told their share of snake stories and issued warnings about another insidious threat: drifting mounds of fire ants that stuck together in clumps atop floating debris, anxious to jump to the next available passerby.

During Florence, *USA Today* reported on a Coast Guard rescue operation in Columbus County, where the team arrived just in time for one resident who owned ten beagles. They were found in cages with water rising above their chests. "If we would have gotten here just a few minutes later, I don't know if these guys would have made it," remarked one rescuer. One by one, the beagles were loaded into the boat, but "the rescue turned into a comedy skit of sorts" when the pups all splashed overboard, causing the crew to chase them down in the waist-deep water. All made it safely back into the boat.

Animal shelters suffered their share of flooding during Florence too, and one man traveled hundreds of miles to help. Tony Alsup, a trucker from Greenback, Tennessee, had converted an old school bus into a traveling shelter for dogs and cats. He'd been active in rescuing hundreds of animals during Hurricanes Harvey in Texas and Irma in Florida. He arrived in South Carolina in time to save more than sixty dogs and cats, most of which came from flooded or otherwise overcrowded shelters. Alsup rounded up more "leftover" dogs before transporting them to a friend's private shelter in southern Alabama. His plan: return for more. The *Washington Post* chronicled his journey, in which he made it clear that he always has more room. His Facebook post during the trip: "NO ONE LEFT BEHIND. Love y'all, mean it."

Many who have survived the frightening passage of a hurricane have done so with man's best friend at their side. During Hurricane Fran, one woman reported that her dog whimpered and barked, waking her just moments before a tree crashed through the roof and crushed her bed. During Hurricane Ione in 1955, rescuers in Jones County located a frail elderly man trapped in a rising flood by zeroing in on the bark of his faithful companion.

Sometimes dogs have been known to even save themselves. During Hurricane Fran's visit to North Carolina, Al's Auto Salvage in New Bern was guarded by Petey, a junkyard dog all of ten inches tall. Skip Crayton, owner of the shop, gave him that name because of his resemblance to the mascot on the television show *Little Rascals*. On the Friday night after Fran roared through the state, water inside the auto salvage building rose sixteen inches above the floor. The following morning, when Crayton arrived at the shop, he opened the door and out came Petey—covered up to his neck in mud and oil. Crayton reasoned that the dog must have swum for six to eight hours continuously, keeping his head just above water to stay alive. Petey slept for two days.

Urban search-and-rescue team members from Missouri Task Force One remove an apprehensive dog from a flooded home in Lumberton during Hurricane Matthew. (Photo courtesy of FEMA.)

Estimates for the total economic impact of Hurricane Fran vary, with several government agencies offering estimates above $5 billion. Calculating these totals for a major storm is an immense task that can sometimes take months to complete. Even then, the variables are many, and historically the estimates usually lack precision. In addition to the measurable costs in damaged or destroyed property, there are hidden and indirect costs, such as lost wages, agricultural losses, and the lingering impact on tourism along the coast. On the other hand, there are positive impacts on some segments of the economy, such as the construction trades, which typically experience a boon after major hurricanes.

According to National Weather Service reports, Fran caused at least $5 billion in damages to property, timber, and agriculture in North Carolina alone. The North Carolina Division of Emergency Management placed the total at $5.2 billion. In addition, early estimates from other states affected by the storm were as follows: South Carolina, $40 million; Virginia, $350 million; Maryland, $100 million; Pennsylvania, $80 million; West Virginia, $40 million; and Ohio, $40 million. By those measures, the sum total for Fran approached $6 billion, placing it among the costliest hurricanes in U.S. history at that time.

But perhaps most significant was the loss of thirty-seven lives, directly or indirectly due to the storm. In North Carolina, twenty-four fatalities were reported: three from drowning, twelve related to fallen trees, and nine due to other storm-related events. Three people died in Onslow County, including L.Cpl. Steve Sears, an Arkansas native who was out driving with two fellow Marines on the night of the storm. The trio became disoriented in the torrential rains, attempted to drive their Mustang over the high-rise bridge to North Topsail Beach, and were swept into the raging sound. After escaping the sinking car, one of the men made it back to land and one grabbed a tree and was rescued nine hours later, but Sears drowned.

The deaths were geographically distributed along Fran's path. Several victims were killed when large trees crashed through their homes, including teenager Cristina Marie Foust in Onslow County, Donald Davis in Benson, Mary Bland Reaves in Raleigh, and eighth grader Curtis Wayne Warren in Alamance County. In Duplin County, Rose Hill resident Marion Rouse was killed and her husband injured when their chimney collapsed onto them as they sat in their den. When the couple were discovered some nine hours later by members of the Rose Hill Fire Department, Marion was found on her couch, which had crashed through the floor. Her husband, though still alive, was pinned under a pile of bricks from the fallen chimney.

Responding to an emergency call at the peak of the storm, nineteen-year-old Bahama volunteer firefighter Ricky Dorsey was another of Fran's tragic

An employee of Al Smith Mazda is offered a boat ride by rescuers after floodwaters swept through the Wake Forest Road area near Hodges Street in Raleigh after Hurricane Fran. (Photo by Gary Allen. Courtesy of the Raleigh *News and Observer*.)

victims. He was killed when a falling tree landed on his truck as he was driving down Stagville Road, north of Durham. After the storm, as the cleanup got underway, Zebulon native Walt DeYoung died while attempting to clear debris from his mother's home in Raleigh. DeYoung, a youth hockey coach, was deeply gashed on the legs by a falling tree and later bled to death. A Raleigh teen drowned while swimming in the flood-swollen Crabtree Creek, and a Greensboro man was found floating near the damaged remains of the Scotts Hill Marina in Pender County. He apparently had been helping a friend board up his home, when he was swept off a deck and drowned.

One of the storm's more memorable tragedies was that of Georgia Greene. The seventy-five-year-old Surf City woman lived alone in her mobile home and depended on round-the-clock nurses to provide her care. As the evacuation of Topsail Island got underway, Greene refused to leave, stating that she had never left for a storm before. As Fran swept over the island, it demolished her home, tossing the ninety-pound woman into the raging waters, her mattress beneath her. For hours she drifted through the flooded marsh, enduring the worst of the hurricane's winds and rains. The following day, she was found by rescue workers, still aboard her mattress and still alive. She was taken to a local hospital but died the following day. Cause of death: hypothermia.

Without doubt, Fran's visit to the state established it as the new benchmark for hurricanes in North Carolina—at least for a while. It may not have been the strongest storm to hit the Tar Heel coast in the twentieth century, but its tremendous toll exceeded that of the previous hurricane to set the standard,

Hurricane Hazel. It had such a significant impact on such a large number of people that a whole new generation of North Carolinians will forever be prepared to reminisce whenever the topic comes up. For decades to come, they'll tell their children and their grandchildren, "I remember Fran!"

TAKEAWAYS

- *With hurricanes, experience is indeed the best teacher.* It's an old adage, often attributed to Julius Caesar, that relates well to our understanding of hurricanes. In just four years during the late 1990s, North Carolina was pounded by Bertha, Fran, Bonnie, Dennis, Floyd, and Irene—a rough period that tested all aspects of the state's hurricane response. It's tough consolation, but communities that suffer through storms and floods more frequently use their experiences to grow their capabilities and better prepare for future storms. Their partnerships become well established, they beef up their infrastructure, their fiscal and logistical plans are more refined, and their past experiences help them cope with new challenges. Conversely, communities that enjoy long quiet periods between significant hurricanes can be more vulnerable once a major disaster hits. Mike Sprayberry, former director of North Carolina's Division of Emergency Management, calls it "hurricane amnesia."

- *The pre-staging of equipment, personnel, and supplies before a hurricane strikes was a transformative strategy for more effective disaster response.* When a dangerous hurricane threatens the Carolinas today, emergency managers know that positioning equipment and supplies in the right places ahead of the storm allows them to better respond to immediate needs. This was one of the important lessons learned following Hugo's visit, and it made a big difference during Fran. It makes perfect sense, because getting food, water, ice, fuel, generators, and other critical supplies to hard-hit areas is a challenge in the chaos following a storm, especially when roads are closed, and communications compromised. National Guard troops, utility crews, search-and-rescue teams, heavy equipment, aircraft, and mobile field hospitals are just a few of the assets that are often deployed in advance of a threatening hurricane.

- *Beach nourishment has been shown to help protect beachfront property during storms, but its growing popularity poses difficult questions for the future.* Long understood to be expensive and controversial, sand nourishment projects have nevertheless become common on many Carolina beaches. They're an engineered remedy that helps sustain tourism and can help reduce a

hurricane's destructive impact on oceanfront structures. Wrightsville
and Carolina Beaches received federal funding to rebuild their beaches
and dunes following Hazel, and the U.S. Army Corps of Engineers has
maintained them ever since. During Fran, the dunes on these beaches were
consumed by design, but erosion around buildings—the most likely cause
of structural failure—was minimal. But federal funding for maintaining
the projects is expected to fade in years to come, even as sand-pumping
costs escalate. And some beaches are better candidates for it than others.
Nourishment projects are very expensive, especially when they're placed
on high-energy beaches that may erode more quickly and require more frequent replenishment. In the long run, some won't be sustainable and will
face numerous continued challenges: escalating costs for local taxpayers,
dwindling federal support, the lack of adequate sources of sand, rising sea
levels, and the ongoing risk of rapid sand loss due to cycles of hurricanes
and nor'easters. Looking decades ahead, East Carolina University coastal
and marine geologist Stan Riggs challenges the long-term strategy: "What
you'll have then is not a barrier island, you'll have an engineered island. . . .
Retreat in some of these areas is still absolutely on the table."

• *Insurance affordability and availability will always be key issues for those living in hurricane-prone areas.* Hurricanes Bertha and Fran struck just a few
short years after Hurricane Andrew—a megadisaster that sent shock waves
through the insurance industry. Following the 1992 storm, the U.S. insurance market changed almost overnight, as carriers realized they had grossly
underestimated hurricane risk in Florida. This led to national trends for
stronger building codes, more carefully managed coastal exposure, the
introduction of hurricane deductibles, the rapid evolution of sophisticated
catastrophe modeling, and a larger role for government in insuring coastal
property. Huge numbers of claim payouts following a string of storms in
2004–2005 caused further disruption, making insurance unavailable for
many and causing dramatic premium increases. Since that time, insurers,
regulators, legislators, and homeowners have continued to navigate the
economics of hurricane risk, especially regarding wind coverage near the
coast. Homeowners today face escalating costs, with most holding separate
policies for fire, wind, and flood. Now the insurance industry is recalculat-
ing again, anticipating the impact of a changing climate on future claims.

• *The buyout of flood-prone properties has been a successful strategy but with
limitations.* As the Neuse River spread its banks into Kinston following Hurricane Fran, floodwaters poured into homes in the Lincoln City
neighborhood, displacing hundreds. Like in many other communities built

on floodplains, residents could have made repairs, but the low elevation of their properties meant they'd likely flood again. One year after the storm, and with help from FEMA, the state purchased and razed 360 of Kinston's most flood-prone homes, removing the chance of repeated damage—a process planners call "managed retreat." Across eastern North Carolina, more than 5,000 homes were ultimately purchased and torn down after Fran and Floyd, and another 1,000 were elevated, in what became the nation's largest single-state acquisition program. Another 2,000 have been purchased since Matthew. But people who have been displaced must relocate to suitable housing, not always an easy find in rural communities. Buyout programs are effective but costly, and there's a tremendous gap between what these programs can financially support and the many thousands of properties in the Carolinas that might be good candidates.

CHAPTER THIRTEEN

HURRICANE FLOYD,
SEPTEMBER 1999

"Here we go again."

In mid-September 1999, that was the common refrain when it was first suggested Hurricane Floyd might be headed toward the Carolina coast. Even before Floyd emerged in the Bahamas as a massive, frightening, near–Category 5 hurricane, Tar Heel storm watchers had had their fill of recent tropical weather. Memories of Bertha and Fran in 1996 were fresh, and some parts of North Carolina were still recovering three years later. The Cape Fear region had been visited by Hurricane Bonnie in 1998, a strong Category 2 that made landfall near Bald Head Island and did its own dance northward along the coast. And by the time Floyd made its sweeping turn toward the Carolinas in September 1999, residents of eastern North Carolina had already been saturated (and frustrated) by a meandering Tropical Storm Dennis. This combination set the stage for what would become a new benchmark Carolina hurricane disaster.

Like a few others chronicled in this book, Hurricane Floyd's massive toll was in part due to its pairing with this earlier tropical cyclone—Hurricane Dennis, which had weakened to a tropical storm by the time it approached North Carolina. Through the early weeks of summer 1999, tourism was booming for most of the resort properties and beach businesses that cater to seasonal crowds on the Carolina coast. Even though another active hurricane season had been forecast for the Atlantic, vacationers packed the beaches to soak up the sun and play in the surf. But property agents noted that those interested in summer beach house rentals seemed less interested in late August bookings—partially due to the potential threat of yet another hurricane strike.

As coastal residents and vacationers looked ahead to the approaching Labor Day holiday, their attention was soon focused on Dennis, a larger-than-average storm that formed near the Bahamas on August 24 and reached hurricane strength two days later. It produced near-hurricane conditions at the Abaco Islands on the twenty-eighth and then intensified later that night, building sustained winds of 105 mph. It maintained Category 2 intensity for the next

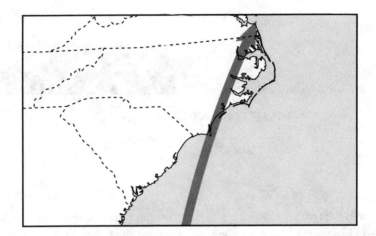

Larry Torrez wades through chest-deep waters near a home on South Hillcrest Drive in Goldsboro. In communities submerged by Hurricane Floyd, residents were forced either to wait patiently for rescue or to move about under treacherous conditions. (Photo by Brian Strickland. Courtesy of the *Goldsboro News-Argus*.)

two days while moving parallel to the southeastern U.S. coast about 115 miles offshore. As it began its approach to the Carolinas, it slowly weakened and moved to within about sixty miles of that frequent hurricane target, Cape Fear. For a while, it looked like the beaches from Wrightsville to Topsail would catch another direct hit.

Dennis was never a classic tightly wound hurricane. Westerly wind shear persisted throughout much of its course, and its large, forty-mile-wide eye was often poorly defined. Once the storm closed in on North Carolina on August 30, it encountered a midlatitude trough that steered it toward the north and northeast, pushing it out to sea off Cape Hatteras. This was good news since it also weakened, and the nearby beaches were spared landfall. But Dennis's large wind field extended for 200 miles in every direction from the storm's center, pushing tropical-storm-force winds of 45 to 65 mph onto the coast.

On September 1, Dennis was downgraded to a tropical storm as it drifted over the offshore waters of the Outer Banks. Storm-force winds, waves, and steady rains buffeted the coast, where residents suffered through the storm that wouldn't go away—which the press appropriately dubbed Dennis the Menace. Steve Lyons, the Weather Channel's senior meteorologist, told the *Virginian-Pilot*, "It is meandering out there. It's a tumbleweed, heading back from whence it came. But this is going to be a long, drawn-out ordeal. It's going to be here for another few days."

After drifting erratically for two days, the unpredictable storm began to intensify again and did another about-face—this time turning northwest, directly toward Cape Lookout on the North Carolina coast. The reintensification continued throughout the storm's last dash for land, though it never again reached hurricane strength. Tropical Storm Dennis finally moved ashore over Core Banks on September 4 and tracked inland, weakening to a depression as it dissipated over central North Carolina on the following day.

Though not a hurricane at landfall, the storm's first passage near the North Carolina coast on August 30 may have produced sustained winds of near-hurricane force along portions of New Hanover, Carteret, and Dare Counties. At Frying Pan Shoals, automated equipment recorded sustained winds of 94 mph, gusts to 112 mph, and a barometric low of 977 millibars (mb). Other high gusts were measured elsewhere along the coast during this period, including 111 mph at Wrightsville Beach, 98 mph at Hatteras Village, 91 mph at Cape Lookout, 89 mph at Oregon Inlet, and 87 mph at Harkers Island Bridge.

As Dennis approached, stalled, and meandered, it produced heavy surf, severe erosion, and coastal flooding from Brunswick County to the Jersey Shore. Areas along the Neuse River reported tides of eight to ten feet above normal on August 30, and portions of the Pamlico River saw similar flooding on September 4. Longtime residents in some areas said that these were the highest water levels they had seen since the September hurricane of 1933. In Craven, Pamlico, and Beaufort Counties, some locations experienced more severe flooding during Dennis than from Hurricanes Bertha, Fran, or Bonnie.

Though Dennis never made landfall as a hurricane, its impact on North Carolina was still significant. In addition to the widespread flooding of the state's sounds and eastern rivers, the Outer Banks were particularly hard hit, hammered by high winds and waves that endured for more than 140 hours. The beach towns of Hatteras, Rodanthe, Nags Head, and Kitty Hawk were pounded through almost a dozen lunar high tides, periods when heavy surf carved away sand and overwashed streets and yards. Beachfront erosion was heavy in Rodanthe, where waves destroyed an oceanfront swimming pool and claimed at least five houses. These houses had already been condemned, but after the storm, one resident described them as "physically missing." Overwash severed the main artery on Hatteras Island—the tenuous pavement of Highway 12. Just north of Buxton, waves also carved away a 3,000-foot section of Highway 12 near Canadian Hole, an area often prone to ocean overwash. The storm forced the postponement of the scheduled relighting ceremony at the Cape Hatteras Lighthouse, but the lighthouse weathered the storm without a problem, having been recently relocated to its new site 1,500 feet away from the Atlantic.

In Carteret County, the hardest-hit areas were at the county's eastern end, where strong northeast winds pushed Pamlico and Core Sound waters onto land. Cedar Island residents suffered through severe flooding on the storm's first pass, then endured more high water when landfall occurred five days later. They referred to the two events as Dennis I and Dennis II. One resident reported that the water in his front yard was "up to the top of the steering wheel" of his car. Most agreed that the storm's first pass brought the greatest flooding.

Across Beaufort, Pamlico, and Hyde Counties, roadways were impassable due to high water, just as they had been during Bertha, Fran, and Bonnie. Because of the regular flooding in recent years, the Raleigh *News and Observer* reported that some Belhaven citizens had "started measuring hurricane high-water marks like some people measure the growth of their children." A pole in Bud O'Neal's drugstore was labeled for comparison. "This is Bertha and here's Dennis," O'Neal told reporters. "Not as bad as Fran. Bad enough though."

Six deaths were attributed to Dennis, including four surf-related drownings in Florida and two automobile fatalities in North Carolina. Injuries were widely reported during the six-day storm, especially in those communities that suffered the greatest flooding.

Though not on the same scale as any of the great Tar Heel storms, Hurricane Dennis (and then Tropical Storm Dennis) will be remembered by many as the flood before the flood. It wore people down simply by lingering for so long, affecting easternmost North Carolina twice within a week. Ultimately, it was the storm's rainfall over a broad area that became the bigger story. At Ocracoke, more than nineteen inches were recorded during Dennis, and other Down East communities reported six to twelve inches. Though these rains provided a welcome break from the drought conditions that had gripped the state throughout the summer, they also saturated the soils and filled eastern North Carolina's creeks and rivers, priming them for the greater disaster that followed two weeks later—the record-breaking floods of Hurricane Floyd.

There were thirteen people on the roof, that cold stormy night.
It was dark, and every sound you would hear would scare you. My dad, my uncle, and my grandpa had to wade through the water to get to the boat.
My dad got gook and gunk all over him when he got back. The water had made a hole in the ground, my uncle fell in it. It scared all of us. We thought he was a goner.—Abby McDonald, from "Spooky Waters," a 1999 essay for her seventh-grade class at Jones Middle School in Trenton, North Carolina

In the days following the dissipation of Tropical Storm Dennis, the weather in eastern North Carolina returned to its normal pattern for late summer: hot, humid, and peppered with frequent afternoon thunderstorms. Rivers, streams, and ditches across the eastern counties flowed heavily with water from Dennis's rains. Saturated soils took in what they could but gave up the excess to flow downstream. More showers fell through early September, with some counties receiving as much as ten additional inches over the course of one week. These rains refilled creeks and swales and set the stage for the arrival of a more ominous rain maker—and monstrous flood producer—that would later be recognized as one of North Carolina's greatest disasters.

Hurricane Floyd emerged from the central Atlantic at the peak of the 1999 season and developed into the year's most awesome hurricane spectacle. It was a moderately busy year amid an extremely active period of tropical activity. The 1999 season produced twelve named storms, eight of which became hurricanes. Five of those were major hurricanes—Bret, Cindy, Floyd, Gert, and Lenny—which all reached Category 4 strength, a phenomenon rarely observed in the Atlantic. And the active 1999 season capped off a dizzying five-year stretch that produced more Atlantic hurricanes than any similar period in recorded history until that time. From 1995 through 1999, forecasters at the National Hurricane Center worked around the clock to keep up with sixty-five named storms, forty-one of which were hurricanes, twenty of them major with winds

exceeding 110 mph. A number of these storms eventually affected North Carolina, including Hurricane Fran, which established itself as the new standard for
Tar Heel hurricanes in 1996. But records are made to be broken, and it didn't
take long—just three years—for Hurricane Floyd to replace Fran as the state's
preeminent weather event.

Floyd's course to America can be traced back to a tropical wave that formed
off of western Africa on September 2. Growing steadily in size and strength,
Floyd became a hurricane the morning of September 10. Its westward course
steered it well north of the vulnerable islands of the eastern Caribbean and
far enough north to also avoid Puerto Rico and Hispaniola. While gathering
steam on its approach to the eastern Bahamas, Floyd amassed a considerable
volume of tropical moisture and grew to become a large, dynamic hurricane.
Little or no wind shear and a ridge of high pressure aloft provided the setting
for the storm's intensification. Satellite photos told the story as this monster
reached its meteorological peak on September 13. With maximum sustained
winds of 155 mph and a barometric low pressure of 921 mb, Floyd was a border-
line Category 5 when it moved to within just 300 miles of the central Bahamas.

All eyes in the eastern United States were fixed on this large and dangerous
cyclone, whose own eye was as pronounced as that of any classic hurricane.
The storm's size was immediately impressive too: televised reports in Florida
compared satellite images of Floyd with pictures of Hurricane Andrew from
1992. Though the two storms reached a similar intensity at nearly the same
position in the Atlantic, Floyd's diameter was about three times what Andrew's
had been, covering an impressive swath of the western Atlantic. Hurricane-
force winds extended more than 125 miles out from the eye, and the overall
storm measured more than 400 miles across. Its formidable size and strength
commanded the full attention of everyone with a television or radio from the
eastern Bahamas to Florida and the southeastern U.S. coast.

Bahamians were the first to be blasted by the storm. On the night of September 13, Floyd changed heading and turned toward the west-northwest, passing
only about thirty miles north of San Salvador and Cat Island. Fortunately,
some weakening occurred during the evening, and Floyd struck the Abaco
Islands with at least Category 3 winds. Few news reports filtered out of the
islands during the storm, but it later came to light that many beachfront properties were devastated. At least one Bahamian was killed, and damages were
widespread throughout the affected islands.

Emergency managers and residents on Florida's east coast were anticipating the worst and scrambling to execute their plans. A hurricane watch was

issued for portions of the Florida coast on the morning of the thirteenth; this watch was shifted northward and upgraded to a warning later that day. The storm appeared to be lunging toward the Cape Canaveral area, and most people on the eastern side of Florida packed their cars and fled. Almost seventy shelters opened throughout the coastal counties, and another seventy were put on standby. From Miami to Jacksonville, a mass exodus was underway as 1.3 million people attempted to flee the path of the storm. Highways were jammed with cars, NASA's Kennedy Space Center was shut down, and for the first time in its twenty-eight-year history, Walt Disney World in Orlando closed.

The hurricane continued to spin toward the northwest, but as it took a gradual turn and the hours rolled by, it became apparent that Florida would be spared a direct hit. Hurricane warnings were extended northward as the storm's center tracked parallel to the coast. As the eye passed 110 miles east of Cape Canaveral early on September 15, a data buoy rode mountainous seas 120 miles offshore, measuring fifty-five-foot waves every seventeen seconds. Floyd was still large and dangerous, and now it was edging up the coast toward the Carolinas.

Massive evacuations continued around the clock in the coastal regions of Georgia, South Carolina, and North Carolina. As Floyd neared South Carolina's Lowcountry, many residents near Charleston fled with high anxiety. They still held vivid memories of Hurricane Hugo, the similar Category 4 storm that had struck the region almost exactly ten years earlier. Once again, highways were packed with cars, trucks, and campers that crept inland at a pedestrian pace. Because state officials in the departments of transportation and public safety hadn't reached an agreement on a lane reversal plan before the storm, Interstate 26 was not set up for one-way flow. As a result, motorists in one section traveled just fifteen miles in four hours. Some even left their cars to engage in fistfights on the highway median. Evening news broadcasts focused on the approaching storm but highlighted the frustrations of road-locked evacuees who spent long hours trying to escape the freeways and find available hotel rooms.

Evacuations along the North Carolina coast were just as thorough, though they involved smaller populations and fewer headaches. In all, the hurried inland flight of millions of residents stretching from South Florida to the Virginia coast was the largest and most complete on record. Some estimates suggested that almost 3 million people along the southeastern seaboard left their homes and moved to safer quarters in advance of the storm. Emergency planners and government officials were awed by the magnitude of the evacuation. Joe Myers, Florida's emergency management director, told the *Miami Herald*,

"In the truest sense, this probably has become the largest peacetime evacuation in U.S. history, and certainly in the state of Florida. This is the first time we've ever had a complete evacuation on either coast."

While forecasters watched the storm hour by hour, North Carolina coastal residents listened to each news update with a familiar sense of dread. Though Floyd had weakened from its strong Category 4 peak, it was still a dangerous hurricane as it passed by the Georgia coast. And its future course was now of greater concern to the Tar Heel State. Storm-weary inhabitants from Brunswick County to the Outer Banks were accustomed to plotting hurricanes with curving tracks; they knew that the more Floyd edged toward the west, the less likely it became that it would curve harmlessly out to sea. Fortunately, though, the storm slowly weakened throughout the day on September 15, with sustained winds dropping from 140 mph to 110 mph. But Floyd was so large that even as its breezes still fanned parts of South Florida, its outer rainbands were spreading over New York State. It was during this time, while the storm was still a full day away from landfall, that drenching rains began to fall across eastern North Carolina.

About the time Floyd made its turn just off the Florida coast, emergency managers and local meteorologists began to issue dire warnings for the Carolina beaches—or wherever landfall might eventually occur. Storm surges in excess of fourteen feet were discussed, and residents along the state's barrier islands prepared for the worst. But the continued drop in the hurricane's intensity throughout September 15 was good news for those who owned property at the coast. With Floyd's weakening trend and its downward transition to a Category 2 storm, a sense of relief suffused hurricane watchers everywhere. Though still oversized when viewed from space, the once-mighty cyclone no longer packed the punch of a killer—or so it seemed.

Floyd finally made landfall around 3:00 A.M. on September 16 at Cape Fear, a point of land that seems to draw hurricanes like a magnet, having been the scene of recent landfalls during Bertha, Fran, and Bonnie. As Floyd approached the coast, it lost much of its eyewall structure and became less well organized. Reconnaissance aircraft recorded maximum sustained winds of 105 mph at the time of landfall, though no reporting stations experienced sustained winds of that speed. The storm's center dragged along the New Hanover shoreline and then moved inland over Pender and Onslow Counties. Later that day, it passed over New Bern and Washington in North Carolina and over extreme southeastern Virginia, where greater Norfolk was also pounded by heavy rains. Floyd then weakened to a tropical storm and accelerated toward the north-northeast, skirting along the Delmarva Peninsula, up the New Jersey coast, over Long

Island, and into coastal New England. By the eighteenth, Floyd became part of a large extratropical low over the North Atlantic and was no longer a distinct storm.

At first look, Floyd was not a meteorological marvel when it came ashore in eastern North Carolina. The storm's loss of strength before landfall was a blessing to those who had watched it teeter near Category 5 territory just days before. Winds gusted above 100 mph in numerous locations, but wind-related damages were not significant. Still, at the New Hanover County Emergency Operations Center, a peak gust of 130 mph was reported, and an instrument atop the eight-story Blockade Runner Hotel in Wrightsville Beach produced an unofficial reading of 138 mph. A more reliable measurement of a 112 mph gust was recorded at Kure Beach at 2:20 A.M. on September 16, just moments before the eye of the storm passed over. The automated Frying Pan Shoals station, located about thirty miles southeast of Cape Fear, reported sustained winds of near 100 mph for a twenty-minute period.

Other reports of peak gusts included 96 mph at the U.S. Army Corps of Engineers' research pier at Duck, 91 mph at Cape Lookout, 86 mph at the Wilmington National Weather Service office, 82 mph at Cherry Point, 80 mph at Oak Island, and 71 mph at Myrtle Beach. In addition to these fixed weather stations, a special mobile research team was positioned on the coast to gather data and study Floyd's impact. The University of Oklahoma's Doppler on Wheels team set up its portable instruments on Topsail Beach, where team members recorded sustained winds of 96 mph and gusts to 123 mph during the early-morning hours of the sixteenth. The lowest barometric pressures reported in North Carolina were 959 mb at New River Air Station near Jacksonville and 960 mb at the Wilmington Airport. Remarkably, this reading in Wilmington makes Floyd the most intense storm ever measured at that location by barometric pressure, which was lower than during Hazel, Fran, or Florence.

Floyd's lessened intensity at landfall also helped reduce the overall impact of tidal surge on the North Carolina coast. According to a report from the Corps of Engineers, Oak Island in Brunswick County was the hardest hit, suffering a measured surge of 10.4 feet. A measurement of 10.3 feet was taken on the sound side of Masonboro Island—ten inches less than the level recorded after Fran. Tides ran nine to ten feet above normal from Fort Fisher northward and six to eight feet above normal on the beaches of Onslow and Carteret Counties. Beach erosion was significant along the entire coast, with some barrier islands faring better than others. And as with most hurricanes, it wasn't just the ocean beaches that experienced high water. The Neuse and Pamlico Rivers and the Pamlico Sound were hit by a surge of six to eight feet.

As the storm's most potent rainbands swept over eastern North Carolina, radar screens up and down the coast lit up with the bright greens, yellows, and reds that signify intense weather. Forecasters monitored their instruments for the early signs of tornado development—and there were plenty such signs to keep them busy. The Newport office of the National Weather Service issued a total of twenty tornado warnings, and ten twisters were verified by spotters in the area. Most of these came during the period from 4:00 P.M. to midnight, several hours before the eye of the storm reached land. One of the stronger tornadoes struck Hobucken in Pamlico County. The Weather Service rated it as an F2 on the Fujita scale, which is used by meteorologists to measure tornado severity (the scale was updated in 2007 and is now known as the Enhanced Fujita scale). The Hobucken twister heavily damaged or destroyed several structures, including a mobile home, a house, three churches, and a school. Another tornado in Emerald Isle destroyed two houses and heavily damaged three others. Four tornadoes were spotted near Wilmington, and others were confirmed in Bertie and Perquimans Counties.

Without question, Floyd's winds, tides, and tornadoes were dramatic and destructive, particularly along some portions of the coast. But in more than two dozen counties, residents experienced an even greater threat that would later prove to be the catalyst for Floyd's most disastrous legacy. This was, of course, the unending rain that accumulated in ditches, creeks, and rivers, eventually swelling into a great flood. The rains, which in some areas lasted more than sixty hours, fell over a region whose soil was already saturated beyond capacity by Dennis's earlier downpours. River levels were already high when Floyd's first steady showers began to fall. As reports of rain accumulations across the region began to come in, Weather Service officials and emergency planners began to issue a steady flow of flood watches and warnings.

The excessive rainfall that swamped eastern North Carolina before and during Floyd was the result of the storm's massive size and the timing of its approach. A strong trough of low pressure had moved in from the west as the hurricane came ashore, wringing extra moisture from the atmosphere and dumping it overland. Hurricane researcher William Gray described the trough's influence in the Raleigh *News and Observer*: "The same kind of thing happened during Hurricane Hazel in 1954. It is a particularly bad weather pattern that can transform a relatively weak hurricane [into] a terrible one, and a terrible one into a catastrophic one."

Because rains began well in advance of Floyd's eventual landfall, total storm accumulations were very large. In Wilmington, rainfall was measured at 13.38 inches on September 15, establishing a new one-day record for that location. A new twenty-four-hour record was set there as well when 15.06 inches fell between 3:00 A.M. on the fifteenth and the morning of the sixteenth. The storm total for Wilmington was 19.06 inches, and a remarkable 24.06 inches were recorded in Southport, establishing a new North Carolina tropical cyclone rainfall record. According to Weather Service reports, rainfall totals averaged between 14 and 16 inches across many inland counties. Other extreme measurements included 19.01 inches in Bladen County, 16.52 inches in Brunswick County, 16.06 inches in Myrtle Beach, 15.65 inches in Rocky Mount, 13.80 inches in Zebulon, 12.99 inches in Tarboro, and 12.86 inches in Greenville.

Thanks to the combined rains of Dennis and Floyd, several locations in North Carolina also established new one-month precipitation records. Wilmington registered 23.45 inches for September, beating out the old single-month record of 21.12 inches set way back in July 1886. September was also the wettest month on record in Raleigh and Durham, where the measured 21.80 inches broke a 112-year-old record. This total was well above the 16.65 inches that fell in September 1996 when Hurricane Fran rolled through the Triangle. Other cities across the east also endured astronomical monthly rainfall totals. Snow Hill in Greene County received 35.29 inches in September, Greenville had 27.36 inches, and Kinston had 23.03 inches. Normal monthly averages for this region are around 5 inches. In addition to these hefty totals, Floyd's rains set new records in Pennsylvania, New York, and Connecticut.

The magnitude of the flooding disaster became apparent in the hours and days after the heaviest rains passed. Because there was no place for water to drain through already saturated soils or overfilled rivers, floodwaters began to back up into streets, homes, farms, businesses, and interstate highways. The waters rose quickly in some areas and more slowly in others. Many of the flood victims were taken by surprise—some were asleep in their beds when they were awakened by the sensation of water on their backs. Others endured the worst flooding days after the storm when rivers finally crested. Along Floyd's path and across at least a dozen Tar Heel counties, an epic flood held the entire population in its clutches.

Within days, media reports began to refer to the disaster as a "500-year flood." The waters were the highest in the memories of just about everyone who lived near the banks of eastern North Carolina's rivers and creeks. Not surprisingly, several reporting stations along the Neuse, Tar, and Northeast Cape Fear Rivers established all-time flood records in the days following Floyd. At Kinston, the Neuse River crested at 27.71 feet on September 23—more than thirteen feet above its flood stage. This eclipsed the previous record of twenty-five feet set in July 1919. The new record was also more than three feet above the peak flood levels of Hurricane Fran. Kinston and much of the Neuse River basin suffered severe flooding for over three weeks. Water levels did not drop below twenty feet until October 10. The river was still above flood stage on October 17, one month after Floyd's passage, when heavy rains associated with Hurricane Irene fell across the east. Irene (not to be confused with the 2011 storm of the same name) made landfall in Florida on October 15 and tracked just off the Carolina coast before heading out to sea.

The Tar River crested in Rocky Mount at 31.66 feet, more than ten feet above flood stage. On September 21, the Tar crested in Greenville at 29.74 feet, more than sixteen feet above flood stage. The flooding in Greenville surpassed by more than five feet the previous record, set in 1919. At Chinquapin, the Northeast Cape Fear River also set a new record, rising to 23.51 feet on September 18. This was more than seven feet above the river's crest during Fran. In all, at least nine U.S. Geological Survey river stations in North Carolina set new flood records, along with one in Virginia, six in New Jersey, one in Delaware, and two in Pennsylvania. And of the more than 200 streamgages monitored in North Carolina, twenty were destroyed during the storm.

Initial data from the U.S. Geological Survey indicated that at least eleven of its monitoring sites in North Carolina exceeded 500-year flood levels, a term used by hydrologists to indicate flood-recurrence intervals. For a particular location, a ten-year flood has a 10 percent chance of occurring in a given year, a 100-year event has a 1 percent recurrence rate, and a 500-year flood has only a 0.2 percent chance of happening in a given year. But preliminary U.S. Geological Survey data suggested that 500-year flood levels were reached in Ahoskie, Rocky Mount, Hilliardston, White Oak, Enfield, Tarboro, Lucama, Hookerton, Trenton, Chinquapin, and Freeland. Months after the storm, however, those 500-year flood estimates were revised by officials at the U.S. Geological Survey. After reviewing many outdated and inaccurate flood maps, they determined that Floyd may have been more of a 150- or 200-year flood at some of these locations.

But regardless of the flood's eventual place in history, its effects were indisputable. The high water covered so many roads, bridges, and highways that entire communities were cut off from the outside world. By the time the rivers crested, nearly all major roads in Duplin, Jones, Pender, Greene, Lenoir, Craven, Pitt, and Edgecombe Counties were impassable. Among the major transportation arteries blocked by flooding were U.S. 70 in Kinston; U.S. 17 in Washington, Pollocksville, and portions of Brunswick County; U.S. 264 between Greenville and Washington; U.S. 64 in Edgecombe County; U.S. 24 in Beulaville and Kenansville; Interstate 40 in Pender County; and Interstate 95 near Rocky Mount. At the peak of the flood, Department of Transportation officials reported that 1,400 eastern North Carolina roads were impassable. Bridges washed out in dozens of places, and asphalt crumbled in others, creating submerged driving hazards that were invisible to motorists. Across eastern North Carolina, 283 bridges were damaged by the storm, and seventeen were completely washed away or undermined. The impassable roads complicated the disaster by slowing relief efforts in many cities, forcing drivers to make elaborate detours and delaying the delivery of food and supplies for days. Five shelters—three in Edgecombe County and two in Pitt County—were completely isolated by flooding and could only be supplied by helicopter. By late October, weeks after the storm, 232 of the state's roads were still closed to traffic.

Tragically, submerged roads proved to be the most dangerous places in the disaster—they were responsible for most of the storm-related deaths in North Carolina. People put too much faith in the heft of their vehicles and underestimated the depth of the water, the swiftness of the currents, and the risks associated with trying to drive over roads they couldn't see. Some of these dynamics were described in a report in the *Virginian-Pilot*, with help from FEMA and the American Red Cross:

> Water weighs 62.4 pounds per cubic foot and typically flows downstream at 6 to 12 miles per hour. When a vehicle stalls in the water, the water's momentum is transferred to the vehicle. For each foot the water rises, 500 pounds of lateral force are applied to the vehicle. . . . The biggest factor, however, is buoyancy. For each foot the water rises up the side of the vehicle, it displaces 1,500 pounds of water. In effect, the car weighs 1,500 pounds less for each foot of rising water around it. In other words, 2 feet of water will carry away most vehicles.

Submerged roadways were only part of the problem. Within hours of the storm's arrival, thousands of residents in more than a dozen Tar Heel counties found themselves trapped in their homes by rising water. Many were shocked to find the coffee-colored fluid edging into their yards—especially those who had never seen floodwater in their neighborhoods. But for many, the worst flooding came during the night—many slept as the floods entered their homes. Along with the rising waters came a witches' brew of leaked gasoline, sewage, and other contaminants that spread a pervasive stench through virtually every flooded area. Thousands were forced to flee their homes and escape to nearby high ground—if they could find any. Many of those ousted by the flood made their way to rooftops and treetops to await rescue. Across eastern North Carolina, thousands of men, women, and children, along with dogs, cats, and other family pets, waited for hours on steeply pitched roofs that became islands in a sea of muddy water. In countless neighborhoods, floodwaters buried cars and trucks and most anything else less than eight feet tall. Homes in Greenville, Tarboro, Princeville, and Rocky Mount were submerged beyond recognition, with waters in some locations standing more than fifteen feet deep.

Rescue teams formed quickly and fanned out across more than a dozen eastern counties. The task of rescue coordination was massive and involved state emergency managers, the National Guard, the U.S. Coast Guard, the U.S. Navy, and virtually every division of the state highway patrol, county sheriff's departments, local police, and fire and emergency service personnel that was available. National Guard units from as far away as Georgia, Kentucky, and Texas arrived to provide aid. Hundreds of volunteers joined forces with government officials to scour the countryside in search of stranded flood victims. Through long days and nights, they patrolled neighborhood streets and rural areas in bass boats and small skiffs, looking for isolated families and stranded individuals. Nearly fifty rescue helicopters were put into service by various branches of the military, focusing primarily on Rocky Mount, Princeville, and portions of Jones, Pitt, Greene, and Duplin Counties where the flooding was the worst. At one point, there were so many choppers in the skies over Rocky Mount that one Coast Guard helicopter hovered high above the rest, doing nothing but air traffic control.

At the Army National Guard logistical staging area in Kinston, more than 1,000 Guardsmen helped carry out hundreds of flight missions in the first days after the storm. In addition to rescuing stranded storm victims, they helped deliver food, water, and medical supplies to shelters and neighborhoods cut off by flooding. In Greenville, choppers lifted hospital employees to a medical supply warehouse that was isolated by the flood. There the workers were lowered to the ground, where they retrieved nearly two dozen large boxes of doctors' bags and other supplies for distribution to hospitals and clinics around the area.

The dramatic rescues during this time were unlike any others in North Carolina's hurricane history. By midafternoon on September 17, almost 1,500 stranded residents had been plucked from rooftops and treetops by rescue teams. Among them were about 500 people in Jones County, 500 in Duplin County, 300 in Edgecombe County, and dozens more in Beaufort, Pitt, Craven, and Greene Counties. At least 400 of those rescued had been lifted out by helicopter, some in the black of night. One man held on to the branches of a shrub for nine hours, screaming for help, until rescuers finally reached him. "It was the most terrifying experience I ever had in my life," Dunbar resident and evacuee Leatha Norman told the Associated Press. "I felt like I was going to lose my family and my life."

But as the hours rolled by, reports filtered in that thousands more were stranded and in need of rescue. By Saturday, September 18, officials in Edgecombe County reported that more than 3,500 residents had been rescued in that county alone. Renee Hoffman, spokeswoman for the state's emergency management office, described the process for the Raleigh *News and Observer*: "It is neighbor rescuing neighbor in a lot of situations out there. There is no way we have a firm number of people who are waiting. We assign a flight to pick up a certain number of people and they find others along the way. This is a find-people-as-you-find-them situation." In many locations, pilots donned night-vision goggles and continued to fly around the clock in search of stranded victims. After nineteen straight hours of rescue missions, Lt. Robert Keith of the Coast Guard told the *Virginian-Pilot*, "We'd be flying to one spot where the sheriff said someone was waiting for us, and we'd fly over all of these people—rows and rows of people with flashlights, waiting on their rooftops, click, click, clicking for us to come help."

Some motorists on Interstate 95 in Nash County were among those rescued in dramatic fashion. Sherry Boyer, a Pennsylvania resident who was traveling the interstate on the morning after the storm, died of a probable heart attack when her van stalled in a four-foot-deep torrent that covered the highway. A motorist attempting to assist her waded into the current with a heavy chain to attach to her van but was carried away into deep water. Jim Howell, a local volunteer firefighter who happened on the scene, watched as the man was swept over the highway and into the woods. Using his handheld radio, Howell called for help, and within minutes, a twin-rotor Marine helicopter was lowering a Marine to rescue the man. Soon after the man was pulled to safety, Boyer's van was recovered, but attempts to revive her were unsuccessful. Then, as Howell and others were still gathered on the edge of the flooded highway, several truckers attempted to cross the deepening stream that covered both north- and southbound lanes. Within minutes, two large trucks lost control in the shoulder-deep water, drifted sideways into the median, and stalled. A second Marine chopper soon arrived and hoisted the truckers to safety, one by one.

Several of the helicopter crews involved in rescue missions were later honored by the army and navy for their heroism during the floods. They were recognized for saving scores of lives, dropping rescue swimmers into dangerous areas, flying as close as five feet to high-tension electrical lines, and showing great compassion for the victims they rescued. Never before had missions of

A Marine rescue helicopter airlifts a desperate trucker from the cab of his rig after Hurricane Floyd's floodwaters covered both lanes of Interstate 95 in Nash County. (Photo by Chuck Liddy. Courtesy of the Raleigh *News and Observer*.)

this kind been deployed on such a large scale in North Carolina. Though many of the rescue teams had acquired their expertise in places such as Kuwait and Nicaragua, they were clearly moved by the destruction they witnessed in their own country. Many of the victims they rescued were also emotional about their airborne evacuations. One young Greenville resident even decided to join the navy after his family was saved by the crew of a hovering chopper: Derek Latham, a senior at J. H. Rose High School, enlisted after watching his mother and two sisters pulled to safety from their flooded home. "That was the moment that I decided joining the Navy was what I wanted to do," Latham told the Raleigh *News and Observer*. "The only thing I would like to do is the same thing they did for my family."

Many of the storm's most daring rescues were linked to tragedy. As rains poured over eastern North Carolina on September 17, Mitchell Piner and his fifteen-year-old stepson, Gary Williams, were on their way to visit a friend when their truck was swept off N.C. 41 just outside Wallace. The swollen waters of Rockfish Creek formed a strong current that smashed the truck into a nearby tree. Piner and Williams managed to crawl out of the cab through the back window, but both soon struggled to keep their heads above the swiftly moving waters. Erasmo Mencias, a fifty-one-year-old construction worker from nearby Magnolia, witnessed the truck's demise and jumped into the raging flood when he heard shouts for help. He managed to find Williams and grab him in a bear hug, inching him up a tree to wait for more rescuers. While the creek waters continued to rise, Mencias held the teenager tightly for more than thirty minutes until the Wallace Volunteer Fire Department arrived with a boat. Mencias had saved Williams's life, but unfortunately Piner became one of Floyd's many drowning victims. For Mencias, a strong swimmer who used to set lobster traps off the coast of Honduras, saving this boy from drowning was not a first. He had rescued four people in a similar way in Honduras during the floods that followed Hurricane Fifi in 1974.

Another of the storm's dramatic rescues was reported by the Raleigh *News and Observer*:

Pender County, along I-40, 4:30 P.M.: Burgaw Creek, Rockfish Creek, and other streams washed over one of Eastern North Carolina's main arteries. Powerful currents of knee-high water streamed across the highway, flooding dozens of cars and sweeping at least one Pender County motorist away, apparently to his death.

Highway Patrol Commander R. W. Holden, the agency's top cop, waded along the highway Thursday afternoon near Wallace, ordering eastbound motorists to turn back. "It's too dangerous," he told them. Behind Holden, a rescue effort was under way. The driver of a minivan tried to cross the flooded westbound lanes near Wallace. Witnesses said the van was swept off the shoulder into a ditch that Rockfish Creek had turned into a torrent.

The roof of the van disappeared under the water. Another motorist, Matt Wilde of Wilmington, dove into the water to try to save the driver. But the waters quickly swallowed Wilde, too. For more than a half-hour, Wilde clung to a tree while troopers tethered to a truck swam in to get him.

Troopers tried several times to get a rope around Wilde and swam under the waves in an attempt to reach the van. Highway Patrol Sgt. Terry Carlyle tried to smash the window of the van with a crescent wrench, but the current was too strong and he couldn't break the van open. Other motorists ran down the highway to volunteer their arms and backs in the rescue effort.

At 5:20 P.M., the rescuers pulled Wilde out of the current. Carlyle hugged Wilde, who was shaken but uninjured. "You did a great job," Carlyle told him as Wilde gazed back at the water where the van had disappeared, its driver almost certainly drowned.

In dozens of communities, emergency workers and volunteers ventured door to door in small boats in search of marooned flood victims. They rounded up fleets of bass boats, aluminum skiffs, canoes, inflatable Zodiacs, and even Jet Skis to search submerged neighborhoods and rural homesteads. In places such as Rocky Mount, Tarboro, and Princeville, where the flooding was most extreme, rescuers described steering small boats over the tops of submerged backyard fences, clotheslines, storage sheds, and swing sets. The flooding was so deep that some reported bumping their engine propellers on the tops of sunken pickup trucks. Another rescue worker recognized the blue lights atop a sheriff's deputy's car "at least two feet" below the murky water. Those searching for stranded victims usually didn't have to travel far, and countless runs were staged day and night to deliver families and their pets to safety on higher ground. According to MSNBC News, rescuers in Duplin County fanned out on Jet Skis, and their wakes "helped scare off deadly water moccasins that wriggled through flooded windows of mobile homes."

Emergency workers and volunteers tirelessly repeated their efforts for days after the storm. Most were very successful. One particular rescue mission on the night of the hurricane failed, however, becoming the single greatest tragedy of the Floyd disaster.

As the hurricane's drenching rains swamped Edgecombe County on the night of September 16, residents in the small community of Pinetops watched the waters rise into their streets and yards. Even in the dark of night, many could see that their homes would soon be filled with the overflowing waters of Town Creek. Ben Mayo, who loved to fish the creeks near his home, scrambled to launch his flat-bottomed boat to rescue his neighbors and family. After collecting eight other people and transporting them to safety, Mayo returned to his home amid the storm's pounding winds and rain. There he loaded his wife, daughter, granddaughter, and several neighbors into his small boat for the short ride to higher ground. But with twelve people on board, the small skiff soon capsized in the shifting currents of the flood. Tossed into the pitch-black water, only half of the boat's passengers were able to scramble to the safety of a nearby bank. Drowned in the flood were Mayo, his wife Vivian, his daughter Keisha, his five-year-old granddaughter Teshika Vines, and two young neighbors, Cabrina and Destiny Flowers. Mayo, who was well respected in the Pinetops community, had died while trying to help others survive the storm.

Though helicopters, boats, and National Guard transport trucks were the vehicles most often used to retrieve stranded flood victims, members of one Pitt County family found a resourceful way to save their neighbors. Charles Davenport of Pactolus took the advice of his son and used his Hagie crop sprayer to maneuver through high water and muck to rescue about sixty-five residents. The sprayer, which features a six-foot ground clearance, managed the high water without problems since the engine and power train were above the flood. Davenport's stepson, Chris Sawyer, backed up the machine—its spray arms folded upward—to his neighbors' front porches and offered rides to high ground. Driving the machine was sometimes treacherous, but Sawyer moved slowly and cautiously. Eventually, flood currents became too swift for the safe operation of the vehicle, but by then most of the neighbors had been transported to safety.

One of the most dramatic rescues of Hurricane Floyd took place a full day before landfall, in the open Atlantic some 300 miles east of Jacksonville, Florida. The eight men aboard the oceangoing tug *Gulf Majesty* knew that the storm was on their heels but made the mistake of thinking they could outrun it. On the morning of September 15, the tug's crew cut loose its 750-foot barge when waves the size of four-story buildings flooded the tug's engine room. After notifying the Coast Guard by radio, the crew abandoned the sinking ship and launched into heavy swells and 60 mph winds. As the men clambered into their bright orange life raft, a wave dashed the raft away from the tug, separating three of them from the five who had made it safely aboard. With their tug now rapidly foundering, the three had no choice but to jump into the raging Atlantic.

Meanwhile, about 140 miles away, huge swells broke over the flight deck of the aircraft carrier USS *John F. Kennedy*. Along with a small fleet of other navy ships, the *Kennedy* was at the time moving out to sea to avoid the wrath of Floyd and its near–Category 5 winds. Having a clear fix on the *Gulf Majesty*'s emergency locator beacon but no ships in the area, the Coast Guard radioed the *Kennedy* to ask for help in rescuing the tug's hapless crew. The massive carrier turned back toward the approaching storm and readied a pair of SH-60

Seahawk helicopters for the mission. The two choppers sped toward the lost ship and zeroed in on the emergency beacon. When they arrived, they found the three men in the water desperately clutching a broken broomstick to stay together. Then, as if taking his cue from the pages of Sebastian Junger's *The Perfect Storm*, navy rescue swimmer Shad Hernandez jumped into the raging seas amid thirty-five-foot swells to save the three men. The rescue went smoothly, and within eleven minutes Hernandez and the three crewmen were safely on their way back to the *Kennedy*.

After returning to the ship to refuel, the helicopters turned back to search for the five crew members still at sea. The men were later found clinging to their raft, eight hours after their tug had gone down. Storm-beaten and exhausted, they had barely held on to the raft as it rode up and down mountainous waves that sometimes folded it in half. Once again, navy rescue swimmers went into the water and successfully hoisted the men to safety. Of the many helicopter missions that took place during or after Hurricane Floyd, few were as daring as the rescue of the *Gulf Majesty*'s crew.

The storm's unprecedented flooding across a broad portion of eastern North Carolina brought misery and destruction to dozens of cities and towns. Among the hardest hit was the historic Edgecombe County town of Princeville, where floodwaters were perhaps deeper and the devastation more complete than in most other locations. Princeville, which had been founded on the banks of the Tar River by former slaves after the Civil War, was submerged when floodwaters burst through a protective dike in seven places. The town of 2,100 residents was quickly swamped by waters that measured close to thirty feet deep in some locations. The inundation buckled roofs, stacked cars on top of one another, and swept at least a dozen houses off their foundations. Surviving homes and businesses were coated with a heavy layer of foul-smelling mud that later proved nearly impossible to remove. More than 600 homes were heavily damaged.

One of the challenges faced by town residents was the recovery of hundreds of caskets unearthed by the flood. The sealed coffins floated out of their graves and were swept about the town, along with propane tanks, appliances, and other household flotsam. While the floodwaters were high, crews working from boats gathered the wayward caskets and tethered them to trees and poles. Two weeks after the storm, 129 caskets had been recovered and taken to a temporary morgue, where a team of forensic experts made the necessary identifications. The morticians were aided by relatives, who supplied information about clothing and jewelry worn by the deceased. Ultimately, some 224 caskets were recovered, of which 174 were positively identified. All were later reburied. Elaine

Wathen of the North Carolina Division of Emergency Management told the Associated Press, "It's something we've never dealt with before. We wanted to be sure we did everything right and had the utmost respect for the remains."

By the end of September, most of the water had receded from the tattered streets of Princeville, but few residents were able to return to their homes due to the extent of the destruction. And just when it seemed things couldn't get any worse, a wave of looting hit the town. Thieves made off with truckloads of stolen items from more than a dozen flood-damaged homes. Princeville's small police force, which had lost two of its three patrol cars to the flood, sought help from FEMA to pay for four temporary officers to provide additional security. About this time, disheartened residents were given a boost when civil rights leader Jesse Jackson and American Red Cross president Bernadine Healy visited the devastated town. Jackson delivered a rousing speech to the 300-plus residents who were still sleeping in a local gymnasium. Though the waters were mostly gone, it would be many more months before residents would return to their homes. According to the Raleigh *News and Observer*, Jackson lifted spirits by mixing "poems, prayers, and promises in his trademark style." Jackson chanted to the crowd, "We can make it. Say after me: 'I am somebody.' Through the rain, through the flood: I am somebody. We can make it. We can make it. Keep hope alive. Keep hope alive."

For several months after Floyd, Princeville served as a focal point for many issues surrounding post-storm recovery and reconstruction. By November, town officials were still wrestling with the question of whether to rebuild the protective dike and replace damaged homes or to participate in federally sponsored buyouts. The buyouts offered by FEMA would have provided funding to relocate many of the town's residents to other neighborhoods out of the 100-year floodplain. If that option had been selected, it would essentially have broken up the historic town. After extensive debate, the Princeville Board of Commissioners voted 3–2 to ask the U.S. Army Corps of Engineers to repair its dike. Construction was completed by the summer of 2000, and many of the flooded homes were repaired.

On September 18 in nearby Tarboro, dozens of residents walked or rode bikes into town to watch the Tar River crest about twenty-two feet above its nineteen-foot flood stage. As in other towns built on the banks of eastern rivers, Tarboro's downtown business district was submerged to a level that far exceeded any flooding in memory. And like people in so many other communities hit by the flood, hundreds of Tarboro residents were rescued by boat and helicopter in the first days after the storm. Many who escaped said the waterline was "just above the light switches" in their homes. They gathered in emergency shelters overflowing with despondent families who could hardly believe what was happening. Initially, some 2,000 refugees filled Tarboro High School, which had no running water and no electricity. As the hours and days crept by, food, drinking water, and personal effects were in short supply, and hot showers were nonexistent. But for many, the greatest need was to know the whereabouts of relatives and friends. In many instances, men were rescued by helicopter hours after their wives and children had been taken to safety, so family members spent long nights searching for one another by sending messages through police and shelter officials. No one was keeping lists of who had been rescued and what shelter they had been taken to.

Edgecombe County officials set up a makeshift operations center near a jail where refugees were to be dropped off after being rescued by helicopter. But with the power out, Coast Guard and other military pilots had trouble seeing the improvised landing field in the dark. To solve the problem, sheriff's deputies parked their patrol cars around the field and flashed their blue lights to guide the pilots to the ground. Officers were called away, however, when reports came in that the Kmart near Tarboro High School was being looted. When they arrived at the scene, they found hundreds of local residents sleeping in their cars in the oversized parking lot, which was on a patch of high ground. Apparently, some had broken into the store—not to steal merchandise but to use the bathroom.

Shelters throughout the area were brimming with storm survivors. By midnight on September 17, more than 5,000 people were sprawled across the gymnasium and cafeteria floors of several Edgecombe County schools. With access to television, radio, and other news media very limited, accurate reports about the disaster were few and hard to come by. Along with their many other duties, shelter officials spent considerable time trying to quell rumors. As the days passed, word spread that a tuberculosis outbreak was underway and that several area shelters were set to close. Another rumor held that refrigerated trucks being guarded by the National Guard near a local hospital contained the bodies of flood victims. The trucks merely contained food.

On September 20, FEMA opened disaster-recovery centers in a handful of the hardest-hit cities, including Tarboro. Lines formed quickly as flood victims waited to sign up for whatever aid was available. Those who still had telephone service registered via FEMA's toll-free phone number, while others could only register in person. As they stood in queues that stretched out into the street, they swapped painful stories about the flood and shared tips on where to find ice and fuel. Patricia Foreman, a home day-care operator whose east Tarboro home was destroyed in the flood, managed to keep her loss in perspective.

After describing her own ordeal, she told the *News and Observer*, "But I know a woman who's really bad off. Her house is gone, her momma's house is gone, her sister's house is gone, and her babysitter's house is, too."

Among the many public buildings swamped by floodwaters was the Edgecombe County Courthouse. Water filled the courthouse basement and saturated 130 years' worth of legal records. After the waters were gone, county workers were left with the formidable task of recovering and restoring the damp and moldy papers that filled rows of file drawers. To accomplish the task, they sought help from state officials and a recovery contractor from Texas. After thousands of documents had been sorted in a downtown Raleigh parking lot, the files were loaded into a refrigerated tractor trailer and trucked to the contractor's facility in Fort Worth. There, they were freeze-dried and disinfected. Held under pressure at −20 degrees Fahrenheit, the moisture in paper turns to ice, which then evaporates. After undergoing this process, the records were left in better shape than they would have been after normal air-drying. The same procedure was used in other cities where books and important records were soaked by the hurricane's floods.

The worst flooding in Rocky Mount's history spread throughout the town, overtaking major highways and businesses and inundating entire neighborhoods. Like so many of Floyd's victims, most of those who watched the waters creep into their homes had no flood insurance—many had felt they wouldn't need it. Warehouses filled with goods were buried in floods that covered their roofs. Stores and stockrooms held soaked merchandise on the highest shelves. The Food Lion on U.S. 301 was submerged by five-foot-deep waters, and store managers assessed the damage from a small raft they maneuvered inside the store. Along with the residents of many other hard-hit cities in the east, the people of Rocky Mount scrambled to escape the rising water, climbing onto roofs and launching small skiffs in the darkness of the storm. Their memories of Floyd are filled with images of unrecognizable neighborhoods and the constant thumping sounds of choppers in the sky.

In Rocky Mount, as in so many other flooded communities, ordinary people took action to rescue their families and neighbors. Fire, police, and other first responders were overwhelmed with calls for assistance, and they, too, took extraordinary measures to save lives. Rocky Mount fire chief Ken Mullen described his initial shock when someone in the dispatch center called him over to ask what to do about the eighty-seven callers needing rescue—at a time when all trucks and firefighters were already out on calls: "Do you go get the guy who's standing on top of his car, and the water's rising, or do you go to the mother with three kids who has water rising in the first floor of her home?"

Rocky Mount fire chief Ken Mullen stands with his crew outside their station. Though nine of Mullen's firemen lost their homes to Floyd's floods, they stayed on the job throughout the event and are credited with saving many lives in the city.

One Rocky Mount citizen was credited with saving the lives of eighteen neighbors, many of them elderly. Kurt Barnes saw floodwaters quickly surround his home and knew his entire neighborhood would soon be swamped. He knew his only chance to save himself and his neighbors was to swim through the rising currents to reach his jeep parked on high ground and retrieve his boat from his nearby father-in-law's home. The currents were swift, but Barnes managed to swim through the torrent, zigzagging from tree to fence post until he reached the jeep. After quickly returning with the boat, he then motored house to house, calling out for neighbors and loading them into his small boat. During this time, a large pecan tree collapsed into the flood, popping sparks and tangling wires through the flooded neighborhood yards.

Barnes continued in the dark, pulling neighbors through windows, along with their pets and personal effects wrapped in plastic garbage bags. One family waited on their front porch in shoulder-deep water with a very small baby. He drove his boat onto the porch, and the young mother handed him her baby wrapped in a blanket. At that moment, she stepped off the porch and disappeared in the dark water. Instinctively, Barnes held the baby in one arm and reached down with the other to lift the mother out of the water and into the boat. Barnes remembered, "She had a head full of hair. So I got ahold of her hair and pulled her back up!"

But perhaps Barnes's most dramatic rescue came during the peak of the storm, when he returned to his neighborhood for a family whose home was filled with more than six feet of water. They had stood on their kitchen bar and cut a hole in their ceiling, through which they had climbed into their attic. Barnes called for them, but they were too frightened to leave. With the help of another neighbor, Barnes swam into their home and coaxed them down from the attic, all while treading water in the kitchen. One by one, the mother, child, and father finally came down and were carried out of the house, ducking underwater briefly to get through the doorway. As they pulled away in the boat, the young girl squealed at the sight of her frantic pet collie treading water behind a high fence. Barnes pulled his boat to the fence, reached over and grabbed the dog, and placed him in the bottom of the boat. "When we picked that dog up to put him in the boat, he didn't bite us, but when we set him down in that boat, buddy, he ate us up," he recalled. Barnes was later recognized with the 2000 North Carolina Governor's Award for Heroism.

After the storm passed and the cresting Tar River subsided, state officials moved quickly to create temporary housing for thousands of displaced flood victims. An undeveloped ninety-acre tract in an industrial park north of Rocky Mount was selected as the future home of hundreds of Edgecombe County refugees. In the days following the storm, workers labored around the clock to build gravel roads, install utilities, and prepare the site for more than 300 travel trailers. The "FEMA city" was operational by September 22, and exhausted storm victims were soon back in livable quarters. One of the first to move in was Princeville resident Mattie Jones, who had been staying in a school shelter in Tarboro since the storm. She told the Raleigh *News and Observer*, "It may not look like much to other people, but to me it's a castle. First thing when I got the keys in my hand, I said 'Oh, thank you God, a house, a bathroom, a bed, quiet.'" At the time Jones moved into her trailer, her Princeville home was still underwater.

Downriver in Greenville, more record-breaking floods forced thousands out of their homes. Among those ousted were almost 5,000 East Carolina University students living in apartments near the Tar River. Though flooding struck some parts of the city and left others untouched, it caused problems everywhere. Late on Friday, September 17, rising water near the river short-circuited a critical transmission station, cutting power to Greenville's 48,000 electric customers. On the following Tuesday, when the flooding reached its highest level, the city's water plant shut down and water was unavailable. Thousands initially sought refuge in Red Cross shelters across Pitt County, but eventually many were moved to temporary housing around the city. Some moved in with area residents and students whose homes were not flooded. National Guard troops arrived to assist with rescue efforts and took up residence on the East Carolina campus. The university suspended classes, parents' weekend was canceled, and the Pirates' nationally televised football game with the University of Miami was moved to Carter-Finley Stadium in Raleigh. Classes did not resume until September 29, almost two weeks after the storm.

Flooding in Greenville was far worse than anyone could remember. Some apartment buildings were flooded up to the second-floor level, and many structures were filled with murky water well above doorknob level. All around town, emergency workers in small boats rescued hundreds of isolated residents. More than 6,000 homes suffered some flooding damage. When the waters finally receded, piles of furniture, carpets, and appliances filled side streets near the river. City engineers estimated that 50,000 cubic yards of trees and storm debris would need to be hauled away. Pitt County residents worked for weeks to clean up the mess. As in so many other communities across the region, Greenville residents spent long hours washing mud and mold from their walls, floors, and furnishings.

About the time the flooding was at its peak and utilities were shut down, an unexpected explosion rocked Greenville. On September 22, a gasoline truck outside Pitt Memorial Hospital went up in flames while refueling fire department pumper trucks. No one was injured in the blast, and the hospital did not catch fire. The fire department pumpers were being used at the time to run a makeshift water system for the hospital. Water from a rehabilitation pool was used to keep toilets flushing and other equipment functioning, while bottled water was stockpiled for drinking. Like thousands of other area residents, hospital staff made the best of a very difficult situation.

As the flooding worsened across the eastern counties, some residents became desperate. After a National Guard convoy delivered drinking water to Greenville on Sunday, September 19, a second convoy was scheduled to deliver food and water on the following day. The unarmed crew ran into trouble, however, when the convoy was chased down by carloads of anxious residents who pulled out guns and baseball bats, demanding food and water. The police were later called in, but provisions were left with the residents, some of whom had not eaten for days.

Communities all along the Neuse River were under siege because of flooding. Waters rose to record levels in portions of Goldsboro, and flooding in Seven

U.S. representative Eva Clayton shows reporters the extent of flooding inside a home scheduled for reconstruction after Hurricane Floyd. Mold is already growing on the walls, clearly
marking the flood level. Many flood victims reported waters rising "above the light switches"
in their homes. (Photo by Dave Gately. Courtesy of FEMA.)

Springs swamped all but four of the town's ninety-four homes and businesses.
In Kinston, the flooding far surpassed that of Hurricane Fran, bringing diesel-
fouled floodwaters into hundreds of homes, shops, motels, and restaurants.
Rising more than thirteen feet above flood stage, the Neuse spread beyond
its banks and crept over U.S. 70, forcing that major artery to close between its
intersections with N.C. 55 and U.S. 258. Two bridges were undermined, and
many people in the city were isolated from the outside world. Though some
towns and cities experienced flooding that lasted perhaps a week, Kinston's
high waters endured for more than three weeks.

When the overflowing Neuse first surged across U.S. 70 on September 21,
two nearby motels were filled with customers, many of whom were evacuees
from other areas. Before the rising waters inched above the hoods of their cars,
many of the guests at the Days Inn and the Super 8 fled for higher ground.
Later, three National Guard trucks plowed through the deepening waters of
the Super 8 parking lot to urge a few remaining residents on the second floor
to leave. Some refused to go, while others were carried to local shelters. Other
businesses along the U.S. 70 corridor were similarly swamped. Landmarks such
as the Neuse Sport Shop and Kings Restaurant were filled with muddy floodwaters that reached well above tabletop level.

A frightened toddler is comforted by a Vance County Rescue Squad member after being airlifted to safety by the U.S. Coast Guard following Hurricane Floyd. (Photo courtesy of the U.S. Coast Guard.)

Though cities and towns along the Tar, Neuse, and Northeast Cape Fear Rivers suffered the most during Floyd, dozens of other communities across eastern North Carolina were affected as well. In all, the National Weather Service reported that the downtown areas of at least thirty North Carolina towns were flooded. The heavy damages were not limited to communities along major rivers but included towns such as Vanceboro, flooded by Little Swift Creek; Grifton, flooded by Contentnea Creek; Windsor, flooded by the Cashie River; and Trenton and Pollocksville, flooded by the Trent River. Across Jones County, where flooding in Trenton was "the worst in memory," almost 1,000 people were housed in five shelters that included schools, a church, and a former topless bar.

In Windsor, the normally placid Cashie rose about one foot every two hours until it finally swamped virtually every business along King Street, the town's main drag. According to the *Virginian-Pilot*, at Jake's Barber Shop, where Jake Mitchell has cut hair since 1943, the flood "climbed more than 8 feet up the walls, knocked out the front window and sucked two big wooden cabinets into the street." It trashed an IGA supermarket, flooded the town hall and county newspaper office, and filled two insurance offices with four feet of water. Local residents commented afterward about the surprising nature of the flood, noting that even the insurance agencies didn't have flood insurance on their offices.

But river flooding was not the only destructive force associated with Floyd. Along portions of the coast, tidal surges caused heavy damages, especially on Oak Island in Brunswick County. Not since the awesome storm surge of Hurricane Hazel in 1954 had this resort community suffered such destruction. Oak Island took the brunt of the storm as landfall was just a few miles to the east. The heaviest damages occurred along the ocean beach, where Floyd's ten-foot storm surge and battering waves knocked down scores of cottages, scuttled two fishing piers, and filled streets with deep sand. According to town officials, forty houses were destroyed, 290 more were heavily damaged, and another 250 were left in need of repairs. Throughout much of the community, homes built under the protection of oak and pine trees showed little evidence of Floyd's effects.

Along the hardest-hit stretch of the beach, several homes collapsed into the surf, while others were completely missing. Half-buried debris was scattered about the strand, having been tossed out of demolished vacation homes. Mattresses, televisions, bicycles, and washing machines were among the recognizable objects that lined what used to be Beach Drive. The kitchen of the popular Windjammer Restaurant was knocked into the surf, and the town's oceanfront boardwalk and gazebo complex were gone. The Long Beach Pier, which once claimed the title of the state's longest fishing pier, was cut down some 300 feet by crashing waves (it was sold and demolished in 2006). The Ocean Crest Pier lost about 500 feet.

On nearby Holden Beach, about five houses were destroyed and another fishing pier was heavily damaged. At the Brunswick Community Hospital in Supply, a large section of roofing was torn off during the storm, just when a pregnant woman was about to deliver. Rainwater poured into the building's air-conditioning system, and the expectant mother had to be transferred out of the hospital amid high winds. This was the second time within a year that the hospital had lost its roof: Hurricane Bonnie's high winds had peeled back the covering in 1998.

In Shallotte, flooding from the Shallotte River filled downtown streets to a depth of eight feet. At least three families were rescued from their rooftops by boat soon after the storm passed through. The flooding tore away a sixty-foot portion of N.C. 130 just south of town, and high winds ripped the steeple off the nearby First Baptist Church. Some Shallotte residents sat quietly on their porches and watched floodwaters fill their yards, rising only to fire shotguns at water snakes that occasionally swam by.

A bit farther south, in Horry County, South Carolina, Floyd's impact was a bit less severe. Storm surge measured just three feet at the beaches, but heavy rainfall and flash flooding caused problems across large sections of the county. Chest-deep waters were reported at the Pine Lakes Country Club in Myrtle Beach, and up to four feet of water entered the Azalea Lakes apartments. As in North Carolina, some of the worst flooding arrived days after the storm; high waters on the Waccamaw River in Conway flooded hundreds of homes. Ten days after Floyd's landfall the Waccamaw River gage reached a peak of 17.61 feet, flooding downtown Conway, Jackson Bluff, Pitch Landing, Savannah Bluff, and Lees Landing.

At Carolina and Wrightsville Beaches, damages were moderate—not nearly as extensive as those left in the wake of Hurricane Fran. At the northern end of Wrightsville, erosion brought Mason Inlet to within about ten feet of the foundation of the imperiled Shell Island Resort, which had been temporarily protected by a wall of sandbags. Winds peeled away large patches of stucco on many of the island's homes and businesses, and sound-side docks and piers were twisted and buckled by hefty tides. Some ground-level apartments were flooded by two feet of water.

In the days following Floyd, isolated damages were reported in dozens of other coastal communities. On the Cape Fear River below Wilmington, several barges loaded with munitions broke free from their docks at the Sunny Point Military Ocean Terminal and were scattered by the storm. One ran aground across the river at Fort Fisher and had to be unloaded and dislodged from the marsh. At Topsail Island, where recent hurricanes had caused extensive ocean overwash, Floyd again cut three new inlets across the fragile beach. Most of the man-made protective dunes on the northern end of the island were leveled by high tides. In some locations, dunes had already been swept away by Hurricane Dennis, exposing homes and roadways to Floyd's thrashing waves. Onslow County experienced losses not only at North Topsail but throughout other communities where swollen creeks flooded homes and businesses. In all, the county reported 118 structures destroyed, 202 with major damage, and another 471 with minor damage.

Up the coast in Carteret County, most of the communities that suffered extensive flooding during Dennis were spared a repeat disaster. The western beaches, though, were hit hard by an eight-foot storm surge that left cottages teetering on the edge of severely eroded dunes. In addition to being hit by a twister that struck Emerald Isle and damaged several homes, the island was battered by waves that destroyed piers, undermined septic tanks, and carved away several more feet of precious sand. Officials later reported that, across the county, seventeen homes were destroyed, 275 suffered major damage, and another 610 had minor damage.

Perhaps as significant as the number of lost structures was the even larger number of oceanfront properties that were left dangerously exposed to future storms. Floyd's impact on the frontal dunes of Pine Knoll Shores, Indian Beach, and Emerald Isle was dramatic; hundreds of homes and condos were left standing at the edge of the sea at high tide. With almost no protective dunes remaining in some locations, homeowners feared the loss of their investments should another hurricane or severe winter storm strike the area.

As Floyd spun into eastern Virginia on the night of September 16, record rains fell across the Tidewater region, resulting in severe flooding, rooftop rescues, and property destruction not unlike that experienced in North Carolina. Some vehicles, swept from flooded highways, capsized and sank. Even one Virginia state trooper in Southampton County had to abandon her cruiser and swim to safety when she was washed off of U.S. 58. At one point, more than 300 roads across the state were closed. A fifty-foot section of road collapsed into Lake Powell when a dam near Williamsburg broke. Flooding was worst in Franklin, where nine to twelve feet of water filled the downtown district. Statewide, almost 6,000 homes were damaged to some degree by the storm. In addition to at least one fatality linked to the flooding, two Virginians were killed by falling trees.

Though several mid-Atlantic states suffered through Floyd's blustery winds and heavy rains, massive rainfall over north and central New Jersey created another pocket of disaster far from the storm's original point of landfall. More than a foot of rain, accompanied by wind gusts of over 60 mph, affected the region and extended into the suburbs north and west of New York City. But by far the hardest-hit area was Bound Brook, New Jersey, where the swollen Raritan River filled the business district with up to fifteen feet of water, forcing hundreds onto rooftops and setting the stage for still more dramatic rescues. The Raritan reached a record crest of forty-two feet, some twenty feet above flood stage. Working from small boats and helicopters, rescue teams pulled people from second-floor windows and rooftops throughout the day on Friday, September 17, and continued the treacherous work into the night. More than 1,000 people were evacuated. Fires burned out of control in the business district, as firefighters could only watch the flames from aboard their Jet Skis. Eventually, helicopters from New York arrived to drop water on the fires. A nearby water company was shut down, leaving tens of thousands of New Jersey residents without water for days. Across the state, 251 structures were destroyed in the storm and another 8,300 were damaged. Four residents were drowned in what officials at the time described as "the single largest disaster to ever affect the state of New Jersey."

Back in North Carolina, emergency management officials struggled to deal with myriad problems, including a burgeoning health concern: what to do with the thousands, if not millions, of dead pigs, turkeys, and chickens drowned by the flood. In several eastern counties where large swine and poultry operations make up much of the agricultural economy, Floyd left behind a putrid mess. Carcasses of drowned hogs floated through submerged forests and farmlands, in some cases intermixed with a few exhausted animals that had managed to survive and gather on rooftops. From the air, windrows of dead pinkish hogs were visible below, and the numbers were astounding—early estimates suggested that upward of 30,000 swine had drowned. In addition, 2.4 million chickens and 700,000 turkeys died in the storm. This massive agricultural loss also posed a dangerous environmental threat that required quick attention.

State agricultural officials, working together with the Division of Emergency Management, arranged for large portable incinerators to be delivered to several eastern North Carolina farms where the animal problems were the worst. The incinerators, wood-fired metal boxes that resemble oversized garbage dumpsters, are capable of burning up to 4,000 pounds of carcasses an hour. Crews gathered the dead animals from around the countryside, sometimes towing them behind small skiffs and piling them into large mounds with front-end loaders. Veterinarians and public health officials were present to monitor each burning operation. Over a period of several days, thousands of animals were collected and destroyed to minimize the risk to public health.

Though most of the dead hogs, turkeys, and chickens were gathered and burned in the first days after the flood, other serious environmental concerns lingered for weeks. While flooding homes, cars, and businesses, the storm's rising waters had also washed solvents, oils, paints, and household cleaners from hundreds of sunken homes. They also submerged at least fifty hog-waste lagoons and twenty-four municipal waste-treatment plants covering a dozen counties. Millions of gallons of sewage from the lagoons flowed into the mix, causing some flood victims to become nauseous while they sat for hours awaiting rescue. At least five hog lagoons collapsed, including one in Duplin County that spilled an estimated 2 million gallons of waste into the Northeast Cape Fear River.

Flooded municipal plants caused similar problems by spilling untreated sewage into creeks and rivers in Cary, Smithfield, Hillsborough, Wake Forest, Zebulon, Kenly, Sanford, Maysville, Pink Hill, Fremont, Grifton, Goldsboro, Greenville, Wilson, Kinston, Jacksonville, and many other towns. In Wayne County, a ruptured dam carried with it at least 200 feet of sewer line. Unknown quantities of waste from thousands of home septic tanks also leached into the flood. A variety of contaminants leaked from submerged automobiles. Vehicles trapped in the flood were not the only culprits: dozens of flooded junkyards filled with rusting wrecks also contributed to the pollution. Industrial chemical spills were reported at six plants, including sites in Castle Hayne and Riegelwood. Because of the broad scope of the flood, the state's overfilled rivers carried with them a toxic soup of contaminants that spread wherever the waters went. Emergency workers began smearing Vicks VapoRub under their noses to cope with the stench. From the air, chopper pilots commented on how the Neuse and Tar Rivers seemed to glow with an iridescent sheen that reflected light in a rainbow of colors. Water-plant and well contamination was another area of grave concern, and residents in most affected counties were urged to boil their drinking water or to drink only bottled water. In the weeks following the storm, health officials began testing wells and municipal drinking-water plants as they came back online.

Fortunately, the most immediate environmental concerns did not materialize. No outbreaks of disease from tainted water were reported. According to area researchers, the rivers and sounds within the flooded area rebounded rapidly. Low oxygen levels killed only around 150 fish in coastal rivers. The state's fishing industry, which was expected to suffer terribly from the storm, actually fared well. The "dead zone" of low-oxygen, low-salinity water that had been present in the Pamlico Sound shortly after the hurricane dissipated within several months. Though state officials had predicted losses totaling millions of dollars in several fisheries, some fishermen instead reported near-record catches, and the commercial fishing industry had a good year overall. State officials tested fish and shellfish from several coastal areas and found no unsafe toxin levels. The entire industry fought false perceptions and worked to get the message out: North Carolina seafood was safe to eat.

After the floodwaters receded and the obvious pollutants had been cleaned up, environmentalists and state officials still questioned the long-term environmental impact of the storm. Groundwater, they felt, could be affected for years to come, and new testing programs were established. Water-quality monitoring was expanded across the eastern counties, including a program that uses state

The Tar River swallowed whole communities in the days following Hurricane Floyd, forcing many onto their roofs. Members of this Pactolus family could only reach their home by boat. (Photo by Dave Gately. Courtesy of FEMA.)

ferries to monitor algal growth and oxygen content in the Pamlico Sound. In December 1999, state legislators funded $27 million for environmental cleanup projects across the flooded region. Locations included eleven junkyards, thirty-five hazardous-waste sites, 277 old landfills, and 139 underground storage tanks.

Lawmakers realized very quickly that the Floyd disaster had amounted to an economic catastrophe for the state. After the storm, assessment teams fanned out to survey damage across the east. But with roads blocked and some neighborhoods flooded for weeks, totaling the damages was a time-consuming and difficult task. It was easy to see, though, especially from the air, that rebuilding eastern North Carolina was going to require massive amounts of state and federal aid. Of the thousands of flooded homes, state officials knew that very few were covered by flood insurance. President Bill Clinton declared sixty-six North Carolina counties disaster areas, paving the way for federal relief. In the weeks following the storm, Governor Jim Hunt established the Hurricane Floyd Redevelopment Center to coordinate reconstruction efforts and to monitor the flow of money to devastated communities. He then prepared his request to the U.S. Congress: the state was seeking a whopping $5.3 billion in federal aid to get people back in their homes and fund the long recovery process.

But Hunt's proposed federal aid package was trimmed back and divided into two parts: a request for $1.7 billion for immediate needs and $2.1 billion for long-term relief. Eventually, Congress came through with a total of around $2.2 billion, far less than had been expected. While lobbying for additional federal aid continued in Washington, immediate needs were not being met across the flood zone. This left Hunt and local lawmakers with little choice but to find additional money within the state. On December 15, 1999, the general assembly convened a special session to address the funding shortfall. Out of the session came a special $836 million appropriation of state funds to provide safe housing, help farmers and small businesses, protect public health, clean up environmental hazards, and aid public schools and local governments.

At the Water Resources Research Institute's annual conference in 2000, the governor's point man for the recovery, Floyd Redevelopment Center director Billy Ray Hall, gave the keynote address, in which he talked about Floyd's overall economic impact. Hall estimated that the disaster caused $5.5 billion in damages to North Carolina alone. A total of 63,000 homes were flooded, 7,300 were destroyed, and a quarter of a million people were displaced. Most significant, though, was Hall's assertion that it would take eight to ten years for eastern North Carolina to fully recover from the storm.

Officially, the National Hurricane Center placed the cost of Floyd at $6.5 billion in the United States. In 2011, the total was revised to $6.9 billion, with the vast majority of the losses in North Carolina. These figures rise even higher if lost wages, lost retail sales, and other tangential economic factors are considered. FEMA later calculated $4 billion in lost business revenue in North Carolina alone. Calculations from other government agencies varied, but however they were measured or estimated, one thing became clear: no hurricane in North Carolina history had left behind this much destruction or caused this much economic loss. Floyd topped Fran to become the state's costliest disaster to date.

Floyd was particularly hard on farmers, and some small-farm operators were at risk of losing their way of life after the storm. Agricultural losses were huge, totaling between $800,000 and $1 billion. State agriculture officials estimated that half the year's crops of peanuts, cotton, soybeans, and sweet potatoes were lost, along with 40 percent of the tobacco harvest. But more than just crops and livestock were destroyed. After surveying the damage and talking to state officials, North Carolina Senate president pro tempore Marc Basnight told WRAL News, "This is worse than the Great Depression. At least when the Depression was over, those folks still had their land, the vegetable plots, maybe a hog tied up out back. Many of these people, when this is over, will have nothing."

Fortunately for thousands of needy storm victims across the east, a massive outpouring of private support began flowing into the hardest-hit communities in the weeks following the storm. Churches, schools, civic groups, and families throughout the state—and from other states—collected truckloads of food and supplies for flood victims. Collection sites popped up everywhere, and soon leagues of volunteers were sorting, boxing, and delivering goods to makeshift distribution centers in cities such as New Bern, Kinston, and Rocky Mount. Nonperishable foods, diapers, water, clothes, and cleaning supplies were among the more popular items donated. Soon after the storm made landfall, Governor Hunt established the North Carolina Hurricane Floyd Relief Fund as a conduit for cash contributions. A statewide telethon raised $2.2 million, special collections made the rounds at Sunday church services, and individuals dug into their pockets to support the cause. In all, the fund received more than 66,000 contributions from around the world and raised over $19 million. This figure dwarfs the $70,000 raised following Hurricane Fran in 1996.

After the floodwaters receded and the scope of the disaster could be better understood, the long, grueling process of rebuilding began. Throughout the fall and winter, some homes in Princeville, Tarboro, and other hard-hit cities were gutted for reconstruction or torn down. As federal money and low-interest loans trickled in, damp and crumbling Sheetrock was pulled out, electrical wiring was replaced, and homes were put back into livable condition. Crews of volunteers from around the country were organized to help with the construction. Church groups, Habitat for Humanity volunteers, college students, and reassigned state employees rolled up their shirt sleeves and went to work rebuilding homes. In many areas, the federal money went toward buyouts in which homes and land in the most flood-prone areas were purchased and residences were torn down. FEMA representatives estimated that as many as 10,000 flooded properties could ultimately be bought, though only about half that many were purchased in the first year after the storm. The buyouts removed thousands of families from high-hazard areas, protecting them from the risks of future floods. The result was that some neighborhoods became ghost towns, with only one or two occupied homes in a community that once had fifty or more.

Though the economic impact of Hurricane Floyd in North Carolina was staggering, the heartbreaking loss of life in the state was the greater tragedy. The state medical examiner counted fifty-two fatalities, most caused by drowning in inland areas. This made Floyd the deadliest hurricane disaster in North Carolina since the Great Asheville Flood of 1916 (though it's unclear exactly

Lonnie Smith, a twenty-three-year-old Marine stationed in New Orleans, drove over 1,000 miles after Hurricane Floyd to check on his family in Hubert, North Carolina, before flood-waters stalled his minivan on N.C. 258. Two fellow Marines used their truck to pull Smith from the flood. Driving in floods is hazardous, and well over half the fatalities attributed to Floyd in North Carolina involved motorists attempting to navigate submerged roads. (Photo by Don Bryan. Courtesy of the Jacksonville *Daily News*.)

how many North Carolinians died in that event). Initial reports on Floyd from the National Oceanic and Atmospheric Administration counted a total of fifty-six deaths in the United States and thirty-five direct fatalities in North Carolina, though later reports counted seventy-six deaths in the United States. More than a dozen lives were lost in other states, including six in Pennsylvania, six in New Jersey, three in Virginia, two each in Delaware and New York, and one each in Connecticut and Vermont. But no matter whose fatality figures are used, Floyd's death toll was still the largest of any U.S. hurricane since Agnes swept from Florida to the Northeast in 1972, killing 122.

In North Carolina, reports of fatalities began to trickle in during the first hours after the storm made landfall. Then, as the flooding worsened and roads became lakes, frustrated drivers fell prey to swiftly moving currents, and the list of storm victims grew longer. Among all the painful lessons learned from the Floyd disaster, none was more critical than understanding the deadly con-sequences of driving through floodwaters. Well over half of the state's storm-related fatalities happened when motorists attempted to drive over submerged roads.

Struggling to stay alive, hogs from a farm near Trenton await rescue on the roof of a swine barn as floodwaters from the Neuse River surround them. The following day, state officials called for reinforcements as they battled to save farm animals across eastern North Carolina from the waters of Hurricane Floyd, the worst agricultural disaster in the state's history. (Photo by Mel Nathanson. Courtesy of the Raleigh *News and Observer*.)

Most of the deaths occurred within the first few days after Floyd made landfall, but because the high waters lingered, reports of fatalities continued to emerge weeks after the storm. Understandably, most of the dead were victims of freshwater flooding in inland areas. In a summary report on Floyd, the Hurricane Center noted that 86 percent of deaths were due to inland flooding, 55 percent were vehicle related, and 80 percent were male. These figures follow a trend that has emerged in recent decades, wherein most hurricane deaths are caused by freshwater flooding away from the coast—a far cry from earlier decades, when powerful storms drove storm surges into unprepared coastal communities, killing hundreds.

Enhanced satellite view of Hurricane Floyd off the Carolina coast. (Photo courtesy of the National Oceanic and Atmospheric Administration.)

One might expect that a particular U.S. state or region would experience a true benchmark hurricane only once in a generation. But for thousands of North Carolinians, especially those whose homes were destroyed, two major hurricane disasters within three years was a perplexing and exhausting experience. Though both Hurricanes Fran and Floyd were truly memorable events in Tar Heel history, each had its own unique recipe for destruction and misery. Floyd's impact on the state established it without question as North Carolina's greatest disaster until that time.

TAKEAWAYS

- *Rainfall prior to a hurricane's arrival boosts inland flooding.* Hurricane Floyd will always be remembered as a great flood, but its impact was made far worse by the heavy rainfall that fell across eastern North Carolina associated with Tropical Storm Dennis just two weeks earlier. These rains soaked the soil, filled creeks and ditches, and raised river levels in many of the same areas later hit by rains from Floyd. In the days and weeks before Hurricane Matthew, similar heavy rains soaked the ground and raised rivers in south central North Carolina. In both cases, rivers eventually crested to record levels, thanks in part to earlier downpours.
- *Slow-motion disasters: For some Carolina communities, peak river flooding arrives days after a hurricane rolls through.* More than a dozen river basins

drain across the Carolina coastal plain toward the Atlantic, some crossing state lines. Gravity moves these rivers at a modest pace over the gentle slope of the land, even once they're overfilled by heavy rains. This was evident after Hurricanes Fran, Floyd, Matthew, and Florence—downstream cities and towns saw peak flooding days after the hurricanes had passed. Following Hurricane Floyd, peak flooding in Kinston struck on September 23, a full week after the hurricane crossed North Carolina. After Florence, a new river crest record was set on the Little Pee Dee River in Galivants Ferry, South Carolina, on September 21, one week after that storm's landfall.

- *Urbanization alters the floodplain and increases flooding risk.* The epic floods that spread across eastern North Carolina during Floyd were unlike anything seen in the region in memory. Floodwaters not only reached record levels but in some places lingered for weeks. Following the shock of the storm, many residents wanted to know why. There are many reasons the floods reached these levels, and key among them is what planners call "urbanization," where over time natural lands are converted by clearing, draining, damming, paving, and building. In simplistic terms, the country starts to look more like the city, with homes, roads, and shopping centers built over what was once forest or farmland. Rainwater can't penetrate pavement, so it runs off quickly and is concentrated in pools that only slowly seep into soil. Road construction sometimes has an unintended damming effect, inhibiting the natural flow of runoff. The steady pace of urbanization continues in the Carolinas, challenging engineers, builders, and local governments to consider the potential flooding impact of their projects, especially on other downstream communities.

- *Inaccurate and outdated flood maps contributed to the massive losses during Floyd and continue to be a threat in the Carolinas.* Inland flooding brought on by hurricanes is a recurring threat in the Carolinas and in many parts of the southeast United States. Community building standards rely on FEMA-approved maps to delineate levels of risk from river flooding and storm surge so that home and business owners can assess risk, prepare, and take protective measures—such as purchasing flood insurance. Floodplains change over time as the landscape is altered and new flood events are recorded, requiring map revisions. After Floyd, North Carolina officials determined the state's flood maps were woefully outdated, a contributing factor in the scope of losses. Similar findings followed Hurricane Matthew. State officials found that only 23 percent of the 2,615 homes with applications for rebuilding through North Carolina's federal block grant program were located within FEMA-defined floodplains. A later report from the U.S. Department of Homeland Security's inspector general found that 58 percent of flood maps nationwide were either outdated or inaccurate. Analysts say there's a built-in lag, as it can take about five years for new maps to be drawn in inland areas and up to ten years near the coast. If you're relying on these maps for base flood elevations, you may be using old information.

- *Military resources and personnel have become essential for effective hurricane response and recovery.* The Carolinas are fortunate to be home to tens of thousands of U.S. troops, housed at bases such as Camp Lejeune, Fort Bragg, Shaw Air Force Base, Joint Base Charleston, U.S. Coast Guard Base Elizabeth City, and others. Thousands of additional National Guard troops live and work in the Carolinas. During times of crisis such as a major hurricane disaster, they play a critical role in saving lives, providing logistics and transport, clearing and protecting property, and distributing humanitarian aid. It's not just the men and women who serve; they bring with them critical resources that make their work possible, such as high-water Humvees for flooded road navigation, planes and helicopters for damage assessment and search-and-rescue missions, generators for emergency power, and countless other assets. Today's state-organized disaster plans include National Guard command at the highest level, ensuring seamless integration with state and local resources.

- *Hurricane floods sometimes cause environmental damages that are challenging to track and often obscured by the surrounding chaos.* During major inland flooding events, floodwaters pour through farms, junkyards, factories, waste-treatment plants, warehouses, and industrial complexes that were never intended to be inundated. Seeping from them are a toxic mix of animal waste, human waste, chemicals, and toxins that move through the floods, eventually either flowing downriver to sounds and the ocean or soaking into the soil as floodwaters dry. Sewage spills from waste-treatment plants are usually monitored and reported, as are potential spills from coal ash ponds operated by Duke Energy. During Floyd, hog lagoons were in the news, as several dozen breached, releasing millions of gallons of hog waste into waterways. Countless other smaller spills and contaminations undoubtedly went unreported. Additionally, the tremendous volume of vegetative debris that washes into rivers with floodwaters consumes oxygen as it decays, sometimes creating fish kills that show up well after the storm's passing. Fortunately, the massive volume of rainwater that creates the flood greatly dilutes contaminants and moves them downstream, where they're further diluted at the coast. But it's believed there may be a lasting toll from heavy metals and industrial chemicals that may linger in soils and waterways for years.

• *Driving on a flooded road is perhaps the most dangerous thing you can do during or after a hurricane.* If there's one takeaway that's more important to remember than others, this is it. It seems logical when a governor or other official urges the public to "turn around, don't drown," during a hurricane flood. Yet during Hurricanes Floyd, Matthew, and Florence— all inland flooding nightmares—vehicular drowning was a leading cause of death. More than half the fatalities during Floyd were motorists or their passengers who became caught in swirling floodwaters. Many were swept off roadways by relatively shallow but swift-moving currents; others lost control when their cars sank into unseen washouts. Even four-wheel-drive trucks and SUVs are no match for the dangers that lurk on and around submerged roads.

CHAPTER FOURTEEN

HURRICANE MATTHEW,
OCTOBER 2016

Bob Simpson was a scientist and innovator. As a meteorologist and hurricane forecaster, he was a leading voice behind the move to increase funding for hurricane research in the 1950s. Simpson was at the center of efforts in the early 1960s to establish what would later become the National Severe Storms Laboratory—one of several important developments that helped improve weather forecasting through the period. By the late sixties, he had become deputy director, and then director, of the National Hurricane Center (NHC) in Miami, where he took on reorganizing the nation's nerve center for tropical weather. He had a passion for hurricane science, but he also understood forecasters' important role in communicating accurate and timely information to the public. It was during this time that he worked with engineer Herbert Saffir to develop the Saffir-Simpson scale—the 1-through-5 classification that we still use today to "rate" hurricane intensity.

Since its launch in the early 1970s, the public has embraced the rating concept. We intuitively know there are strong hurricanes and weaker ones, and the Saffir-Simpson scale helps sort it out. A forecast for an approaching Category 1 storm shouldn't be taken lightly but doesn't create the same level of worry as a Category 4 or 5 might and justly so. The scale is designed around the potential for destruction from wind, with the understanding that hurricanes with higher sustained winds are normally stronger storms with lower barometric pressures and higher storm surges at the coast upon landfall. Since its inception, the public has largely viewed the rating system as a measure of overall severity.

But over the years, several major U.S. disasters revealed the rating scale's underlying flaw—it underplays the threat posed by flooding rains in lower-category storms. In 1985, Hurricane Juan swamped Louisiana as a Category 1, flooding thousands of homes, businesses, vehicles, and crops. With $1.5 billion in damages, it became the fourth-most costly U.S. hurricane until that time. In 1994, Tropical Storm Alberto drifted over northwest Florida, Alabama, and Georgia, bringing record flooding to the region and causing thirty-two

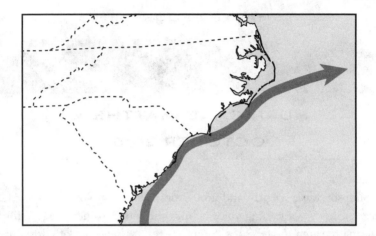

Search-and-rescue teams from across the Carolinas and from other states were deployed throughout flooded communities during Hurricane Matthew. This team from Missouri plans their next move on a flooded Lumberton street. (Photo courtesy of FEMA.)

fatalities and $1 billion in losses—all from a tropical system that never attained hurricane status. In the Carolinas, there have been similar events—once-powerful hurricanes that weakened but still delivered massive rain-induced floods. Floyd in 1999 (Category 2) was a prime example, on the lower end of the Saffir-Simpson scale but among the greatest flood events in Carolina history.

It happened again in 2016. Hurricane Matthew, a formidable Category 5 in the Caribbean, Category 4 in the Bahamas, and Category 3 as it passed near Florida, managed to skirt land as it moved northward toward the Carolinas. The eye remained just off the Florida and Georgia coasts, placing the storm close enough to pound beachfront communities with hurricane-force winds and high surf. It slowed and continued weakening as it tracked northward, and by the time it made landfall at Cape Romain on October 8, its winds were greatly diminished. The center of the Category 1 hurricane only briefly touched land in South Carolina before slipping back offshore, tracking close to the Brunswick County beaches in North Carolina and heading out to sea the following day. Matthew never made landfall in the Tar Heel State. Even though it was a minimal hurricane whose eye barely touched the coast, it's still counted among the Carolinas' greatest hurricane disasters.

The 2016 Atlantic hurricane season started early and stayed busy. The Carolinas had already felt the effects of four tropical cyclones in the months before Matthew arrived. Bonnie, Colin, Hermine, and Julia or their remnants had swept through the region and caused lots of problems. Tropical Storm Bonnie dumped copious rains over South Carolina at the end of May, temporarily shutting down Interstate 95 in Jasper County and flooding dozens of homes and businesses. In mid-September, the remnants of Tropical Storm Julia caused similar problems in northeastern North Carolina, where nearly seventeen inches of rain fell in three days. Swift-water rescue teams pulled 138 residents from flooded homes in Bertie County. Heavy rains fell through central North Carolina at the very end of September too, playing a key role in the events to come. Matthew arrived a bit later and became the first October hurricane to make landfall north of Florida since Hazel in 1954 (Hurricane Sandy in 2012 lost hurricane status prior to landfall in New Jersey).

Matthew emerged in the western Atlantic near the Lesser Antilles on September 28 and quickly deepened to become a Category 5 just two days later, on the thirtieth. It peaked as a Category 5 with sustained winds of 165 mph and a barometric pressure of 934 millibars (mb), making it the strongest hurricane in the region since Felix in 2007. It also set another record during its peak: at just 13.4 degrees north latitude, it was the lowest latitude at which a hurricane of this intensity had ever been observed in the Atlantic basin. With its rapid intensification, Matthew grabbed news headlines more than a week before it ever reached the Carolina coast.

The potent storm tracked northward out of the deep Caribbean and went on to become the season's deadliest. It first claimed lives in Columbia, Saint Vincent and the Grenadines, and the Dominican Republic. On October 4,

Matthew struck Haiti, causing the greatest disaster and humanitarian crisis there since the devastating earthquake of 2010. Category 4 winds blew down homes and power lines while heavy rains produced deadly mudslides, with the heaviest losses on the Tiburon Peninsula. Along the southern coast, even well-built concrete homes were no match for the storm tide's cresting waves. In Les Cayes, high winds tore away the roof of the local hospital. Across Haiti, more than 120,000 homes were destroyed by winds, tides, and mudslides; more than 300,000 were left homeless and over 500 lives were lost.

As it neared Cuba, the storm center was expected to pass close to the U.S. Navy base in Guantánamo Bay, prompting the evacuation of 700 military family members. The region was then hit hard—hundreds of homes were destroyed by storm surge flooding, though no direct deaths were reported. Wind gusts of over 170 mph were recorded in Jamal. Damages in Cuba approached $2 billion, mostly in Guantánamo Province. News reports of Matthew's power and destructive toll in the islands gave hurricane watchers on the U.S. East Coast reason for concern.

Once the storm tracked past the Bahamas, Florida braced for possible landfall. As Matthew edged closer, thousands of Floridians fled their homes and filled school shelters in a dozen counties. Governor Rick Scott told reporters, "The storm has already killed people. We should expect the same for Florida." In a rare move, Disney World and Universal Studios in Orlando both closed in anticipation of a possible strike from the storm. But it wasn't just Florida residents who were concerned. Forecast models extended the hurricane's track northward to the Carolinas. On October 4, South Carolina governor Nikki Haley ordered more than a half million residents to flee the state's low-lying coastal areas, and North Carolina governor Pat McCrory issued similar orders. The following day Georgia governor Nathan Deal ordered a mandatory evacuation of the entire Georgia coast, the first such order since Hurricane Floyd's approach in 1999. Jeff Masters, Weather Underground's meteorology director, told the Associated Press, "There's no question it's going to have major impacts. Is it going to be devastating or just major-damaging? That depends. A few degrees difference in the hard-to-forecast track as it hugs the coast could make the difference between a $1 billion storm and a $10 billion one."

After Matthew passed through the northwestern Bahamas as a Category 4, an approaching midlatitude trough over the central United States helped steer the storm toward the north-northwest, just offshore of and parallel to Florida's east coast. Residents in Miami and Fort Lauderdale breathed a sigh of relief, as a slightly more westerly track would have pushed the major hurricane inland upon them. Thanks to an "eyewall replacement cycle" (a common occurrence in strong cyclones in which an outer wall cloud forms and replaces the inner wall, or eyewall), Matthew began weakening, its eye expanding to forty miles in diameter. Still, as the hurricane's center slid by just offshore, the western edges of its circulation pounded the Florida coast from West Palm Beach northward.

Sustained hurricane-force winds were felt along the barrier beaches and immediate coast as the hurricane lumbered by. Gusts reached 105 mph at Cape Canaveral. National Weather Service surveys after the storm determined that Category 2 sustained winds likely occurred over the mostly unpopulated coastal areas of northern Brevard County. Storm tides ranged from three to seven feet above mean high water, which in many locations was several feet above ground level. Oceanfront properties were inundated, and some businesses were forced to close. At Mayport, the tide was the highest since 1898. In Saint Augustine, four feet of water filled the streets, flooding Flagler College. As the storm swept the coast, a frightening rumor quickly spread through social media that dozens of alligators and crocodiles had escaped their enclosures at the nearby Saint Augustine Alligator Farm—but fortunately, it was only a rumor; all remained safely in their lagoons.

Damages mounted all along the storm's path. Matthew's churning waves left severe erosion along much of the coast. In Palm Beach County alone, the losses to beaches and dunes were estimated at $29 million. In Brevard and Volusia Counties, which were closest to the storm center, eighty homes were destroyed and more than 500 suffered heavy damage. At the Kennedy Space Center at Cape Canaveral, saltwater intrusion caused several million dollars' worth of damages to NASA's rocket launch facilities. Winds damaged the roofs of buildings throughout the site, but officials were generally thankful that Matthew passed by offshore; the Cape Canaveral complex has never been directly hit by a major hurricane. Two Floridians were killed during the storm, both struck by falling trees.

Even so, with the energy wrapped inside this dangerous storm, Matthew was a fortunate near miss for Florida. The NHC's warnings were extended up the coast, and beachfront communities in Georgia and the Carolinas completed their evacuations. The storm weakened to Category 3 strength as it passed thirty-five miles east of Vero Beach; it was a Category 2 by the time it tracked by Jacksonville Beach late on October 7.

Fifty miles off the Georgia coast, Matthew took a hard turn toward the northeast and slid along the South Carolina coastline—still just offshore. It was steadily weakening—but also growing in size. In its summary report, the NHC noted, "As Matthew gained latitude, its wind field expanded, spreading hurricane-force wind gusts across the coastal regions of southeastern Georgia and southern South Carolina, especially on the barrier islands where category 2 wind gusts occurred." The storm's slow, steady pace and position close to shore kept everyone guessing what its next move might be.

Late on the morning of October 8, Matthew finally drifted overland near Cape Romain, just south of McClellanville. But just three hours later, it was back at sea, tracking toward the east-northeast as a Category 1 hurricane. By remaining offshore, and with maximum winds continuing to diminish, Matthew appeared to be another dodge-the-bullet-type hurricane that might spare the Carolinas the kind of disaster once feared. It edged by North Carolina's Brunswick County beaches, where the storm center passed just a few miles below Southport on the morning of October 9. It continued to hug the North Carolina coast, slipping just past Cape Lookout and out to sea later in the day.

All through this period, Matthew was weakening but also transitioning into an extratropical system. As it skirted the South Carolina coast, the midlatitude trough approaching from the west caused an increased pressure gradient, elevating wind velocities even as the storm was losing its tropical characteristics. During and after its brief landfall in South Carolina, and even though it was a minimal hurricane, Matthew's large western eyewall extended well inland, resulting in sustained hurricane-force winds and significant sound-side storm surge flooding across eastern North Carolina, especially along the Outer Banks. Among the peak recorded gusts were 103 mph at Winyah Bay and 97 mph at Nags Head. Interaction with this trough also caused the storm's cloud shield and heaviest rains to shift from the southeastern to the northwestern side of the circulation. From late on October 7 through the day on October 9, this shift spread heavy rainfall well inland over much of the southeastern United States. The combination of these forces set the stage for the widespread and disastrous floods that covered eastern portions of the Carolinas.

As it passed along the coast, Matthew moved through several lunar tide cycles and left extensive erosion and storm tide destruction from Hilton Head to Virginia Beach. At Fort Pulaski, near Savannah, a new peak tide record was set (measured since 1935) at 4.9 feet above mean higher high water—breaking the old mark set in 1947. Most coastal areas in South Carolina saw tides measuring three to five feet above normal, causing widespread damage to homes, businesses, bridges, and watercraft. The Sea Islands south and east of Beaufort were hit hard, with tides scouring out some roads and causeways, including the Harbor Island Bridge to Hunting Island. Eight boats were swept over U.S. 21, and four more were carried onto the runway at the Beaufort County airport. The National Weather Service noted that on Hilton Head Island, storm surge flooding reached the Harbor Town Golf Course, "located more than 500 feet inland from the small harbor and more than 1,000 feet from the coast." Wind damage on the island was heavy too—an estimated 120,000 trees were downed in the storm. In all, Hilton Head suffered more structural damages than anywhere in South Carolina: more than 3,700 homes and businesses were hit by fallen trees or flooding, and nearly 400 structures incurred damages greater than 50 percent of their assessed value.

Isle of Palms suffered heavy beach erosion and overwash, as did Edisto Island, where five feet of sand covered some roads and more than seventy homes were undermined or significantly damaged. Officials determined that Matthew's surging tides moved the island's beachfront inland nearly two city blocks. In Charleston, tides swirled around City Market and officially measured 3.51 feet above mean higher high water, high enough to rank among the top five highest tides recorded in the city. One boat sank in the Ashley River; others were driven aground nearby.

Not surprisingly, the combination of Matthew's destructive winds, storm surge, and rain-induced floods caused major problems northward along the coast, especially near the area of landfall. From McClellanville to Little River, countless roads, bridges, and railways were blocked by downed trees and power lines or submerged by freshwater floods. At Pawleys Island, ocean surge flooded the town hall, and two to four feet of sand covered long stretches of Springs Avenue. In Horry County, major flooding on the Waccamaw and Pee Dee Rivers drowned the area around Socastee, just west of Myrtle Beach, sinking streets and businesses in knee-deep floodwaters. More than 1,000 residents fled to shelters. At Myrtle Beach, battering waves and storm surge wiped out most of the 1,000-foot Springmaid Pier; the Surfside Beach pier also suffered heavy damage. Even an EF0 tornado contributed to the impact in North Myrtle Beach, causing minor damages to homes and businesses. Like in most every community near the hurricane's path, power outages in Myrtle Beach were widespread. The local ABC television affiliate, WPDE-TV, resorted to streaming on Facebook Live to inform its viewers after losing power on the afternoon of October 8.

Two days earlier, on October 6, with the news that Matthew was forecast to continue weakening as it slid past Florida, local officials in North Carolina were understandably relieved. Learning of the expected drop from Category 4 to Category 1 intensity and a track that might take it out to sea, Governor Pat McCrory said he was "cautiously optimistic" about the hurricane. Across the state, most emergency managers and local officials felt well prepared for a Category 1 that was expected to dance by just off the coast. And it was in that region, across North Carolina's coastal counties, where media attention was focused in the hours before the storm's arrival. As Matthew tracked closer, with a drop in intensity and a northeasterly turn, its much-feared winds and storm surge at first appeared to be less of a threat. But the broadscale spread of the storm's western cloud mass ensured that winds, rains, and tides would stir up plenty of trouble across the eastern counties of the Tar Heel State.

Winds in Brunswick and New Hanover Counties, nearest the storm center, were surprisingly less severe than those on the Outer Banks, farther north, away from the center of circulation. Peak gusts in Southport (59 mph) and Wilmington (70 mph) were not as great as those at Ocracoke (84 mph), Duck (85 mph), and Nags Head (97 mph), thanks to Matthew's interaction with that approaching front. Still, after hours of pounding winds and steady rains, the manager of one Brunswick County Comfort Suites hotel found it all to be just too much. The property was fully booked with utility linemen and local evacuees, along with forty-five pets. As the storm raged, the hotel's walls began to lift and crack open, forcing the manager to go door to door to evacuate all 123 guests. All safely escaped out a back stairwell and retreated to a nearby shelter at South Brunswick High School.

Storm tide impacts in North Carolina were impressive for a Category 1 hurricane, though inundation levels varied significantly by location. On Oak Island, tides washed away eight-foot dunes in some sections and knocked down at least a third of the Oak Island Pier. Coastal areas south of Cape Hatteras saw tides rise two to four feet above ground level. The highest record in this region was on the Cape Fear River in downtown Wilmington, where much of Water Street was underwater. A maximum of 3.53 feet above mean higher high water was reported, eclipsing the old record for that location set during Hazel in 1954 (Matthew's mark translates to 8.17 feet above mean lower low water). But even higher levels were observed on the sound side of the Outer Banks, where the average inundation was estimated to be four to six feet above ground level. The U.S. Coast Guard Station on Hatteras Island, located on Pamlico Sound, recorded a peak water level of 5.76 feet above mean higher high water. Along Hatteras Island, massive ocean waves pounded the beachfront while wind-driven tides, combined with heavy rains, produced significant inundations across most of the region's beach towns. Sound-side docks and piers were battered and destroyed up and down the shore from Ocracoke to Corolla. N.C. 12, so often a victim of hurricanes and nor'easters, was closed and impassable from south Nags Head to Hatteras Village. The North Carolina Department of Transportation reported that deep standing water covered much of the road for the entire length of Hatteras Island.

On the northern Outer Banks, high winds toppled trees and power lines and ripped away shingles, but structural damages mostly involved deck and dock washouts due to sound-side flooding and beachfront erosion. Winds gusts up to 90 mph caused minor damages to about 500 homes in Duck. In Southern Shores, massive amounts of tree debris filled the streets and had to be removed to allow emergency vehicle access. Freshwater flooding and sound-side inundations were common in Kitty Hawk, Nags Head, and Duck, though it was the eye-popping beachfront destruction in the area that made news. Matthew's pounding waves ate away portions of N.C. 12 in Kitty Hawk, leaving short stretches of asphalt dangling over the Atlantic. As far north as Hampton Roads, Virginia Beach, and Norfolk, downed power lines and fallen trees blocked streets, frustrating drivers and leaving plenty of work for cleanup crews. Even though Matthew's center passed more than 100 miles to the southeast, storm surge flooding and power outages in Virginia Beach combined to cause a major sewer line break—resulting in a 2-million gallon spill near Linkhorn Bay.

Like hurricanes on the Carolina coast sometimes do, Matthew left a few curiosities in its wake, especially along the ocean strand. In South Carolina, a U.S. Air Force explosives team was called in to Folly Beach after the storm to safely detonate a cache of Civil War–era cannonballs unearthed by the scouring tides. On Oak Island, residents walking the beach found an oversized homemade raft constructed of wood, string, plastic foam, and empty water jugs. Inside were flour bags labeled "Product of Cuba," leading local officials to speculate that it was likely a raft once used by desperate refugees fleeing that island nation, some 1,500 miles away. Some pondered the fate of its occupants.

Thanks to steady downpours throughout September from the remnants of Hurricane Hermine, Tropical Storm Julia, and another shot of heavy rain in south central North Carolina on September 28, many streams and rivers across the region were already running near or above flood stage by the time Matthew's rains first began to fall. Jeanne Robbins, assistant director for data at the U.S. Geological Survey's South Atlantic Water Science Center, told UNC-TV, "In addition to the tremendous rainfall associated with Hurricane Matthew, rain that fell prior to Matthew in September led to higher than normal streamflows and wet soils that had limited capacity to absorb more rainfall." Much like Tropical Storm Dennis had set the stage for the Hurricane Floyd disaster, these September rains no doubt contributed to Matthew's record-setting floods.

Though Matthew only briefly tracked onshore in South Carolina, its rains extended some 250 miles inland as it passed. Rainfall totals, measured over the duration of the storm, were impressive near the coast in places such as Hilton Head Island (16.58 inches), Edisto Island (16.90 inches), Charleston (10.48

inches), Myrtle Beach (12.69 inches), and Wilmington (6.59 inches). Rains spread inland in South Carolina, swamping communities such as Reevesville (13.05 inches), Darlington (12.71 inches), Dillon (13.88 inches), Marion (15.02 inches), and Mullins (15.57 inches). But the storm's broad northwestern cloud mass poured even greater amounts over the coastal plains in North Carolina. Extreme totals were recorded in Fayetteville (15.62 inches), Hope Mills (17.05 inches), Garland (18.52 inches), Elizabethtown (18.85 inches), Kinston (16.50 inches), and Goldsboro (15.48 inches). The highest storm total was recorded in Evergreen: 18.95 inches.

The National Weather Service described these rains as "historic." They began to fall across the Carolinas well before Matthew's landfall and continued even as the hurricane slipped out to sea off the coast. Several locations established new twenty-four-hour rainfall records, including Florence (11.74 inches), Dillon (17.22 inches), Lumberton (12.53 inches), Fayetteville (14.00 inches), Tarboro (9.50 inches), and Raleigh (6.45 inches). Weather Service reports described the rapid accumulation: "Rainfall rates increased to one to two inches per hour early in the morning of October 8th and stayed there for most of the day, leading to exceptional flash flooding. The first reports of significant flooding arrived between 7:00 and 8:00 A.M. with road closures reported in Garden City, Marion and Florence, SC. By 9:00 A.M. storm-total rainfall amounts were already approaching 10 inches in portions of Williamsburg County, SC. Flooding became widespread by late morning with road closures reported in Wilmington, Whiteville, and Pembroke, NC and in Conway, SC."

The disastrous floods that hit the Carolinas were not a total surprise. The NHC began describing anticipated inland flooding as "life-threatening" on October 7 as Matthew was passing east of Cape Canaveral. At the time, local officials across eastern North and South Carolina, most of whom were quite familiar with the flooding risks in their communities, monitored the forecasts and prepared for high water. The National Weather Service's Southeast River Forecast Center issued daily forecasts for rivers across the region, but rain events such as Matthew's are challenging to predict—to know how much rain will fall, over how large of an area, and over what period of time. With Matthew, all these factors exceeded expectations. Early river forecasts vastly underestimated the event, though subsequent updates provided greater accuracy as more rainfall data was factored. In the end, runoff from these rains pushed U.S. Geological Survey streamgages to new river flood records at twenty-eight separate locations in eastern North Carolina and five in South Carolina—eighteen of which had been in operation for decades.

In the communities nearest these expanding rivers, Matthew's floodwaters spread far beyond the bottomlands, creating historic inundations that affected areas local residents never knew could flood. In many sections of North Carolina, high-water levels exceeded those of Hurricane Floyd, the last great flood to affect the state. Among the North Carolina locations setting new flood crest records after Matthew were the Lumber River at Lumberton (28.00 feet on October 9), near Pembroke (13.43 feet on October 11), and at Boardman (14.43 feet on October 11); Town Creek near Pinetops (28.63 feet on October 9); Little River at Manchester (32.19 feet on October 10); Black River near Tomahawk (27.92 feet on October 10); and Neuse River at Smithfield (29.09 feet on October 10), near Goldsboro (29.74 feet on October 12), and at Kinston (28.31 feet on October 14). At numerous other rivergage locations, flood levels recorded during Matthew were the second- or third-highest in history.

In South Carolina, new records were established on the Waccamaw and Little Pee Dee Rivers, including measurements near Conway (17.89 feet on October 18) and at Pawleys Island (10.34 feet on October 17). The record at Pawleys Island exceeded Matthew's storm surge at that location by almost a foot.

Understandably, the widespread flooding surprised many residents and challenged emergency workers. But it wasn't just flash floods during the storm—some of the greatest flooding impacts occurred days after Matthew's passing as rivers continued to swell from the added burden of upstream runoff. Lumberton flooded two days after Matthew's arrival. On the Waccamaw in South Carolina, the new peak record was made a full week after the storm. Along the Neuse, Goldsboro remained above flood stage for six days and Kinston almost two weeks. These lingering floods, reminiscent of, but in many cases eclipsing those of, Hurricane Floyd became the primary focus for response and recovery efforts in Matthew.

As Matthew's rains first began to pile up across eastern North Carolina, inspectors and engineers from the state's Dam Safety Program were already on high alert. They're familiar with the dams in their regions, and as Matthew approached, they kept a watchful eye—especially on those dams considered "high hazard" across the eastern half of the state. Heavy rains often pose a threat, and the excessive totals associated with Matthew pushed many small lakes and ponds to the brink. Unfortunately, there were at least seventeen dam failures in North Carolina during the storm, thirteen of which were in the Cape Fear River Basin (there were about forty dam failures in North Carolina during Hurricane Floyd). An earthen dam on J. C. Keith Lake in Fayetteville was breached, as were dams at Rhodes Pond, Wilson Lake, Watson Lake, Herndon Pond, Mirror Lake Drive, and others. A breached dam at Mount Vernon Estates was discovered during a flyover. About 100 downstream residents were

Patrick Hager, a Savannah district structural engineer with the U.S. Army Corps of Engineers, surveys a road washout at Fort Bragg after Hurricane Matthew. (Photo courtesy of the U.S. Army Corps of Engineers.)

evacuated when a spillway ruptured at the privately owned Woodlake dam near Vass. No lives were lost directly as the result of any dam breaches during Matthew.

More than 3,200 dams, most privately owned, are monitored across North Carolina. About 1,200 of these are listed as "high hazard"—dams that could potentially cause loss of life or property should they fail—and another 735 are classified as "intermediate hazard." South Carolina has about 2,400 dams, not all of which were regulated before Matthew's arrival. In fact, in the years just before the hurricane, South Carolina's dam inspection program was ranked among the nation's worst, employing only a handful of staff inspectors. The severe flooding that struck the state in October 2015 caused more than fifty dam failures, forty-five of which were in Richland and Lexington Counties. Flooding associated with these breaches put the state's inspection program under a microscope. Then, about twenty-five more dams failed the following year during Matthew. Within weeks of the storm, a new bill moved through the South Carolina legislature designed to strengthen the state's dam oversight and inspection programs. Some new funding was approved, but critics contend that perhaps 1,000 potentially hazardous South Carolina dams still pose risks. In 2021, South Carolina Emergency Management director Kim Stenson noted, "That program has made a lot of progress and expanded their operation considerably over the last few years. I'm not sure we're where we need to be, but they're doing much better in that area."

As challenging as the 2015 floods had been in South Carolina, Matthew's rains pushed several of the state's eastern rivers even higher. In Colleton County, the Edisto River spilled its banks, but the highest water and most significant flooding was in areas surrounding the Little Pee Dee and Waccamaw Rivers. Flooding shut down nearly 500 roads across several counties and chased thousands of residents from their homes. One of the hardest-hit small towns was Nichols in Marion County, located just a few miles above the union of the Lumber and Little Pee Dee Rivers. Matthew's rains turned this sleepy town on a "modest bluff" into a raging torrent. The Charleston *Post and Courier* reported that "Matthew's winds did little damage in Nichols, but heavy rains caused more than a half-dozen upstream dams to breach. By the time the flood reached Nichols, the rivers might as well have been one stream—running 4 feet high down the streets." All 261 of the town's homes were left uninhabitable, most coated with a black, moldy crust left behind from a mix of floodwaters, fuel, fertilizer, and sewage. Six months later, nine out of ten Nichols residents still couldn't return to their homes due to the extent of the damages.

Retiree Billy Jones was one of those Nichols residents who watched the water rise quickly. "When it come, it come. It was just a matter of minutes," he told the *Post and Courier*. For the seventy-eight-year-old, who had lost his wife just months before, Matthew was devastating. Months after the flood, he struggled with the reality of his dilemma: he didn't have the money to rebuild, and he also didn't qualify for FEMA help because his home was in the floodplain and he didn't have flood insurance. Early in 2017, he struggled to think about his scuttled home: "Everything is gone. The duct work, the heat pump. They disconnected the water and sewer. They tore out the flooring, the kitchen cabinets, piled them in the street."

Similar scenes could be found across other parts of Dillon, Marion, Williamsburg, and Horry Counties, though the extent of flooding was appreciably greater across the border in North Carolina. Matthew's rains extended inland well beyond the Triangle and bore down on the Lumber, Cape Fear, Neuse, and Tar River Basins. Much like the destruction caused by high waters on the Pee Dee and Waccamaw, record-setting floods devastated communities across eastern North Carolina, including Smithfield, Rocky Mount, Goldsboro, Wilson, Princeville, Greenville, Kinston, Fayetteville, and Lumberton.

A Horry County Fire and Rescue vehicle inches down a flooded road to reach someone requiring medical attention near Conway on October 8, 2016, just as Hurricane Matthew was making landfall at Cape Romain. (Photo by Sgt. Jorge Intriago. Courtesy of the South Carolina Army National Guard.)

If there was any one area that could have been considered an epicenter for these historic floods, it might have been the communities surrounding the Lumber River in Robeson County, North Carolina. Lumberton, the county seat, was devastated by flooding that came as a surprise to many. Four feet of water filled homes and businesses across a city whose citizens could least afford disaster—Robeson County ranks among North Carolina's poorest. After receiving a remarkable ten inches of rain on September 28, the additional ten to fifteen inches that fell in Cumberland, Hoke, Moore, and Robeson Counties during Matthew lifted the Lumber to all-time-record levels, topping the old record in Lumberton by more than three feet. In this city of 22,000, the flood began overnight on October 9 and expanded quickly, closing back roads, city streets, and miles of Interstate 95. Many residents were surprised to wake up on Monday, October 10, and find water lapping at their doorsteps. Resident Nikia Moore told WRAL News, "I heard a noise, which is what woke me up out of my sleep. When I got up, the water was coming in the house. We had to get out." Moore hardly had time to react. She put her baby on her shoulder and left "with just the clothes on her back."

Few places in South Carolina were hit by more severe flooding during Hurricane Matthew than the town of Nichols. Members of the South Carolina Army National Guard navigate flooded roads to evacuate town residents on October 10, 2016. (Photo by Sgt. Jorge Intriago. Courtesy of the South Carolina Army National Guard.)

Lumberton City Council member John Cantey, a lifelong resident, was also caught off guard by the flood. He told the Raleigh *News and Observer*, "We went to bed Sunday night thinking the worst had been done. Then we woke up Monday morning, there was water all in the streets and water coming in the house. I grabbed what I could. I told my dog, if it gets bad, you get up on that bed. I left some food and water and then I had to run start knocking on doors around the community, saying, 'Get out! Get out! Get out!' I was the last one out of the neighborhood. They had to come get me with a boat."

In the mid-1970s, flood-control projects were put in place that essentially divided Robeson County into drainage districts. In Lumberton, a nearly three-mile-long earthen dike was constructed along the west bank of the Lumber River to help prevent flooding. Matthew's record river crest sent floodwaters high along the berm—but it wasn't a breach that flooded Lumberton so quickly, as some media reported. Instead, the rising river pushed water through an opening left for railroad tracks near Interstate 95, spilling into the city and rising several feet in just a few hours. It flooded four public housing developments along with other apartments and homes, launching a major swift-water rescue event that would ultimately save hundreds.

Within hours, floodwaters swirled around buildings and covered the wind-shields of parked cars. Dozens of residents were seen standing on their roofs awaiting rescue. Others clung to porches and second-story windows, where they prepared to evacuate in small boats manned by local firefighters and state-spon-sored swift-water teams. National Guard helicopters buzzed overhead, part of a multibranch search-and-recovery effort that was highly successful in find-ing and extracting trapped motorists and homeowners. Governor McCrory even ordered the airspace over Robeson County restricted, including the use of drones, to allow the rescue choppers space to do their work. It was during this time that the governor told the *New York Times*, "I wouldn't assume that there aren't people clinging to life right now in houses that are underwater that we have yet to reach, especially in lower populated areas. That's what my major concern is." In all, about 1,500 Lumberton residents were evacuated from their homes by air and by small boat—many of them elderly. Six school shelters housed the victims—some at full capacity—until one school, Carroll Middle, was threatened by flooding. Evacuees were quickly relocated to other sites.

Flooding shut down movement around the city and cut off basic services. The combination of power outages and high water shut down 911 call systems in numerous North Carolina counties, including Bladen, Moore, and Robeson. More than three feet of water filled the offices of the *Robesonian* newspaper, destroying furniture and equipment in the pressroom and forcing the paper's editor to relocate to a Charlotte hotel room. Like so many others who worked straight through disaster, the paper's reporters continued to do their jobs, re-laying critical local news reports through social media and online. Power out-ages lingered, and the Lumberton water treatment plant was overwhelmed, knocking out the municipal water supply. Given the extensive damages to the plant and waterlines in the county, it's not surprising the system was down for weeks—finally reopening in early November.

Record-setting floods covered many parts of nearby Cumberland County, home to Fayetteville and Fort Bragg. In Spring Lake, the U.S. Geological Sur-vey reported a remarkable feat: the streamgage on the Little River recorded two new record flood events over a two-week span. The first record was set on September 29—following the deluge of the night before—when water levels topped thirty-one feet, two feet greater than the previous record from 1945. Then, following the rains of Matthew, a new record was established on October 10: 32.19 feet. These floods spelled trouble for nearby residents, who watched waters rise "higher than ever known before," sinking dozens of homes and businesses.

A North Carolina Army National Guardsman helps evacuate a Lumberton resident from his flooded apartment during Hurricane Matthew. (Photo courtesy of the North Carolina National Guard.)

In nearby Fayetteville, it was more of the same. Eleven dams across the county gave way under pressure from nearly fifteen inches of rain, sending torrents through forests and neighborhoods and over highways, essentially dividing the city into several large islands. Floodwaters rose five feet inside Paye Funeral Home. Caskets floated into a pile, and solid-oak pews in the chapel were found stacked "on top of one another like pick-up sticks." Eighty secondary roads across Cumberland County were submerged, many with hidden dangers: washed-out sections lurked beneath the surface. Swift-water rescue teams stayed busy, supported by units from as far away as New York, New Jersey, and Ohio, pulling 700 flood victims to safety across the county—nearly eighty in Fayetteville alone. Many others were saved by friends and neighbors who owned small boats.

Fayetteville police broadcast live on Facebook during the rescue of a woman and child whose car was trapped by high water on Robeson Street. U.S. Coast Guard helicopters plucked others from rooftops. Large military vehicles were also useful, especially during the rescue of a woman who held on to a tree for nearly three hours after her car was swamped by floodwaters. Fayetteville residents Candace and Sharon Thompson led eight children to safety through deep water along Murchison Road, and Candace later told the *Fayetteville Observer*, "We were up to our necks in water." And it wasn't just people who needing saving. The Raleigh *News and Observer* reported that Governor McCrory and his wife saw an October 8 news helicopter video of a dog swimming endlessly in floodwaters and were "riveted by the coverage." They were relieved when they heard the dog managed to climb into a tree and was later rescued by the Coast Guard.

Over in Hope Mills, a bizarre rescue played out for one trapped navy veteran, thanks to his twin brother in Austin, Texas, some modern technology, and a stroke of luck. Chris Williams was awakened late on October 8 when floodwaters burst through his kitchen door and knocked over his refrigerator. With his dog, he fled to his second-floor converted attic as five feet of water filled his home. He couldn't leave and had no phone service. As he told the *Washington Post*, the only person that knew he was there was his brother Craig, some 1,300 miles away. Chris was able reach his brother through Facebook Messenger, but neither could get through to 911 to alert authorities. Chris and his dog spent the night in the dark, waiting.

The following morning, Quavas Hart, an Afghanistan veteran from Fayetteville who didn't know the brothers, decided to fly his drone around the area to record video of the floods. He posted several still photos on Twitter and included the hashtags #HopeMills and #HurricaneMatthew. Down in Austin, Craig anxiously scrolled through tweets from the area. He picked one of Hart's photos to send to his brother—one that happened to include his flooded house. Chris quickly replied to his brother, letting him know his house was in the photo. Craig then alerted Hart via Twitter. "I couldn't believe this guy was way in Texas, and he just happened to see his brother's house on the Internet," Hart told the *Post*. Hart messaged Chris and asked him to wave out the window the next time the drone passed by, which he did, confirming the location. Hart then spotted a boat operated by a FEMA rescue team. "I told them, 'There's a guy in this house. Follow the drone.'" Minutes later, rescuers pulled Chris and his dog from his second-floor window, ending his fourteen-hour ordeal.

Over a span of days, floodwaters swirled through other communities within reach of the Lumber and Cape Fear Rivers. In Columbus County, massive evacuations were required in Fair Bluff, where 85 percent of the town was flooded by the rising Lumber River. Much of Bladen County was swamped too, forcing evacuations and water rescues in Kelly, Clarkton, Elizabethtown, White Oak, Tar Heel, and Bladenboro. In Pender County, the swollen Black River—a tributary of the Cape Fear—flooded numerous homes, forcing the rescue of thirty-two residents, twenty-three by helicopter. Similar rescues took place near Shallotte once floodwaters backed up the Lockwood Folly River. Just days earlier, as Matthew was spinning along the coast, two fishermen had been rescued from an island in the river after their boat, *Kokopia*, ran aground. The U.S. Coast Guard had dispatched a helicopter from Savannah, and its crew lifted the two to safety around midnight on October 8.

Matthew's destructive floods reached well inland in North Carolina too, washing out a twenty-foot-wide section of N.C. 97 in eastern Wake County. The bulging Little River breached the dam and washed out the roadway at Little River Park, a Zebulon landmark that dates back to 1871. On October 9, swift-water teams rescued two trapped motorists on Holly Springs Road south of Raleigh. In Johnston County, flash flooding kept emergency personnel hopping as rapidly rising water from the Neuse River spilled across highways, farms, and neighborhoods. One section of Interstate 40 remained closed for seven days. Near Smithfield, more than 200 people were rescued, many from their car tops. Roads across the county were washed out, some with tragic results. A car with five people aboard ran off N.C. 42 and sank; four passengers were rescued after they were found clinging to trees, but a fifth did not survive. Another motorist perished trying to cross a flood-covered bridge on Interstate 95. Longtime residents noted that flooding in Smithfield was the highest in memory, higher than during Fran or Floyd. Arnold McLain, who'd lived in Smithfield for fifty years, told WRAL News the Neuse was the highest he'd ever seen. "I've seen it flood along the river, but never over here."

In Goldsboro, the rise of the Neuse took a few days, finally reaching a new record crest on October 12. Flooding forced the evacuation of nearly 800 inmates from the minimum-security Neuse Correctional Institute, a not-so-uncommon occurrence during high-water events (evacuations were necessary during Floyd too). Environmental groups watched closely as thousands of gallons of water flowed into the Neuse from a pond at a retired Wayne County Duke Energy power plant after flooding caused a sixty-foot breach in an earthen retaining wall. Most of this water was from a cooling pond rather than a coal ash pond—a far more serious contamination threat had there been a breach. Duke Energy reported that none of its coal ash pond sites in North Carolina spilled into waterways following Hurricane Matthew, though environmentalists challenged that assertion in a debate over the types of contaminants released in Goldsboro.

As the Neuse rose to record heights, Goldsboro was the scene of one of Matthew's most unsettling deeds—the flood-induced desecration of Elmwood Cemetery. At the peak of the flood, the cemetery's metal entrance gate was submerged. As floodwaters receded, left behind were thirty-six unearthed caskets that had been buried in surface vaults. All were recovered, but because the caskets had drifted about, officials had a difficult time identifying them. Eighteen were eventually identified and reburied in their previous locations. But the other eighteen were kept in refrigerated storage for over a year while officials attempted to record and match DNA profiles with family members. Ultimately, the unidentified were buried in a new section of the cemetery, leaving some family members outraged and distraught. After two years, DNA matching was still underway. Similar disinterring occurred following Hurricane Floyd, prompting state officials at the time to require identifying tags for all future burials—though the caskets unearthed by Matthew had been interred prior to the change in law.

Another disturbing outcome from Matthew's extensive flooding was the loss of large numbers of chickens, turkeys, and other livestock. Agricultural officials estimated that 100,000 chickens drowned in Wayne County alone. Much like during Floyd, the impact across eastern North Carolina was staggering: according to the North Carolina Department of Agriculture, thirty-five farms in fifteen counties lost 1.9 million chickens and turkeys. In addition to the financial losses, farmers faced the daunting task of disposing of the dead birds—a messy and environmentally challenging undertaking. Total agricultural losses in North Carolina, including crops, timber, and livestock, topped $400 million. In South Carolina, total agricultural losses were close to $500 million, with significant damage to cotton and timber.

Flooding from the Neuse reached many small towns and crossroads communities that dot the landscape in the east, some all too familiar with hurricanes. The population of Seven Springs dropped from around 200 to about 120 after Hurricane Floyd sank homes and businesses there in 1999. Some chose to rebuild; others moved away. Nearly two decades later, floodwaters from Matthew were at least a foot higher. Once again, the survival of this small community was threatened as more homes were damaged and more residents decided to leave. Resident Ivey Outlaw told the Raleigh *News and Observer,* "It [Floyd] was supposed to be a 500-year event. It wasn't supposed to happen again in our lifetime." Rich in history and proud of its endurance, Seven Springs had seen its population grow to about seventy by 2020, with some homes elevated to better survive future floods.

Matthew's next victim along the Neuse was the city of Kinston—much like Goldsboro, flooded by high waters that surpassed those of Floyd. As rainfall accumulates in the central part of the state, the Neuse River's downhill flow toward the coast slows over the coastal plain as the land flattens out. It takes time for the flooding to peak there—Matthew's record river crest in Kinston wasn't reached until October 14.

A lot had changed in Kinston after Floyd, most notably the buyout and removal of nearly 800 flooded homes in the vibrant Black community of Lincoln City, which were razed in early 2000 with help from FEMA. Moving those families from perilous locations no doubt reduced Matthew's toll, but flooding still cut the city in half and submerged countless homes and businesses. Popular U.S. 70 establishments such as Kings Barbeque and Neuse Sport Shop were hit hard again, though their owners had time to prepare. Russell Rhodes, owner of Neuse Sport Shop, said his employees had removed about 75 percent of the shop's merchandise before the flooding hit. Thirty-three inches of water filled his store; twenty-eight inches were measured there after Floyd.

Over the years, most Kinston residents have shown their resolve through the floods and rebuilt and repaired their homes after each event. Matthew was perhaps their greatest test. Some, such as Thurman Taylor, recalled the journey through two decades of hurricane disasters. Taylor described to the Raleigh *News and Observer* how he remembered "having to kill snakes" in his house after Fran. He and his sister then moved into a new home on higher ground, but that was destroyed by Floyd. The two then moved into another home, expecting to stay dry in the next flood. But after Matthew, they were again surrounded by floodwaters. He told the paper, "We've spent our life moving higher and higher and higher."

The Tar River was another North Carolina waterway to spill its banks and send life-threatening floodwaters across streets and neighborhoods. Again, like during Floyd, Rocky Mount was hit hard by flooding that caught many off guard. During Matthew, city firefighters reported 472 water rescues, including five dogs. But unlike during Floyd, when the fire department had to improvise to pull people from flooded homes and cars, the city had since invested in equipment, personnel, and training. During Matthew, the Rocky Mount Swiftwater Emergency Rescue Team went to work, outfitted with three boats, twenty firefighters, and specially designed dry suits, deploying alongside swiftwater teams from Chapel Hill and other locations. These were just some of the rescuers later recognized with the prestigious Higgins and Langley Memorial Award for Outstanding Achievement presented by the International Association of Water Rescue Professionals during its annual conference in 2017. The recognition was welcomed by the consortium of agencies involved, including local law enforcement and fire department teams, state-organized swiftwater teams, FEMA rescue teams, and the North Carolina helo-aquatic rescue teams, which included military rescue operations from North Carolina bases.

The North Carolina Division of Emergency Management reported that the state effort during and after Matthew included 400 personnel, seventy-seven boat teams, and twelve aircraft. Across the state, 2,336 people were pulled from floodwaters, mostly in Cumberland, Robeson, Bladen, Columbus, Johnston, Wayne, Nash, and Edgecombe Counties.

One rescue that drew a lot of media attention happened when a sixty-three-year-old nurse was saved by a National Guard search team after her car slid into a flooded ditch in Wilson County. After she left the long-term care facility where she worked at about 11:30 P.M. on October 8, her family called authorities when she didn't make it home. Riding atop a Humvee over dark, flooded roads, her rescuers traced her route and finally heard her call for help. She was spotted holding on to a tree, where she had clung for three hours after her car submerged. A rescue boat soon arrived, and she was transported to a local hospital—suffering from hypothermia but glad to be out of the treacherous water. State emergency management director Mike Sprayberry was grateful for the good news but used the opportunity to remind the public of the dangers of driving on flooded roads. It was a simple message: "Turn around; don't drown."

It was about that same time that volunteer firefighters, law enforcement, and Coast Guard helicopters teamed up to rescue around 200 residents in and around Pinetops. Town Creek, a tributary of the Tar River, had swollen to more than one mile wide, forcing surprise evacuations in the middle of the night along Bynum Farm Road. This was another community that had been hit hard by flooding during Floyd. Pinetops mayor Stephen Burress told the Raleigh *News and Observer* Matthew's floods matched the levels he saw back in 1999: "I swear, the water came to the exact same place."

It's only natural for residents and local officials to compare Matthew's floods to those of Floyd. In many cases, the two floods struck the same businesses, the same neighborhoods, and the same people. During Floyd, no community was hit any harder, or received more media attention, than Princeville, in Edgecombe County. Flooding had heavily damaged 600 homes there after the town's protective dike had washed out, sending Tar River floodwaters over their roofs. In the aftermath, residents were offered buyouts and the opportunity to relocate, but in the fall of 1999 town commissioners voted 3–2 to return and rebuild, and reinforcements to the protective dike were completed the following summer. Princeville's 2,000 residents rebuilt their homes and moved back in, hoping to put the "500-year flood" behind them. But Hurricane Matthew, some seventeen years later, gave them a heart-wrenching case of déjà vu.

On October 9, authorities issued a mandatory evacuation of Princeville, a reasonable precaution given the threat of Matthew's flash floods and the town's flooding history. Hundreds of evacuees filled Tarboro High School, where they waited. Three days later, the waters reached their peak. This time, Princeville's protective levee held, but flood levels along the Tar River were so great that high water managed to flow around it, sinking hundreds of homes. The National Guard's 875th Engineer Company set up a pumping system to remove water from the town, using six pumps running twenty-four hours per day. By the time town officials were able to return to get a look at the damages on October 18, 76 million gallons of water had been pumped back into the Tar River. The historic town settled by freed slaves was covered in dried mud and debris, the town hall had once again been flooded to the roofline, and high water had destroyed three of the fire department's five engines. Assessment teams inspected homes and marked them with colored tags to indicate the level of damage. Of the more than 700 homes in Princeville before Matthew, about 400 received red tags, indicating severe damage. Two years later, about 500 residents had returned. Some had restored their homes better than before, while other dwellings sat vacant, surrounded by tall weeds. State hazard mitigation specialist Calvin Adkins told WRAL News, "In the beginning, you had more people saying they were not coming back. As time went by, all that old feeling left and it was reality then. This is home for me."

The Tar River also overflowed into Greenville and brought high water to those sections with a flooding history. Officials ordered evacuations for about one-tenth of the city's 90,000 residents and set up barricades to block off evacuated areas, carefully monitoring movement in and out. In places such as the Meadowbrook neighborhood, families fled by boat as floodwaters crept inside their homes—forcing some to stay away for weeks. Some of the homes in this section were flooded "over the roof." Flooding covered runways, shut down the Pitt-Greenville Airport, and forced the closure of numerous roads around the county. East Carolina University happened to be on fall break during this time, though some students later returned to find their apartments and belongings soaked by Matthew's floodwaters.

In the aftermath of Matthew's visit to the Carolinas, the scope of recovery efforts was vast—state and local governments in both states, along with FEMA and a host of charitable and service organizations, went to work implementing their plans. As with most major disasters, housing was an immediate need. Shelters were near capacity in many communities, though their populations steadily decreased in the days and weeks following the worst of the flooding. In North Carolina, 109 shelters had opened in thirty-five counties, housing over 4,000 evacuees. The final shelter closed on November 14. Across northeastern South Carolina, seventy-seven shelters housed up to 6,500 evacuees. Once the floods finally receded, many residents found they couldn't return home and had to make arrangements to stay with family and friends.

Both states opened disaster recovery centers in the hardest-hit regions to help victims sort out their options and apply for aid. Just as had occurred after Floyd and every other hurricane disaster, the process took an emotional toll. When a WRAL News reporter visited Princeville nearly two years after Matthew, she found positive signs of recovery and lingering fear: "Grit, backbreaking work and sheer willpower mingle with anger and frustration at the red tape, the hoops and uncertainty that has gone on for 22 months and counting." Natalie Bess, Edgecombe County's director of disaster recovery, described how the beginning of hurricane season brings flashbacks and worry for Matthew victims: "We still have people now that get really anxious when it rains. We are talking about infrastructure and finance, but the people are really still dealing with the ramifications of what happened."

Matthew's economic toll was massive, considering its extensive journey through the Caribbean, Haiti, Cuba, the Bahamas, and the southeastern United States. Dollar estimates vary by source, but most list the total above $15 billion. Of that amount, $2.8 billion was estimated in Haiti, making Matthew the costliest hurricane in that nation's history. The NHC estimated $10.9 billion in losses in the United States, ranking Matthew just inside its list of the top twenty costliest U.S. hurricanes (adjusted to 2020). In North Carolina, fifty counties received federal disaster declarations, and 100,000 homes and 19,000 businesses were damaged or destroyed. South Carolina reported more than 40,000 structures damaged and had twenty-six federally declared counties. Reinsurance intermediary Aon Benfield, using its impact forecasting model, analyzed Matthew's losses based on physical damage to homes, businesses, vehicles, infrastructure, and agriculture as well as on business interruption losses. The group found that North Carolina had the greatest losses, with a $5 billion toll. Florida's losses were $2.3 billion, South Carolina's $2 billion, and Georgia's $1 billion. Aon Benfield also determined that only 30 percent of the hurricane's total financial cost was covered by public and private insurance, a lower-than-expected ratio for tropical cyclone events. The report concluded this was largely due to the nature of the damages: "In the state of North Carolina, the most prolific flood damage occurred well inland where the vast majority of residents did not own National Flood Insurance Program (NFIP) policies."

In North and South Carolina, the effort to obtain and deploy funding needed for recovery was protracted and messy. Typically, states rely on significant federal assistance after natural disasters, and the needs for Matthew were great. Unfortunately, the process became mired in red tape and partisan bickering and moved slowly, delaying rebuilding and mitigation efforts across both states. In North Carolina, Governor McCrory submitted a nearly $1 billion request for assistance to Congress in the fall of 2016, hastened to meet the deadline for a short-term federal budget resolution to avoid a government shutdown. FEMA provided some funding that was helpful in debris cleanup and other needs, but in April 2017 North Carolina's newly elected governor, Roy Cooper, wrote to President Donald Trump to "express shock and disappointment in the lack of federal funding" that had been allocated. By August of that year, the U.S. Department of Housing and Urban Development had announced additional allocations, bringing the total block grant funding for the state to $236 million (the Department of Housing and Urban Development had a similar package for South Carolina at $221 million). Just weeks later, in September 2017, $130 million in aid for North Carolina was frozen due to the "deluge of claims" that resulted after Hurricanes Harvey and Irma. In May 2018, eight Republican North Carolina legislators wrote to Governor Cooper condemning the slow progress in spending the Matthew funds, noting the extremely frustrating and difficult challenges faced by the hurricane's victims as they waited for relief. But red tape continued to dog the process. More than a year later, in August 2019, and nearly three years after Matthew, Mike Sprayberry, North Carolina's emergency management director, told the Raleigh *News and Observer*, "We have a difficult time managing expectations when [Housing and Urban Development] puts out a news release and says 'We are awarding $168 million to the state of North Carolina for [Community Development Block Grant–Disaster Recovery] for mitigation' [in April 2018] and we still don't have a Federal Register so that we can write a staff action plan so that we can turn it in for approval so we can get the money to be executed." By this time, Hurricane Florence had already paid a visit to the Tar Heel State, layering additional major funding requests onto a system that was already struggling to provide victims relief. The *Winston-Salem Journal* editorialized that spending delays in North Carolina were "caused by a lack of institutional knowledge about Community Development Block Grant–Disaster Recovery funds, intended for long-term housing and infrastructure recovery. Before Matthew, the state had not received this kind of funding since 2003." Ultimately, the Cooper administration addressed the issue with creation of the North Carolina Office of Recovery and Resiliency to manage and coordinate the recovery process.

Much like in North Carolina, many of South Carolina's hardest-hit areas were also among its poorest. Over this same extended period, federal agencies allocated almost $400 million in disaster aid to help victims of Matthew in places such as Marion and Horry Counties. But years after the storm, many residents still had not moved back into their homes. Local leaders said that many who were displaced simply scattered and never received the information they needed to apply for aid. Others gave up, overwhelmed by the required paperwork. Some held a long-standing distrust of government, depressing aid applications. By the time the window of opportunity for applications closed, many South Carolina families with heavily damaged homes still had not applied. For those that did apply there were other barriers, such as flood zone requirements for elevating homes and the required purchase of National Flood Insurance policies—both of which were beyond the means of many affected families.

Though Matthew's financial impact was great, the loss of nearly 600 lives was tragic on a different scale. Matthew became the deadliest Atlantic hurricane since Hurricane Stan in 2005. By far the largest number of fatalities was in Haiti, where torrential rains, mudslides, and storm surge struck a mostly unprepared population, causing more than 500 deaths. The NHC's preliminary report noted a total of 585 direct deaths for Matthew, with thirty-four in the United States. It counted twenty-five in North Carolina, four in South Carolina, two each in Florida and Georgia, and one in Virginia. The center also reported eighteen indirect deaths associated with the storm in the United States. The North Carolina Division of Emergency Management placed the total number of deaths in the state at thirty-one, and South Carolina officials listed five for their state. Most of these fatalities occurred in inland counties, many miles from the effects of storm surge. As with Hurricane Floyd, most deaths in the Carolinas occurred when people attempted to drive their vehicles on flooded roads—with some even attempting to drive around posted barricades.

In North Carolina, fatalities were reported in Bladen, Columbus, Cumberland, Gates, Granville, Harnett, Johnston, Lenoir, Pitt, Robeson, Rowan, Sampson, Wake, Wayne, and Wilson Counties. In South Carolina, deaths were reported in Dillon, Florence, Marion, and Richland Counties. Among the tragedies: two men drowned when their vehicle plunged into floodwaters covering a washed-out Bladen County road; a seventy-four-year-old man drowned after driving around a barricade and into a rain-swollen creek in Harnett County; a woman drowned in a flooded ditch after also driving around barriers in Lenoir County; a Wake County man was killed when a falling tree struck the truck he was driving; in Robeson County a man apparently drowned after he fell into a large hole left by an uprooted tree and was unable to climb out; a seventy-one-year-old Lenoir County man drowned while trying to rescue a horse from a flooded ditch; a female passenger drowned after her husband attempted to drive through floodwaters in Robeson County; and a sixty-six-year-old man

Swift-water rescue teams, working for local emergency services, evacuate flood victims from a Fayetteville neighborhood during Hurricane Matthew. Some homes in the area were filled with five feet of water. (Photo courtesy of the North Carolina National Guard.)

near Columbia, South Carolina, drowned after being pinned facedown in standing water under his electric wheelchair. Along with many others, these tragic events occurred despite pleas from local officials to shelter during the storm and avoid driving on flooded roads. Other tragedies became part of Matthew's legacy: During the worst of the flooding in Lumberton on October 10, a North Carolina state trooper shot and killed a hostile resident who drew a handgun on officers involved in search-and-rescue efforts. And tragically, a Fayetteville public works employee died on November 29—seven weeks after Matthew's arrival. He was making repairs to an earthen dam at McFayden Lake when the Bobcat he was driving overturned, pinning him underwater.

Residents in eastern North and South Carolina will long remember Hurricane Matthew and the surprising broadscale flooding that sank their communities. As time goes by, memories for some may be conflated with memories of Hurricane Florence, which caused similar floods in many of the same areas just two years later. Like Hurricane Floyd at the end of the last century, Matthew taught us a few things about public expectations and how a storm that might appear weak can turn out to be the disaster of a lifetime. With Matthew, the public's initial interpretation of Bob Simpson's hurricane rating scale was misplaced, and government officials and emergency planners became more vocal about the scale's use. Just days after the storm spun away from the North

Carolina coast, Governor McCrory stood next to a massive sinkhole in Cumberland County and told reporters that the way the NHC rates hurricanes must change. "Rain kills," he told WTVD News. He noted that once people heard the storm had dropped from a Category 4 to a Category 1, they let their guard down. "They say, 'Well, that's not going to be any problem,'" he said. Research has shown that inland flooding has surpassed storm surge as the primary killer in U.S. hurricanes. Even *Popular Science* magazine considered Matthew "curiously underrated," saying, "While Matthew didn't produce many iconic scenes of palm trees felled by high speed winds, it proved immensely destructive, robbing people of their lives and homes."

Partly in response to Matthew's impact, the National Weather Service made some changes to its forecasts beginning with the 2017 hurricane season. Storm surge watches and warnings are now issued separately from hurricane alerts, and inland flood threats have been made more visible in maps and forecast warnings. The NHC also began highlighting forecasts from its sister agency, the Weather Prediction Center, which focuses on excessive rainfall outlooks and local flood warnings. These changes mean that though the Saffir-Simpson scale will remain an important measurement for storm strength from a wind perspective, new emphasis will be placed on inland flood risk and coastal storm surge. Craig McLean, assistant administrator for oceanic and atmospheric research at the National Oceanic and Atmospheric Administration, told UNC-TV, "The best forecast can be scientifically brilliant, but if the public doesn't understand how to use it with a state of readiness and preparedness to respond, and then recover after an event, we haven't fully done our jobs."

TAKEAWAYS

- *Beware the weakening hurricane—and never underestimate a Category 1 storm.* Destructive hurricanes are often perceived as windstorms, vicious weather systems that knock down trees and wreck coastal properties. That's frequently the case in places such as the Caribbean or South Florida and sometimes in the Carolinas. The Saffir-Simpson scale was created to help gauge how severe those windstorms might be. But high winds aren't the only worry. Tropical cyclones spinning into the midlatitudes often lose power as they pass over cooler waters, diminishing their top winds—yet they can still muster billions of dollars in property damage and claim multiple lives from rain-induced flooding. In the Carolinas, that's become a frequent scenario; Matthew and Florence were both low-category hurricanes that set records for rainfall, river flooding, and property destruction. Though we may be grateful when a hurricane weakens before it arrives, it doesn't mean the threat has ended—and each storm's rainfall potential is different.

- *Slow-moving hurricanes tracking along the coast pass through multiple lunar tide cycles.* For coastal communities, storm surge is a primary threat from any hurricane. The timing of a storm's approach becomes critically important, as arrival during a time of high tide adds considerably to the surge, whereas landfall at low tide reduces its impact. Forecasters usually emphasize this when issuing storm tide warnings, and coastal residents are wise to watch for this alignment. When a hurricane tracks slowly along the coast, such as Matthew's trek from Florida to the Carolinas, it moves through multiple tide cycles. If its forward pace is slow enough, coastal communities may experience the surge through more than one high-tide period—subjecting properties to increased flooding risk.

- *Public and private dams across the Carolinas pose serious risk when a rainmaker hurricane strikes.* Not all hurricanes produce history-making rains. Some are relatively "dry," causing limited freshwater flooding. Others, such as Matthew, pour drenching rains across broad inland areas, causing memorable floods. Among the threats state officials in the Carolinas monitor closely during "wet" hurricanes are large numbers of dams, both public and private, some of which are at risk of failure once heavy rains push their limits. Most are constructed of earth and are subject to erosion and degradation during heavy downpours. Once a dam breaches or fails, millions of gallons of stored water behind the dam rush downstream, potentially flooding neighborhoods and putting lives at risk. During the October 2015 floods in South Carolina, more than fifty dams failed, resulting in historic flooding damage in Richland and Lexington Counties. Twenty-five more dams failed in the state during Matthew, and at least seventeen breached in North Carolina. Officials in both states manage dam inspection programs, with each dam rated for its potential to do harm. "High hazard" dams understandably receive the most attention—they are those that pose a risk to life or property should they breach. Improvements in these inspection programs have been welcomed in recent years, but risks remain—and people living near high-hazard dams should be especially attentive.

- *Well-trained and well-equipped swift-water rescue teams have become essential lifesaving components of hurricane response in the Carolinas.* When floodwaters from Hurricane Floyd surprised residents across eastern

North Carolina in 1999, first responders performed remarkably. In places like Pinetops, Rocky Mount, and Chinquapin, door-to-door rescues were necessary to remove residents from submerged homes. In many cases rescues were launched by friends and neighbors who quickly gathered small fishing boats, farm tractors, and anything they could find to navigate flooded neighborhoods. Local fire departments, the state highway patrol, and sheriff's deputies were busy with rescues too, sometimes relying on borrowed boats and equipment. Thankfully, military resources were also heavily involved. It was one of the great lessons from Floyd, and since that time, federal, state, and local agencies in the Carolinas have dramatically improved water-rescue capabilities through investments in training and equipment. During Matthew and Florence, dozens of highly trained swift-water rescue teams were deployed across the Carolinas with great success, including teams from other states.

• *Emergency managers often face unexpected challenges—such as disaster mortuary services.* Seasoned emergency managers know to expect the un-expected: each hurricane disaster brings its own surprises. During Hurri-cane Floyd, when hundreds of caskets were disinterred by flooding, officials in North Carolina faced an issue they hadn't seen before. Adding to the challenge were the high emotions of family members whose loved ones had been unearthed. More caskets were tossed by floodwaters during Matthew and Florence. Identifying the remains for these can be an uneasy task, usually requiring DNA matching, since burials prior to the 1990s seldom included any identifying information on the caskets. Mortuary laws in North Carolina were adjusted after Floyd, including the elimination of ground-level vaults for new burials—the kind dislocated during Matthew.

• *Communications before, during, and after hurricanes continue to evolve, especially through the age of social media.* When Hurricane Hazel ap-proached the Carolinas in 1954, general warnings were issued for the southeast United States. Most coastal interests in the Carolinas got the message, though for some it came last-minute from friends and neighbors or through late-night phone calls. Today, hurricane forecasts are issued days in advance, followed by an avalanche of news coverage preceding every storm. Online news outlets, cable networks, local television affiliates, radio, and Facebook are some of the countless sources the public turns to for information. During a storm, high winds and flooding can knock out electricity and phone service, potentially threatening life safety. But once restored, our mobile phones are critical lifelines—for calls but also for internet access. Along with the regular public, state and local governments and news outlets now turn to social media to relay critical information amid the chaos of a hurricane disaster. Tweets have led to rescues, Facebook posts have detailed dam breaches, and overall, the public's access to timely information has never been better.

CHAPTER FIFTEEN

HURRICANE FLORENCE,
SEPTEMBER 2018

On October 18, 2016, less than two weeks after Hurricane Matthew socked the Carolinas with historic flooding, North Carolina governor Pat McCrory stood before reporters in the capitol to announce the formation of the Matthew Recovery Committee. The committee's charge was to raise funds for those in need, rebuild critical infrastructure as quickly as possible, assess the storm's impact on agriculture and other industries, develop plans for further legislative funding, and "implement a comprehensive strategy for how to rebuild towns and communities in a sustainable way." The governor was optimistic: "Rising waters can crumble our roads and flood our communities, but they cannot wash away our resilience or spirit to rebuild." He added that the committee's work would include evaluating where and whether to rebuild in some areas. He told the Raleigh *News and Observer,* "What I don't want to have is have this happen again."

Unfortunately, and all too quickly, it did. No blue-ribbon panel or government agency could have anticipated the arrival of another, even greater flood just two years later—one that set new records in the Carolinas for rainfall, river flooding, and destruction. This was Hurricane Florence.

In many ways, the Florence disaster was spun from Matthew's blueprint. Both were powerful hurricanes at sea that weakened to Category 1 intensity as they reached the Carolinas. They both were influenced by approaching fronts, causing them to shift their course and slow their pace. With some exceptions, neither is remembered for its extreme winds; instead they're remembered as crawling rain makers that pushed rivers to record levels, causing them to spill their banks and inundate communities across the coastal plain. Floodwaters covered interstate highways and rushed into areas never before known to flood. To varying degrees, the two storms largely affected the same river basins in eastern North Carolina and northeastern South Carolina, namely the Tar, Neuse, White Oak, Cape Fear, Lumber, and Yadkin–Pee Dee. Both hurricanes were slow-rolling disasters; in some areas they were at their worst under blue skies, days after the rains had ended. The two hurricanes, twenty-three months

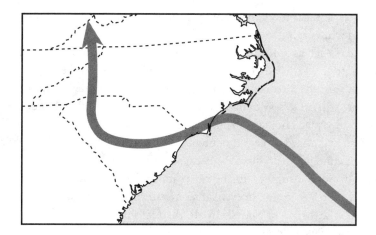

Robert Simmons Jr. escapes his flooded New Bern neighborhood with his kitten Survivor on September 14, 2018. This Raleigh *News and Observer* photo spread quickly on social media and helped convey to a national audience the anguish felt by victims of Hurricane Florence. (Photo by Andrew Carter. Courtesy of the Raleigh *News and Observer* / Associated Press.)

apart, tested the skill and endurance of first responders, many of whom were engaged in daring rescues and recoveries during both. Government agencies large and small were also tested, challenged to meet the overwhelming needs of the storms' victims. Together, Matthew and Florence effectively traumatized some of the Carolinas' most vulnerable communities, wrecked small-town economies, and left more than ninety dead in the two states—many of whom drowned while trying to drive on flooded roads.

In places such as Smithfield, Goldsboro, Kinston, Fayetteville, Lumberton, Wilmington, Myrtle Beach, and Conway, residents relived the nightmares of Matthew during Florence's extended visit. Across a broad region, Matthew repairs were still underway or had recently been completed when Florence came ashore. Sadly, many homes and businesses were damaged by both, forcing their owners to make hard choices about rebuilding or relocating. They brought devastating economic consequences, because many flooded properties were not covered by flood insurance during either storm. Florence was more than just a repeat of Matthew, it was an even larger disaster that compounded the myriad problems Matthew had caused. In all, the Carolinas suffered through three devastating years of flooding that began with the great South Carolina flood of 2015. Matthew and Florence followed soon after, and the three events each set new records and changed our understanding of natural disasters in the region.

Florence formed in a familiar spot for midseason storm development: the warm waters near the Cape Verde islands in the eastern Atlantic. It was identified as a tropical depression on August 31 and within twelve hours it was a named tropical storm. It slowly organized itself over a period of days, reaching hurricane status on September 4 some 1,200 miles east-northeast of the Lesser Antilles. Florence reached twenty-five degrees north latitude on the sixth, though it was still only halfway across the Atlantic (no other storm in history had ever moved so far north while so far at sea yet still made landfall on the U.S. East Coast). It was about this time that it began its first cycle of rapid intensification. The following day Florence reached Category 4 strength while still several days east-southeast of Bermuda. But strong southwesterly wind shear began tearing the hurricane down, knocking Florence back to tropical storm intensity by September 7. After briefly encountering a shortwave trough that bumped it toward the northwest, Florence set a westward course. The shear abated, and the storm quickly restrengthened, with sustained winds eventually gaining 60 mph in just twenty-four hours on September 10. An "exceptionally strong and long-lived" ridge of high pressure over the North Atlantic influenced the track.

Florence's rapid intensification and projected course captured everyone's attention along the mid-Atlantic coast. At 11:00 P.M. on September 8, the five-day forecast map from the National Hurricane Center (NHC) showed Florence making landfall somewhere in the Carolinas as a major hurricane. Over the next days, storm watchers from Hilton Head to Virginia Beach anxiously waited for tropical updates that offered ever-more-alarming news. Florence was strengthening, reaching peak intensity at 150 mph on September 11, some

725 miles east-southeast of Cape Fear. Confidence in the forecast track was increasing, and Florence appeared headed to the Cape Fear region, possibly as a Category 3 or 4 hurricane.

News media, government officials, businesses, and residents across the Carolinas' coastal counties went on high alert. Not only was Florence expected to possibly arrive as a powerful, Hazel- or Hugo-like storm, but its anticipated trajectory appeared to track well inland, with potential for heavy damage in cities and counties miles from the coast. Some could see a new "benchmark" disaster in the making. High surf was building along the beaches, though the storm was still days away. Rescue crews saved fifteen people from rough waters at Wrightsville Beach. Dare County issued a mandatory evacuation on September 10. The following day, classes were canceled at East Carolina University, North Carolina State University, and the University of North Carolina at Chapel Hill. South Carolina governor Henry McMaster ordered an evacuation of the state's entire coastline, which included the reversal of eastbound lanes of Interstate 26, boosting the flow of cars out of the Charleston area. North Carolina beach communities also prepared evacuation orders. Chief meteorologist Greg Fishel told his WRAL-TV viewers, "We haven't seen anything like that approaching the coast, assuming this is close to being correct, since Hazel. This is certainly going to make a stronger approach, in terms of wind speeds the way it looks now, than Fran did."

With Florence edging closer to the coast, preparations intensified. On September 11, North Carolina governor Roy Cooper stepped up his warnings with a first-ever state evacuation order for North Carolina's barrier islands (evacuation orders are normally the responsibility of local governments). He told the Associated Press, "This storm is a monster. It's big, and it's vicious. It is an extremely dangerous, life-threatening, historic hurricane. The waves and the wind this storm may bring are nothing like you've ever seen. Don't bet your life on riding out a monster."

By this time, disaster preparations were fully in motion. FEMA placed an operation center at Fort Bragg, where swift-water rescue teams were staged in anticipation of severe flooding. The Global TransPark in Kinston was another hub of activity, where relief supplies and crews were pre-positioned. Duke Energy announced that up to 20,000 line workers were preparing for "attack restoration" in anticipation of massive power disruptions. Anheuser-Busch and Miller-Coors shipped in 500,000 cans of water, and relief organizations such as the American Red Cross and Salvation Army prepped for feeding and shelter operations. The value of pre-staging personnel, equipment, and supplies is one of the great lessons learned from hurricanes past.

Meanwhile, forecasters closely watched their computer models and saw conditions that might weaken and slow the storm. NHC director Ken Graham warned that Florence was expected to weaken, slow down, and linger, potentially making it less like Hazel or Fran and more like Matthew. Some saw comparisons with 2017's Hurricane Harvey in Texas, which dumped a record-breaking sixty inches of rain in parts of the state and caused more than $100 billion in damages. University of Miami hurricane researcher Brian McNoldy described to the Associated Press how Florence was shaping up: "I think this is very Harvey-esque. Normally, a landfalling tropical cyclone just keeps on going inland, gradually dissipating and raining itself out. But on rare occasions, the steering patterns can line up such that the storm slips into a dead zone between troughs and ridges."

It's not uncommon for strong storms like Florence to fluctuate in intensity as they go through eyewall replacement cycles, which Florence did on the night of September 10. On the eleventh the storm was less well organized, but forecasters expected some restrengthening and were still anticipating landfall near Wilmington with at least Category 3 winds. Coupled with an expected stall upon landfall, Graham told the Associated Press on the morning of the twelfth, "this one really scares me. It's one of those situations where you're going to get heavy rain, catastrophic, life-threatening storm surge, and also the winds." The NHC increased its rainfall forecast to fifteen to twenty-five inches, with up to "35 inches in isolated locations." That ominous forecast, perhaps even more so than anticipated winds, caught the attention of most everyone across the Carolinas. And, since Florence was on a somewhat unusual path—heading toward the coast from the east instead of taking a more typical southerly approach—there was little likelihood that it could make a last-minute turn and curve safely out to sea. It was about this time that recording artist Jimmy Buffett posted a photo on Instagram of himself and a friend after a surfing session at Folly Beach, quoting his song, "I ain't afraid of dying. I got no need to explain. I feel like going surfing in a hurricane." He also added, "On a serious note—respect mother nature, please be safe and listen to your local authorities."

As the hours passed, Florence's winds gradually diminished and its forward speed slowed, as predicted. Residents from Charleston to Cape Hatteras watched to see where landfall would be. Nearly 1 million people had evacuated from coastal areas, including beachfront towns and communities with a history of river flooding such as Fayetteville, Lumberton, Kinston, and Princeville. Finally, at an excruciatingly slow pace, Florence made landfall near Wrightsville Beach around 8:00 A.M. on September 14, with 90 mph winds and a barometric pressure of 956 millibars (mb). From Wrightsville the storm center briefly drifted southwestward through Wilmington and then westward across Brunswick County, reaching the South Carolina border more than twelve hours later—a distance of only sixty-five miles. In another twelve hours, the center passed Conway. Florence, a lumbering giant of a storm, was drifting west and somewhat south at a pace equal to that of a brisk walk.

During this short journey it continued to weaken, even while pouring copious rains across much of the Carolinas. As it entered South Carolina it transitioned to a tropical storm, then a tropical depression. The storm center passed just south of Florence and tracked across the state, making a slow turn to the west-northwest, then north, and eventually northeast. The depression accelerated around the periphery of a narrow high-pressure system just east of the Outer Banks, causing it to curve over western North Carolina, eastern Tennessee, western Virginia, and eventually western West Virginia, where it became extratropical. It continued its northeasterly turn; remnants of the once-mighty storm finally dissipated over Massachusetts on September 18.

The weakening that Florence experienced before landfall came as a welcome relief for coastal storm watchers. Facing down a possible Category 3 or 4 hurricane just three days earlier was unnerving for many. Most had expected Florence to be a major hurricane upon arrival; after all, sea surface temperatures in this part of the Atlantic were running well above normal—about 2.7 degrees Fahrenheit above, which might have further stoked the storm. But forecasters had another theory. In addition to the eyewall replacement that occurred on the eleventh and caused some weakening, NHC forecasters determined that the above-normal sea surface temperatures were fairly shallow, which allowed cold water upwelling and mixing to deplete energy from the hurricane. By September 12, the storm's eye had grown to nearly thirty miles across, another sign of weakening. But much like during Matthew, these changes were coupled with the storm's expanded size. Though peak winds dropped considerably in the days and hours before landfall, the outer wind field grew larger, making Florence an oversized hurricane as it passed inland.

Florence will always be remembered in the Carolinas for its epic floods, brought on by days of relentless rains. But the hurricane's winds, storm surge, and embedded tornadoes also caused problems in many eastern and coastal communities. All the peak winds were recorded on September 14, the day of landfall. Some of the maximum gusts recorded included 106 mph at Cape Lookout, 105 mph at Fort Macon, 105 mph at the Wilmington airport, 105 mph in Southport, 100 mph in downtown Wilmington, 92 mph in Hampstead, 77 mph in Cherry Grove Beach, 69 mph in Lumberton, and 61 mph in Myrtle Beach. Unlike hurricanes that breeze through in just a few hours, Florence's crawling pace meant these communities were pounded by high winds for extended periods—compounding the damage to structures, signs, trees, and power lines. The heaviest wind damages were found from Cape Lookout south, across Carteret, Onslow, Pender, New Hanover, Brunswick, and Columbus Counties in North Carolina and Horry County in South Carolina. As would be expected from near–100 mph gusts, thousands of trees fell across the region, snarling power lines and blocking countless streets and highways.

Tides associated with Florence's arrival on the North Carolina coast were most extreme not on the ocean beach but along the southern and western shores of Pamlico Sound and the banks of the Neuse River and its tributaries. Relentless easterly winds piled water into the area, effectively blocking the normal flow of the Neuse and sending destructive floodwaters into New Bern. National Weather Service reports described the highest storm surge levels as nine to thirteen feet. U.S. Geological Survey (USGS) storm tide pressure sensors deployed in the Neuse at New Bern recorded a peak of 10.4 feet above mean higher high water (MHHW). This storm tide combined with extreme rainfall in the area to devastate New Bern and surrounding communities with some of the worst flooding in the city's long history. Along other parts of the river and nearby communities on Pamlico Sound, maximum storm surge inundations ranged from eight to eleven feet above ground level. Many portions of Pamlico, Hyde, and Beaufort Counties experienced this flooding tide. Other storm tide measurements were recorded by the USGS, including at Johnnie Mercer Pier at Wrightsville Beach, 7.4 feet above MHHW; Emerald Isle on Bogue Sound, 7.0 feet above MHHW; and Beaufort, 3.8 feet above MHHW. In South Carolina, the highest storm tide reading was 3.8 feet above MHHW on the Waccamaw River at Murrell's Inlet. The National Weather Service noted that storm surge measuring over four feet eroded beaches and damaged property between Cape Lookout and Cape Fear. Because of the storm's slow movement along the coast during and after landfall, higher-than-normal tides were experienced on the beaches, rivers, and sounds over several lunar tide cycles.

Tornadoes are always a potential threat during hurricanes. Florence produced a lot of tornadic activity that was carefully tracked and evaluated by the National Weather Service. Over the period of September 13–17, forty-four tornadoes touched down in three states. Most were classified as EF0, the minimum rating on the Enhanced Fujita scale, the measurement used to rate tornado wind speeds and resulting damage. These EF0 twisters had winds of 65–85 mph, strong enough to knock down some trees and cause minor damages. Sixteen EF1 tornadoes were reported, whose wind speeds were likely in the 86–110 mph range. Among these were a tornado in Pender County on the fifteenth that passed over an occupied mobile home, briefly lifting it off the ground; a tornado in Columbus County on the sixteenth that tore away roofs and snapped more than forty eighteen-inch pine trees above the ground; a tornado on the same day that carved a fifty-foot-wide path near Elliot Place in New Hanover County, snapping about twenty eighteen-inch trees; and another tornado in Wilmington that touched down and caused significant tree damage near the Forest Hills community, the same area that had experienced heavy tree damage during the passage of the eyewall two days before. In all, the Weather Service recorded twenty-seven tornadoes in North Carolina, six in South Carolina, and eleven in Virginia. The most severe was the only EF2 (111–135 mph winds) observed during Florence. It touched down in Chesterfield County, Virginia, just south of Richmond, on September 17. This twister turned deadly after overturning cars, ripping away roofs, and downing power lines—it caused the collapse of a commercial building, where one deceased victim was later found.

During Florence's four-day visit to the Carolinas, the destruction caused by scattered twisters, fierce winds, and extreme tides began to accumulate. But unfortunately the disaster was better defined by the broadscale, record flooding that followed the storm's unprecedented rainfall. More than ten inches fell over a broad region, with totals exceeding twenty inches measured in numerous locations from near the North Carolina–South Carolina border eastward across southeastern North Carolina.

Tropical cyclone rainfall records for any given location are often shown in one of two ways: twenty-four-hour rainfall total or total rainfall over the duration of the storm event. Because the drenching rains from Florence fell over a period of days, the latter provides a better measure of the hurricane's impact. With the storm's slow movement after landfall, rainbands moved inland and "trained" over a narrow swath roughly from Wrightsville Beach to Elizabethtown. It was along this stretch that accumulations of more than thirty inches occurred. A new North Carolina tropical cyclone rainfall record was set near Elizabethtown, where 35.93 inches were recorded. This surpassed the previous record of 24.06 inches set in Southport during Hurricane Floyd. Similarly, a new South Carolina accumulation record was set at Loris: 23.68 inches. This total surpassed the previous tropical cyclone record of 17.45 inches set near Lake Jocassee during Tropical Storm Beryl in 1994.

Some of the highest storm-total accumulations were recorded in North Carolina in Elizabethtown (35.93 inches), Swansboro (34.15), Gurganus (31.58), Jacksonville (30.65), Wilmington (30.18), Hoffman Forest (29.63), Hampstead (29.52), Oak Island (26.98), and Whiteville (25.91), and in South Carolina in Loris (23.68), Cheraw (23.21), and Marion (19.56).

As Florence began to churn over southeastern North Carolina, everyone could see that the storm's steady downpours were going to be trouble. Flood-weary residents in communities that had suffered through Matthew knew that river levels would rise and more destructive floods were inevitable. As the hurricane spun toward South Carolina, updated forecasts for rainfall totals were shockingly high. In Lumberton, *Robesonian* editor Donnie Douglas told the Associated Press, "People are tired. I'm tired. Our community has gotten swatted around. . . . The county collectively is traumatized by what happened, and what might be happening again. I guess we need to build an ark." Even with fresh memories of Matthew's floods on their minds, many in the hardest-hit areas were shocked at the extent of Florence's flooding. It was a common refrain heard from residents: "How could we have two 500-year floods in two years?"

Flooding problems began right away and escalated in the days following landfall. Much like with Matthew, the flooding was focused in south central North Carolina and northeastern South Carolina, again targeting the Tar, Neuse, White Oak, Cape Fear, Lumber, and Pee Dee River basins. The USGS, in cooperation with the National Weather Service, carefully monitored and reported rivergage levels and issued forecasts that provided vulnerable communities with a timeline for flood peaks. The USGS monitors nearly 500 streamgages across the two states, eighty-four of which counted flood peaks from Florence among their top five events of record. According to the USGS, Florence produced thirty-three new record river peaks across the region, including twenty-two in North Carolina and eleven in South Carolina. In many locations, records set during Matthew were surpassed. USGS hydrologist Toby Feaster concluded in his summary report for Florence, "Since several of the streamgage sites we analyzed had more than 30 years of historical data associated with them, it was interesting that a majority of the number one and number two records were from back-to-back flooding events." Among the new records: The Waccamaw River in Freeland, North Carolina, set a new peak record on September 19, with water levels at 22.61 feet, the highest at that location since at least 1940. In South Carolina, the Little Pee Dee River in Galivants Ferry set a new peak record on September 21, one week after landfall, at 17.21 feet. This was the highest measurement there since record keeping began in 1943 and, according to an NHC report, is likely the highest there since at least 1928.

In addition to recording peak flood levels, these gages also measured stream-flow rates—the volume of water moving past a fixed point. Not unexpectedly, Florence established new records for streamflow too. Record-setting stream-flows were measured at twenty-eight locations in the Carolinas: eighteen in North Carolina and ten in South Carolina. In the weeks following the flooding, dozens of USGS personnel fanned out across the disaster zone to document high-water marks and verify their gage measurements. These water marks—thin lines of mud and debris left on buildings and structures—provided verifiable evidence of peak flooding levels.

As the hurricane struck the Tar Heel coast and slowly crept into South Carolina, floodwaters chased residents from their homes while property damages from winds, tides, and tornadoes began to pile up. Some described Florence as a slow-motion disaster, with some locations slammed on Friday and in recovery by Sunday while others were hit hardest on the following Tuesday and Wednesday. No one community bore the brunt of destruction; each affected city and town faced its own challenges. Because of their size and proximity to landfall, Wilmington and Wrightsville Beach were initially the focus for much of the national media attention as the hurricane raged.

At the Wilmington International Airport, a 105 mph wind gust was the second-highest ever recorded at that location (a 135 mph gust was measured there during Hurricane Helene in 1958). Florence's winds were relentless, taking a toll on Wilmington's trees and power lines to an extent not seen there since Fran in 1996. Maneuvering on city streets quickly became treacherous, not only because of flash flooding, downed trees, and dangling power lines but also due to the large number of intersections without working stoplights. More than 150 roads in the city were closed. At its peak, flash flooding put three feet of water into homes in the Northchase neighborhood. In the Wrightsboro and Ogden communities, 350 water rescues were performed on September 14 and 15.

Along the Wilmington riverfront, waters from the Cape Fear River covered docks and poured into streets and parking lots, putting Water Street two feet under. A peak tide measurement of 3.60 feet above MHHW was recorded there on September 14, setting a new record for that location and eclipsing the all-time record set during Matthew by less than an inch. Once upstream flooding worked its way downriver, a second Cape Fear River peak was recorded in Wilmington just two days later, measuring 2.65 feet above MHHW, good enough to make the top ten peak levels for that location. (Surprisingly, flooding associated with Category 1 Hurricane Isaias in 2020 established a new river crest record for Wilmington at 4.35 above MHHW.)

As the hours and days passed, Wilmington "became an island," largely cut off from the outside world. Flooding blocked major roadways into the city, and power and internet outages kept many residents in the dark. There was a bit of chaos when one Harris Teeter grocery store on South College Road found a way to reopen on the fifteenth after electricity was briefly restored over a two-block area. A mob of 500 storm-weary customers rushed the store—seizing on their first opportunity to resupply in days. Overall, food, water, ice, and fuel were hard to find. New Hanover County officials announced on September 16 that food and water would be flown into the city but that some distribution centers would need to be moved because of the lack of access. The city's water plant nearly exhausted its supply of generator fuel, threatening a shutdown, but additional fuel was located just in time. It took ten days before electric power was fully restored in Wilmington.

On September 18, four days after landfall, twenty trucks arrived from Fort Bragg delivering meals ready to eat, water, and tarps. By this time some two-lane roads into the city had reopened, but access was again blocked when state officials closed U.S. 421 at the New Hanover–Pender county line. On September 20 state officials announced, "There is not a safe, stable, reliable route for the public to get to and from Wilmington."

Damages around the city were staggering. Stately oaks were split and broken, some with massive limbs leaning into houses or crushing cars. City officials estimated that 1.2 million cubic yards of vegetative debris required hauling and disposal. At least two commercial buildings in the downtown area lost their roofs. The roof of the Bellamy Mansion Museum peeled away, and heavy water damages occurred when rains poured through to the basement. Other antebellum homes near downtown suffered similar water intrusion. Around the city, some described the wind damage as worse than that of Hurricanes Diana (1984), Fran, or Floyd. Gas station canopies toppled, fences and signs were downed, and virtually every New Hanover County public school suffered some combination of wind and water damage. The University of North Carolina Wilmington was hit hard by the storm, with more than $140 million in reported damages to buildings, grounds, and vehicles. Among the biggest losses was a large science building, Dobo Hall, which lost part of its roof and was flooded by nearly thirty inches of water. Seventeen other university buildings suffered significant damages, including thirteen apartment buildings so badly damaged they were later demolished. The hurricane toppled so many trees across campus that even basic access to roads and buildings was impossible. A report was later issued on the storm: "The university has weathered many storms before, but it has never suffered the extent of damage that hurricane Florence wrought."

Even when roofs remained intact, Florence's continuous blowing rains seeped into homes and businesses through walls, windows, doors, vents, and chimneys. Many residents described how wind-driven water had found a way to permeate their exterior siding and damage interior wallboard. For these homeowners, it was an insidious and unexpected disaster—water intrusion was often not evident until weeks had passed, when mold began to grow. Accumulating rains also gushed into garages and crawl spaces, damaging subfloor insulation, ductwork, and electrical systems. Leaking roofs were a common problem too, even for critical workers in fire departments, city offices, and medical facilities.

Reporters for the Wilmington *Star-News* had always thought of their concrete building on South Seventeenth Street as an impenetrable fortress, ready for any storm—until Florence. Initially, roof leaks in the building were captured in trash cans. But as the rains continued, ceiling tiles collapsed, putting staff and their computers and other electronic equipment at risk. Then, as the hurricane's eye passed over Wilmington, the newspaper's three large generators stopped working. Fortunately, the *Star-News* team got some help from their friends at WWAY-TV and a local Hampton Inn, where reporters were able to relocate with their computers and continue publishing news updates from the storm. Editors took the matter seriously: "We've had a weighty legacy to maintain: The *Star-News* is the oldest daily newspaper in continuous publication in North Carolina. Since 1867, nothing has stopped us from publishing."

Florence's impact was widespread, and reports of damages continued to pile up over a period of days. Among the calamities, officials estimated that over 22 million gallons of untreated sewage overflowed into area waterways. Duke Energy also reported that a coal ash storage pond at a decommissioned coal plant was overtopped, spilling about 2,000 cubic yards of toxic ash—enough to fill about two-thirds of an Olympic-size swimming pool. An earthen dam at Sutton Lake breached in several locations, draining the lake into the Cape Fear River and shutting down Duke's natural-gas power plant, which relied on the lake water for cooling. As had occurred after Hurricane Matthew, Duke Energy officials, environmental groups, and regulators later examined the impact of the breaches and quarreled over any potential harm to the environment.

As Florence moved onshore, its slow drift southwest meant that beachfront communities had to endure several flooding high-tide cycles. On Carolina and Kure Beaches, heavy beach erosion cut ten-foot escarpments into the dunes. Kure Beach Pier suffered only minor damages. On the north end of Masonboro Island, large waves washed away about twenty feet of dunes. On Wrightsville Beach, erosion and overwash were considered minor, though numerous pricey beach homes and condominiums suffered significant water damages from wind-driven rain. Sliding-glass doors were particularly vulnerable.

Up the coast on Topsail Island, the impact was mixed. Some streets in Surf City were covered by several feet of sand, and about three-fourths of the town's homes suffered minor damages. In the town of Topsail Beach, erosion was not as severe, and property damages were lighter than expected. Topsail Beach mayor Howard Braxton was relieved, given Florence's size and power and the media attention it had received. He told the Wilmington *Star-News*, "People expected their homes to be completely washed away."

Mainland Pender County, however, was not so fortunate. In describing the impact there, the National Weather Service said Florence was "the worst flooding event in local history." Hundreds were rescued from swamped neighborhoods on September 14 and 15 during the initial flash floods. After a few more days, as rivers approached record levels, an even larger-scale rescue effort was launched—one of the largest in North Carolina history. On September 19, the Northeast Cape Fear River crested at 25.57 feet at Burgaw, setting a new all-time record and exceeding the crest from Hurricane Floyd by more than three feet. A fourteen-bed mobile hospital was set up in a parking lot after Pender Memorial Hospital was flooded and evacuated. Many homes and businesses outside of the 500-year floodplain were inundated with three to four feet of water. Over 1,000 additional residents had to be rescued by boat, helicopter, and military Humvee. Pender County sheriff Carson Smith announced that anyone needing evacuation should call 911 and "be prepared to wave a towel or flashlight or set off a flare to signal an approaching helicopter." He told the *Star-News*, "You've got to hang on a little bit longer. We're going to get through this."

Pender County residents who remembered Floyd were shocked and saddened to realize that Florence's floods would be far greater. N.C. 53 was covered by seven feet of water. Portions of Interstate 40 resembled a wide river, and a 300-foot section of U.S. 421 was washed out near the New Hanover County line. The swollen Cape Fear River caused water to back up in Black River and Moores Creek, sending waist-deep floodwaters into the communities of Currie and Canetuck, where more rescues took place. The town of Atkinson was also badly flooded and isolated by submerged roads. Officials at nearby Moores Creek National Battlefield said floodwaters there were two to three feet higher than during Matthew or Floyd. Pender County Emergency Management later reported that there were 3,882 flood-damaged structures across the county, ninety-six of which were completely lost. Total property damages were estimated at $270 million.

Warning coordination meteorologist Steve Pfaff from the National Weather Service's Wilmington office described his encounter while doing survey work in western Pender County a week after Florence's landfall: "There's an individual there who told me, 'I don't know what to do.' His aunt was buried sixteen years ago and her casket had floated up, so he was dealing with that. Then he told me how he had just finished, two weeks before Florence, fixing all the damage to his home from Matthew. Two weeks before. And then he lost everything again."

As floodwaters finally receded along Interstate 40 on September 22, firefighters near Wallace found themselves performing a bizarre task: using their fire hoses to wash away thousands of dead fish left behind on the highway. Days before, boats were navigating this stretch of the interstate in waters several feet deep. Local officials at first were perplexed. Samantha Hardison, a volunteer firefighter with the Penderlea Fire Department, told the *Washington Post*, "When the chief got the call, he was like: 'Wait, are you serious? You're kidding, right?'" Her Facebook post, which included photos of countless dead fish on the roadway, added, "Well, we can add 'washing fish off of the interstate' to the long list of interesting things firefighters get to experience!"

Just south of landfall but well within reach of Florence's heaviest rainbands, Brunswick County was also swamped by the storm. Widespread flash flooding on September 14 and 15 struck about thirty homes in the Stoney Creek neighborhood. Some of the most dramatic scenes were near N.C. 133 in Boiling Springs Lakes, where Sanford Dam breached on the evening of the fifteenth, spilling water from Patricia Lake, North Lake, and Pine Lake across the roadway, washing out bridges and sections of pavement. Other bridges along N.C. 133 and N.C. 87 were also damaged. In Southport, fallen trees damaged homes and businesses while floodwaters washed out portions of Moore Street, Willis Drive, and West Eleventh Street. By September 17, as the flooding continued, Brunswick County was divided into three separate "islands." Though power had been restored in some areas and skies were beginning to clear, city and county officials had their hands full with dangerous highway conditions and a public anxious to travel in to check on homes and boats.

On the Brunswick beaches, winds knocked down trees and whisked away shingles and siding, but overall damages were relatively light. Beach erosion was modest thanks in part to protective sand dunes that had been rebuilt following Matthew. At Bald Head Island, erosion was more severe, as was roof and awning damage on several large homes. Riverside flooding on the island extended for days after landfall as the bulging Cape Fear pushed destructive tides into marshes and the village harbor. Downed trees blocked the island's canopied roads; local officials reported that the amount of storm debris requiring removal was the greatest in the town's history. Electricity on the island was out for two weeks.

In Jacksonville, well north of the storm's Wrightsville Beach landfall, flash floods and destructive winds made Florence among the city's most memorable hurricanes. Downed trees blocked city streets and tangled power lines, and at least one Onslow County family had to be rescued when a large tree fell through the roof of their home. In the hours just before the hurricane reached the coast, about seventy people, including infants and children, as well as some pets were evacuated by emergency workers from a collapsing hotel. Police and fire personnel forced their way into some rooms of the Triangle Motor Inn after its roof was compromised and parts of the structure crumbled. Hours later, flash floods struck low areas of the city, prompting the rescue of more than three dozen residents from homes and apartments. Officials put out a call for volunteers with flat-bottomed boats to assist the city's water rescue team. The flooding caught motorists by surprise. Thirteen occupants in two vehicles were later hoisted to safety from flooded county roads by a helicopter crew called in from Coast Guard Air Station Elizabeth City.

In Carteret County, Newport received nineteen inches of rain in a twenty-four-hour period during landfall on the fourteenth. The floods came so quickly that many became trapped in their homes in waist-deep water. Residents said the water rose several feet in under an hour. The Newport Fire Department joined with units of the National Guard to complete about 400 water rescues. Assistant chief James Ainsworth told the *Asheville Citizen-Times*, "As far as I know, there has never been flooding like this in Newport. It was overwhelming, but we just got to work and didn't think about it." Most of those rescued were taken to a shelter at Newport Middle School. One volunteer group launched a rescue operation after the Carteret County Humane Society put out a call for help on Facebook. Staff were trapped on the second floor of their Hibbs Road shelter. A group known as the "Cajun Navy" mobilized in small boats to rescue all shelter inhabitants, including two workers, forty-three dogs, eighty cats, and fifteen chickens.

New Bern was another city to feel Florence's early wrath. As the hurricane approached the coast, continuous easterly winds blew across Pamlico Sound, creating wind-driven storm tides that pushed floodwaters from the Neuse River into city streets. Drenching rains added to the flood levels throughout town. New Bern had seen floods before, but longtime residents were adamant that Florence was "the worst in memory." While broadcasting live hurricane coverage the night before landfall, WCTI-TV news anchors and crew learned they had to evacuate their television studios as floodwaters crept inside. Meteorologist Donnie Cox remained on air at first, interpreting the latest radar loops even as water began to cover the floor. But as the water continued to rise, he, too, evacuated and the broadcast switched over to a Myrtle Beach affiliate. This was the first time the Glenburnie Drive studios had flooded since they

Mike Morgan pilots a boat through the flooded town of Pollocksville on September 18, 2018, days after the arrival of Hurricane Florence. (Photo by Gray Whitley. Courtesy of the USA Today Network.)

A North Carolina National Guard Humvee maneuvers through a flooded neighborhood in Beulaville on September 15, 2018. Military assets played a key role in Hurricane Florence response and recovery, just as they have with other hurricanes in the Carolinas. (Photo courtesy of the North Carolina National Guard.)

were built in the late 1950s. Just after midnight, the station tweeted that all employees were safe: "Little rough but we're all out."

Severe flooding struck dozens of New Bern homes and apartments that night, trapping frantic residents in darkened second-floor rooms and attics. Water was ten feet deep in some places. The swollen Neuse and Trent Rivers remained blocked by Florence's surge, sending floodwaters into neatly renovated historic homes as well as nearby public housing. Emergency calls poured into the 911 call center, and at 2:30 A.M. on the fourteenth the city tweeted, "WE ARE COMING TO GET YOU. You may need to move up to the second story, or to your attic, but WE ARE COMING TO GET YOU." About 200 residents were pulled to safety before dawn the next day. Rescue teams stayed busy through the morning, removing another 160 residents from second-floor windows, attics, and rooftops. Calls continued to pour in from families needing help, but some turned to social media. One woman tweeted, "If anybody could help . . . our cars is under water and so is our house. Stuck in attic. Phone about to die please send help to 611 Watson ave, new bern. NC." Friends later confirmed that the woman and her family were safely rescued.

As with most hurricane disasters, national media outlets sent correspondents to the Carolinas for Florence's arrival. Among them was a reporter for the *New York Times* who wrote about the scene in New Bern: "'As long as it doesn't come up to the second floor, we'll be fine,' said Cynthia Diraimondo, who had left her steadily flooding one-story home Thursday afternoon to join two families in a two-story dwelling up the street. The water level rose inside the house overnight, reaching about 7 feet. It receded a bit by morning, she said, but she knew it would come back again."

On the morning of September 14, just as the hurricane was pushing inland over Wilmington, New Bern resident Robert Simmons was in a boat, fleeing the flooded home where he had spent a stressful night. He told the Raleigh *News and Observer*, "We done been through Bertha, Fran, Irene, Matthew. . . . And this is the worst it's ever been, is this part right here." Cuddled in the hood of his jacket was his kitten, which he named Survivor. When the *News and Observer* published the photo of a storm-drenched Simmons and his companion, it instantly became an iconic image for Florence, likely seen around the world as a reflection of the struggles underway in eastern Carolina.

After the storm passed and the tides receded, New Bern residents faced a long and difficult recovery. Mayor Dana Outlaw told reporters that at least 4,200 homes and 300 businesses sustained damages, and 1,200 residents had been forced into shelters. On September 18, President Donald Trump joined Governor Cooper at New Bern's Temple Baptist Church, where they helped

distribute hot meals to a crowd of storm-weary residents. During a short brief-
ing on recovery efforts, Trump thanked the governor and first responders, telling the group, "Whatever we have to do at the federal level, we will be there,
and you know that 100 percent."

As the days passed, residents returned to their flooded homes and went to
work removing wet carpeting, ruined furnishings, and cherished keepsakes.
Piles of debris lined the roadsides in many neighborhoods. One storm victim,
Shirley Jones, was profiled on Facebook Live by WCTI-TV reporters as she
stood next to a pile of soggy furniture and trashed belongings from her Second Avenue home. Emerald Isle resident Roy Brownlow saw the interview and
contacted the station with an offer to help. A meeting was arranged, during
which Brownlow offered to restore Jones's antique dresser. Some weeks later,
he returned with the finished piece to the delight of the owner. Brownlow told
the reporter, "I'm not a professional by any means, something I do on the side,
and I thought I can help out in this opportunity." Jones was delighted: "You
just don't know that used to be my grandmother's and I thought it was lost and
they came and fixed it. Thank you, Jesus, they came and fixed it."

Flooding hit other nearby communities in similar fashion. Video posted online the night of the thirteenth showed storm waves splashing on the windows
of a house in Belhaven. In Beaufort County, North Carolina, some 300 people
were rescued from flooded homes. Docks and seawalls along the southern
banks of the Neuse and the western reaches of Pamlico Sound were pounded
by waves and badly damaged or destroyed. Pamlico County suffered extensive waterfront damage, with at least three vessels sunk. Mostly rural Jones
County suffered too, with two public schools badly flooded and later deemed
unrepairable; a new state-of-the-art school to replace them was completed in
2019. Trenton was hit hard by record flooding on the Trent River, inundating
the Jones County courthouse and jail along with 106 homes—all but twenty of
the town's households. As Florence arrived, emergency crews sprang into action
rescuing those trapped by fast-rising floodwaters.

State officials at the emergency operations center in Raleigh monitored the
storm closely and used the Flood Inundation Mapping and Alert Network to
help them make decisions about moving resources and issuing evacuations. The
online system, accessible by the public, uses updated weather data and rivergage information to predict when and where flooding poses the greatest threat.
They knew Florence's initial flash flooding on the thirteenth, fourteenth, and
fifteenth, some of which was influenced by storm surge near the coast, would
abate and be followed by major river basin flooding. On the fifteenth, John
Dorman, assistant director of North Carolina Emergency Management, told

WRAL News, "Even though this storm is dropping down into South Carolina, Charlotte and the western part of the state are going to experience some significant flooding as well. This is a statewide event."

Upstream from New Bern, flooding along the Neuse had been expected, given the hurricane's slow drift overland and the weather service's ominous rainfall forecasts. Residents from Smithfield to Goldsboro and Kinston were disheartened at the prospect of a Matthew replay. Overall, Florence's peak high water along the upper Neuse turned out to be somewhat less extreme but still presented dangerous conditions for motorists and caused heartbreaking losses for those whose homes and businesses were flooded. Florence's peak floods in these areas arrived days after the inundation of New Bern. In Goldsboro, the Neuse crested at 27.60 feet on September 19, more than two feet below the record mark set during Matthew and one foot below the peak during Floyd. In Kinston, the Neuse peaked at 25.78 feet on the twenty-first, two and a half feet lower than the record set during Matthew and almost two feet below the highest water in Floyd—but still high enough to flood U.S. 70 and cause widespread destruction.

Goldsboro received about fifteen inches of rain with Florence, and the Neuse lingered above the eighteen-foot flood stage there for nearly a week. Floodwaters spilled into streets and neighborhoods that had seen high water before and seemed to stay there. After initial flash floods had subsided, most everyone knew a second round of water would come with the river crest. Volunteer firemen went door to door in vulnerable neighborhoods urging residents to evacuate, handing out flyers that compared Florence with Matthew. Some left; others decided to stay. When the river crested on the nineteenth, flooding disinterred a small number of caskets at Elmwood Cemetery. Businesses with sandbagged doorways struggled to keep the water out. Two people were rescued after they drove their vehicle onto a flood-covered road near Grantham. They escaped their vehicle and attempted to swim away and were later found hanging on to trees. Two tornadoes were confirmed in the area too, one that caused damage near Elm City and another that touched down near Goldsboro at 6:00 A.M. on the seventeenth.

Downriver in Kinston, the high water peaked two days later on the twenty-first. Residents used the advance notice to their advantage. They watched and waited, some making what preparations they could—sandbagging doorways and moving personal items to higher floors. Along the U.S. 70 corridor, businesses such as Neuse Sport Shop started preparations early to move merchandise off the floor or out of the store, readying for the inevitable flood. Owner Russell Rhodes had been through it all before with Floyd and Matthew. At its

North Carolina governor Roy Cooper meets with state and local officials in Wilmington to coordinate response efforts for Hurricane Florence. (Photo by Sgt. Wayne Becton. Courtesy of the North Carolina National Guard.)

peak, Florence put about two feet of water inside, considerably less than the thirty-three inches during Matthew but still enough to require a monumental cleanup. Once the floodwaters receded, his team was prepared to squeegee the remaining "Neuse juice" out of his 74,000-square-foot store, dry the floors and walls, and then restock. Rhodes told *Our State* magazine the total effort cost about $1 million in manpower, trucking costs, employee wages, and lost sales. Amazingly, the store was open to the public again in a few short weeks.

As the river rose, roads in many parts of Lenoir County were covered and impassable, especially on the south side of the river. U.S. 70, the main thoroughfare from Raleigh to Morehead City, was covered for several days. Seven Springs had been devastated by Matthew and was still trying to rebuild when Florence again chased people from their homes and caused more damage. All through the region, the muffled whir of helicopters could be heard in the distance. National Guard choppers ran regular missions along the river using infrared cameras to detect the body heat of stranded victims. State officials later reported that through this period, 3,000 members of the National Guard assisted 1,000 search-and-rescue personnel across the state, using thirty-six helicopters and over 200 boats to rescue victims of the flood.

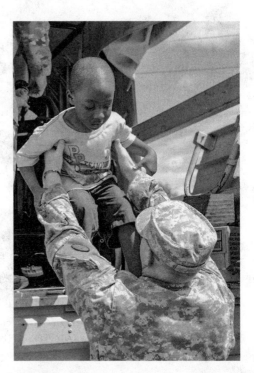

Soldiers of the 252nd Armored Regiment and the 230th Brigade Support Battalion shuttle adults, children, and their pets across high water on U.S. 17 between Wilmington and Bolivia on September 18, 2018. (Photo by Sgt. Odaliska Almonte. Courtesy of the North Carolina National Guard.)

A resident assesses the damage from a road washout in Boiling Spring Lakes, North Carolina, after Hurricane Florence. The Brunswick County community, known for its fifty spring-fed lakes, was transformed when its Sanford Dam failed during the storm, causing a chain reaction of other dam failures that emptied its lakes. Rebuilding the dams and reestablishing the lakes would take years. (Photo courtesy of the North Carolina National Guard.)

Florence's incessant rains caused problems in the Triangle area too, as did whipping winds as the storm tracked well to the south. Not surprisingly, power outages were widespread, hampering traffic where stoplights were out. The City of Raleigh posted photos of huge downed trees at Dix Park and at the Rose Garden near Cameron Village. Johnston County's sewage system was overwhelmed by heavy rains, causing a spill of more than 100,000 gallons of untreated wastewater into a tributary of the Neuse. Flash flooding in Durham and Chapel Hill covered busy streets and highways, shutting down traffic and stranding motorists. On the seventeenth, emergency teams evacuated Chapel Hill residents from Camelot Village, Brookwood Apartments, Airport Gardens, Booker Creek Apartments, and Ridgefield Apartments. Eastgate Shopping Center was flooded too, as business owners said the water rose at "an astounding rate." In Durham, the Eno River rose well above its banks, flooding nearby communities and forcing more evacuations. Fire department personnel, using trucks and small boats, went door to door evacuating residents in the Old Farm, River Forest, and Old Well neighborhoods. GoDurham buses transported people from flooded homes and apartments. Flooding forced the closure of Interstate 85 near Cole Mill Road.

One Durham business owner had an idea to help boost the rescue efforts. Boat dealer Branden Patrick, owner of N.C. Marine, contacted one of his suppliers—Lowe Boats out of Lebanon, Missouri—to see if it might provide some loaners to help North Carolina fire departments complete water rescues. Instead of providing loaners, Lowe delivered five new small boats with motors and trailers, valued at $55,000. They were distributed to fire departments in White Lake, Laurinburg, and Newport, and one was donated to the North Carolina Baptist Men. White Lake fire chief Dale Brennan called the donation a "morale booster" after his crews put in long hours rescuing flood victims from the Kelly and Rowan communities. He told *Bladen Online*, "We still know there are people down there, and we're going to get them."

Heavy, enduring rains put fire departments on alert across numerous counties. In Harnett County, flooding on the Lower Little River near the Cumberland County line closed roads and forced evacuations on the fifteenth. Emergency workers went door to door urging vulnerable residents to relocate to a shelter in Lillington. A pregnant woman, her husband, and her one-year-old were all rescued from the roof of their car when they were swept into deep water on Autry Road. In Hoke County, west of Fayetteville, flash floods closed roads while a dam failure prompted more evacuations downstream. County officials asked for assistance from Fort Bragg to remove people from neighborhoods below McLaughlin Lake. Fire crews rescued several people from flooded homes in Randolph County, as well as the occupants of three vehicles that became overwhelmed by floodwaters from the surging Deep River. Tragically, flooding as far west as Union and Anson Counties became deadly once rains pushed the Rocky and Pee Dee Rivers beyond their banks. In Union County, two storm-related fatalities were recorded: a one-year-old boy drowned after his mother drove around a barricade and into deep floodwaters (the mother was later charged), and an eighty-eight-year-old man drowned when he drove his vehicle into a flooded creek. In nearby Anson County, a passenger drowned in a car that plunged into a roadway washout. Anson County was also the scene of a storm-related train derailment on the sixteenth. Heavy rains washed out portions of track near U.S. 74 in Lilesville, tossing three CSX engines onto their sides and upending several railcars. The conductors were transported to a local hospital with minor injuries.

In Scotland County, a mandatory evacuation was ordered for neighborhoods below two vulnerable dams. The dam at Richmond Hill Pond did breach on the seventeenth, lifting floodwaters up to U.S. 74—one of many roads in the area closed due to high water. Flooding washed out a section of Main Street in Laurinburg, undermining walls and damaging several businesses. At one point, the county's 911 call center was overwhelmed with urgent calls for help. Over a two-day period, there were nearly 250 water rescues, yet fewer than five had been reported in the county in the previous thirty years. One fatality was reported: a swift-water team from Raleigh recovered the body of a man who was believed to have drowned when his car was washed off a county road.

As with Matthew, some of Florence's worst flooding occurred in the Cape Fear River basin, on the Deep, Little, South, Black, Northeast Cape Fear, and Cape Fear Rivers as they wind their way from the Sandhills region and south central plains toward the coast. On the fifteenth, while rains continued to pour across the Carolinas, Cumberland County officials ordered evacuations for about 7,500 residents living within a mile of the Cape Fear and Little Rivers. By midmorning, flooding had forced the highway patrol to close northbound and southbound lanes of Interstate 95 from Fayetteville to Dunn. At one time or another over the span of a week, over ninety miles of the heavily traveled north–south route were shut down in North Carolina. Another twenty or so miles of the interstate were closed in South Carolina, though not all at the same time.

Near the Cumberland-Harnett county line, the swollen Little River spilled into homes and covered primary roads. As the river rose, Erwin homeowner Kurt Reed watched as floodwaters slowly inched past his outbuildings and toward his house. He told WRAL News, "This is unbelievable compared to

Matthew. It's been a creeping death." Nearby, homeowner Angie Wood had a similar experience. After watching the rising river swallow up her yard, barn, and home, she told reporters, "You know it's coming, but you don't know how bad and you don't know how fast. . . . And you can't stop it. When they said higher than Matthew, we still never anticipated this."

Dam failures in this region were a worry again too, just as they had been with Matthew. According to the National Weather Service, of the more than 160 high-hazard dams in North Carolina, seven were in areas that received more than fifteen inches of rain during Florence. Lake Upchurch in Fayetteville was one of several lakes identified by officials requiring the release of water to prevent catastrophic dam failure. The release into Rockfish Creek added to the flow that residents described as a "mad torrent." Crowds gathered at sunset on the seventeenth to watch the bulging Cape Fear pass under the Person Street bridge in the neighborhood of East Fayetteville. As water reached the underside of the bridge the following afternoon, the Department of Transportation closed it down. A nearby railroad trestle then trapped stacks of floating trees and other storm debris, turning the trestle into a dam and forcing floodwaters to spread around it, into downtown. Ultimately, the Cape Fear crested in Fayetteville on the nineteenth at 61.58 feet, more than thirty inches above the level during Matthew and high enough to rank as the fifth-highest crest at that location since record keeping began in the 1880s. The peak record was a remarkable 68.90 feet, recorded in September 1945.

Finally, on September 20, after floodwaters began to recede, some Cumberland County residents were able to return to their homes. With Matthew's woes still on their minds, many found a second round of mud and destruction absolutely heart wrenching. Stephen Thomas, whose home had been hit hard by flooding from the Little River during Matthew, returned to find heavy damages after Florence. Like many who suffered from both hurricanes, Thomas's experience was emotionally (and financially) draining. As he inspected his property, he told WRAL News, "In the house, floors are buckled, the corner walls are buckled, the refrigerator is laying on the floor. Everything is just destroyed. . . . Brand-new cabinets just installed. I spent $20,000 fixing it and repairing it and it's all gone."

Farther downstream, Bladen County was another trouble spot. The combination of flash flooding and downed trees shut down scores of roads and highways across the county during and immediately after the hurricane's arrival. This area also experienced some of Florence's largest rainfall accumulations, with a storm total of nearly thirty-six inches measured near Elizabethtown. Flooding from the Cape Fear then slowly crept in, reaching a new record crest of 30.68 feet at lock 1 near Riegelwood on September 21, a full week after Florence's landfall. In Bladenboro, floodwaters burst storefront windows and washed away large sections of railroad track, while high winds toppled the steeple of Galeed Baptist Church. So many roads were underwater throughout the county that it became difficult for emergency crews to move about. Adding to the calamity, and in addition to power outages, both landlines and cell phone service were compromised in the area. As the river continued rising, another logjam formed at the U.S. 701 bridge over the Cape Fear.

Some of the most dramatic flooding was in and around Kelly. Evacuations had reduced the town's population, normally around 800, to just more than 100. Largely isolated by flooded roads in the first hours of the storm, some residents later found a way to return home, only to be trapped by water that was still rising. One family of five was found desperately clinging to tree branches in chest-deep waters not far from their heavily damaged home. They were rescued by a crew from Wild Florida, an airboat tour company that had joined a flotilla of emergency responders and neighbors who were out in boats looking for victims. Rescuer Jordan Munns said when the team turned off the noisy airboat motor to listen for calls for help, they heard the family's faint cries in a remote area of flooded forest. "They thought this was it," Munns told WFTV News. When they reached the family sometime after dawn, they found the father with his eight-year-old son on his shoulders, his pregnant wife with their four-year-old daughter on hers, and a sixty-year-old uncle cradling a dog. All were brought safely to an area shelter.

Days later, on the evening of the twentieth, Kelly was again swamped when a thirty-foot-wide breach on a levee by the Cape Fear sent floodwaters into town. Emergency personnel contacted the North Carolina National Guard, who along with the U.S. Coast Guard began rescue operations with eight CH-47 Chinook and UH-60 Black Hawk helicopters. Using night-vision goggles and running missions throughout the night and into the following morning, crews airlifted more than 100 people and thirty-three animals to safety. Some were able to board helicopters that had landed, while others were hoisted into hovering choppers. It was a frightening ordeal for the evacuees, who were flown to Kinston where they spent the night, only to board buses for a return to Bladen County shelters the following day. One of the evacuees, Brittney Simpson, told WECT News, "It just hurts. It's something you can't explain, you just have to leave it behind. Your safety is more important. I have two kids, my mom and my grandma and my brother so I can't be selfish and stay home. We gotta go."

In Sampson and Duplin Counties, flooding also reached across highways, farms, and neighborhoods, surpassing levels experienced during Floyd, the previous record flood for the area. At Chinquapin, the USGS gage measured a new record crest of 25.77 feet, more than two feet greater than Floyd's high mark. Flooding closed roads and turned towns into islands on the fifteenth, just as swift-water teams arrived to perform rescues of stranded motorists and trapped homeowners. A sixteen-member team from California, with rescue experience during Hurricanes Katrina in New Orleans and Harvey in Houston, had been deployed to Kenansville but never quite made it. They arrived in Beulaville just in time to save three women and a girl from a sunken pickup truck. They followed that effort with the rescue of a man found clinging to a tree in twelve feet of water, who had been swept off the road by the swollen Northeast Cape Fear River. Beulaville fire chief Joey Carter, who watched the rescue from the water's edge, told the *Asheville Citizen-Times*, "If they hadn't been with us, we couldn't have done a thing for that man—not a thing. These guys got stranded here with us, and it was a blessing. They got stranded where they were needed."

Not surprisingly, similar scenes were found throughout Robeson and Columbus Counties, where gusty winds and early flash floods were followed by devastating high water later in the week. The Lumber and Waccamaw Rivers ultimately pushed well above flood stage and set new records. In Robeson County, where Matthew's floods had been devastating, it was as a good sign that local shelters filled up quickly as Florence approached. As people were hearing the forecasts, seeing the rain start to fall, and thinking about how Matthew had upended their lives, a wave of anxiety swept through Lumberton even before Florence's first floods appeared. Alexis Haggins was one who feared the worst. Reporters for the Associated Press told her story in 2018:

Alexis Haggins initially thought she'd stay put in the apartment she shares with two friends in a low-lying area devastated in 2016. The elementary school around the corner was deemed a total loss, shuttered and now sits abandoned. Many of the houses remain vacant and boarded up.

But then she couldn't stop reliving that terrible day when Matthew's floods came. She was driving when all of a sudden the water was up to her windows and the car started drifting. Haggins jumped out and took off on foot. She was beaten by falling limbs and pelting rain. Power lines fell around her, and she was sure she would be electrocuted. The mud sucked off her shoes, so she walked for miles barefoot until her soles were so bruised she could barely stand for days.

On Friday, she felt panic bubbling up. She imagined herself again up to her waist in water, fearing certain death. "If I would have to walk out of this house and into a flood, I would probably just drop to my knees and start crying," she says. "I can't do it again. I can't. I would just give up."

Before Florence's landfall, crews built a protective dike around the Lumberton water plant to try to prevent a repeat of the inundation during Matthew, when the plant was knocked offline for thirty days. National Guard troops and Lumberton city employees, with the help of local citizens, also filled more than 5,000 sandbags to block an entry point near Interstate 95, where floodwaters had poured into the city in 2016. Ultimately, the barrier failed to keep Florence's floodwaters out. The Lumber River at Lumberton crested on September 17 at twenty-nine feet, exactly one foot higher than the previous record set during Matthew. The impact was devastating, with homes and businesses so deeply engulfed that some suffered total structural collapse. The National Weather Service reported that flooding in the Mayfair neighborhood just north of the city was eight feet deep. Lumberton Rescue reported evacuating about 400 residents from flooded homes; about 100 more were saved from flooded vehicles and "open waters" that in many areas were chest deep. The nearby town of Pembroke also suffered heavy damages, as did roadways across the county that buckled under the rush of water. As many as 2 million gallons of untreated sewage were believed to have spilled in Lumberton and Saint Pauls, adding to the dangers of floodwater exposure. Robeson County Emergency Management reported that at least 500 structures across the county were damaged by the flood.

For residents of Columbus County, Florence caused similar chaos and is considered by most to be the "worst storm in history." Flanked by the Lumber River to the west and the Waccamaw River to the east, this largely rural county was swamped from every direction. As the storm center tracked just a few miles to the south across Brunswick County on the fifteenth, Whiteville, Lake Waccamaw, and surrounding areas took the brunt of the hurricane's core winds and rains. By the morning of the sixteenth, the county's secondary roads were impassable, covered with fallen pines and rising water. The Lumber River at Boardman peaked on September 18 at 14.36 feet (just under the level during Matthew), while the Waccamaw River at Freeland crested two days later on the twentieth, setting a new record at 22.47 feet, three feet higher than the previous record set during Floyd.

Like in other areas, rescue efforts in Columbus County took place in different places on different days. By the morning of the sixteenth, about ninety residents across the county were safely evacuated from homes struck by trees and flash flooding. In Tabor City, fifteen more residents were evacuated from flooded homes that evening, with many more occurring over the next two days.

The U.S. Coast Guard rescued 116 people from flooding that swamped the Crusoe community on the eighteenth. The Wilmington *Star-News* reported that even the highest ground in Acme, Delco, and Riegelwood was underwater. Floodwaters inside one Riegelwood business were nine feet deep. Fair Bluff was also hit hard by the rising Lumber River, which split the town into two isolated sections. In Whiteville, Soules Swamp flooded the southern parts of the city. At Magnolia Missionary Baptist Church, church leaders reported four feet of water in the sanctuary and five in the fellowship hall. Swift-water rescues were needed along Water Tank Road near Delco, where homes were flooded "up to the rooflines." These victims were just more of the 5,200 North Carolinians rescued during the storm.

At Lake Waccamaw, it was the storm's initial blow that did the most damage. High winds over the lake produced a seiche, a storm-surge-like sloshing effect that battered boats, docks, and boathouses, sending waves into homes that circle the shore. The Whiteville *News Reporter* said the storm "destroyed nearly every pier and boathouse on Lake Waccamaw, sending water across Waccamaw Shores and Canal Cove Drive for the first time in memory." The winds also toppled countless large trees, some crashing into lakefront homes and adding to the destruction. About 80 percent of homes on the lake were damaged by trees, flooding, and the battering effect of dislodged docks and watercraft.

Though much of the media coverage during Florence was focused on North Carolina, where epic flooding and daring rescues made headlines, northeastern South Carolina was also hit with a wave of extreme flooding. As the storm center inched across the border and tracked upstate, rainfall totals in South Carolina were impressive—though generally less than those measured to the north. More than twenty-three inches were recorded in Loris during the storm; gages measured nearly twenty inches in Marion and just over eighteen in Dillon. More than fifteen inches were recorded in Myrtle Beach and on Pawleys Island. These rains brought flash flooding on their own, but because rivers in this region flow down from North Carolina, the accumulated rains from a broad area lifted them to record levels in many South Carolina communities. In most areas, these peak floods arrived days after those upstream. The Waccamaw, Little Pee Dee, and Great Pee Dee Rivers spread well beyond their banks and left heavy damages from Chesterfield County to the Grand Strand.

Among the portions of South Carolina to first feel Florence's effects was Horry County, home to Myrtle Beach. Much of the county is crisscrossed by rivers, creeks, and swamps, with the Waccamaw River flowing down from North Carolina and the confluence of the Lumber and Little Pee Dee Rivers holding the greatest flooding potential. As the storm rolled through, Loris was one of the first communities to suffer. On September 16, as the center of Florence spun through the county, city officials felt optimistic. But the following day, after an exhausting night of water rescues, Loris fire chief Jerry Hardee told the *Tabor-Loris Tribune*, "I have never in 66 years seen anything like it. . . . About 10:30 last night we were good, the ditches were in good shape, the city was draining good." Hardee's crews got a few calls for water rescues in areas that have historically flooded. "Then we started getting calls to places we've never had problems before. We had five units out at a time. This went on to daylight." With the help of the South Carolina National Guard, Loris firemen responded to nearly 100 water rescue calls through the night. An emergency shelter was opened at the public safety building to house the grateful evacuees.

Though these floods might have surprised some people, ample warnings had been issued across the region. Governor McMaster had for days stressed the potential flooding risks because of the storm's size, speed, and trajectory. Orders had gone out to evacuate especially vulnerable communities such as Nichols. On the sixteenth, Department of Transportation workers and National Guard troops worked for hours in drenching rain to fill large sandbags on a one-and-a-half-mile stretch at the U.S. 501 bypass bridge over the Waccamaw River near Conway. It was ten days later, on September 26, that the gage at that location reached its all-time peak of 21.16 feet, more than three feet higher than the previous record crest set following Matthew. As the Waccamaw spread beyond its banks, the impact in Conway and neighboring communities was horrific. Stop signs were completely underwater; fish swam in the streets. In its Hurricane Florence summary, the National Weather Service office in Wilmington described some of the destruction in Horry County:

> Nearly 1,000 homes and businesses near the [Waccamaw] river were flooded, many severely. Homes in the Polo Farms neighborhood off SC highway 905 were flooded five feet deep when the Waccamaw River backed up Simpsons Creek. Aberdeen Country club in Longs and the Bradford Creek neighborhood off Highway 544 also flooded with up to three feet of water entering homes. On September 26 raw sewage flowed from the Conway Wastewater Treatment Plant into a tributary that feeds into the Waccamaw River. The community of Dongola in western Horry county was isolated for ten days. The flood wave continued to create devastation as it moved downstream through the towns of Bucksport and Socastee. The Silver Fox Landing Development near the Intracoastal Waterway had water up to eight feet deep in homes.

Connie Parrish's home in Socastee, near the Intracoastal Waterway, had flooded during Matthew and was hit again after Florence. "We lost all of our

On September 24, 2018, one week after Hurricane Florence's landfall, the Polo Farms community off S.C. 905 in Longs, South Carolina, sits in deep standing water due to widespread flooding in the area. (Photo by Jason Lee. Courtesy of the *Sun News* / Associated Press.)

furniture. We lost all of our clothes. I lost everything," she told WMBF News as she recalled the latter storm's intrusion into her home. "The washer was turned upside down and it was in the other room. It actually floated to another room, their refrigerators turned upside down." Like so many others, Parrish and her family didn't have flood insurance. At the time, her home wasn't designated as being in a high-risk zone for flooding. And she didn't qualify for Small Business Administration loans, an alternative many without flood insurance use to pay for home repairs. She was left in tears, with few options. Her home was ultimately torn down.

Emergency management officials later reported that 361 homes in Conway and 1,580 homes in the rural portion of the county were damaged. Conway fire chief Le Hendrick told WCSC News the city hadn't seen many rescues, largely because his firefighters had urged vulnerable residents to leave their homes well before the worst flooding began. In Georgetown, flooding from the Waccamaw and Great Pee Dee Rivers finally reached its peak on September 28. Damages in the area were not extensive, though one fatality was reported on September 16 when a truck overturned in deep water where a barrier had been removed. In Marion County, sandwiched between the Great Pee Dee and Little Pee Dee Rivers, flooding was severe in Nichols, Gresham, and Brittons Neck. Local officials reported that flooding in Nichols was "much worse" than had occurred during Matthew; about 150 homes that had been refurbished since the 2016 flood were damaged again.

One of the many tragedies reported from Florence's journey through the state occurred on September 18, on U.S. 76 between Nichols and Mullins. Two sheriff's deputies were transporting two patients to a mental health center in Darlington when their van encountered swift-moving floodwaters and was swept off the highway into deep water. The deputies quickly scrambled onto the roof of the van, but despite persistent efforts to open the doors to free the patients, floodwaters rose too quickly—the victims remained trapped inside and drowned. The deputies were later found by swift-water rescue teams. Ultimately, the deputies were terminated and charged in the deaths, as state investigators alleged they took an unapproved route and drove around a marked road barrier.

About 400 homes were damaged by flooding around Dillon, and one submerged-vehicle fatality was reported nearby on the nineteenth. Flooding along the Lynches River forced the evacuation of more than 2,000 residents in Florence County, though most later returned to find their homes in good order. Two residences were destroyed, and fifty-two others were damaged by rising water. Gusting winds early in the storm ripped away shingles and toppled trees and fences, affecting hundreds of properties across the county. In Darlington County, twenty-one homes received major flood damage, as did more than two dozen roads and bridges. A bridge on New Hopewell Road collapsed, and numerous other roadway washouts were reported. The dam at Lake Darpo was damaged, pushed to its limits by the nearly twenty inches of rain that fell across the area. Farther inland and upriver, about 200 more homes were damaged by rising water from the Great Pee Dee in Marlboro County.

In Chesterfield County, where more than sixteen inches of rain were recorded, numerous automobile accidents were credited to the storm—two of which were blamed on roads crumbled by the rush of flash flooding on the sixteenth. On S.C. 145 near the North Carolina border, a driver plunged into a hole in the road, tossing his car onto its side near a swollen creek. As floodwaters swirled around him, he managed to pull his girlfriend and two young children out of the car through the driver-side window. They escaped the incident with only minor injuries. On another stretch of the same road, a truck driver was extremely lucky to survive his watery encounter. He made the mistake of attempting to push through a submerged stretch of the highway, unaware of the missing asphalt beneath him. The local sheriff's office later posted a photo online of the tractor trailer, which had dropped several feet into a deep washout. Deputies had helped the driver escape through a side window and later reported that he was badly shaken by the experience—and talking of giving up driving trucks for good.

By late September, as river levels across the Carolinas began to finally return to normal, recovery efforts were getting underway in the hardest-hit communities. The scope and scale of the flood damage was unlike anything seen in the Carolinas before, even though many seasoned emergency planners had worked through complex recoveries following the 2015 floods in South Carolina and, more recently, Hurricane Matthew. Across both states, federal and state agencies, local governments, nonprofits, faith-based groups, utilities, local businesses, and private citizens worked tirelessly to meet the challenges left in Florence's wake. As always, power restoration was a priority. Duke Energy, working with dozens of electric cooperatives, unleashed brigades of line crews to repair damaged transmission lines, poles, and substations. Many of these crews had been pre-staged within targeted areas and were bolstered by workers and equipment from across the southeast. In some communities, residents were astounded at how quickly power was restored.

Housing was another immediate priority, as thousands of displaced residents faced the daily challenges of living in emergency shelters that were only intended to operate on a short-term basis. At one time more than 26,000 evacuees filled over 200 shelters in North and South Carolina, five times the total number of occupants during Matthew. Shelters operated in schools, churches, municipal buildings, and even in the Lawrence Joel Coliseum in Winston-Salem. Many were managed by teams of volunteers from the American Red Cross. In the storm's aftermath, state and local officials, partnering with local churches and relief organizations such as the Red Cross and Salvation Army, worked to relocate evacuees into temporary housing. Some victims lost all their possessions, including clothing, so the need for donated goods was great. Fortunately, generous and compassionate people from across the Carolinas and beyond responded to the need. In Wilmington, local leaders were appreciative but made a timely plea: send money, not clothes. Tommy Taylor, executive vice president of United Way of Cape Fear, told the *Anderson Independent-Mail* that in the short term, cash contributions were best—clothes would need to be cleaned, sorted, stored, and distributed, and there "are not enough dry places to fit donations in Wilmington."

Damage assessment was another critical priority, linked to the states' efforts to funnel critical funding to the right places for humanitarian needs, debris removal, infrastructure replacement, and emergency repairs. Teams in both states compiled damage reports that told a grim story, detailing losses to homes, businesses, roads and bridges, agriculture, and industry. Florence was one for the record books, especially in North Carolina. A total of 44,700 buildings were damaged, 8 percent of which were completely destroyed. Overall damages in the Tar Heel State topped a whopping $22 billion, more than four times the toll from Matthew, easily making it the costliest hurricane in state history. FEMA reported in 2020 that more than $2 billion in state and federal aid were ultimately distributed to North Carolina families and communities for the disaster, including $632 million in flood insurance claims, $134 million in FEMA grants to homeowners, $408 million in Small Business Administration loans, and $629 million to reimburse state and local governments and aid nonprofits in fifty-one affected counties. Additionally, FEMA provided no-cost travel trailers for temporary housing to 656 households in the thirteen hardest-hit North Carolina counties.

Agricultural damages in North Carolina were staggering. A post-storm review from the Office of State Budget and Management found $1.3 billion in direct losses to crops and livestock, and another $1 billion in indirect losses. Again, this sum far surpassed the $400 million in damages following Matthew. State agriculture commissioner Steve Troxler told the Raleigh *News and Observer*, "We knew the losses would be significant because it was harvest time for so many of our major crops and the storm hit our top six agricultural counties especially hard." Among the casualties in North Carolina after Florence were 4.1 million chickens and turkeys. Over 5,500 hogs died—more than twice the number lost during Matthew but far fewer than the nearly 30,000 that died during Floyd. In 2020, there were more than 9.3 million hogs in the state.

In South Carolina, more than 8,000 homes had FEMA-verified property losses, with nearly half of those homeowners receiving housing assistance. According to NHC reports, total damages in South Carolina equaled those from Matthew at $2 billion, though an analysis from real property analytics firm CoreLogic pegged the number at $5.5 billion in the Palmetto State. Damages were largely east of Interstate 95 and north of Interstate 26, with Horry County recording the greatest number of losses. Agricultural damages totaled $125 million, mostly to soybeans, cotton, and equipment. Nineteen counties were federally declared eligible for public assistance, with eight also declared for individual assistance.

With most large-scale disasters, recovery usually plays out over months and years, and Florence was no exception. Many homeowners, after dealing with the immediate shock of losing so much to the flood, felt an agonizing state of limbo set in as they waited to hear from funding agencies, insurance adjusters, contractors, and building inspectors. Some waited for months or just gave up on those services in highest demand such as roofing contractors and tree removal companies. Volunteer groups and faith-based organizations stepped in to help, especially in the days and weeks following the storm, by providing feeding

Recovery efforts following major disasters always rely on the generosity of others, including those willing to donate supplies and volunteer their time. Following Hurricane Florence, Samaritan's Purse volunteers were on the ground in New Bern, providing flood victims much-needed support. (Photo courtesy of Samaritan's Purse.)

stations, debris cleanup, and home repair in some of the hardest-hit neighborhoods. Some larger-scale projects were held until state or federal funding was released. But slowly, the battered communities across the Florence zone began to rebuild. In North Carolina, the last of the state's 2,500 closed roads was reopened near Mount Olive in April 2019—seven months after the hurricane.

Florence once again provided more evidence of the dangers of driving on flooded roads. Freshwater drowning was the leading cause of death, and almost all of the flood-related fatalities reported in North and South Carolina involved vehicles. According to the NHC, Florence caused fifteen direct fatalities in North Carolina, four in South Carolina, and three in Virginia—twenty-two in all—with all but five linked to driving on flooded roads. The NHC also reported thirty indirect fatalities in the Carolinas. But others tallied the death toll differently. State officials reported a sum of fifty-nine deaths: forty-five in North Carolina, eleven in South Carolina, and three in Virginia. The Raleigh *News and Observer* described the North Carolina chief medical examiner's approach: "If the time, place and circumstances of someone's death were determined by the storm, then it gets counted."

Selected Record River Crests in the Carolinas (through 2021)

Location	Flood stage	Peak during Floyd	Peak during Matthew	Peak during Florence
Tar River at Rocky Mount, N.C.	21 feet	**31.66**	28.73	16.19
Tar River at Greenville, N.C.	13 feet	**29.74**	24.46	12.21
Contentnea Creek at Hookerton, N.C.	13 feet	**28.28**	24.15	18.98
Cashie River at Windsor, N.C.	8 feet	**18.52**	16.63	4.99
Neuse River at Smithfield, N.C.	15 feet	26.72	**29.09**	18.91
Neuse River at Goldsboro, N.C.	18 feet	28.85	**29.74**	27.60
Neuse River at Kinston, N.C.	14 feet	27.71	**28.31**	25.78
Cape Fear River at Wilmington, N.C.	5.5 feet	7.31	8.17	8.28*
Cape Fear River at Fayetteville, N.C.	35 feet	38.38	58.94	61.58†
Northeast Cape Fear River at Chinquapin, N.C.	13 feet	23.51	19.98	**25.77**
Northeast Cape Fear River at Burgaw, N.C.	10 feet	22.48	17.81	**25.57**
Little River at Manchester, N.C.	18 feet	N/A	32.19	**38.30**
Lumber River at Lumberton, N.C.	13 feet	17.50	28.00	**29.00**
Lumber River at Nichols, S.C.	20 feet	N/A	27.01	**27.36**
New River at Gum Branch, N.C.	14 feet	25.12	20.61	**25.76**
Trent River at Trenton, N.C.	14 feet	28.42	23.77	**29.28**
Black Creek at Quinby, S.C.	10 feet	N/A	16.46	**17.36**
Waccamaw River at Pawleys Island, S.C.	10.5 feet	N/A	10.34	**11.35**
Waccamaw River at Conway, S.C.	11 feet	17.61	17.89	**21.16**
Little Pee Dee River at Galivants Ferry, S.C.	9 feet	12.11	17.10	**17.21**

Record levels are in **bold**. All measurements in feet.

Thirty-three new river crest records were set across the Carolinas following Hurricane Florence, often topping marks set during Hurricanes Floyd and Matthew. In some locations, records set during those earlier storms still stand. (Source: National Weather Service / National Oceanic and Atmospheric Administration.)

* Cape Fear River at Wilmington: record level set during Florence was surpassed during Hurricane Isaias on August 4, 2020 (9.03 feet)

† Cape Fear River at Fayetteville: record of 68.90 feet was set in September 1945

USGS hydrologic technician Rob Forde flags a high-water mark above the eaves of the Presbyterian Church of the Covenant in Spring Hill, North Carolina, in the wake of flooding brought on by Hurricane Florence. (Photo courtesy of USGS.)

Following Hurricane Sandy in 2012, scientists and policy makers began promoting this broader approach when counting deaths in hurricanes—counting not only those due to wind and flooding but also those caused by the conditions a storm leaves behind. In 2017, the Centers for Disease Control and Prevention issued new guidance for how to document disaster fatalities, eliminating direct and indirect distinctions and expanding the count to include victims who died during evacuations and storm cleanup and those whose natural deaths were exacerbated by the stress of the event. Ilan Kelman, a researcher at the Institute for Risk and Disaster Reduction at University College London, told the *News and Observer*, "We want to stop disaster deaths. To do that, we need to understand who is dying, why they are dying and what intervention we could do in order to stop them from getting into situations in which they end up dying."

The fatalities recorded during and after Florence included a range of tragic events spread across a broad area. Those attributed to vehicular drowning were most common, but others were equally tragic. Among them: a homeless Wilmington man riding a moped was hit by a truck on U.S. 74 in Columbus

County while evacuating ahead of the storm—the first death attributed to Florence; a Wilmington mother and her eight-month-old son were killed when a tree crashed into their home as the storm made landfall; a Horry County couple succumbed to carbon monoxide poisoning after operating a generator at their home; a seventy-eight-year-old Kinston man was electrocuted while connecting extension cords to his generator in the rain; a sixty-one-year-old woman was killed when her truck hit a downed tree branch that crossed a Union County, South Carolina, highway; a seventy-seven-year-old Lenoir County man was blown down while checking on his hunting dogs; a Fayette-ville couple died in a house fire started by candles they were burning while power was out; a sixty-nine-year-old Hampstead man died after falling from his roof while cleaning up storm debris, and a forty-seven-year-old Duplin County man died in the same manner; an eighty-five-year-old Wilmington man died following a septic shock infection from a wound he received from a tree branch while cleaning up his yard; and a three-month-old child was killed when a tree fell on a mobile home in Gaston County, some 240 miles from where Florence made landfall. Other deaths were attributed to heart attacks, automobile acci-dents, and even suicides, including a sixty-nine-year-old Robeson County man who took his own life after his home was badly flooded by Florence. He had suffered major damage in Matthew as well.

Florence easily ranks among the very worst of all Carolina hurricanes. After causing nearly five dozen fatalities and flooding more properties in North Carolina than any previous storm, it redefined how we think about hurricane disasters in the region. On the heels of Matthew, it is remembered by a genera-tion as "the great flood that came after the other flood." Many remember the incessant rain, the slow, crawling pace of the storm, and the record high water that isolated cities such as Wilmington and covered neighborhoods never be-fore known to flood. Those who suffered damage to their homes wish they could forget. Before the damage estimates were even complete, North Carolina governor Roy Cooper told the Associated Press, "For overall damage, it would be hard, at the end of the day, I think, to find a rival for this storm."

TAKEAWAYS

• *Records were made to be broken.* Recording weather data, counting the losses, and measuring the impact from hurricanes helps us understand the scope of each event. Extremes sometimes surpass what might seem pos-sible, but over time, history has shown that new storms eventually set new marks—especially with the improved data collection methods in use today.

It may take many decades (or not), but one day a hurricane in the Carolinas will likely surpass Hugo's record South Carolina storm tide or Florence's record river crests. It's news no one wants to hear: expect more big storms.

- *It could have been worse.* No one likes to hear this either. As dire as Florence's visit to the Carolinas was, it's frightening to consider the what-ifs: What if it hadn't weakened prior to landfall and had arrived on the coast as a Category 4 and then slowly crept into South Carolina as a massive rain maker with far more destructive winds? What if previous rainfall had pushed rivers to flood stage before Florence arrived, as had been the case with Floyd and Matthew? Or what if Florence had struck over Labor Day weekend, when coastal resorts were near capacity? Most never ponder worst-case scenarios such as these, but forecasters and emergency managers in the Carolinas have.

- *Low-income communities suffer the most.* Hurricane disasters such as Fran, Floyd, Matthew, and Florence have proven most devastating for those who have the least. Much of this comes with the territory: the coastal plains in North and South Carolina both are vulnerable to hurricanes and happen to include some of the poorest counties in each state. Just as important, across many parts of this region, low-income and minority populations have historically been relegated to cheap, less desirable lands that are low in elevation—in floodplains. Recent FEMA studies confirm that low-income homeowners are disproportionately likely to live in flood-prone areas. Flood insurance premiums are often beyond their means, putting them in further jeopardy when rivers rise.

- *Just because it's never flooded before, doesn't meant it can't.* Ample evidence of this emerged during Florence. This is a good match with another truism: if it's flooded before, it will flood again.

- *Computers, data, and scientific rigor save lives.* Hurricane forecasting has evolved over the years, with the goal of saving lives and property. Advances in technology have been key. Today's watches and warnings from the National Weather Service and NHC are easily taken for granted, but there's an impressive universe of data collection, computer modeling, and visual interpretation behind each forecast. Scientists are building ever-larger data sets and creating increasingly sophisticated computer models for studying the atmosphere and ocean. Their work is yielding new insights into hurricane behavior, the risks of rising seas, and the anticipated effects of a changing climate. During Florence, forecasters used real-time rainfall updates to model river crest levels by time and location—helping state officials move resources to the most vulnerable areas and remove the public from danger. It's just another recent example of how forecasters are using science and technology to inform and protect the public.

- *A 500-year flood isn't what you think.* There is plenty of unfortunate confusion surrounding this often-used term. Many believe a 500-year flood must be an ultrarare event, perhaps only happening once every 500 years. But that's not what it means. In the 1960s when the U.S. government launched the National Flood Insurance Program, probability ratings were established to determine risk levels for different parts of the country. Organizers chose to designate floodplains with a 1 percent annual exceedance probability, meaning that in any given year, there's a 1 percent chance that flooding will reach or surpass a certain elevation. It became known as a "100-year flood." The same applies for a 500-year flood zone: in any given year, there's a 0.2 percent chance of water reaching or surpassing that level. Each year the probability remains the same—it doesn't really matter what happened the year before. And floodplains shift over time with land use changes, climate cycles, and other factors, requiring regularly updated maps. Because of the confusion, some forecasters have backed away from using the term.

- *Don't misinterpret your flood zone designation.* Anyone owning or purchasing a home should know their flood zone, as determined by FEMA flood maps for their community. Higher-risk areas (in the 100-year, or 1-percent-chance, zone) begin with the letters *A* or *V*, and if you live in one of these zones and have a federally backed mortgage, flood insurance is a requirement. Moderate-risk flood zones are designated with the letters *B* or *X* (shaded), while low-risk zones are designated with the letters *C* or *X* (unshaded). Flood insurance may not be required in these areas, but that doesn't mean there's no risk of flooding. In Florence, more than half of all flood-damaged properties were in these low-to-moderate zones. Critics contend that residents in zone X, for example, often have a false sense of security about their level of risk. Hurricanes such as Florence and Matthew, extreme as they were, proved devastating to many who likely felt they just didn't need flood insurance.

- *The low rate of flood insurance coverage in the Carolinas sustains our vulnerability.* It was a factor long before the epic floods of Matthew and Florence. Too few homes and businesses are covered by a flood insurance policy, due to a variety of factors. Though the National Flood Insurance Program is subsidized by Uncle Sam, many people of low-to-moderate incomes living in floodplains are unable to afford the premiums. Those owning homes with paid-off mortgages sometimes drop coverage that's not required.

Others are misinformed, unaware that regular homeowners' policies don't cover damages from rising water. And as stated above, some whose homes fall outside the high-risk zones have a false sense of security and don't consider flood insurance a priority. Without that insurance, flood victims such as those in Matthew and Florence are left with huge repair bills that can devastate their personal finances.

CHAPTER SIXTEEN

FUTURE STORMS

The future has a way of arriving unannounced.—George Will

For the most part, we tend to think of the future in the near term—plans for next week, events scheduled in the coming months, or perhaps some general thoughts about what retirement might be like. The changes coming over the next forty, sixty, or eighty years are a little hard to fathom. But institutions such as governments and major corporations must take a long view and develop plans based on their best understanding of future conditions. Their long-term thinking allows them to not only invest wisely but also shape their own destinies.

Today, much attention is rightly focused on how a changing climate is affecting our planet and how it will impact our future. In 2021, historic wildfires, killer heat domes, and deadly urban floods made front-page news, and the National Oceanic and Atmospheric Administration reported that July 2021 was the earth's hottest month on record—prompting some to proclaim that climate change is here now. There's an urgency about that message, though the worst aspects of a warming planet will play out over many decades. The alarm bells started ringing years ago, and now emerging science offers an ever-more-detailed view of what to expect. More institutions are taking the matter seriously, and the voices have been building for some time: this is a global climate *crisis*. Curbing greenhouse gas emissions is the priority, and the consequences of not meeting that challenge are far-reaching. At the top of the list of concerns are the expected impacts of rising sea levels on coastal populations and the costs and consequences of more destructive hurricanes.

North and South Carolina have long been prime targets for menacing tropical weather. Big storms, far more than the fifteen profiled in this book, have plagued the region for centuries. But as years roll by, even "memorable" hurricanes tend to fade into history. While for some there's a tendency to think recent hurricane disasters in the Carolinas are something shockingly new and different, in reality they're only the latest episodes in a rinse-and-repeat cycle

Hurricane Florence, as viewed from the International Space Station. (Photo courtesy of NASA.)

that has no end. What is new and different is how continued growth in the Carolinas over the last decades has placed more people and property in harm's way. Coupled with an influx of residents with limited hurricane experience, it's easy to see why emergency management officials remain concerned about what future storms might bring.

The threat of more devastating hurricanes is often presented as one of the most serious climate-related perils we face. After his Oscar-winning documentary *An Inconvenient Truth* was released in 2006, Vice President Al Gore famously said, "What changed in the United States with Hurricane Katrina was a feeling that we have entered a period of consequences." Anthropogenic climate change and its influence on tropical cyclone activity have remained in the news ever since. More recently, some pundits and advocates for climate action have put forward the idea that epic hurricanes such as Sandy, Harvey, Florence, and Ida were *the result of* global warming.

From a historian's perspective, that thinking seems flawed. Big, powerful, and destructive hurricanes are nothing new. It's not that there has been no influence; that seems unlikely given that the earth's seven warmest years on record have all occurred since 2014. But how climate change is communicated is important, and some clarity is needed. To sort this out, we'd need to look more closely at what the science is really telling us about warming oceans and rising seas and how they might affect future Atlantic hurricanes—especially those tracking toward the Carolinas.

Even before considering the effects of a changing climate, to get an idea of what to expect regarding hurricanes in the Carolinas in the next 100 years, a good place to start is to look back at the last 100. There have always been powerful hurricanes along these shores, and knowing the tumultuous events surrounding their visits gives us good perspective on the different kinds of impacts we might expect in years to come. No two storms are the same—and our plans and preparations should factor in a wide range of possibilities. Pounding storm surge on the coast, fierce and destructive winds, embedded tornadoes, and widespread, rain-induced river flooding across inland counties are the obvious threats, though with each hurricane these impacts will vary greatly by degree and location. North and South Carolina's coastal counties will always bear the brunt, but every corner of both states holds some risk for future hurricane destruction.

Before the 2021 hurricane season began, Chris Landsea, chief of the Tropical Analysis and Forecast Branch of the National Hurricane Center, offered his perspective on what the Carolinas might expect in the future and what role a changing climate might play. Scientists such as Landsea make their case using an array of ever-more-sophisticated computer forecast models, run out over decades, which factor increasing amounts of carbon dioxide, methane, and other greenhouse gases. There is, of course, some uncertainty with such modeling, but the models' growing consistencies offer compelling and even surprising results. The first important observation regarding future hurricanes was quite unexpected.

"The number of tropical storms and hurricanes around the world and in the Atlantic is expected to stay the same or even decrease. That's true for the number of tropical storms, it's true for hurricanes, and may be true for major hurricanes—Categories 3, 4, and 5—that cause 80 percent of the damage," says Landsea. The two thoughts behind that conclusion: it's expected that around the globe there will be more dry or stable air for hurricanes to fight through, and in the tropical Atlantic there'll be increased wind shear that will help thwart the development of emerging tropical storms. Though climate change might not add to the total number of storms, the status quo is nothing to celebrate—each Atlantic season could still average twelve to fourteen named storms and six or seven hurricanes.

A cursory review of the Atlantic hurricane record from the National Oceanic and Atmospheric Administration's Atlantic Hurricane Database, or HURDAT, website would seem to suggest that tropical activity is already

Future hurricane floods in the Carolinas will again require "boats in the streets," just as they have during past storms, such as Hurricane Ione in 1955. (Photo courtesy of the George H. and Laura E. Brown Library, Washington, North Carolina.)

trending upward, with a doubling in the number of tropical storms and hurricanes over the last 100 years. That increase might appear to be linked to climate change, but Landsea cautions against that assumption: "The reality is that we measure tropical storms and hurricanes so accurately today, compared to 100 years ago. Back then we had no satellites, we had no radar, we had no hurricane hunters, we didn't have buoys moored over the open ocean—we really were primitive in the way we observed tropical storms and hurricanes." Landsea and others at the National Hurricane Center know that earlier records are incomplete, and they've run calculations on what's been missed. They found that once they account for the tropical storms and hurricanes that were missed due to lack of information—open-ocean hurricanes and the short-duration, one- or two-day tropical storms that fizzle out at sea—the trend disappears. Landsea summarized, "You've kind of got to throw out the shorties, which are not very consequential anyway, and then add in the medium to long-lived ones you've missed because of the lack of satellite pictures before the 1970s. So when you do that, instead of a massive doubling in the number of tropical storms and hurricanes, it's flat."

Regarding intensity, though, Landsea says we can expect a future with stronger hurricanes. Warmer ocean and atmospheric temperatures will provide the necessary fuel. But here's the good news: the values are relatively small. "We're looking at 3 to 5 percent stronger [storms] by the end of this century. So as an example, a 100 mph hurricane might be a 105 mph hurricane at the end of the century because of global warming. That sounds small, and I would argue it is fairly tiny, compared to natural changes in hurricanes we've seen." So the news is mixed—in decades to come, we should expect the same number or fewer storms, but they'll be slightly stronger. Landsea added, "At the very high end, Categories 4 and 5, that are pretty rare, those may increase in numbers."

This correlates with Landsea's views on a storm such as Katrina, which some still hold up as a "climate-change-induced disaster." Landsea explained it this way to *PBS NewsHour* in 2005: "We certainly see substantial warming in the atmosphere and oceans over the last several decades, on the order of 1 degree Fahrenheit, and I have no doubt that a portion of that, at least, is due to greenhouse gas warming. . . . Hurricanes like Katrina and Rita may have been stronger due to global warming but maybe by 1 or 2 mph. At least that is what the theory and the numerical modeling suggests to us today." Since Katrina, further study has reinforced Landsea's views on the incremental change. He told the *Palm Beach Post* in 2019, "Global warming likely added one percent to Hurricane Michael's Cat 5 power, or one or two mph. This is a fairly small increase."

One area of concern that's being carefully studied is the idea that future hurricanes, influenced by global warming, will produce more rain. Hurricanes Harvey in Texas (2017), Florence in the Carolinas (2018), and Ida in Louisiana and the Northeast (2021) each set new precipitation records, motivating many to make the connection with a warming climate. Harvey and Florence were extremely slow movers overland, a huge factor in the production of their staggering rainfall totals. But researchers urge caution about making assumptions regarding recent hurricanes. Katherine Hayhoe, a climate scientist at Texas Tech University, told PolitiFact in 2017, "Nearly every scientific study agrees that, as the world warms, on average the amount of rainfall associated with hurricanes will increase. . . . These studies require painstaking, detailed analyses that take years to complete so there is nothing we as scientists can say right now about the extent to which human-induced change was involved in determining Harvey's path, or even whether it was at all."

Future hurricanes may indeed be bigger rain makers. Some studies in recent years have shown slowing trends for tropical storms, while others have predicted that blocking weather patterns—systems that cause hurricanes to slow or stall—may become more common in a warmer world. Recent studies have shown tropical cyclones are shifting closer to the poles, while others have documented hurricanes' increasing impact on deep inland areas following landfall. Also concerning were reports in 2019 that new modeling predicts significantly reduced vertical wind shear along the U.S. East Coast in the decades to come. Vertical shear in this region acts like a "speed bump" to landfalling hurricanes, preventing them from intensifying before they strike.

In 2019, researchers at the University of North Carolina at Chapel Hill, led by professor Hans Pearl, published a study of high-precipitation events in North Carolina since 1898. They found that six of the seven greatest totals occurred in the last twenty years. Three of those events, Hurricanes Floyd, Matthew, and Florence, defied statistical expectations. "With less than a 2% chance of three such events occurring in a twenty-year period, either North Carolina has been very unlucky, or the historical record used to define storm statistics is no longer representative of the present climatic regime. . . . Our observations are consistent with observations elsewhere and with predicted changes in a warming climate. Moreover, rather than attributing a particular event to global warming, we should consider whether a warming climate made these events more likely, which our records suggest is the case for coastal NC," the authors concluded.

Researchers around the globe continue to study how weather will change in the years to come. Though Landsea and others expect global warming's impact on hurricanes to be meaningful but not extraordinary, he notes other influencers of future storms: "One is natural climate variability, from the Atlantic Multidecadal Oscillation, where we see a two-to-one swing in the number of major hurricanes."

The Atlantic Multidecadal Oscillation—also known as the Atlantic Multidecadal Variability—is a cycle of long-duration changes in sea surface temperatures in the North Atlantic, with cool and warm phases that may last for twenty to forty years at a time and cause temperature fluctuations of about 1 degree Fahrenheit between extremes. These natural changes are thought to have been occurring for at least 1,000 years. The most recent shift to the warm phase happened in 1995, after which a significant increase in Atlantic tropical storm activity (especially major hurricanes) was observed. An earlier cool phase, which lasted from the early 1960s through the early 1990s, was a period with far fewer tropical storms and hurricanes in the Atlantic. The barrage of hurricanes that hit Florida in the 1940s and the Carolinas in the 1950s occurred during the previous warm phase.

Like the better-known interannual El Niño and La Niña southern oscillation in the tropical Pacific, which changes every two to seven years, the Atlantic

Multidecadal Variability has a pronounced effect on Atlantic hurricane activity. The good news? Though no one is offering predictions, the current warm phase is expected to end sometime before 2035. But what follows is unknown: Will the cycle revert, reducing overall tropical activity? Or will the steady rise of global temperatures mask any potential Atlantic cooling? Steve Pfaff, warning coordination meteorologist for the National Weather Service in Wilmington, sees that possibility: "I think the big question is even if we do transition to a cool phase, will that be tempered by a higher level of greenhouse gases in the atmosphere? The projections look like it should at least counter that, or at least the ones that do form could be more intense." Even if the cycle does shift, keep in mind that monster storms will still blast ashore during the Atlantic Multidecadal Variability's next cool phase. Recent examples of cool-phase hurricanes include Category 5 Camille (1969), Category 4 Hugo (1989), and Category 5 Andrew (1992).

Hurricanes of the future, regardless of their number or strength, will strike coastal communities in the Carolinas that are grappling with another serious issue—rising sea levels. It's a prominent topic in the climate change discussion, with dramatic implications for millions of people worldwide. Ocean levels rise as warming temperatures cause ice on land to melt (mostly the Greenland and Antarctic ice sheets), transferring fresh water to the sea; warmer temperatures also cause ocean water to expand, taking up more space. Globally, the level has gone up about one inch per decade over the last 100 years. Landsea puts that in perspective: "It doesn't sound like much, but in areas where the terrain is pretty low-lying, even a foot over several decades is a big deal. And the concern is that sea level rise is going to accelerate, so that instead of an inch a decade, maybe it would be two or three. Places that don't have much elevation, that are less than a few feet above sea level, are the ones at risk for having more flooding, more often."

Evidence of this slow creep is already apparent along the Carolina coast if you know where to look or talk to people who've lived there long enough to witness the change. Down East old-timers tell stories about hunting when they were young in hardwood bottomlands that have since become marsh. Travel farther east toward North Carolina's Outer Banks and you'll pass through the Alligator River National Wildlife Refuge, where scientists have been studying "ghost forests," large tracts of dying trees, swallowed by the steady rise of salty ocean water. In a 2021 Duke University study, researchers found that the refuge has lost 11 percent of its tree cover to rising sea level since 1985, an area equal to 35,000 football fields. The most prominent die-off was recorded in 2012, likely due to extreme flooding in the region following Hurricane Irene in 2011.

Emily Ury, one of the study's authors, told the Raleigh *News and Observer*, "Like all living organisms, trees die. But what is happening here is not normal. . . . Within months [after Irene], entire stands of dying and downed trees were visible from space." Ghost forests can be found along other portions of the Carolina coast; large tracts on the Savannah River between Georgia and South Carolina are also the scene of ongoing university research.

It's worth noting that changes in sea level are not the same everywhere. Some locations, such as South Florida and the Gulf coast, will experience a more rapid rise than other parts of the United States. For the Carolinas, there are notable differences up and down the coast. In the *North Carolina Climate Science Report*, produced in 2020 by North Carolina–based climate experts and published by the North Carolina Institute for Climate Studies, researchers stated that sea level on the state's northeast coast has risen twice as fast as along the southeast coast. The rate has been 1.8 inches per decade at Duck, North Carolina, since 1978 and 0.9 inches per decade at Wilmington since 1935. The report affirms a continued rise: "Increased flooding, due largely to sea level rise, will disrupt coastal and low-lying communities. By the end of the century, these areas will experience high tide flooding nearly every day and a substantial increase in the chance of flooding from coastal storms." The analysis considered different greenhouse gas emission scenarios (low to high), and found that under the higher scenario, "storm-driven water levels that have a 1% chance of occurring each year in the beginning of the 21st century may have as much as a 30%–100% chance of occurring each year in the latter part of the century." That's not good news for the many coastal communities already witnessing flooding king tides.

Rick Luettich, director of the University of North Carolina Center for Natural Hazards Resilience, was a member of the advisory panel that prepared the *North Carolina Climate Science Report*. He added, "Coastal North Carolina is so flat it's close to sea level to start with. It doesn't take much sea level rise to really add up. . . . We're seeing more and more of what we call 'sunny day flooding,' or just high tide flooding." Luettich also believes the regional differences in sea level rise will become less of a factor in the future. The differences are mostly the result of the underlying geology of the regions, with some land areas subsiding while others are stationary or even rising. "Over time that differential actually goes away, because the rate of sea level rise is starting to accelerate. At some point the actual rise of sea level is large enough that the nuanced difference of the settlement in the northeast versus the southeast becomes mute, so they all go up at a rate that's pretty close to the same."

A range of greenhouse gas emission scenarios are part of the second volume of the *Fourth National Climate Assessment*, produced by the U.S. Global Change Research Program in 2018. The authors concluded that global sea level is "very likely" to rise by 1.0 to 4.3 feet by the year 2100. If warming cannot be curtailed, the report's authors make a bleak prediction: "Under higher emissions scenarios (RCP8.5), global sea level rise exceeding 8 feet (and even higher in the Southeast) by 2100 cannot be ruled out." The report also described that prospect as a "low probability, high consequence risk."

Along the South Carolina coast, the rate of increase is attracting attention —sea level is up 1.07 feet in the past 100 years and is ten inches higher than it was in 1950. But the rate is accelerating, with a rise in Charleston Harbor of approximately six inches in the last twenty years and an average of about half an inch per year over the last decade. Researchers believe sinking coastal land (subsidence) is responsible for a good portion of the increase. According to analyses for Charleston's Sea Level Rise Strategy, "In the 1970s the city of Charleston experienced an average of 2 days of flooding per year, but now it is projected that the City would experience 180 days of tidal flooding by 2045." Officials estimate that each flooding event costs the city around $14 million (2020 dollars).

Much of Charleston's history with flooding hurricanes has been detailed in this book. But the city is now battling rising water even without cyclones nearby. Shannon Scaff, Charleston's emergency management director, described the problem in 2021: "King tide events seem to be happening more frequently, and the range is increasing. . . . You get a heavy summer rain shower, and before you know it, at 4:30 in the afternoon the crosstown is flooded and has to shut down. That's a major thoroughfare; that's the artery, really, right through the medical district. We've got pumps running, we've got barricades out, trying to reroute traffic, and it's a giant mess, and it's pouring down rain. That only needs to happen a few times before you realize you've got problems."

Along with Miami, Norfolk, and other coastal cities, Charleston is on the front lines in the battle against a changing climate. Its Office of Resiliency and Sustainability has launched an ambitious agenda to reduce the impacts expected in the years to come. Since 2019, the city has invested $385 million in drainage improvements and flood protection measures, including elevating the low Battery seawall. In 2020, the U.S. Army Corps of Engineers came forward with a bold proposal: a $1.75 billion, eight-mile-long barrier to be built around the Charleston peninsula to a height of twelve feet above sea level. The plan includes funding for a floating breakwater and for elevating homes not behind the seawall. In 2021, the city gave a green light for the concept, though reaction from the public has been mixed. It could be years before the plans are finalized and approved (if they are) and funding is secured (with costs sure to rise), but Charleston is being proactive about its future. Scaff added, "The projection for sea level rise over the next fifty years is what's got us concerned. It's increasing exponentially. With heavy rain events and hurricane seasons becoming more active, there's a duty to act.... We have to remember, it took us 300 years to get here; the fix is not going to happen overnight. And it's very, very expensive."

With the seawall likely years away, some Charleston homeowners have already taken action. More than two dozen historic homes had been elevated by the end of 2021, and city leaders believe hundreds more might need to be raised. Officials with the Historic Charleston Foundation were originally opposed to the idea but changed their views and joined city leaders in describing the rising sea level as an "existential threat."

Efforts to prepare for these future consequences, such as those underway in Charleston, are examples of improving community *resiliency*. City and county governments that work to strengthen their planning processes, capabilities, and infrastructure can better prepare themselves for future natural disasters. It's become a focus for local governments, such as that of Charleston, and for businesses, universities, and others—including the state of North Carolina. In 2018, Governor Roy Cooper issued Executive Order 80, which led to the release of the North Carolina Climate Risk Assessment and Resilience Plan, "a comprehensive effort to address climate change vulnerability." That same year the state created the North Carolina Office of Recovery and Resiliency to manage recovery efforts and help communities with adaptive planning.

Those who work in resiliency are quick to point out that their efforts involve far more than planning engineered solutions such as seawalls. "One of the things I've learned over the last five to ten years is just how all-encompassing resilience is," says Luettich, who also serves as the lead principal investigator for the Department of Homeland Security's Coastal Resilience Center of Excellence. "Part of it is 'So we got whacked yesterday.' Now we're confronted with 'Do we just do over what we did before, and hope for something different, by building it back like it was?' Or have we learned something, and make changes for a better outcome?"

Jessica Whitehead, former director of North Carolina's Office of Recovery and Resiliency, echoes that broader idea: "We take a holistic approach to resilience. Some think resilience is the time it takes you to recover from a disaster. ... We think very broad. Resilience helps us to maintain and improve our quality of life and to have healthy growth for everyone. You have these durable systems, economic systems, or social systems, or environmental systems, and conserve resources not just for present but for future generations."

Whitehead and others have worked with local governments across eastern North Carolina to enhance their planning processes and bring new ideas to the table. Physical projects such as levees, floodgates, and other flood-control measures are often on the minds of local leaders. Nature-based solutions have become popular in recent years, such as living shoreline projects and constructed wetlands to help manage excess floodwaters. But Whitehead urges community leaders to consider how to diversify and strengthen their economies, effectively plan for growth, manage future environmental concerns, and strengthen their communities' social fabric to help them better endure future disasters. "How do we help you build capacity to be successful for the long haul? It's often not something you can go and take a picture of, and cut a ribbon on, and have it in the paper, but it's absolutely what you need for the long term. Think broader about what climate change is going to throw at us, and what the next storm is going to be," she says.

At North Carolina State University's College of Design, Gavin Smith teaches classes focused on natural hazards, disasters, and climate change adaptation and leads efforts in coastal resiliency across the university. As the former director of the Coastal Resilience Center for Excellence and with extensive experience in past hurricane recoveries, he provides real-world context to help his students understand the complexities of good community planning and design. "In many cases communities have designed themselves, I would argue, in ways that reflect the climate of the past," Smith contends. He understands the breadth of the challenge:

> Creating more-resilient communities is all about good governance. We often think of federal and state actors influencing local development, and there are examples of that, like the large-scale buyouts and resettlements in programs that follow disasters. But local governments have within their tool kits a whole slew of land-use tools and techniques they can employ to reduce risks. . . . They can make choices about where and how building should take place. They can adopt more stringent land-use plans. . . . But we find that after disasters it's not about the tools they possess; it's also the political will to take action. Sometimes that's difficult to achieve in the aftermath of a disaster.

Following destructive hurricanes, city and county governments often face pressure to rebuild as quickly as possible, even while funding can be slow to arrive. Smith added, "It shouldn't surprise us that often local governments make, some would say, suboptimal choices. In the aftermath of disaster, it takes a lot of political will to slow down and think through 'What is the best option for the community?' including options that are informed by long-term, deep community engagement. . . . It's also important for them to realize all these choices are inherently political. And they affect people's lives directly."

Matthew's and Florence's flood-related property losses extended well outside of the 100-year floodplain, calling into question the reliability of the flood-mapping system and its use for decision-making purposes. As described earlier, thousands of flooded properties were not covered by flood insurance, leaving home and business owners in financial peril. Florence, in particular, exposed shortcomings in a system where flood insurance is vastly undersold. "It's a challenge to educate local governments and property owners that these maps are a static depiction of an inherently dynamic system. Floodplains change, flood maps are not perfect; nor does it mean that if you're on either side of the line, inside or outside of that 100-year floodplain, that you will or won't get flooded. . . . If you rely on those maps over longer time scales they're going to incentivize development to a certain standard that probably is inadequate," says Smith.

With experience in hazard mitigation that predates Hurricane Fran, Smith also understands the shortcomings in our approach to funding. "In the U.S. and in North Carolina, we tend to emphasize the post-disaster receipt of dollars to take action, and we invest virtually nothing on the front end to do good, pre-disaster hazard mitigation, disaster recovery, and climate change adaptation planning. We're just not investing enough," Smith says. The hope is that may change with more communities taking a long view and investing the time and money to better prepare for future hazards.

Growth and investment across the Carolinas help sustain economic vitality, and everyone wants to see "smart growth." Sometimes, though, disasters shine a bright light on past decisions that in retrospect may not have been that "smart." Like everywhere, in South Carolina questions sometimes arise about how and where development should occur. Kim Stenson, director of the state's emergency management division, was candid in a 2021 interview: "My personal opinion is that we're probably building more houses in flood-zone areas than we should, and they could have problems eventually. That's not a problem that's going to solve itself. But it's very unpopular politically; people like living by the water. You know, in South Carolina, like everybody else, we're very pro-business. Part of being pro-business is being pro-building, and they're going to build where people want to live, and many times that's by the water."

Stenson and others at the state level are making progress, however, in addressing the risks of future floods. Among recent efforts was the 2019 creation of the South Carolina Floodwater Commission, an eighty-member panel of scientists, planners, policy makers, and business leaders charged with identifying solutions to reduce the impact of future flooding in the state. Among their recommendations: address deferred maintenance of the state's drainage systems, beginning with 244 projects in thirty-one counties; incentivize green infrastructure, such as storm-water wetlands and living shorelines; construct artificial-reef demonstration projects to mitigate coastal erosion; coordinate the sharing of available river modeling data; and develop a "capacity-building program to assist under-resourced local governments in identifying solutions." The commission's report also addressed the challenges that come with growth: by 2100, an additional 5.8 million acres of South Carolina's urban and suburban land will have been developed, a 305 percent increase over developed areas in 2010. The report concluded that this growth "has significant consequences for flood management and community resilience."

Stenson identified other areas of focus for his division—including some that have been problem areas in the past. Before the 2015 floods, South Carolina had not operated emergency shelters in many years, and the "growing pains" of operating shelters through recent flood events helped the state better prepare for future disasters. Stenson believes evacuation compliance in South Carolina is still pretty low, perhaps because of past overevacuation of some areas, leading to public reluctance. He also said the state is working to improve flood inundation modeling, bolster its online geographic information system Palmetto, further strengthen its dam inspection and safety program, and continue to improve logistics and communication regarding the pre-staging of equipment and supplies. Stenson added that the recovery aspect has been an "enduring mission" for his office, with well over $1 billion in federal funding coming to the state for disaster recovery in recent years. He added, "We're still working issues from five or six years ago, in terms of the recovery piece."

One of the concerns emergency managers often face is hurricane complacency among the public they serve. Complacency can build over time in the years between landfalling storms but is also a factor when residents weather near-miss hurricanes and become desensitized to the threat. After televised pleas to the public before approaching storms, Charleston emergency management director Scaff often hears a troubling response: "We have this misconception here in the city of Charleston: 'I didn't leave for Hugo and I'm not leaving for this one.' And that really bothers me. . . . Because of the complacency that exists in our community, with new people here that don't understand, with young people who like the excitement of it, with older people that were here for Hugo and say they wouldn't leave for this one, we have the makings, the potential, for a Katrina. We really do."

Scaff has seen changes in public attitude too, and his concerns go deeper: "What I hear as I talk to some of the community, [is that] they've lost confidence in decision-makers, they believe things are politically driven, they've lost confidence in the media. . . . From the citizens' perspective, the motives of the decision-makers and those entrusted with providing them information are being questioned. It's further encouraging people to just blow it off."

Even though the public's general knowledge about hurricanes has probably never been better, and sources for up-to-the-minute information are abundant, forecasters and government leaders still face challenges in communicating the risks of each storm. At the National Weather Service, over the last decade forecasting has evolved to become "impact based"—focusing on the kinds of impacts expected from winds, rains, and tides. And there's been a major effort to ensure that forecasters, emergency managers, and government leaders present a unified message. Pfaff says it's not good enough to just issue forecasts and hope for the best; knowing if they're understood by the public is critical. "You're seeing this agency put a lot of value in social science, human behavior. We want to know the best ways to communicate, so that someone is clear of what could happen but also makes the right decision based on the information. . . . Integration of social science is helping shape the message and it's also helping shape the graphics," says Pfaff.

In North Carolina, emergency management professionals have been engaged with so many disaster recoveries in recent years that multicolored Gantt charts are needed to keep track of all the activity. State emergency management director Mike Sprayberry described his division's role before the 2021 season: "It's all about coordination, it's all about partnerships. First of all, you can't be successful in a response or recovery without volunteers. Volunteers are the base; they make things happen. We also rely heavily on our private-sector partners; we've got about a thousand of them now. . . . So really we're the lead, but the bottom line is we're here to coordinate all the different assets. With our counties, it's a pull system, not a push system. We don't ever want to push a bunch of resources down somebody's throat."

Sprayberry knows there's now heightened awareness about hurricanes and flooding, especially across the East, and sees North Carolina's investments in resiliency as the right strategy: "We need to be deliberate and thoughtful in how we develop along the coast, along rivers, along other bodies of water, because as time goes on, and the climate warms, we're going to have more precipitation, sea level will rise, and it's going to create issues. We need to remember storms like Matthew and Florence, going into the future." With firsthand knowledge of the impressive work of swift-water teams and first responders in those floods, Sprayberry added, "The best rescue is the one you don't have to make."

All through these pages have been examples of the economic hardship hurricanes have leveled on the Carolinas. Sunken boats, flooded homes, broken

Hurricane Isaias stacked up boats in Southport Marina on August 4, 2020. Isaias was a Category 1 hurricane that caused extensive damages in Myrtle Beach, Ocean Isle, Holden Beach, Bald Head Island, and Oak Island. It spawned fifteen tornadoes in the Carolinas, including an EF3 that touched down in Windsor, North Carolina, claiming two lives and injuring fourteen. Isaias struck during the COVID-19 pandemic, requiring additional safety protocols for first responders, shelter operations, and cleanup crews. (Photo by Ken Blevins. Courtesy of the USA Today Network.)

dams, lost crops, and untold other property damages stack on top of lost wages and other indirect costs. Eventually, billions in federal and state dollars help fund recoveries, but unmet needs abound. Hurricanes of the future will be no different, though the costs are sure to escalate. Jane Harrison, economist for North Carolina Sea Grant, has worked with eastern North Carolina communities through recent disaster recoveries. "I see the future of how storms affect our area as kind of 'the haves and the have-nots,'" she says. "If you have enough wealth and resources in terms of insurance, and you own your home and you're not a renter, then you're probably going to be alright. You'll figure it out, and it may be a pain in the rear for a year or two as you rebuild, but you'll get through the process and make it out the other side."

Harrison has seen the impact of Matthew, Florence, and Dorian on less affluent, rural communities too, where residents don't have all the resources they need to bounce back: "Since the Great Recession [in 2008], and it's been over a decade, in some places like Lumberton and a lot of northeastern rural counties, they have never gotten back to where they were. The hurricanes were just one more disaster piled on. . . . Some, they're not necessarily coming back. Are they going to be what they once were anytime soon? They almost have to reinvent themselves in terms of their economic base." While overall the state is growing rapidly, several northeastern North Carolina counties lost more than 10 percent of their population between 2010 and 2020.

Smith sees the potential for the gap to widen. He sees future dollars being invested to help prepare cities such as Charleston, Hilton Head, or Wilmington, but less populated, rural communities could be overlooked. "We need to invest more on the front end from federal, state and regional partners to assist smaller communities. One of the real challenges, especially in eastern Carolina, is how do we advance this idea of rural resilience? Those communities with high risk and modest-to-low capacity, to me, that's the big question," says Smith.

In Hurricanes Floyd, Matthew, and Florence, eastern counties in the Carolinas suffered their greatest losses from rising water. That will be the case in future storms, too, especially if hurricanes become even bigger rain makers. The large percentage of homes without flood insurance coverage in these areas will be an ongoing burden through future hurricane disasters. North Carolina insurance commissioner Mike Causey put the numbers in perspective, and it's a statewide issue: "When Hurricane Florence hit in September 2018, less than 135,000 families had flood insurance [in North Carolina]. That's less than 2 percent, so that hit me really hard, when you realize all the places that were flooded, that had never flooded before. That's when I came up with a slogan: 'If it rains where you live, you need flood insurance.'"

Following the storm, Causey and his team partnered with the North Carolina Rate Bureau and the insurance industry to develop flood insurance classes for real estate agents and insurance professionals, with available continuing education credits. "When it started, we asked how many thought they needed flood insurance, and almost nobody raised their hands. But when they finished four hours later, we asked the same question, and everybody raised their hand."

Causey also says National Flood Insurance Program policies are no longer the only option; private carriers are increasingly offering their own flood policies or flood riders. According to a 2021 report by Policygenius, the cost of a National Flood Insurance Program home policy varies depending on risk and other factors but averages about $700 a year in the United States. But that average rate was calculated before a major overhaul of the program in October 2021. Under the revised plan, flood insurance rates more accurately reflect each property's unique flood risk. Some policy owners have seen their rates go down, while many have seen increases. David Maurstad, deputy associate administrator for the National Flood Insurance Program, told CNBC, "What we found out was that many folks with lower-value homes were paying more than they should, and those that had higher-value homes were paying less than they should. And we have a responsibility to make sure that we have actuarily sound, fair, and equitable rates." Private policies have distinct differences, and may be more costly, so comparison pricing is a must. But affordability of any policy remains the primary barrier that perpetuates the likelihood of more devastating flood-induced financial losses in the Carolinas.

We know future hurricanes will cause great economic harm. One way to think about the next big storm is to perform a what-if analysis of past hurricanes. What if Hazel or Hugo were to strike the Carolinas today? What would the economic impact be? It turns out that Landsea, along with Roger Pielke and other researchers, were among the first to review historic hurricanes and make normalized projections for their cost in today's dollars. The most recent updated list, *Normalized Hurricane Damage in the Continental United States: 1900–2017*, factors changes in population, per capita wealth, and inflation in the counties affected by the storms. This methodology offers a glimpse of what the direct dollar impact of past U.S. hurricanes might be were they to strike today. At the top of the list is the Great Miami Hurricane of 1926, a potent Category 4 that rolled through Miami and later struck the Mississippi coast, with an astonishing normalized cost of $229 billion (all figures in 2017 dollars). The Galveston Hurricane of 1900 ranks second at $135 billion; Katrina is third at $114 billion. Among the hurricanes profiled in this book are Hurricane Donna (no. 11) at $46.7 billion; Hurricane Hazel (no. 13) at $31.9 billion; Hurricane

Hugo (no. 19) at $24.4 billion; Hurricane Floyd (no. 32) at $13.4 billion; Hurricane Fran (no. 38) at $10.7 billion; and Hurricane Matthew (no. 43) at $8.3 billion (Hurricane Florence will be included in future updates). The report's authors offer this perspective: "The United States should expect much larger hurricane damage in its future, of this there is certainty. . . . Whatever the future brings, addressing vulnerability to hurricanes will remain a permanent priority for communities along the U.S. Gulf and Atlantic coasts."

Many in the Carolinas have lived through painful and difficult challenges brought on by recent hurricanes and floods. Unfortunately, there'll be more to come in the years ahead. With each disaster, though, there's a different kind of resiliency that emerges—a resiliency of the human spirit. Bolstered by the kindness and generosity of others, it's uplifting to see examples large and small of storm-weary Carolina residents bouncing back, rebuilding, and looking past the disaster that surrounds them. The transition often begins with the outpouring of support from friends and neighbors and the hard work of volunteers who make personal sacrifices to lend a hand. It's a resiliency that can overcome despair and move communities forward. North and South Carolinians hold a deep love for where they live, too—the thought of packing up and moving far away is never a consideration for most.

While cities such as Wilmington, Myrtle Beach, or Charleston might garner more attention and resources after a hurricane disaster, smaller, rural communities must be more self-reliant and generate resiliency from within. "It's so complicated on the ground after the TV cameras go home, and there you are with a tarp on your roof and insurance to deal with," says Karen Amspacher, founding director of the Core Sound Waterfowl Museum and Heritage Center in Harkers Island, North Carolina. Amspacher has deep Down East roots and has built her life around community connections, especially with those remote communities overlooking the broad waters of Core and Pamlico Sounds: "They are real people. They're working people that struggle, that love their communities, that love their heritage, that understand that Hatteras and Buxton, and Ocracoke and Harkers Island, are connected by that water, not the road, not some travel brochure, not some bull somebody put in a movie. It's that water, and living close to the earth, and being vulnerable but strong."

Amspacher remembers that following Hurricane Florence, a group from Hatteras wanted to come down to Carteret County to help with cleanup, even though they knew there was nowhere for them to stay, no electricity, and travel would be treacherous. The next morning two truckloads of men showed up with "generators, sleeping bags, and chainsaws" to help clear roads and repair homes. The very next year, Hurricane Dorian slammed the Outer Banks, and

Coastal communities in the Carolinas have seen their share
of hurricanes over the years. Hurricane Dorian's storm tide
at Ocracoke was the highest in a generation, as evidenced by
the water-mark sign added on the wall of the Village Craftsmen store in 2019. (Photo by Amy Howard. Courtesy of
Village Craftsmen, Ocracoke, North Carolina.)

Amspacher recalls the response: "It's really an unsung story. The crowd from
Cedar Island and Davis Shore, that crowd was in the boat by two o'clock that
afternoon with chainsaws, generators, and artillery, headed to Ocracoke. They
knew it was bad, really bad. . . . They have become the best of friends, that little
clump from Davis, and a little clump from Hatteras. They find themselves having no choice but to help each other out, because there's not a whole lot of help
coming in from the outside."

It may be the most important takeaway from this look at hurricanes past
and future: people across the Carolinas will always find a way to rebound
from hurricanes, through their own hard work and determination and with
the support of others. Our storm history offers countless examples of neighbor

helping neighbor; of heartfelt generosity; of first responders risking their own lives to save others; of dirty, difficult, and back-breaking work that manages to get done; and of government leaders who genuinely want to improve readiness and make our communities stronger. All will continue to be essential in the aftermath of hurricanes to come.

One story that comes to mind offers a small glimpse of that community spirit. Janice Bailey, a retired nurse and Red Cross volunteer from Maryland, happened to be visiting her niece in Kinston when Hurricane Floyd's floods struck the city. Recognizing the tremendous needs around her, she ended up staying four months to volunteer and assist the local community. Bailey remembered, "I helped out down at a local church for a while, distributing clothes to people that needed them. We had these big vans of clothes and supplies that people had collected from all over. One man who was there got a jacket out of a box, and there was a note pinned to the collar. It said something like, 'God bless you. Look in pocket.' In the pocket was an envelope with two folded-up twenty-dollar bills. That poor old man started laughing and crying at the same time."

ACKNOWLEDGMENTS

This book was prepared with the help of a wide variety of publications and sources and the outstanding cooperation of many individuals and organizations. Special thanks are extended to those who gave their time for interviews, and to those who assisted me in collecting photographs, stories, weather reports, and historical records. Whenever possible, appropriate credit has been provided for quoted sources and photographs.

A variety of museums, libraries, universities, newspapers, nonprofits, government agencies, and individuals have graciously contributed photographs and other helpful information. These institutions and individuals are recognized with each photograph, and their outstanding cooperation and timely efforts are appreciated.

Also deserving thanks for their assistance are interviewees, hurricane survivors, and those with unique perspectives on the storms, including Janice Bailey, Alton Ballance, Billy Ray Cameron, Tom Ditt, Craig Fugate, Lewis Hardee, Ed Harper, Steve Harned, Jerry Helms, Governor Jim Hunt, Dorothy Ipock, Steve Lyons, Max Mayfield, Richard Moore, Hugh Morton, Ken Mullen, Joe Pelissier, Ed Rappaport, David Redwine, Tony Seamon, Eric Tolbert, and Harry Warren. Special thanks are also offered to the scientists, educators, government officials, and policy makers who have taken time to share their views with the author and readers. Their candid insights on climate, risk, and resiliency offer valuable perspective to help us better understand the future of hurricanes in the Carolinas. These include Karen Amspacher, Mike Causey, Jane Harrison, Chris Landsea, Rick Luettich, Hope Mizzell, Steve Pfaff, Stan Riggs, Spencer Rogers, Shannon Scaff, John Shelton, Gavin Smith, Mike Sprayberry, Kim Stenson, Jessica Whitehead, and Robert Young.

A NOTE ON SOURCES

The profiles presented in this book rely heavily on the painstaking research and writings of earlier historians. Two important storm histories—Ivan Tannehill's *Hurricanes: Their Nature and History*, published in 1938, and David Ludlum's *Early American Hurricanes, 1492–1870*, published in 1963—provided details for many of the early hurricanes described here. Other important references are regional books including David Stick's *Graveyard of the Atlantic* (1952), Walter Fraser Jr.'s *Lowcountry Hurricanes* (2006), Rick Schwartz's *Hurricanes and the Middle Atlantic States* (2007), and the author's own *North Carolina's Hurricane History*, fourth edition (2013). All are valuable compilations for any student of hurricane history.

Equally important are records produced by a variety of government agencies. These include National Weather Service bulletins, journals, and publications, especially the U.S. Weather Bureau's catalog of *Monthly Weather Review* and the National Hurricane Center's collection of hurricane summaries. The National Oceanic and Atmospheric Administration's *Deadliest Atlantic Tropical Cyclones, 1492–1996* provided useful detail. Another important source was the National Weather Service technical memorandum *A Historical Account of Tropical Cyclones That Have Impacted North Carolina since 1586*, originally researched by Charles Carney and Albert Hardy and later updated by James Stevenson. Carney and Hardy included numerous uncredited quotations and stories, most of which were borrowed from newspapers and other historical documents. Some of those have been repeated in this book. A similar compilation produced by South Carolina Sea Grant, *A History of Storms on the South Carolina Coast* by Laylon Jordan, Robert Dukes, and Ted Rosengarten, was also helpful.

Every effort has been made to assure the accuracy of the meteorological data provided. Online records available from the National Oceanic and Atmospheric Administration Hurricane Research Division's Atlantic Hurricane Database (HURDAT) and Atlantic Hurricane Reanalysis Project were essential to that effort. Working with a team of leading scientists and researchers, the reanalysis committee has compiled new information that led to changes in track and/or intensity for some of the hurricanes profiled in this book. It was through its efforts that Hurricane Gracie, for example, was upgraded from Category 3 to Category 4 in 2016—fifty-seven years after it struck the South Carolina coast.

Other government agencies provided helpful reports, statistical summaries, and other assistance. These include the South Carolina Emergency Management Division, South Carolina Climate Office, South Carolina Sea Grant, City of Charleston Emergency Management, North Carolina Division of Emergency Management, North Carolina Office of Recovery and Resiliency, Hurricane Floyd Redevelopment Center, City of New Bern, North Carolina Sea Grant, North Carolina Department of Insurance, North Carolina Office of the Chief Medical Examiner, U.S. Geological Survey, FEMA, National Climatic Data Center, U.S. Global Change Research Program, and Coastal Resilience Center of

Excellence in partnership with the University of North Carolina at Chapel Hill and the U.S. Department of Homeland Security.

Special thanks are also extended to a broad collection of newspapers, magazines, television stations, and other news outlets whose reporting provided historical context and compelling firsthand accounts of the disasters profiled in this book. These include ABC News, the *Anderson Independent-Mail*, the *Asheville Citizen-Times*, the Associated Press, the *Atlantic* magazine, the *Beaufort Gazette*, the *Beaufort News*, Bladen Online, *Carolina Skywatcher*, the *Carteret County News-Times*, the *Cary News*, the *Charleston Courier*, the Charleston *News and Courier*, the Charleston *Post and Courier*, the *Charleston Times*, the *Charlotte Observer*, CNBC, CNN, the Columbia *State*, the *Fayetteville Observer*, the Franklin, Va., *Tidewater*, the *Georgetown Times*, the *Georgia Republican*, the *Goldsboro Messenger*, the *Goldsboro News-Argus*, *Good Morning America*, the *Greensboro Daily News*, the Greenville *Daily Reflector*, the *Hatteras Monitor*, the Jacksonville *Daily News*, *Lowe's Storm 2000*, the Manteo *Coastland Times*, the *Miami Herald*, MSNBC News, the Myrtle Beach *Sun News*, NBC News, the New Bern *Sun Journal*, the *New York Times*, the *North Carolina Gazette*, the North Carolina Herpetological Society newsletter, North Carolina Sea Grant's *Coastwatch* magazine, the North Carolina State University *Technician*, the *Orlando Sentinel*, *Our State* magazine, the *Outer Banks Sentinel*, the *Palm Beach Post*, PBS *NewsHour*, the *Pee Dee Times*, PolitiFact, *Popular Science* magazine, the *Raleigh Minerva*, the Raleigh *News and Observer*, the *Raleigh Observer*, Reuters News Service, the *Robesonian*, *Sea Chest* magazine, the *South Carolina Gazette*, South Carolina Sea Grant's *Coastal Heritage* magazine, *State* magazine (N.C.), the *State Port Pilot*, the *Tabor-Loris Tribune*, the *Topsail Voice*, UNC-TV, *USA Today*, the *Virginian-Pilot*, the *Washington Daily News*, the *Washington Gazette*, the *Washington Post*, WAVY News, WCTI News, the Weather Channel's *Storm Stories*, Weather Underground, *Weatherwise* magazine, WECT News, WFTV News, the Whiteville *News Reporter*, the *Wilmington Morning Star*, the *Wilmington Messenger*, the Wilmington *Star-News*, the *Wilson Daily News*, the *Winston-Salem Journal*, the Winston-Salem *Union-Republican*, WITN News, WMBF News, WRAL News, and WTVD News.

Other valuable reference materials include books and articles from a variety of sources, including *Ships in the Streets: The Charlestown Hurricanes of September 1752*, by Amy Glen; letters from Vice President Aaron Burr, National Archives, Washington, D.C.; *Joshua's Dream*, by Susan Carson; a letter from Governor Tryon to Lord Hillsborough from *Colonial Records, Tryon's Letter Book*; excerpts from *An Archaeological and Historical Reconnaissance of U.S. Marine Corps Base, Camp Lejeune*, by Thomas Loftfield and Tucker Littleton; *History of South Carolina*, by David Ramsay; "An Act of Providence," a widely published article by John Sanders; *The Atlantic Hotel*, by Virginia Doughton; *The Outer Banks*, by David Stick; various articles by Carteret County author Sonny Williamson; reports from the American Red Cross, including Clara Barton's *The Red Cross in Peace and War*; "Sea Islands Hurricane," an article in the 1894 edition of *Scribner's Magazine* by Joel Chandler Harris; *The Storm Swept Coast of South Carolina*, by Mrs. R. C. Mather; records from the Charleston Preservation Society; *The Great Sea Islands Storm of 1893*, by Bill and Fran Marscher; letters from the Louis T. Moore Collection at the New Hanover

County Public Library; *Sailin' with Grandpa*, by Sonny Williamson; *Ocracokers*, by Alton Ballance; *The Great Bahamian Hurricanes of 1899 and 1932*, by Wayne Neely; "The Great Atlantic Hurricane," an article in the *Hatteras Monitor* by Rhonda Roughton; "Hurricane Survival on Hatteras," an article in *State* magazine by Sybil Skakle; several Bill Sharpe articles in *State* magazine; *The Hurricane and Its Impact*, by Robert Simpson and Herbert Riehl; *Hurricane Hazel Lashes Coastal Carolinas*, edited by Art Newton; *Making a Difference in North Carolina*, by Ed Rankin and Hugh Morton; portions of *Duke Power Annual Report* (1989); reports from the Natural Hazards Research and Applications Information Center; *The Savage Season*, a special report from the Wilmington *Star-News*; the North Carolina Herpetological Society newsletter; *Fran*, a collection of essays from LeAnne Smith's seventh-grade class at Topsail Middle School; "Spooky Waters," an essay by Jones Middle School seventh grader Abby McDonald; *Reflections of the Outer Banks*, by Donald and Carol McAdoo; the *North Carolina Climate Science Report*; the final report from the South Carolina Floodwater Commission; and the *Fourth National Climate Assessment*.

INDEX

Page numbers in italics refer to illustrations.

by, 1, 77, 167, 177, 184–93, *192*, 202, 214,
215, 216, 252, 300, 347; flooding from,
179, 180, 181, 182, 184, 190, 191, 193,
194–200, 215–16, 219, 220, 228, 243,
246, 256; and Hurricane Bertha, 1, 77,
172; Hurricane Florence compared to,
294; intensity of, 149, 178, 179, 180, 183;
landfall of, 178, 179, 181; path of, 88, 178,
179, 182, 191; rainfall of, 182, 183, 189,
190–91, 194–96, 200, 203, 227; seabirds
caught in, 148, 206; size of, 182; storm
surge of, 181, 182, 183, 184, 185, 187;
studies of, 180–81; tides of, 179, 182, 184,
187, 189, 190; winds of, 154, 178, 179, 181,
182–84, 186, 189, 190–92, *191*, 193, 194,
198, 200, 202, 299
Hurricane Frances (2004), 88, 142
Hurricane Gert (1999), 221
Hurricane Ginger (1971), 156, 177
Hurricane Gloria (1985), 156
Hurricane Gracie (1959): destruction
caused by, 133, 136, 142–43; flooding
from, *134*, 136, 138, *139*, 142; intensity
of, 135, 136, 159; landfall of, 135, 136, 139;
path of, *134*, *141*; tide of, 130, 136, 138,
142; and tornadoes, 139–42; winds of,
135, 136–37, *137*, 138
Hurricane Harvey (2017), 142, 210, 283,
294, 315, 331, 334
Hurricane Hazel (1954): as benchmark,
128, 132, 133, 183, 214; destruction caused
by, 1, *2*, 34, 35, 78, 109–12, *110*, 113, 115,
115, 116, *116*, 117–20, *117*, *121*, 122–23, *123*,
126, 127–28, *128*, *129*, 133, 135, 161, 184,
186, 187, 226, 346; fiftieth anniversary
of, 119; flooding from, 112, 118–19, 122,
123–26, 181, 182, 208, 266; historical
marker for, *2*; Hurricane Donna compared to, 149, 150; Hurricane Florence
compared to, 293, 294; intensity of, 34,
106, *107*, 108–13, 181, 183; landfall of,
109, 113, 116, 124, 149, 261; path of, 76,
107, 109, 111–13, 115–16, 127, *141*; stories
of, 97, 98–99, 118–19, 122–23, 125, 128,

131–32; storm surge of, 109, 113, 116, 118,
120, 122, 124–26, 184; tide of, 109, 124,
130, 149; winds of, 109, 111, 112, 113, 116,
119, 120, 122, 124, 125, 126, 127, 154
Hurricane Helene (1958), 104, *141*, 186, 299
Hurricane Hermine (2016), 267
Hurricane Hugo (1989): beach erosion
from, 167; as benchmark, 132, 223; as
Cape Verde storm, 15, 156; destruction
caused by, 156, 158–62, 164, *165*, 166,
168, 170–71, 179, 191, 194, 202, 346–47;
flooding from, 160, 161–63; Hurricane
Florence compared to, 293; intensity of,
34, 158, 159, 169, 170, 336, 342; landfall
of, 158, 159, 16*7*; path of, 88, *141*, *157*,
169–70; seabirds caught in, 148; size of,
22, 58, *62*, 182; stories of, 97, 132; storm
surge of, 159, 163, 167; tide of, 159–60,
161; utility outages from, 166–67; winds
of, 154, 156–60, 162, 163, 164
Hurricane Ida (2021), 331, 334
Hurricane Ione (1955), *29*, 35, 78, 211, *333*
Hurricane Irene (1999), 214, 228
Hurricane Irene (2011), 35–36, *36*, 336
Hurricane Irma (2017), 210–11, 283
Hurricane Isabel (2003), 35, 99, 205, 209
Hurricane Isaias (2020), 122, 299, *344*
Hurricane Ivan (2004), 88
Hurricane Joaquin (2015), 37
Hurricane Juan (1985), 259
Hurricane Katrina (2005), 64, 142, 315,
331, 334, 342, 346
Hurricane Lenny (1999), 221
Hurricane Lorenzo (2019), 156
Hurricane Matthew (2016): challenges of,
4–5; destruction caused by, 263, 264–70,
270, 273, 274, 285–87, 291–92, 303, 345,
347; domestic animals rescued from, 210,
211, 276, 279; environmental concerns
of, 277, 301; flooding from, 122, 216,
255, 256, 258, *260*, 263–71, 272, 273–81,
285, 286–87, 298, 299, 308, 309, 312, 313,
315–16, 318, 319, *324*, 328, 341, 343; intensity of, 261, 263, 265, 266, 285–86;